HESS, HITLER & CHURCHILL

Also by Peter Padfield

BIOGRAPHY
Dönitz: The Last Führer
Himmler: Reichsführer-SS
Hess: Flight for the Führer
(*in paperback*, Hess: The Führer's Disciple)

NAVAL AND MARITIME HISTORY
The Sea is a Magic Carpet
The *Titanic* and the *Californian*
An Agony of Collisions
Aim Straight: A Biography of Admiral Sir Percy Scott
Broke and the *Shannon*: A Biography of Admiral Sir Philip Broke
The Battleship Era
Guns at Sea: A History of Naval Gunnery
The Great Naval Race: Anglo–German Naval Rivalry, 1900–1914
Nelson's War
Tide of Empires: Decisive Naval Campaigns in the Rise of the West
Volume I: 1481–1654
Volume II: 1654–1763
Rule Britannia: The Victorian and Edwardian Navy
Beneath the Houseflag of the P & O: A Social History
Armada: A Celebration of the 400th Anniversary of the Defeat of the Spanish Armada
War Beneath the Sea: Submarine Conflict 1939–1945
Maritime Supremacy and the Opening of the Western Mind: Naval Campaigns that
Shaped the Modern World 1588–1782
Maritime Power and the Struggle for Freedom: Naval Campaigns that Shaped
the Modern World 1788–1851
Maritime Dominion and the Triumph of the Free World: Naval Campaigns that
Shaped the Modern World 1852–2001

(*As contributor*)
The Trafalgar Companion (ed. Alexander Stilwell)
Dreadnought to *Daring* (ed. Peter Hore)

NOVELS
The Lion's Claw
The Unquiet Gods
Gold Chains of Empire
Salt and Steel

HESS, HITLER & CHURCHILL

THE REAL TURNING POINT OF THE SECOND WORLD WAR – A SECRET HISTORY

PETER PADFIELD

ICON

Published in the UK in 2013 by
Icon Books Ltd, Omnibus Business Centre,
39–41 North Road, London N7 9DP
email: info@iconbooks.net
www.iconbooks.net

Sold in the UK, Europe and Asia
by Faber & Faber Ltd, Bloomsbury House,
74–77 Great Russell Street,
London WC1B 3DA or their agents

Distributed in the UK, Europe and Asia
by TBS Ltd, TBS Distribution Centre, Colchester Road,
Frating Green, Colchester CO7 7DW

Distributed in India by Penguin Books India,
11 Community Centre, Panchsheel Park,
New Delhi 110017

Distributed in South Africa by
Book Promotions, Office B4, The District,
41 Sir Lowry Road, Woodstock 7925

Distributed in Australia and New Zealand
by Allen & Unwin Pty Ltd,
PO Box 8500, 83 Alexander Street,
Crows Nest, NSW 2065

Distributed in Canada by Penguin Books Canada,
90 Eglinton Avenue East, Suite 700,
Toronto, Ontario M4P 2YE

ISBN: 978-1-84831-602-7

Typeset in Adobe Text Pro by Marie Doherty

Printed and bound in the UK by
CPI Group (UK) Ltd, Croydon CR0 4YY

For Jane

Contents

Contents

List of illustrations

Adolf Hitler and Rudolf Hess at a Nazi rally in Weimar in 1936.

Winston Churchill with Viscount Halifax in 1938.

Douglas Douglas-Hamilton, the 'boxing Marquess' of Clydesdale.

Albrecht Haushofer.

James Lonsdale Bryans.

Sir Samuel Hoare with King George VI and Queen Elizabeth.

Colonel Stewart Menzies with his second wife in 1932.

Claude Dansey of MI6 in the 1930s.

Abwehr chief Admiral Wilhelm Canaris.

Kenneth de Courcy.

Carl Burckhardt.

Winston Churchill and Anthony Eden in 1941.

Hitler, Goebbels and Hess celebrating the anniversary of the Nazi 'seizure of power' at the Berlin Sportpalast, January 1941.

The wreckage of Hess's Me Bf 110 at Floors Farm, Eaglesham, Renfrewshire.

The Duke of Hamilton in flying kit.

The Duke of Kent in RAF uniform.

The 'summer house' in the garden of Spandau jail, where Hess died.

The extension flex with which he hanged himself, attached to the window catch.

The lower end of the flex unplugged.

The back of Hess's neck at the post-mortem, showing a horizontal mark more typical of strangulation than hanging.

The 'suicide note' found in Hess's clothes.

Acknowledgements

I HAVE TO THANK Andrew Lownie, my agent, for providing import-ant contacts and documents for this project and for his unfailing support from the beginning. One of those contacts, the late Duc de Grantmesnil-Lorraine, Kenneth de Courcy in this story, was a mine of information on the personalities and politics of the war years, espe-cially Stewart Menzies, head of MI6, the Duke of Buccleuch and Lord Rothschild, patron of the 'Cambridge ring' of Soviet spies. It was only after Grantmesnil's death that I learned he had been given first-hand information on Hess's peace mission by an officer who guarded Hess in captivity.

The late Adrian Liddell Hart, son of Captain Basil Liddell Hart, was generous in sharing the results of his own researches into Hess's mis-sion. The late Duchess of Hamilton, wife of the 14th Duke, provided much information about her husband and the events surrounding Hess's arrival, as did her son, the 15th Duke, and his brother, James Douglas-Hamilton, now Lord Selkirk of Douglas, who wrote a pio-neering book on Hess's arrival, *Motive for a Mission*; I am grateful for permission to quote from letters he published from his father's papers.

Rudolf Hess's son, the late Wolf Rüdiger Hess, besides provid-ing much material assistance, granted permission to quote from his father's letters and alleged suicide note, and released the pathologists who conducted the second autopsy into his father's death, Professors W. Eisenmenger and W. Spann of Munich University, from their oath of silence. In their turn they spent much time and trouble answering my queries, for which I am most grateful.

I am particularly grateful to the late John Howell, who provided the introduction to the informant whose testimony provides the key to the original official cover-up of Hess's peace mission, and who arranged question and answer sessions. Unfortunately the informant, after referring to his former masters (in the Foreign Office or MI6) insisted on anonymity, which I have to honour.

The late Robert Cecil, liaison between MI6 and the Foreign Office during Hess's captivity in Britain, helped enormously with Foreign Office personalities and procedures, as did the late Lord Sherfield (Roger Makins at the time of this story), Sir Frank Roberts, Lord Gladwyn (Gladwyn Jebb) and Lord (David) Eccles, who was adviser to Sir Samuel Hoare in the Madrid Embassy. From the other side of the intelligence divide, the late Drs Wilhelm Höttl, Otto John and Eduard Calic, author of the most insightful biography of Reinhard Heydrich, provided information on Albrecht Haushofer and the German resistance to Hitler, as did my friend, Peter C. Hansen, one-time courier for Admiral Canaris, chief of the *Abwehr*; and I am grateful to Ernst Haiger for much information from his current researches into the Haushofers, especially Albrecht.

Dr Scott Newton provided valuable insights into the personalities and motives of the British 'appeasers', as did John Harris and Richard Wilbourn, whose lateral thinking and persistent investigation into all matters connected with Hess's mission have provided some of the most telling information I have included in this book. I should also like to thank Ron Williams, whose father was involved in the search for peace, for his researches on my behalf, his hospitality and his constant support.

Roy C. Nesbit, co-author of *The Flight of Rudolf Hess: Myths and Reality*, helped enormously with RAF and Messerschmitt technicalities, and was most generous with the results of his own researches. I was helped by former MI6 officers who wish to remain anonymous; by the late Group Captain Frederick Winterbotham, former chief of Air Intelligence; the late Colonel 'Tar' Robertson of MI5 and the 'Double-Cross Committee'; the late Lieutenant Colonel John

McCowan, who was ordered to apprehend SS parachutists on a mission to assassinate Hess in England; by Squadron Leader R.G. Woodman, who investigated Hess's flight into British air space; Maurice Pocock, who was 'scrambled' in his Spitfire too late to intercept the intruder; and Felicity Ashbee, Moira Pearson and Nancy Goodall who helped plot Hess's incoming aircraft. I should also like to thank all those who replied to my original request for information, who are listed in my earlier (1991) biography of Hess.

My wife, Jane, was, as ever, a constant support and did much excellent work on the files in The National Archives; our son, Guy, gave invaluable advice and technical IT support; Mary and David Thorpe provided such generous hospitality at their home near Kew that our visits to the archives were a real pleasure. The final script was edited by Robert Sharman with care, sensitivity and attention to the questions readers might ask, for which I am most grateful.

Finally, I should like to thank the following authors, editors and publishers for permission to quote from published works: The National Archives, Kew, for Guy Liddell's diaries, filed as KV 4/186; Albert Langer-Georg Müller Verlag for W.R. Hess (ed.) *Rudolf Hess: Briefe 1908–1933*; Druffel Verlag for Ilse Hess (ed.) *Ein Schicksal in Briefen*; K.G. Sauer Verlag for E. Fröhlich (ed.) *Die Tagebücher von Josef Goebbels*; and Churchill Archives Centre for permission to quote from the papers of Sir Alexander Cadogan, ACAD 1/1. I have been unable to trace the copyright holder in Lieutenant Colonel A.M. Scott's 'Camp Z' diary at the Imperial War Museum.

Dramatis personae

ATTLEE, Clement   Leader of the Labour Party and a fierce critic of 'appeasing' Hitler. When Churchill came to power in May 1940 Attlee brought Labour into coalition government with the Conservatives. Appointed Lord Privy Seal, later Deputy Prime Minister, he looked after domestic affairs while Churchill ran the War Cabinet.

BEAVERBROOK, Lord   A Canadian who came to England in 1910, entered Parliament as a Conservative and bought the *Daily Express*, the first of several newspapers he acquired and increased in circulation. In 1917 he was raised to the peerage. During the 1930s he promoted 'appeasement' of Nazi Germany, and wobbled in that direction after the outbreak of war, but Churchill, on becoming Prime Minister, harnessed his immense energy by appointing him Minister of Aircraft Production; in this role he made a major contribution to winning the Battle of Britain. Although not in the War Cabinet, he was one of Churchill's closest confidants.

BEDFORD, Duke of   A prominent pacifist. At the outbreak of war, as Marquis of Tavistock, he co-founded the British People's Party advocating an immediate end to war with Germany and the adoption of a monetary policy known as 'social credit'. In February 1940 he travelled to Dublin to discuss peace terms at the German Legation. Later that year he succeeded as 12th Duke. Disliking the family seat, Woburn Abbey – acquired by the government as headquarters for

SOE – he lived at Cairnsmore in Galloway, Scotland. Although kept under surveillance by MI5, he was not arrested as it was felt this would only give his views more prominence.

BLUNT, Anthony Homosexual art historian and member of the notorious Soviet spy ring including Kim Philby, Donald Maclean and Guy Burgess. Recruited into MI5 in June 1940 as personal assistant to Guy Liddell, head of B Division, he passed intelligence to the Russians throughout the war. At war's end he was despatched to Germany by Buckingham Palace on a mission to retrieve sensitive royal documents, thereby it is said, gaining immunity from prosecution when he was unmasked in 1963.

BORMANN, Martin A farm estate manager and *Freikorps* activist, he joined the Nazi Party in 1927, becoming regional business manager in Thuringia. Successfully concealing his coarse appetites and unprincipled ambition he was appointed Rudolf Hess's personal secretary and head of his cabinet in July 1933; he also managed Hitler's finances, so insinuating himself into the Führer's confidence.

BROCKET, Lord Conservative politician from a millionaire brewing family with great estates in England and Scotland. A member of the Anglo-German Fellowship committed to increasing friendship with Germany, he was an active Nazi sympathiser and used by Lord Halifax to convey British government views to the German government. In April 1939 he travelled to Berlin with the Duke of Buccleuch and General J.F.C. Fuller to attend Hitler's 50th birthday celebrations. After the outbreak of war he promoted and financed efforts for a compromise peace.

BUCCLEUCH, Duke of The grandest of Conservative grandees with the largest private landholding in the kingdom and several great houses: Drumlanrig, Dumfriesshire, Bowhill in the Border region (and perhaps by coincidence practically on Hess's flight path in May 1941), Boughton, Northamptonshire, and others. A great friend of Stewart Menzies and on first name terms with King George VI, his sister was married to the king's younger brother, the Duke of Gloucester. He was committed to friendship with Germany on imperial strategic rather than ideological grounds.

BURCKHARDT, Carl   Swiss academic and diplomat. As League of Nations High Commissioner for the Free City of Danzig from 1937 to 1939 he acquired experience of the German demands for living space (*Lebensraum*) in eastern Europe; Hitler told him personally that he wanted 'nothing from the West', but 'must have a free hand in the east'. During the war as a member of the International Committee of the Red Cross based in Geneva he had occasion to visit Germany on ICRC business, and was used as an intermediary for peace overtures by both sides.

BUTLER, R.A. 'Rab'   Conservative politician with a first-class intellect. He supported Chamberlain's policy of 'appeasing' Hitler, and in 1938 was appointed Undersecretary of State for Foreign Affairs. Like many others, he distrusted Churchill, describing him in private after he succeeded Chamberlain as 'a half breed American' and 'the greatest adventurer of modern political history'. He and his senior, Lord Halifax, continued to pursue 'appeasement' clandestinely in 1940 in contravention of Churchill's policy of no negotiation with the enemy.

CADOGAN, Sir Alexander   Passed top in the exams for entry into the diplomatic service in 1908; 30 years later he was appointed Permanent Undersecretary for Foreign Affairs (head of the permanent staff of the Foreign Office) in place of the outspoken anti-German, Vansittart (see below). Outwardly restrained, he reserved often acid assessments of colleagues for his diaries, published posthumously; the originals are held by the Churchill Archives Centre, Churchill College, Cambridge.

CANARIS, Admiral Wilhelm   The son of a wealthy industrialist, Canaris had a distinguished record in the First World War, latterly as a U-boat commander. After the lost war he was active in the clandestine re-building of the U-boat arm in contravention of the Treaty of Versailles. Appointed head of the *Abwehr* (Military

Counter-Intelligence) in 1934, he had by 1938 realised that the *Reich* was being led to disaster, and he began conspiring against Hitler. During the war he passed information to the British Secret Intelligence Service (MI6). With a subtlety of mind unusual in the German naval officer corps, he was an enigma to his colleagues, and remains so to history. He was brutally executed as a traitor in the final days of the war.

CHAMBERLAIN, Neville Conservative politician and British Prime Minister from 1937 to May 1940, when he lost the confidence of the Labour and Liberal parties after British defeats in Norway. He is remembered chiefly for attempting to preserve peace by conciliating, or 'appeasing' Hitler's territorial demands. His choices were limited as Britain's armed services had been run down in the atmosphere of disarmament after the horrors of the First World War, yet his policy demonstrated complete misunderstanding of the determination of the German military leadership to reverse the decision of the first war, and of Hitler's aim for European hegemony.

CHURCHILL, Winston   A descendant of John Churchill, 1st Duke of Marlborough, he was the son of Lord Randolph Churchill and Jennie Jerome, socialite daughter of a New York millionaire; he saw too little of either parent while growing up, which distressed him, and he did not distinguish himself at school. His career as a cavalry officer, war reporter, Member of Parliament and minister in the social reforming Liberal government of 1905–1915 reads like adventure fiction. Subsequently he crossed to the Conservative benches, serving in the post-war Conservative government as Chancellor of the Exchequer. After the government fell he found himself at odds with the party leaders and spent the 1930s writing the biography of his illustrious ancestor, Marlborough, gaining strategic insights which were to illumine his subsequent war leadership, while attempting to convince the government and a complacent public of the need to re-arm against Hitler. On the outbreak of war Chamberlain appointed him First Lord of the Admiralty. Although distrusted by many as an impulsive adventurer, when Chamberlain fell he had sufficient support from all sides to succeed him as Prime Minister. A brilliant conversationalist and orator with an original mind, he yet suffered periods of deep depression which he called his 'black dog'. He has been judged by history as one of the greatest Britons.

CLYDESDALE, Marquis of, Douglas Douglas-Hamilton, eldest son of the Duke of Hamilton, the premier peer of Scotland. He and his three younger brothers, Lords George ('Geordie'), Malcolm and David Douglas-Hamilton all took up flying and served in the Royal Auxiliary Air Force. Clydesdale became the youngest squadron leader of his time and in 1933 was appointed chief pilot for the first ever flight over Mount Everest; with his co-pilot and lifelong friend, D.F. McIntyre, he described the feat in *The Pilot's Book of Everest* (1936). The grass landing strip adjacent to his home, Dungavel House, south of Glasgow, is believed to have been Rudolf Hess's destination on his flight to Scotland. Clydesdale became 14th Duke of Hamilton on the death of his father in March 1940.

COLVILLE, Jock   Seconded from the Foreign Office to 10 Downing Street at the outbreak of war, Colville served Chamberlain and then Churchill as Private Secretary, becoming particularly close to Churchill. The diaries he kept, although this was forbidden in wartime, provide unique insights into life and work with the Prime Minister, the personalities around him and the conduct of the war. The originals are held by the Churchill Archives Centre, Churchill College, Cambridge.

DANSEY, Claude, served as a junior officer in the South African (Boer) War of 1899–1902, latterly in intelligence. He was subsequently recruited into the Security Service, MI5, then joined the Secret Intelligence Service, MI6. Serving in Rome in the 1930s, he recognised dangerous weaknesses in MI6's structure in Europe and set up a parallel intelligence-gathering organisation comprised mainly of business people termed the Z Organisation (his own code-name was 'Z') with a particularly strong presence in Switzerland. After the outbreak of war he was recalled to London by a new head of MI6, Stewart Menzies, who made him his right-hand man (Assistant Chief of the Secret Service).

DE COURCY, Kenneth   Before the war secretary and intelligence officer of the Imperial Policy Group of high Tory landowners, bankers, industrialists and military strategists aware of the disparity between Britain's imperial commitments and her armed forces, and anxious to avoid any continental European entanglement. The group was dissolved on the outbreak of war, but de Courcy retained his influential connections and continued to be the recipient of confidences, which he noted in a diary kept in a locked safe. A friend of Stewart Menzies and the Duke of Buccleuch, both of whom favoured compromise peace with Germany to allow Hitler to attack Russia, he was considered potentially subversive by Guy Liddell of MI5, although never arrested.

DOUGLAS-HAMILTON, Douglas *see* Clydesdale, Marquis of

EDEN, Anthony   Conservative politician who had served in the First World War and worked to prevent a second. Appointed Foreign Secretary in 1935 he attempted to use the League of Nations to curb the dictators, Hitler and Mussolini, but in 1938 resigned over disagreements with Chamberlain's 'appeasement' policy. Churchill recalled him to succeed Lord Halifax as Foreign Secretary at the end of 1940.

GOEBBELS, Josef   A rejected novelist and playwright, he had a PhD from Heidelberg University and was regarded as an intellectual by the old guard of the Nazi Party. Appointed *Gauleiter* (District Leader) of Berlin, and after the Nazis took power in 1933 Minister for Public Enlightenment and Propaganda, in which role he exercised total control over all media. One of Hitler's closest colleagues during the war, and like his leader a visceral anti-Semite, he made speeches and commissioned poisonous films to inspire disgust and hatred of Jews. The diary entries he dictated each day were also informed by propaganda values.

GÖRING, Hermann   A fighter pilot in the First World War, in the final months given command of the famous Fighter Squadron 1 formerly led by von Richthofen. An early convert to Nazism, when Hitler took power in 1933 he was appointed Minister of the Interior for

Prussia; he formed the Prussian Secret State Police (*Gestapo*), using them in ruthless suppression of Communists and other opponents. Also appointed Minister of Aviation, he created a German air force and was appointed its chief in 1935. The following year Hitler commissioned him to head a four-year plan to speed up re-armament, rewarding his success by promoting him *Reichsmarschall* and designating him his successor. Hiding his brutal character under a grossly flamboyant exterior given to lavish entertainment and outlandish costumes, he convinced many from Britain that he would make an acceptable alternative to Hitler, and was the source of numerous peace offensives before and after the outbreak of war.

HALIFAX, Lord Nicknamed 'the Holy Fox' for his devotion to Christianity and the hunt, Hitler mocked him as 'the English parson'. In 1938 on Eden's resignation, Chamberlain appointed him Foreign Secretary to pursue 'appeasement', and was not disappointed. Dedicated to peace at almost any price, he strove for compromise with Germany up to and beyond the outbreak of war. When Chamberlain fell in May 1940, he was Buckingham Palace's choice to succeed as Prime Minister, but his reluctance allowed Churchill to seize the prize. Despite their very different views Churchill retained him as Foreign Secretary in the War Cabinet until the end of that year when he sent him to Washington as British Ambassador.

HAMILTON, Duke of *see* Clydesdale, Marquis of

HASSELL, Ulrich von Career diplomat from the Prussian landed nobility married to the daughter of Grand Admiral von Tirpitz, for whom he had worked as secretary after being wounded in the First World War. Posted as Ambassador to Rome in 1932, he joined the Nazi Party the following year, but became disgusted by Hitler's methods. Recalled home in 1938 he supported opposition groups plotting a generals' revolt to oust the regime. After the outbreak of war he passed messages to the British government through Halifax's envoy, Lonsdale Bryans. He was arrested and executed after the failed July 1944 assassination attempt on Hitler.

HAUSHOFER, Albrecht Academic geographer, the son of Professor Karl Haushofer and his half-Jewish wife, Martha. Rudolf Hess protected him and his brother from the consequences of their Jewish blood; in return Albrecht served Hess as a roving expert on foreign affairs, particularly on British politics and personalities. Keenly aware of the evil in Nazism and hating himself for his complicity with the regime, he also worked for an opposition group. He was executed by Himmler's SS towards the end of the war.

HAUSHOFER, Professor Karl An army general turned academic; on retirement in 1919, he taught Political Geography at Munich University. Developing a Geopolitical doctrine including the necessity for expanding eastwards for living space (*Lebensraum*) to ensure food supplies, and stressing the need for friendship with Britain, he advised Hitler on these lines through Rudolf Hess when both were imprisoned after the failed 'Beerhall Putsch' of 1923. It is evident in Hitler's testament, *Mein Kampf*, and in his policies after coming to power. Haushofer and his wife committed suicide after the lost war.

HAUSHOFER, Martha Daughter of Georg Ludwig Meyer, a German-Jewish businessman, she married Karl Haushofer in 1896 and was mother to Albrecht and Heinz.

HESS, Ilse, née Pröhl. Raised in an upper middle class family in Berlin, she first met Rudolf Hess in 1920 on moving to Munich to take her entrance exams for Munich University. He had just returned from a flying mission against a Communist uprising in the Ruhr and was wearing the field-grey uniform of the *Freikorps Epp*. She knew with an unforgettable clarity, she wrote later, that her life had been directed towards this young man. So it proved: they found they were living in the same pension, and they shared a love of walking and skiing and soon a dedication to Adolf Hitler; she also took on secretarial duties for Hess, and they married in 1927 with Hitler's blessing. After the war she published his letters from captivity in two moving volumes.

HESS, Rudolf Born into the house of a prosperous German import-export merchant in the Egyptian seaport of Alexandria in 1894, and destined to follow his father into the family firm. He attended the small German school in the city until the age of twelve, and after being tutored at home for two years was sent to a boarding school at Bad Godesberg on the Rhine; there he excelled at maths and sciences and developed a love for the music of the German composers, Beethoven in particular. Thence he was sent to a commercial college in Switzerland, and afterwards apprenticed to a firm in Hamburg to learn the practical side of business. But with no desire to follow the path his father had chosen for him the outbreak of the First World War came as a personal emotional release. He volunteered for the army and rose to commissioned rank before transferring to the air force. Germany's defeat came as a profound shock. Enrolling at Munich University to study Political Economy, his life was given a new direction when in 1920 he heard Hitler speak at a meeting of the young National Socialist German Workers' ('Nazi') Party, and promise to restore Germany's honour. He became Hitler's most faithful follower, his co-writer for his memoirs, his secretary and when he achieved power in 1933, his deputy.

HESS, Wolf Rüdiger The only son of Rudolf and Ilse Hess, born in November 1937 and only three-and-a-half years old when his father flew off to Scotland and captivity. After the war he qualified as an engineer and entered government service. He did not see his father again until at the age of 32 on Christmas Eve 1969 he visited him in Spandau prison with his mother. He led a vigorous but ultimately unsuccessful international campaign to have his father freed, edited a volume of his father's letters and wrote two books about his father's mission to Britain and inhumane period of imprisonment. He died in 2001.

HESSE, Prince Philipp of After service in the First World War, Prince Philipp of Hesse studied art history and architecture in Darmstadt, but left without a degree and moved to Rome, where he set up as an interior designer. In 1925 he married Princess Matilda, daughter of the King of Italy. Impressed by Fascism in Italy, he joined the

Nazi Party in 1930 and acted as go-between for Hitler with Mussolini, also as Hitler's art agent in Italy. Both he and his wife were arrested and sent to concentration camps in 1943 as Hitler grew disenchanted with the princely houses; both survived the war.

HEYDRICH, Reinhard, grew up in a musical household: his father, Bruno, was a composer and opera singer who founded the Halle Conservatory of Music; his mother was a piano teacher. He himself became a talented violinist. As a schoolboy false rumours that his father had Jewish blood meant he was taunted as a Jew. Distinctly Aryan in appearance – over six feet tall with blond hair, blue eyes and a long, equine face – he nonetheless tried to distance himself from the jeers by joining aggressively anti-Semitic societies. He entered the navy in 1922 and formed a fateful friendship in the cadet training ship with an officer, Wilhelm Canaris (see above), famed for clandestine re-armament, who inspired him with interest in espionage and intelligence. When Himmler was looking for an intelligence officer in 1931 Heydrich was discharged from the navy, allegedly for breaking a marriage engagement, and engaged to establish an intelligence office for him, soon named the Security Service (*Sicherheitsdienst* or *SD*). It was the beginning of a diabolic partnership between Himmler and his new chief executive that was to define Nazi repression, aggression and genocide: both were morally blind and completely ruthless. Heydrich was assassinated in 1942 by British (SOE)-trained Czech agents.

HIMMLER, Heinrich Born into a middle-class Catholic family, second son of a Munich *Gymnasium* headmaster, he attended church regularly and was a model pupil at school, invariably near the top of his class. The exception was the gym, where he proved physically inept and suffered humiliation. He wanted to become an army officer, but the war ended too soon. Instead he turned to agriculture, but soon lost his job and became swept up in the post-war ferment of nationalist anti-Communist politics in Munich, serving in Ernst Röhm's paramilitary *Freikorps* during the failed 'Beerhall Putsch', subsequently touring rural Bavaria on anti-Communist, anti-Jewish speaking tours for the Nazi Party, and organising protection squads (*Schutzstaffeln* or

SS) for party meetings. His conscientiousness in this role led to his appointment as *Reichsführer-SS* (National Leader-SS) in 1929 just as hyper-inflation was boosting party membership. He forged the SS into a pure-blooded (no Jewish ancestors) praetorian guard loyal to the Führer, attracting many from the higher social classes into the officer corps, including Reinhard Heydrich, whom he made chief of his Security Service. After the Nazis came to power he took over the secret state police (*Gestapo*) and formed a closed triangle of repression: SS–*Gestapo*–concentration camps. Commissioned by Hitler to eliminate European Jewry, he charged Heydrich with the detailed planning of what in 1942 became industrialised murder. Captured at the end of the war, he committed suicide with a poison pill.

HITLER, Adolf   Son of an Austrian customs official who disciplined him savagely and a doting mother who spoiled him. At elementary school he was a leader of other boys playing war games, which he loved, but, sent to a *Realschule* (Technical Secondary School) in Linz, he hated it and failed to apply himself. Characterised by one teacher as stubborn and hot-tempered, he fantasised about becoming a great artist, but when he applied to the Vienna Academy of Fine Arts in 1907, he was rejected. His mother was stricken with cancer and he looked after her until she died, then moved to Vienna, living an indolent life, but painting city scenes, which he sold. Thence in 1913 he moved to Munich, artistic capital of Germany, there greeting the outbreak of the First World War with enthusiasm, and enlisting in the Bavarian infantry. He served with courage as a despatch runner on the western front and was awarded the Iron Cross 1st class, but rose no higher than corporal. In the turbulence after the war he was employed by the army to infiltrate the German Workers' Party in Munich (soon changed to the National Socialist German Workers', or 'Nazi', Party). He proved its most effective orator, and after discharge from the army became principal propagandist and leader of the party, drawing large crowds when he spoke. He played on the resentments and prejudices of his audiences, blaming the lost war and humiliation of the Versailles Treaty on international Jewry. As hyper-inflation ruined lives, swelling both Nazi and Communist Party membership, he struck deals with nationalist politicians and military and industrial chiefs who in 1933 brought him to power to defeat Communism and remove the limitations imposed on the armed forces by the Versailles Treaty. He used the burning of the Parliament building, the *Reichstag*, allegedly by a Communist, to liquidate the rule of law, establish a dictatorship and arm for war to smash Soviet Russia and gain hegemony in Europe. His overriding emotional goal was the purification of German blood; analysis of his writings and speeches suggests he suspected he himself had Jewish blood, but this Hebrew ancestor, if he existed, has never been found. At the end of the war he forced on Europe he committed suicide under the ruins of Berlin.

HOARE, Sir Samuel   High-flying Conservative politician who first entered Parliament in 1910. His health prevented him serving in the First World War, but he learned Russian and was recruited into the Secret Service and served in St Petersburg, then Rome. Between the wars he held senior posts in government: Secretary of State for Air; for India; Foreign Secretary and Home Secretary. A supporter of Chamberlain's 'appeasement' policy, he was subsequently blamed as one of the 'guilty men' opposing re-armament. Churchill dismissed him when he came to power in May 1940, but subsequently sent him as Ambassador to Madrid specifically to prevent General Franco from bringing Spain into the war on the side of the dictators. In this he succeeded, but it was his last appointment. He died in 1959.

HOHENLOHE, Prince Max zu   Descended from one of Germany's oldest and most illustrious princely houses with great estates in the Sudetenland and Spain and a wide circle of social contacts, he was a member of Himmler's influential 'Circle of Friends' supporting the growth of the SS. A friend of Göring, he offered his services as a mediator between Germany and Britain before the outbreak of war, and continued to meet British agents and ambassadors throughout the war, reporting back to the Foreign Ministry in Berlin.

JAHNKE, Kurt   Born into a Junker (landowning) family in the Prussian province of Posen in 1882, Jahnke emigrated to the United

States at age sixteen, joined the US Marines and became a US citizen. During the First World War he worked for the German navy as an intelligence and sabotage agent based in San Francisco, continuing his activities from Mexico after America entered the war. Returning to Germany during a period of secret German armament co-operation with the Soviets in the early 1920s, he worked for the Fourth Department of the Soviet Commissariat for War. Subsequently he created his own intelligence bureau in Berlin, working closely with Admiral Canaris (see above) and in the late 1930s was certainly in touch with the British, including Vansittart's agents. His bureau was merged with Hess's intelligence department under Pfeffer von Salomon before the outbreak of war, but dissolved for an unexplained reason in April 1940, when he was engaged as adviser to Walter Schellenberg, head of foreign counter-intelligence in Himmler's Security Service (SD). Jahnke had a Swiss wife with whom he frequently visited Switzerland. After Hess's flight to Scotland Schellenberg received a detailed report of Jahnke's activities as a top-level British agent who met his contacts in Switzerland. Jahnke denied it. There is no doubt that he and his secretary and agent-runner, Carl Marcus, hated Hitler and Nazism. He was captured by the Russians in 1945 and executed; other reports have him returning to live in Berlin or Switzerland.

KENT, Duke of Prince George, fourth son of King George V, shared with his eldest brother Edward, Prince of Wales (subsequently Edward VIII and, after abdication, Duke of Windsor – see below), admiration for the benefits Nazism had brought Germany, and acted as conduit between Edward and the German Ambassador in London, von Ribbentrop. While taking royal duties seriously, he was also a cocaine-using bisexual playboy who had many affairs with both sexes. Married to Princess Marina of Greece and Denmark, they made one of the most glamorous couples on the international circuit. In April 1940 he joined the staff of RAF Training Command with the rank of Group Captain, subsequently touring RAF bases on morale-boosting visits. He was killed in an unexplained air crash in August 1942.

KIRKPATRICK, Ivone   Of Catholic Irish descent, he was severely wounded in the First World War at Gallipoli; subsequently transferred to propaganda and intelligence duties, he ended the war running a network of British agents from the Netherlands. He joined the Foreign Office in 1919 and served as First Secretary at the British Embassy in Berlin from 1933 to 1938, privy to top-level meetings between British ministers and top Nazis, including Hitler and Hess. In 1940 he was appointed director of the foreign division of the Ministry of Information; behind the official posting he served on the board of SOE after Churchill set up the sabotage and propaganda organisation. An obvious choice to debrief Hess on his arrival in Scotland, there are questions about what he may have omitted from his official reports on these interviews. His memoirs are uninformative. He died in 1964.

LIDDELL, Guy   Son of a Royal Artillery officer, cousin of Lewis Carroll's muse, Alice Liddell, he was studying to be a professional cellist when the First World War broke out. Enlisting in the Royal Artillery, he was commissioned from the ranks and won the Military Cross. Afterwards joining Scotland Yard's Special Branch, he transferred in 1931 to the Security Service, MI5. In June 1940, after Churchill dismissed MI5's Director General and redirected priorities to combat fascist instead of Communist subversion, he was appointed Director of 'B' Division (Counter-Espionage). Dubbed by the intelligence specialist, Nigel West, as 'unquestionably the pre-eminent Counter-Intelligence officer of his generation', the fact that he engaged the Soviet spy Anthony Blunt and the pro-Soviet scientist Victor Rothschild in MI5, and spent much off-duty time with other members of the Cambridge spy ring, particularly Guy Burgess and Kim Philby, led to post-war charges that he was a double agent. Nigel West, who edited his wartime diaries (held at The National Archives, Kew) for publication, strongly refutes the allegations, ascribing the company he kept to social naïvety. He was far from naïve in his professional judgements, and while there is no direct evidence against him, questions will surely remain.

LIDDELL HART, Captain Basil   Leading military historian and strategist, military correspondent of *The Daily Telegraph* 1925–1935 and *The Times* 1935–1939, he believed Britain should not become militarily involved on the European continent, and after the outbreak of war promoted compromise peace with Germany.

LLOYD GEORGE, David   Liberal politician and cabinet minister, as a reforming Chancellor of the Exchequer from 1908 laying foundations for a welfare state. He opposed Winston Churchill, his friend and colleague at the Admiralty, for his determination to outbuild Germany's growing navy, but unlike many Liberals supported Britain's declaration of war in 1914 after the German invasion of Belgium. As Prime Minster from 1916 he prosecuted the war with determination and success. At the Paris peace conference in 1919 he tried to lighten the punishments imposed on Germany, subsequently supporting territorial concessions to Germany, and after Hitler's accession to power praising him for the transformation he had wrought, even if not by democratic methods. After the outbreak of the Second World War he promoted a compromise peace with Germany and expected to succeed Churchill when he fell. He died in 1945.

MENZIES, Stewart   In all probability the son of Captain Sir George Holford, courtier to King Edward VII, who married Susannah Menzies, a favourite at court, in the Chapel Royal, St James, shortly after her husband's death; Stewart was allowed to use Holford's London residence, Dorchester House, as his own. After Eton, where he was president of the prefect society 'Pop', he was commissioned in the Life Guards and fought in the First World War on the western front. After being gassed in 1915 he was transferred to intelligence duties, and after the war joined the Secret Intelligence Service (MI6). Like the Service itself, he considered Soviet Russia a greater threat to British interests than Nazi Germany, and was strongly opposed to war with Germany. He continued to hold this view after he was appointed 'C', as the chief of the Service was known, in November 1939, after the death of the incumbent.

MESSERSCHMITT, Professor Willi   Designer and builder of Nazi Germany's most successful fighter aircraft, the Me 109, and chairman and managing director of the company that bore his name, with works and airstrip outside Augsburg, near Munich. Hess had supported him through a difficult period, and Messerschmitt repaid him by giving him the fighter-bomber Me 110 he required to fly to Scotland in May 1941. He also provided Hess with flying training and all the modifications Hess requested for the aircraft.

MORTON, Major Desmond Served in the Royal Artillery in the First World War. In 1917 he was shot in the heart, but recovered; awarded the Military Cross, he finished the war as ADC to the Commander of British Forces, Sir Douglas Haig. Subsequently he joined MI6. In 1929 he was appointed head of the Industrial Intelligence Centre investigating the arms manufacturing capabilities of the powers. He lived at Edenbridge, close to Churchill's home, Chartwell, and during the 1930s supplied secret reports which Churchill used in his attempts to wake the country to the threat from Germany. When Churchill became Prime Minister in May 1940 he appointed Morton his personal intelligence assistant to keep an eye on MI6, and installed him in an office next to the cabinet room. Morton, a garrulous raconteur given to over-egging his stories, gradually lost influence to Stewart Menzies.

MUSSOLINI, Benito The founder of Fascism in Italy, an authoritarian, ultranationalist movement transcending class; Mussolini, a former socialist, came to power after leading a march on Rome and ousting the government in 1922, providing one of several models for Hitler's dictatorship. Deposed soon after the Allied invasion of Italy in 1943, he was summarily executed by Italian partisans in April 1945.

PHILBY, Harold 'Kim' Notorious member of the 'Cambridge spy ring', including Donald Maclean and Guy Burgess, all said to have been recruited by the Soviet NKVD (later KGB) in the early 1930s while undergraduates at Trinity College, Cambridge, under the influence of Anthony Blunt. It was fashionable for intellectuals to look towards Communism as a panacea for unemployment and the class system in Britain. At the beginning of the war Philby was working as a correspondent for *The Times*. He was recruited into SOE in 1940 and posted to their training establishment at Beaulieu, Hampshire, and was still there in May 1941 when Hess arrived in Scotland. Recruited into MI6 later that year, he supplied secret intelligence to Moscow throughout the war and into the 'Cold War'. Unmasked in the 1950s, he fled to Moscow in 1963, where he died, a hero of the Soviet Union, in 1998.

RIBBENTROP, Joachim von   The son of a Prussian army officer not entitled to the aristocratic 'von'; the fact that he acquired it from a distant relative by adoption later in life reveals much. After a cosmopolitan childhood with no formal education after fifteen, and service in the First World War, winning the Iron Cross 1st Class, in 1920 he married into the family of a leading German *Sekt* (sparkling wine) manufacturer and became a prosperous international wine dealer in his own right. A convert to Nazism in 1932, he impressed Hitler with his knowledge of the world, and in 1935 delighted him when, appointed head of a mission to Britain, he brought back a naval treaty. He was sent to London as German Ambassador in 1936, annoying most of those he met with his pomposity and ignorance of British governance. Two years later Hitler appointed him Foreign Minister, and in 1939 he negotiated the Nazi–Soviet non-aggression pact precipitating the outbreak of war. He was scorned by Göring, Goebbels, Hess and the 'old fighters' of the party. At Nuremberg in 1946 he was sentenced to death and hanged.

ROBERTSON, Major T.A. 'Tar'   After public school and Sandhurst he was commissioned in the Seaforth Highlanders, but resigned after two years, possibly due to debts from high life in London. He joined a City bank, then the Birmingham Police before being recruited into the Security Service, MI5, in 1933. During the Second World War he was head of Section B1a, controlling Nazi spies in Britain who had been 'turned' to work as double agents for the British. The information or disinformation they sent their German stations was decided by representatives of service intelligence chiefs meeting weekly as the Twenty, or XX ('Double-Cross'), Committee under the chairmanship of the Oxford historian, J.C. Masterman. Robertson proved outstanding at running double agents without letting the enemy suspect the deception, thereby influencing key campaigns, and equally talented at inspiring lifelong affection in his own team. He died in 1994.

RÖHM, Captain Ernst   Born in Munich, his father a railway official, he was commissioned in the Bavarian 10th Infantry Regiment in 1908. During the First World War he was severely wounded, bearing the scars for life. Returning to Munich after the war, he served with von Epp's *Freikorps* to depose a Soviet government established in the city. He helped to arm Hitler's paramilitary SA, and in 1923 took part in Hitler's failed 'Beerhall Putsch'. In 1931 Hitler appointed him chief of the SA, which grew under his leadership to an unruly force over 4 million strong, threatening the government and the regular military leadership. Hitler decided in favour of the army and conspired with Himmler and Heydrich to purge the SA, whose leaders they arrested on the 30 June 1934, 'the night of the long knives'. Röhm was among the many subsequently executed.

ROOSEVELT, Franklin D.   President of the United States, first elected in March 1933, barely a month after Hitler became Chancellor of Germany, and noted for his 'new deal' legislation to reverse the economic malaise after the Wall Street crash. Re-elected in 1937, he began a major re-armament programme to deter Japanese expansion in the Pacific. In Europe he viewed the survival of Britain and the Royal Navy as vital for US security, and on 11 September 1939 initiated a personal correspondence with Chamberlain and Churchill, then First Lord of the Admiralty, expressing his support. As Assistant Secretary of the US Navy in 1918, he had met Churchill and regarded him as a 'stinker', but the secret correspondence they exchanged in the opening years of the Second World War was vital for Churchill's strategy and the development of a partnership in which US industry was mobilised as the 'arsenal of democracy'. Isolationist sentiment in America prevented Roosevelt from openly joining the war against the fascist powers, but his industrial and naval support for Britain breached US neutrality in letter and spirit. After winning an unprecedented third term as President in 1941, the Japanese attack on Pearl Harbor followed by Hitler's declaration of war against the United

States propelled America into the war. He died in office just before final victory in 1945.

ROSENBERG, Alfred   Born in 1893 in Estonia, then part of Russia, he was studying engineering in Moscow in 1917 when the Bolshevik Revolution broke out. Romantically attracted to Germany – his forbears had been German – he emigrated to Berlin, thence moved to Munich, where he met Hitler and impressed him with his first-hand knowledge of the Russian Revolution and his conviction that it was caused by the conspiracy of international Jewry which aimed to undermine all governments and seize power throughout the world. He became editor of the Nazi newspaper, *Völkischer Beobachter*, and the party's pre-eminent racial theorist, postulating in his key book, *The Myth of the Twentieth Century* (1930), a race hierarchy with 'Nordic Aryans' at the top and Jews at the bottom, and stressing the necessity for laws to protect Nordic blood from contamination. In April 1941, before the assault on Russia, Hitler appointed him his delegate for Central Planning for the East European area about to be conquered, and after the start of the offensive *Reichsminister* for the occupied east, but he was completely ineffectual against Himmler and regional Nazi governors. He was sentenced to death and hanged at Nuremberg in 1946.

ROTHSCHILD, Victor, grew up at the grand Rothschild mansion, Tring Park, Buckinghamshire. His father, Charles, was a keen naturalist, his uncle, Walter, who lived at Tring, a zoologist, and they awakened in him an early interest in nature; it is said he could identify butterfly species before he could read their names. Educated at Harrow and Trinity College, Cambridge, he developed into a good-looking young man of remarkable academic, musical and sporting talent. He also drove a racing car, played jazz, collected art and 18th-century books and threw champagne parties. Beneath the gilded exterior, under the influence of Anthony Blunt and others of the Cambridge secret society, the 'Apostles', he became a committed Communist, believing in scientific Marxism, and supporting the Soviet Union as potential saviour of the Jewish race threatened by Nazism. After university and a spell of only six months with the family bank, whose ambience bored him, he returned to Cambridge, gaining a research fellowship in Zoology. In 1937 his uncle died and he became 3rd Baron Rothschild and head of the dynasty. On the outbreak of war he applied his scientific mind to sabotage research for military intelligence, and in 1940 was recruited by Guy Liddell of MI5 and set up an anti-sabotage section (B1c). He introduced Blunt to Liddell, who recruited him as his personal assistant. Since Blunt and Guy Burgess sub-leased a flat in a London house Rothschild owned, where Liddell and Kim Philby were visitors, it is not surprising that after the defection of Burgess, Donald Maclean and Philby to Moscow and the unmasking of Anthony Blunt in the 1960s Rothschild was rumoured to be the 'fifth man' in the Cambridge spy ring. There is strong circumstantial evidence in support, but no direct proof has been found. He died in 1990.

SIMON, Lord, a successful lawyer with a cold manner who liked to insist that despite his name he was not a Jew, entered Parliament as a Liberal in 1906 and was soon appointed to government. During the interwar years he served as Foreign Secretary, Home Secretary and Chancellor of the Exchequer. Like Hoare, tarnished as one of the 'guilty men' for supporting 'appeasement', he was removed from the War Cabinet when Churchill became Prime Minister, raised to the peerage as Viscount Simon and appointed Lord Chancellor; this was his last government post. He died in 1954.

STALIN, Joseph   General Secretary of the Central Committee of the Communist Party, *de facto* dictator of Soviet Russia. As a boy he had, like Hitler, suffered physical abuse from a brutal father. He won a scholarship to an Orthodox Seminary at sixteen but once there discovered Marxist literature and joined the Bolshevik Party; subsequently taking part in the Russian Revolution with Lenin, he took over Lenin's political mantle on his death in 1924. Ruthless in purging rivals and promoting his own personality cult, he forced through collective farming and rapid industrialisation by terrible means: in terms of numbers driven from their homes, wiped out by famine, sent to concentration camps in Siberia, worked to death as slave labourers, executed as 'enemies of the state', tortured and murdered by sadists in the NKVD – People's Commissariat of Internal Affairs – and secret state police, Stalin's victims were on a scale Hitler never matched. German historians have argued that his transformation of Russia forced its mirror image, Nazism, on Germany. Vansittart (see below) would not have agreed. Stalin knew Hitler would turn on him eventually; he agreed to the non-aggression pact of 1939, carving up eastern Europe between them, in order to create a buffer. Despite eventual victory over his enemy, he grew increasingly paranoid, and died of a stroke in 1953.

TAVISTOCK, Marquis of *see* Bedford, Duke of

VANSITTART, Sir Robert   A spell at a school in Imperial Germany at the time of the South African (Boer) War when Anglophobia and militarist nationalism poured from all media moulded his view of Germany. In marked contrast to his own school, Eton, he found in German schools and universities 'no real love of sport or games but only of fighting fitness', aloof and inhuman teachers who took pleasure in humiliating their pupils, and spying and 'sneaking' everywhere. He entered the diplomatic service in 1902 and in 1930 was appointed Permanent Undersecretary (non-political head) at the Foreign Office. Realising that Hitler was bent on war, he advocated alliance with France and Soviet Russia to maintain the peace, while using his intelligence sources, including one inside the German Air Ministry, to brief Churchill on German re-armament. He opposed Chamberlain's policy of appeasing Hitler so stridently that in 1938 he was removed from his post and appointed to a non-position designated Chief Diplomatic Adviser; but he retained his intelligence sources and after Churchill came to power in May 1940 played a senior intelligence and propaganda role. A series of his wireless broadcasts published in January 1941 as *Black Record*, arguing that Nazism was a natural outcome of historic German militarism, became the most influential popular manifesto for continuing the fight, and also ran through several editions in the United States. He wrote plays, novels and poetry and died in 1957 while writing his memoirs, never reaching the period of appeasement when his career was so abruptly terminated.

WINDSOR, Duke of   Prince Edward, eldest son of King George V and Queen Mary, ascended the throne as King Edward VIII of the United Kingdom and Commonwealth and Emperor of India in January 1936; he abdicated in December that year and was succeeded by his brother, Prince Albert, who took the title King George VI. The practical reason for the abdication was Edward's insistence on marrying the American divorcee, Wallis Simpson; beneath this lay his open sympathy for Hitler and Nazism and Mrs Simpson's closeness to the German Ambassador in London, von Ribbentrop. Given the title Duke of Windsor, he married Mrs Simpson in France in June 1937 and the couple toured Germany later that year, entertained by Hitler, Hess and other top Nazis. On the outbreak of war he was sent to France with the British Military Mission. After the fall of France Churchill appointed him Governor of the Bahamas to keep him out of the country. He was not forgiven by the British Royal family, particularly Queen Elizabeth, and after the war lived in exile with his wife in France until his death in 1972.

CHAPTER ONE

Death in the summer house

17 AUGUST 1987: to all appearances, just another morning. Prisoner Number Seven eased himself from bed with the painful movements of age. He was 93. His hair was grey and thin on top, his eyes deep-set beneath bushy brows. Once he had been second man in Hitler's Reich. Despite the changes wrought in him by age, those who had seen him then leading the massed ranks of the Nazi Party in ringing acclamation of the Führer would have had little difficulty in recognising him. He believed he was still due the dignity of that station. He had never accepted the jurisdiction of the victor powers at the Nuremberg war crimes trials, nor reconciled himself to his sentence.

Six other leading Nazis confined with him in Spandau jail, West Berlin, had been freed long since. He alone remained, the sole inmate of a cell complex built to house 600, watched over by a prison directorate, warders, guards, kitchen and laundry staff and a platoon of soldiers provided by one of the four victor powers of the war on a monthly rota. August was the American month.

He had been held for just over 40 years in Spandau, in total 14,640 days, and for six years before that in captivity in Britain and Nuremberg, altogether almost half his life span. Appeals for his release made by his family, groups of sympathisers and prominent individuals in the West appalled by the unprecedented length of his imprisonment had been rejected by the Russians. At Nuremberg they had wanted him hanged as a prime mover in the Nazi assault on their country. They had not forgotten nor forgiven;[1] and now, in the Cold War with the West, Spandau provided them with a convenient listening post in the British sector of Berlin.

There had been recent signs of change. A thaw in East–West relations inspired by a new Soviet leader, Mikhail Gorbachev, had been accompanied by hints of clemency for the prisoner in Spandau;[2] and in June the German-speaking service of Radio Moscow had held out the prospect of 'the long-standing endeavours for the release of the war criminal Rudolf Hess soon being crowned with success'.[3] His supporters felt that such a sensational statement must have been approved at the highest level in the Kremlin.

Over the past two decades his living conditions had been rendered easier. He now occupied a double cell, formerly used as the chapel for the seven. The cell door was no longer locked, in case he needed to get out quickly to the lavatory. Beside his bed he had a table with a mug, a ceramic pot with an immersion heating coil for boiling water, the wherewithal for making tea and coffee and an anglepoise reading lamp. On the wall behind the bedhead were large charts of the moon's surface sent to him by NASA in Texas. He had made himself a lay expert in space exploration over the years. The study of history, philosophy and the latest developments in space travel, and brief periods listening to his favourite composers – Beethoven, Schumann, Schubert – on an old record player whose sound was no longer true, had been his release from the emptiness of his solitary confinement without end.

Outside, the garden provided solace. It had been created by the prisoners from a wild area of some twelve acres between the rear of the cell block and the high red-brick wall enclosing the prison grounds. Prisoner Number Four, Albert Speer, formerly Hitler's architect and armaments minister, had designed a scheme of paths and lawns and overseen the planting of roses, forsythia, lavender and hydrangia bushes and lilac trees among the existing trees. Birds flitted among the branches.

Besides the warders who guarded him in shifts, Number Seven had a male nurse to attend him, a Tunisian named Abdallah Melaouhi, who lived in a flat just outside the prison walls. An experienced senior nurse, Melaouhi had looked after the old man in Spandau for five years, and the two had come to trust and like one another. Melaouhi had entered the prison at 7.00 that morning, as he did on most mornings;[4] he now escorted his charge from the lavatory to the wash cell and helped him shower, shave and dress; thence to the First Aid Room or dispensary, where he weighed him, measured his blood pressure, pulse and temperature, trimmed his hair and gave him his daily massage before counting out the pills he was prescribed for hypertension, heart and circulatory ailments.[5]

After escorting him back to his cell, Melaouhi left and went back to his apartment, returning to the prison shortly after 9.00. Meanwhile, the old man lay back on his bed, tired, and dozed off. On most mornings he slept for an hour or so before going out into the garden, but on this morning he stayed in, and later, as it was a Monday, made out his weekly requisition form, this time for 30 packets of paper tissues, three rolls of lavatory paper, a sheet of writing paper and a ruler. The form was handed in to the chief warder at 10.20.[6] Ten minutes later his lunch was wheeled in to the cell block. As always, Melaouhi took the first mouthful, indulging the suspicion of poison the old man had manifested long ago during the first days of his captivity in England. Shortly afterwards he asked Melaouhi to go to the nearby shops in his lunch break and buy a replacement for the ceramic pot he used as a kettle. Melaouhi was logged leaving the prison at 11.07.

At 12.15 a black American warder named Tony Jordan relieved the British warder on cell duty. During the previous American tour of guard duty in April, Number Seven had requested Jordan's dismissal on the ground that the man's poor education, rudeness and antagonism towards him endangered his health.[7] The request had been refused. It was believed among prison staff that the real reason for the complaint was Number Seven's prejudice against black people, manifested on earlier occasions.

The August day was warm and bright. Shafts of sunlight filtered through the small barred windows high in his cell, and at about 1.30 he sought permission for his usual outing in the garden. Jordan helped him dress for the walk – as always a protracted process, finishing with a light tan raincoat and a wide-brimmed straw sombrero hat. He then escorted him slowly to the lift that had been installed specifically to ease his passage to ground level. The two were logged going down together at 2.10.[8]

At the bottom Jordan left his charge and went outside, taking a path through the garden that led to a metal cabin some twelve feet by seven, variously termed the 'summer house', the 'garden house' or the 'resthouse'. Reaching it, Jordan unlocked the single door in the cabin wall facing the prison. There was a small window in the same side; the opposite side facing the perimeter wall of the prison grounds was formed of sliding glass doors. The two ends were windowless. Inside was a straw mat on the floor, two chairs, a bench and a table and four electric reading lamps. Here the old man liked to sit alone, whatever the weather, and read or think or frequently just doze off. The warders, instructed to watch him at all times, usually respected his privacy and sat outside, checking him at intervals.[9]

But this was no ordinary day: it was the last day of the old man's life, and a subsequent Military Police investigation was to find he had been planning it for some time. The witness statements on which this conclusion is based, released a quarter of a century later, leave little room for doubt about the sequence of events.

THE MILITARY POLICE INVESTIGATION

Names have been redacted from the statements; witnesses are identified only by numbers. The American soldier who had the most comprehensive view of the unfolding drama from the beginning is numbered Nine. His post was in observation tower number three of altogether six towers built above the perimeter wall and numbered clockwise in ascending order. Tower number three was opposite and something under 100 yards from the rear of the prison building and the exit from the lift to the garden. When Nine looked towards the prison from his observation platform some 20 feet above ground, the 'summer house' was diagonally to his left some 30 yards away, glass side towards him but partly obscured by the foliage of a nearby tree.

At about 2.20 p.m. his shift supervisor, Sergeant Ten, approached the foot of the tower on his rounds and called up to make sure all was in order. As Nine responded he heard the door at the rear of the prison complex open and saw Jordan emerge alone. The warder walked to the dirt path leading towards the summer house and on reaching the little cabin unlocked the single door on the prison side – although all Nine could actually see from his elevated position was the top of the door swing outwards beyond the flat roof. Jordan, by his own account, supported by the testimony of Sergeant Ten, then went inside and unlocked the glass doors on the side facing Nine's tower before walking back along the path to the prison building and in via the door from which he had first emerged. A moment later he came out and again took the path towards the summer house. Nine noticed that 'as the warder walked to and from the resthouse he was looking around all the time, as though he was checking the area. On one occasion I saw him look directly up at the sky as though he was checking the weather.'[10]

Sergeant Ten meanwhile climbed up Nine's tower to the observation platform and checked the telephone that connected to the prison switchboard. Watching him, Nine heard him exclaim, 'He's out!' and turning towards the prison building saw Prisoner Number Seven, in wide-brimmed straw sombrero and tan raincoat, emerge from the door Jordan had come from and walk slowly with the aid of a cane along the same path leading to the summer house. He stared. He had never seen the prisoner before. 'Allied Prisoner No. 7 took only a few steps at a time and would then stop and look around as though he was looking at the sights,' recalled Nine. 'He would then take a few more steps. On one occasion I saw [him] look upwards at my tower for what I would describe as a quick glance. I would say that it took Allied Prisoner No. 7 about ten minutes to walk from the main prison building to the resthouse where I lost sight of him.'

He had also lost sight of the warder, Jordan. Meanwhile he had alerted US soldier Thirteen at the prison switchboard to the fact that the prisoner was out in the grounds if he wanted to have a look; Thirteen had never seen the prisoner either. Hoping to catch a glimpse of him, Thirteen had another member of the guard relieve him at the switchboard and went out into the garden, walking anti-clockwise past observation towers five and four towards the summer house. As he neared it he saw the warder, Jordan, wearing a blue jacket and tie sitting on a bench by a tree some fifteen feet to the right of the cabin. He walked on, passing the cabin on his right some twelve feet away, noting that the single door was shut. He looked in through the window, but could see no one.

He carried on walking until he came opposite observation tower number three and called over to Nine, 'Can you see him?'

'No, I can't see him, he's inside,' Nine replied – meaning inside the rest house.

'I didn't see him,' Thirteen said before waving his hand and continuing his anti-clockwise walk towards tower number two and back to his post at the switchboard.

By this time Sergeant Ten had left Nine's tower, and the Guard Commander, Lieutenant Three, also on his rounds, had climbed up to the observation platform in tower number three. He witnessed the incident:

> I believe I had been in the tower two minutes when one of the sentries, 13, came up to the bottom of the tower and informed me he had not seen the prisoner in the gardenhouse, although this is a little bit unusual because normally Prisoner No. 7 sits in the gardenhouse in such a way he could be seen through a window located in the wall nearest the prison building ... I did not attach any importance to this at the time.

In the light of subsequent events, Thirteen's observation was crucial. Jordan was sitting outside under the tree; the single door to the cabin was shut and the prisoner could not be seen through the window. It is not surprising the significance was not appreciated at the time. Lieutenant Three left the tower and walked away from the summer house in a clockwise direction to the guardroom by the front gate of the prison.

* * *

A few minutes later, perhaps 2.35 p.m., Jordan got up from the bench and went to the summer house to check on his charge. According to his own statement, looking in through the single window, 'I immediately saw that Allied Prisoner No. 7 was lying on his back on the floor ... slumped against the wall in which the window I was looking in was situated.'

He ran in through the door and saw that the prisoner had one shoulder – 'I think it was the right one' – against the wall, his legs stretched out on the floor and an electrical cable around his neck. This was taut and appeared to be supporting him. The upper end was tied to the window handle. He lifted the prisoner to relieve the tension on the cable and pulled it from around his neck; it seemed to come away quite easily: 'The prisoner's eyes were open and he appeared to be alive. I spoke to him ... He was moving slightly and appeared to understand what I said or at least that I had spoken to him.'

Jordan laid him on his back and placed what he thought was a blanket, but which proved to be the prisoner's tan raincoat, under his head; he undid the prisoner's top shirt buttons and loosened his shirt, afterwards running out to seek assistance.

From tower number three, sentry Nine saw Jordan, without the blue jacket and tie he had been wearing earlier, running towards the prison building, cutting across the grass instead of following the path, but turning before he reached the building and running back towards the summer house. Before reaching it, he turned and again ran towards the prison, this time going inside. Realising something was wrong, Nine alerted the switchboard with the intercom radio that, as in all the observation towers, supplemented the telephone. At much the same time, Jordan called the switchboard from a telephone at the rear of the prison, at the bottom of a spiral staircase leading up to the cell block. The call is logged in the duty warder's log at 14.30, although it was surely later. The '3' of the '30' obscures another, now indecipherable figure.[11]

Lieutenant Three, who had been in the guardroom barely ten minutes since leaving tower number three, replied to Nine's radio call, instructing him to remain at his post; he would deal with it. Jordan meanwhile ran out into the garden and over to Nine's tower, calling up and asking if Nine could do first aid. 'Yes,' Nine replied, and started telling him his orders were to remain at his post, but the warder ran off back to the summer house, thence again towards the prison building.

Lieutenant Three meanwhile left the guardhouse and walked through the garden anti-clockwise past towers numbers five and four to tower number three, where he called up to ask Nine where the warder was. The sentry pointed towards the prison building. Seeing Jordan there, the lieutenant called him over. Jordan, who 'appeared to be panicking', led him to the summer house and in through the single door. Lieutenant Three saw the prisoner lying on the floor on his back under the window, his legs pointing towards the door, his shirt unbuttoned, his head resting on his folded raincoat: 'his eyes were wide open and staring, his mouth was open. To me he appeared to be dead. I went up to him and checked for a pulse on his left wrist. I found a very weak pulse, it was hardly noticeable. He did not appear to be breathing.'

Lieutenant Three ran to tower number three and told Nine to instruct the guardroom that they needed medical assistance right away. The shift supervisor, Sergeant Ten, had come into the garden by this time. Lieutenant Three went over and told him to ensure really tight security, afterwards returning to the summer house, where he found a medical orderly, Four, and the prisoner's nurse, Abdallah Melaouhi, had arrived.

The medic, Four, later testified that he had been called at about 2.40 p.m.; he was certain of the time, he had looked at his watch. Hurrying to his room, he had collected his first aid bag and run into the garden area, meeting Sergeant Ten who had passed him to Jordan, and they had both run to the summer house. He knelt at the prisoner's left side and tried but failed to detect any breathing; he checked the carotid artery, listened to his chest with a stethoscope and felt the radial pulse in his left arm: 'I did not detect any sign of life. Also during my first check, I noticed a red mark around Prisoner No. 7's neck, running under his chin from ear to ear. The mark was pinkish red in colour, about an inch wide all along.'

Afterwards, he and Melaouhi began a two-man artificial resuscitation, the nurse blowing air into the prisoner's lungs, mouth to mouth, while he applied intermittent pressure to the chest to stimulate the heart in a cycle of five compressions followed by two breaths. He told Jordan to fetch oxygen. Some minutes later the warder returned with an oxygen bottle and a second medical orderly, Five, with a box containing the trauma kit. It was now about three o'clock. Attempts were made to get oxygen into the prisoner's lungs by inserting an airway tube from the trauma kit into the prisoner's throat, but the connection did not match that on the oxygen bottle. Instead Melaouhi started breathing into the tube.

MELAOUHI'S PERSPECTIVE

Melaouhi had his own view of the situation. He refused to make a statement to the British Military Police Special Investigations Branch unit, but has since given his side of the story publicly on several occasions – in February 1989 on BBC's *Newsnight*, in 1994 as a solemn declaration to a Berlin notary, and in 2008 in a German language book entitled *Ich sah den Mördern in die Augen!* ('I looked the murderers in the eye!') – leaving little doubt about his interpretation of his former charge's death.

According to his solemn declaration, he was in his apartment just outside the prison gate when the French duty warder rang and told him to come quickly. In his book he described the warder telling him in a hysterical voice, 'Hess has been murdered, no, not murdered!' This can surely be discounted as Melaouhi had not mentioned anything of this sort in his declaration to the Berlin notary. He rushed to the prison gate but was refused admission to the cell block and finally had to run all round the building to the garden where he expected his charge to be at this time of day. Again, in his solemn declaration he merely stated that he had reached the garden house 'with some delay'. The delay was no doubt due to the strict security Lieutenant Three had ordered.

Inside he found everything in confusion, looking 'as if a wrestling match' had taken place. The straw mat on the floor had been pushed back, the table and chairs were overturned and a reading lamp had fallen down. He 'remembered clearly that the flex to the lamp was plugged in to its wall socket'.

This last statement was a feature of all his accounts. If correct it virtually rules out the official account of the prisoner's death.

This was that when Hess entered the cabin alone shortly after 2.30 p.m., one end of an eight-foot-long plastic-coated extension flex for the reading lamps was already tied around the window catch, four feet and seven inches above the floor, and had been for some weeks. Hess simply twisted the flex around his neck, tied a simple overhand knot in it, then slid down the wall causing the knot to tighten. This would not have been possible if the extension flex had been plugged in at the bottom. US Sergeant Eleven stated in his testimony that while familiarising himself with the prison and grounds on his first day of their tour of duty, 1 August, he had seen the flex tied to the window catch, and had noticed it in the same position several times since then.

Returning to Melaouhi's account, Hess was lying apparently lifeless on the floor. Two men whom Melaouhi did not recognise, one large, one small, wearing ill-fitting US Army uniforms stood near the body. This seems to be a description of the US medical orderlies Four and Five, although by the other witness accounts medic Five did not arrive on the scene until after Melaouhi. Jordan, Melaouhi went on, was standing by Hess's feet. He appeared overwrought; his shirt was soaked with sweat and he was not wearing his uniform tie.

Melaouhi knelt to examine Hess, but could find no pulse or breathing. He thought he must have been dead for 30 minutes or more, and asked Jordan, accusingly, what he had done to him.

'The swine is finished,' the warder responded. 'You won't have to work any more night shifts.'[12]

At this point, according to his book, Melaouhi felt suddenly scared, perceiving that he was in the presence of murderers who had killed his patient. For self-protection, to pretend he suspected nothing, he ordered Jordan to fetch the first aid apparatus, and began mouth-to-mouth resuscitation on what he knew to be Hess's corpse. The larger of the unknown Americans knelt with him and pressed down rhythmically on Hess's chest, but with such force that Melaouhi heard the ribs and breastbone crack.

When Jordan reappeared with the first aid kit Melaouhi noticed he had changed his shirt, and although he, Melaouhi, had inspected the first aid apparatus that morning and found it in order, it was now useless, without a battery for the intubation set, and without oxygen.

Such, in essence was Melaouhi's story. In addition, he observed that Hess's physical infirmities would have prevented him committing suicide in the manner described: he walked with a stick, could not rise if he fell and was nearly blind. Above all, he could not raise his arms above shoulder height, and his hands were so crippled with arthritis he could not tie his shoelaces. Melaouhi concluded his solemn declaration: 'I am of the firm opinion that Herr Hess could not have committed suicide as claimed. In my view it is clear that he met his death through strangulation at the hands of a third party.'[13]

The testimony of the US guards virtually rules out his conclusion. None reported a stranger in the prison grounds. The only possible murderer, therefore, was Jordan. On Melaouhi's thesis he must have strangled Hess when letting him into the summer house, quickly arranged it to look like suicide, then gone outside, closing the door behind him and calmly sitting down on the nearby bench. It will be recalled that Thirteen, who had left switchboard duty and gone into the garden for the express purpose of seeing Prisoner Number Seven, saw Jordan in jacket and tie sitting outside the summer house as he approached. Passing the cabin, he noticed the single door closed and saw no sign of the prisoner through the window. The accounts of Jordan's demeanour after he had looked in the cabin and seen his charge with a flex around his neck indicate a radical change: the warder dashed hither and thither in complete panic without a jacket or tie, not knowing what to do. He was either a consummate actor or he had not killed Hess. The latter is surely more likely; indeed, to believe Melaouhi's interpretation it is necessary to postulate a complex conspiracy by the US guards and British and French warders who gave statements to the British Military Police investigation.

BACK TO THE MILITARY POLICE INVESTIGATION

At the time the US medics were called out, the British Military Hospital in Berlin, not far from the prison, was alerted to the emergency with the pre-planned code 'Operation Paradox'. This was logged at 2.50 p.m. About 20 minutes later an ambulance from the hospital and a British medical officer in his own car arrived separately at the prison gate. The doctor, Lieutenant Colonel Six, was met by Jordan, who led him into the garden, telling him that the prisoner had been found hanged. Inside the summer house the doctor found cardiac massage being administered by the medics and oxygen being introduced to the prisoner's lungs through an endo-tracheal tube, although the seal on the tube was faulty and causing a leak. He checked for signs of life, but could find no spontaneous pulse: 'I also saw that the pupils were fixed and dilated and that Prisoner No. 7 was cyanosed – a bluish tinge was present on his exposed flesh.'

US medical orderly Four had already noticed that the prisoner's exposed flesh, initially pale, had taken on a bluish colour, particularly around the lips. The doctor set up an intravenous drip in the prisoner's right arm, then informed the commanding officer of the British Military Hospital that resuscitation had been continuing for some 50 minutes, but there were no signs of life. He was instructed to transfer the prisoner to the hospital. The ambulance had by this time been manoeuvred into the garden, and the prisoner was stretchered in and driven off, the medics and Melaouhi still continuing their resuscitation efforts. Arriving at the hospital at 3.50, Hess's body, as it must now be described, was taken up to his special ward on the second floor. At 4.10 he was officially pronounced dead.

* * *

At 6.45 p.m., some two and a half hours after Hess was pronounced dead at the British Military Hospital, the US prison director, Colonel Darold Keane, rang Hess's son, Wolf Rüdiger Hess, and told him that his father had died at 4.10 that afternoon; he was not authorised to give further details.[14]

It was almost 24 hours before Keane called Wolf Rüdiger again and read out an announcement prepared for the press: a preliminary investigation indicated that his father had attempted to take his own life:

> Hess, as he was accustomed to do, went escorted by a prison warder to sit in a small cottage in the garden of the prison. On looking into the cottage a few minutes later, the warder found Hess with an

electrical cord around his neck. Resuscitation measures were taken and Hess was transported to the British Military Hospital. After further attempts to revive Hess, he was pronounced dead at 16.10. Whether this suicide attempt was the actual cause of death is the subject of a continuing investigation ...[15]

Wolf Rüdiger found the statement unbelievable. Why should his father attempt suicide just as hopes of freedom had begun to open up for him? In any case, like Melaouhi, he could not believe his father could have hanged himself in this way: he was barely able to walk without a stick and a warder's assistance, and was so stooped and stiff he could not look much above the horizontal without overbalancing. And his hands were crippled with arthritis: how could he have looped an electrical flex around his neck and tied it in a knot? And how was it possible he had been left unsupervised for long enough even to attempt it?[16]

It had been evident for years that Hess's death, when it came, would be a political event; consequently a procedure had been laid down by the British directorate, agreed by the other three powers, for an autopsy to be conducted by the consultant forensic pathologist to the British Army, Professor J.M. Cameron. He was on holiday, but was swiftly recalled to fly to Berlin, and began his examination at 8.15 in the morning of 19 August, watched by other medical and military observers from the Four Powers on closed circuit television in an adjoining room.

Apart from marks resulting from the resuscitation attempts, Cameron found 'a circular bruised abrasion over the top of the back of the head' and 'a fine linear mark, approximately 3 in. (7.5 cms.) in length and 0.75 cms. in width' running across the left side of the neck. He also found haemorrhagic spots in the conjunctivae (cornea and inner side of eyelid) of both eyes. Internally, he found 'deep bruising over the top of the back of the head, noted on external examination', 'excessive bruising' to the upper part of the right side of the thyroid cartilage, or voice box, and deep bruising behind the voice box.[17]

Prior to receiving results from analysis of samples of blood and the contents of internal organs, Cameron established that the primary cause of death was asphyxiation, and an official announcement to this effect was put out at 6.00 that evening. With it came a statement that a note found while removing Hess's clothing implied that he had planned to take his own life.

The wording of the note was read out to Wolf Rüdiger Hess on the telephone. He found it clearly bogus. The content was simply out of date: it referred to an incident with Hess's former secretary, 'Freiburg', which had been cleared up long ago, and the letter was signed off 'Euer Grosser' (Your Big One), a form his father had not used since the early 1970s.[18] Wolf Rüdiger suspected it must have been written in November 1969 when his father had been very ill and believed he was dying. The note made reference to the Nuremberg trial, a subject Hess was forbidden to talk or write about, and Wolf Rüdiger concluded it must have been retained by the prison authorities at the time instead of being sent on, and had now been used to forge the 'suicide note'.

Disbelieving the official account, he commissioned a second post-mortem by German pathologists, and when his father's body was handed over for private burial he had it taken instead to the Forensic Medical Institute of the University of Munich. There Professors W. Spann and W. Eisenmenger conducted a second examination.

Their task was not made easy. They were provided with no evidence of how the body had been found or what had happened to it subsequently, and were not given Hess's medical records; nor were they allowed to see the video made during Cameron's autopsy or the X-rays taken previously. Furthermore, many of Hess's internal organs were missing. These included the larynx and upper throat organs which Cameron had found to be so damaged. Nonetheless, Spann and Eisenmenger's initial examination of the neck was suggestive. Whereas Cameron had found only 'a fine linear mark approximately 3 ins. (7.5 cms.) in length ... running across the left side of the neck', they observed at the front of the neck a brownish-reddish marking of variable breadth extending from a high point under the left ear obliquely down to the middle of the throat and around to the right, and at the back an almost horizontal double-track discolouration typical of that left by a single cord squeezing the blood either side to form a tram line effect.[19]

Cameron's report was published later that month. On the basis of the internal damage to Hess's neck and the linear mark about three inches long on the left side, which he described as 'consistent with a ligature', he concluded that Hess had died from 'asphyxia' produced by 'compression of the neck' as a result of 'suspension'[20]. Speculation is no part of the forensic pathologist's task and there is no requirement for a description of how the victim might have met his end or whether the injuries were consistent with the testimony of witnesses, although these things are frequently included in reports. Yet the whole purpose of the swift autopsy procedure laid down by the authorities had been to pre-empt and defuse political controversy. Cameron's report had the opposite effect. His failure to address the circumstances in which the body had been found or the manner in which it might have acquired the deep bruising at the top of the head, or to elaborate on the single-word description of the manner of death as 'suspension' left all substantive questions open: had it been suicide, murder or misadventure?

The Four Powers issued their 'final statement' on the matter on 17 September, a month after the event: 'Rudolf Hess hanged himself from a window latch in a small summerhouse in the prison garden, using an electrical extension cord which had been kept in the summerhouse for use in connection with a reading lamp.'[21] There was no explanation of how the old man might have contrived to do this, nor why he had been left so long unattended. 'The routine followed by the staff,' it was stated, 'was consistent with normal practice.' The statement added that the 'suicide note was written on the reverse side of a letter from his daughter-in-law dated 20 July 1987'.

Wolf Rüdiger found this to be so when the letter was returned to him the following week. Curiously, it had previously been examined by the senior document examiner at the laboratory of the British government chemist, who had concluded, 'there is no reason to doubt that it was written by Rudolf Hess.' The examination had clearly been rushed: the examiner had come from London and studied the letter in non-laboratory conditions at Spandau prison. He admitted to a 'very limited knowledge of the German language', and based his conclusions on 'a marked area of resemblance together with detailed features' which he considered characteristic of the writer and gave him 'no reason to doubt that the author of the questioned writing was Prisoner Number 7.'[22]

Wolf Rüdiger had every reason for doubt. The opinion he had commissioned from Professors Spann and Eisenmenger gave additional grounds. Whereas they agreed with Cameron that death had been caused by 'an operation of force against the neck by means of a strangulation instrument', their observation of the mainly horizontal mark left by this instrument pointed to throttling rather than hanging, or 'suspension', since it was lower than that associated with a typical hanging, and 'obviously not above the larynx'. Moreover, they reported that in their experience such massive damage and haemorrhaging in such diverse areas of the neck organs and muscles as described in Cameron's report were not usual in typical hangings, and even unusual 'not to say rare' in atypical hangings. While they lacked the data which might have allowed them to draw definite conclusions, they recorded that their findings did not conform to those of a typical hanging, although they could not exclude 'a special type of atypical hanging'. They noted the fact that Professor Cameron had not described the course or height of the 'fine linear mark' he had found; nor had he discussed the possibility of throttling.[23] The late Wolf Rüdiger Hess released them from their obligation of confidentiality and in reply to the present author they stated their opinion that in the light of their own findings Professor Cameron's diagnosis of 'suspension' without discussing other possibilities was 'not justifiable'.[24]

Later, Wolf Rüdiger commissioned the eminent British pathologist, Professor David Bowen, to review the conflicting autopsy reports. Bowen came down on the side of the German professors, suggesting in particular that the bruising to Hess's deeper neck tissues was unlikely to have occurred in a suicidal hanging, but was a feature of strangulation. He concluded that 'doubts must remain on the reliability of the official statement' concerning Hess's death.[25]

The bogus suicide note and doubts over the official post-mortem report created just the conditions needed to give credibility to Melaouhi's allegation that Hess had been murdered, particularly as the British Military Police investigation report was not published. Rumours and political disinformation proliferated. Wolf Rüdiger received information allegedly emanating from Israeli Intelligence sources that the murder had been committed by two SAS soldiers on the orders of the British Home Office. A book he wrote, *Mord an Rudolf Hess?* (*Murder of Rudolf Hess?*), publicising the allegation became a bestseller in Germany.[26]

Leaving aside the divergent views of the pathologists as interpretations only, the problem is how to reconcile the statements made to the British Military Police pointing conclusively to suicide with what appears to be a forged suicide note suggesting the prison authorities had something to hide. It is difficult, if not impossible, to imagine the four-power prison directorate agreeing to have a suicide note forged to deflect the political difficulties his death would cause.

A possible answer, the most credible in the author's view, is that the note was indeed written by Hess himself, and was intended to sow doubt and confusion. The Military Police investigation 'Final Report' states that 'Rudolf Hess – Prisoner Number 7, planned well in advance to take his own life'; this is supported by the witness testimony: for instance, the suicide note was found in Hess's pocket after he was pronounced dead at the British Military Hospital; it was written on the back of a letter he had received on 29 July from Wolf Rüdiger's wife, Andrea. But he could not have written it in the short time between his entry to the summer house and US soldier Thirteen passing the window and seeing no one inside. He must, therefore, have penned the note some time before and kept it in his pocket to be found on his death. If so, it can be concluded that he planned maximum embarrassment to the authorities who had kept him locked up for so long.

Such a step would have accorded with aspects of his character. While appearing idealistically naïve, even childish to some, he was also perverse and wily. He would not have survived at the top of the Nazi regime had he not been. Suppose he wrote the note referring to a long-defunct episode with his former secretary, 'Freiburg', and signed it off in a form he had not used for 20 years to indicate to Wolf Rüdiger and his family that it was a forgery. He would have thought it a fitting way to go. If so, the wonder is that at 93, after half a lifetime in prison, he retained the intellectual ability to carry it through.

CHAPTER TWO

The big question

Some doubts about aspects of Hess's death in Spandau remain. More important questions surround the circumstances of his flight to Great Britain in May 1941. The official British and German accounts depict a lone idealist, anxious to restore his position at Hitler's court, flying without Hitler's knowledge or approval unannounced into enemy territory on the off chance of finding the Duke of Hamilton at home at his Scottish seat and ready to talk peace. Obviously he was deranged. Yet doctors who examined him on arrival pronounced him sane and not a drug-taker; moreover how could a lunatic have planned and executed such a precise flight? These questions hardly disturb the academic historical community, which accepts the official account in whole or in part; and that version of events remains the received explanation.

The intelligence specialist, Richard Aldrich, has pointed out that historians who explore the state work under unique conditions: in no other discipline is the researcher 'confronted with evidence precisely managed by their subject'[1] – for the processing of official records for preservation in The National Archives, declassification or destruction offers government departments the means to massage, even to excise the narrative of their more secret activities. In Hess's case the open files have been extensively 'weeded'; this is apparent from documents such as the several inventories of Hess's possessions when he arrived in Scotland, which are now missing from the reports to which they were originally attached; the MI5 report missing its final page or pages; documents described in the initial pages of that report which are nowhere in any files open to the public; the letter from the chief of MI6 with the bottom half neatly removed; and many more. We can only guess at the number of complete files that remain closed to the public or that have actually been destroyed.

The absence of these vital documents provides every opportunity for conjecture, and Hess's extraordinary flight has been the subject of much speculation, ranging from the silly and sensational to the plausible but unproven. Historians reject conclusions derived from the absence of evidence as a resort to the *argumentum ex silentio*. However, in this case there is documentary evidence that papers which were once in the files have been removed, and that others – most notably the documents Hess brought with him, for the existence of which there is incontrovertible evidence – are missing from any files.[2] This is proof of official concealment, although not, of course, of what is being concealed or why.

In these circumstances the only way to the truth is to use the evidence in the open files and the letters and diaries of participants, and credible witness statements to build a picture of Hess's peace mission and its hinterground which fits the provable facts, and most importantly fits Hess's character and absolute devotion to his Führer.

Interpretation of the resulting picture is difficult: important accounts are contradictory, particularly on the German side, and after the event both sides spread deliberately misleading stories. Above all, in the opaque world of clandestine negotiations, that which was said or reported at the time was not necessarily the truth.

Hitler, then master of Europe, could not afford to have it known that he had weakened and sent an emissary to Britain with peace proposals; and many of the highest in British society did not wish it known they had been in favour of negotiating peace with him. It was these people Hess flew over to meet. Much evidence suggests that he was invited. The question is, by those who genuinely desired a compromise peace, or by British intelligence masquerading in their colours?

The facts and deductions presented in this book constitute a significant challenge to the received explanation of what happened in May 1941. Readers may form their own conclusions on these facts and deductions, but without such a challenge, acceptance of the official version continues, and with it misrepresentation of this critical moment when history failed to turn in the way Hess and Hitler and so many in the highest circles of British life wished. It is high time the official story is confronted, for consideration of the path Churchill did not take in 1941 casts a more brilliant light on the morality of the path he did take, the history we know. Hence the sub-title of this book: *The Real Turning Point of the Second World War.*

Apart from that, the story of Hess's mission remains an absorbing mystery.

CHAPTER THREE

Hess

HESS LOVED HITLER. This is the essential key, without which his life story becomes incomprehensible. He adored Hitler. Whatever faults he may have discerned in him and however the more sensitive side of his nature may have recoiled from the abominations later associated with his idol, like a woman who knows her man is guilty yet loves him despite all, so Hess loved Hitler.

Both were veterans of the first war. Both had responded fervently to the call to arms in the first days. Hess had enrolled as a private in the Bavarian Field Artillery, transferring within weeks to the elite 1st Bavarian Foot and receiving his baptism of fire in Flanders before Ypres. He proved a brave infantryman, gaining the Iron Cross, 2nd Class, and earning rapid promotion to *Vizefeldwebel* (literally 'vice-sergeant').[1] As such in 1916 he served in the murderous campaign for the French strongpoint at Verdun. He conveyed something of the horrors experienced here in a poem he wrote later as a memorial to fallen comrades: '... Along the whole front a savage fire ... howled like a supernatural hurricane in which individual blows were scarcely heard.'[2] Today the outlines of trenches in cratered earth can still be seen outside Verdun, and rank upon rank of crosses marking the unidentified dead, mute reminders of the industrialised slaughter which claimed thousands on both sides.

He survived, so severely wounded by shrapnel he was sent back to hospital, thence on convalescent leave, after which he was transferred to the eastern front. Here he was wounded again, twice, on the second occasion by a rifle bullet that passed through his chest almost grazing his heart and his spine.[3] While hospitalised, he was commissioned a lieutenant in the Reserve, but in the meantime he had applied to join the rapidly expanding Flying Corps. He was accepted and in early 1918 began training as a pilot, qualifying in October. By then it was clear the war was lost. Posted to a fighter squadron, he took part in the final battles in the air.

The terms of the armistice dictated by the Western powers came as a deep humiliation. As with thousands of his fellows, Hess was left with a hurt, vengeful sense that the blood and pain and loss of young lives should not have been in vain.[4] Hitler was not yet even a name to him, but he was ripe for the message he would proclaim.

HAUSHOFER

The victorious Western Allies punished Germany by demanding she disarm and pay reparations for the war she had undoubtedly begun, but they did not advance across her borders or stage a martial triumph in Berlin. This permitted German Army chiefs to manufacture a myth that the armed forces had not been defeated in the field, only stabbed in the back by politicians at home. The deception answered Hess's emotional needs, and he found confirmation in Munich, where he went after demobilisation. The Bavarian state government in the city had been toppled before the Armistice, and a republic proclaimed by a Jewish socialist, Kurt Eisner, who had demanded peace.

Conservative and nationalist opposition in the city found extreme expression in the secret Thule Society. The name derived from Ultima Thule, supposed birthplace of the Germanic race; the society's motto was 'Remember that you are German! Keep your blood pure!' The generally professional, wealthy business-class and aristocratic members had to prove racial purity for at least three generations. The society was rabidly anti-Semitic and anti-Communist and its ultimate aim was to unify Europe under the leadership of a greater Germanic Reich. Its symbol was the swastika.[5]

In February 1919, the month Hess arrived in Munich, a young Jew excluded from the Thule and wanting to prove his nationalist credentials assassinated Eisner. Anarchy followed until in April three emissaries from the Russian Bolsheviks seized power and established a Soviet republic in the city, curbing opposition with terror. All three were Jews.

Hess had joined the Thule Society, and in May he enrolled in the *Freikorps* Epp, one of many ex-servicemen's paramilitary formations throughout the country assisting regular central government forces to put down Communist uprisings. Whatever Hess had thought of Jews before, it was during this period of active fighting to liberate Munich from the 'Red' terror that Jews and Bolshevism became indissolubly linked in his mind. So it was for Hitler, Himmler, Röhm and other future Nazi leaders in the city. There is some truth in the assertion that Bolshevism, in its ruthlessness and contempt for ethical restraint, evoked its natural counter force and mirror image in the Nazi Party.

An equally formative and fateful influence on Hess at this time was Karl Haushofer, an army general of intellectual bent, who had been appointed professor to found a department of 'geopolitics' at Munich University. Hess had applied to the university to study political economy, but his introduction to Haushofer was arranged by a friend from his flying training days who had served under the general, and revered him.

Professor Haushofer was a cultivated man of extraordinary charm. As described by one of Hess's later adjutants, he had 'a bewitching way of handling people and an outstanding, fingertip feeling for human relationships'.[6] By contrast Hess was reserved and deeply earnest. 'He laughed seldom,' his future wife, Ilse Pröhl, was to recall of this period, 'did not smoke, despised alcohol and simply could not understand how after a lost war young people could enjoy dancing and social life.'[7] In Haushofer he found a mentor with a very positive message about Germany's future which met his deepest needs, and he fell under his spell, attending his lectures on geopolitics and working as his unpaid assistant. For his part, Haushofer was attracted by the quiet, ardent young man with a first-class war record who so obviously idolised him, and he brought him into his family circle and became like a father to him.

'He is a capital fellow [*famoser Mensch*],' Hess wrote to his mother in June 1920, describing how in fine weather Haushofer always collected him from work before lunch or dinner for a walk together. He had been to dinner with him and his wife – 'who is also very nice' – and their two sons, Heinz and Albrecht, the latter with 'a good English accent. I sometimes take a stroll and speak English with him.'[8]

Twenty-five years later, after a second lost war, Haushofer was questioned about Hess in his university days. 'He was a very attentive student,' Haushofer replied, 'but you see, his strong side was not intelligence but heart and character, I should say. He was not very intelligent.' Asked whether the young man had evinced great interest in the subject matter that he taught, Haushofer responded, 'He had great interest, and he worked very hard, but you see at that time there were all those students' and officers' associations and so the young men were always drawn away from their work.'[9]

Two other older men who influenced Hess during that early post-war period were Dietrich Eckhart and Captain Ernst Röhm. The former was a rabidly anti-Semitic writer, racialist (*völkisch*) poet and wit who held forth at a regular table at the Brennessel beerhouse in Schwabing, the intellectual and artistic quarter of Munich where Hess was lodging; the latter was a regular army officer serving on the staff of the district Army Commander. Each was to play a crucial role in projecting an obscure national-socialist working men's party, the *Nationalsozialistische Deutsche Arbeiterpartei* – the *NSDAP*, or *Nazis* – into national politics: Eckart by recognising the potential of its star orator, Adolf Hitler, and nurturing his gift for inspiring nationalist and anti-Bolshevist sentiment in language ordinary people understood; Röhm by diverting secret army funds and arms into a paramilitary wing of the party to serve as street fighters against their socialist and Communist enemies.

It was probably from one or both of these men that Hess first heard of Hitler. And it was Hitler, rather more than officers' or students' associations, who drew Hess away from his studies.

HITLER

Hess first heard Hitler speak in spring 1920. He had persuaded 'the General', as he called Professor Haushofer, to accompany him to a meeting of the NSDAP at their headquarters in the back room of a beerhouse in a working men's district of Munich. Few if any of those sitting in upright wooden chairs about a bare table were from the social milieu of the General or his favourite student, and Hitler, when he rose to speak seemed no exception: a man of the people with a pale face and sloping shoulders, dark brown hair, small moustache and strange, slightly protruding blue eyes. But when he spoke of German honour and the 'November criminals' who had signed it away at Versailles, his voice rising to a hoarse shriek, he was transformed by the intensity of his feelings. Hess was captivated.

Ilse Pröhl saw him afterwards, 'a new man, lively, radiant, no longer gloomy.' He told her she must come with him to the next meeting of the party: 'I have just been there with the General. An unknown man spoke. I don't remember his name, but if anyone will free us from Versailles, this is the man.'[10]

Haushofer was not impressed. The tirade he heard would undoubtedly have been built around an indictment of the German representatives who had signed the Versailles Treaty at the end of the war as instruments of international Jewry. This would not have troubled Haushofer unduly. His charming wife, Martha, was the daughter of a wealthy Jewish businessman, but he himself was an extreme nationalist, and the Jew as the racial enemy was inherent in German nationalism. It was not so much the message as the crude delivery that offended him; probably he saw Hitler as merely a street agitator.

Hess had no doubts. From that time on he attached himself to Hitler, took a muscular role in protecting his meetings from assaults by socialist and Communist groups, raised a student battalion for the party paramilitary *Sturmabteilung* (SA) and became his most loyal young aide. As such in November 1923 he was given a prominent role in Hitler's attempt to stage a 'national revolution' from the Bürgerbräukeller in Munich. The 'Beerhall Putsch' collapsed in utter failure and some loss of life, but while Hitler and others were arrested and tried, Hess found shelter in Haushofer's apartment then escaped to Austria. The Bavarian authorities had been heavily implicated in the coup; when in consequence the Munich court sentenced Hitler to 'fortress detention' with the possibility of parole after six months, a preposterously short term for high treason, Hess returned to Munich and surrendered himself, reasoning that if caught and sent for trial elsewhere in Germany the length of his sentence would more accurately reflect the severity of the crime. To his mother he wrote that if he went to Landsberg Prison, where Hitler was confined, he would have 'peace to study, interesting company, good fare, a common living-room, individual bedroom, garden, lovely view, so! vvvv'[11] – which was the Hess family laugh sign in correspondence.

So it proved. It is impossible to read his letters from Landsberg without concluding that this must have been the happiest period of his life. Seldom is the subject anything but Hitler, referred to as 'the Tribune' – the tribune of the people. Even those to Ilse Pröhl express fulfilment in devotion to his idol:

> The Tribune looks radiant. His face is no longer so thin. The forced rest is doing him good. He does gymnastics vvvv, bathes, does not smoke, drinks scarcely any alcohol apart from a little beer; here indeed he *must* be healthy without the former stress, with plentiful sleep, fresh air a[nd] a moral state that is far from depressed.[12]

In the fine spring mornings of 1924 he and Hitler 'wandered between the blossoming fruit bushes in the garden' discussing everything under the sun. He was enthralled by Hitler's power of anecdote, continually surprised by the range of his 'knowledge and understanding of subjects not really his own', amused or moved by his extraordinary talent for mimicry. From his letters one would scarcely know that others were in detention with them. Sitting writing at his desk in his bedroom one day, he described hearing Hitler from the adjacent communal living room performing a wartime experience, simulating exploding grenades and machine-gun fire, 'springing ferociously around the room, quite carried away by his imagination.'[13]

A visitor to Landsberg who testified to Hitler's talent for mimicry was the Munich art publisher 'Putzi' Hanfstaengl, one of his earliest followers from the educated classes. He described the repertoire of sounds Hitler deployed when reminiscing about the war, from the single crack of a howitzer or mortar to the whole battlefield din with 'the hammering tack-tack of machine guns'.[14] As a rival for Hitler's favour, Hanfstaengl was made aware of Hess's jealousy: on one occasion when he came to speak to Hitler, Hess, who was sitting beside him, rose with bad grace, seized another chair nearby and started performing gym exercises with it to claim attention.

For his part, Hess received regular visits from 'the General', who brought him books and advised him on issues that came up in discussion with Hitler. Most of these concerned the memoirs Hitler had begun to write, or more accurately dictate, first to his chauffeur, also locked up in Landsberg, then to Hess. These grew into *Mein Kampf*, published in two volumes after his release, an autobiographical polemic shaped by the political and racial dogmas he had absorbed from the nationalist milieu in Munich. The extent of Hess's input is impossible to know. Haushofer was questioned on the point at the end of the Second World War. 'As far as I know,' he replied, 'Hess actually dictated many chapters of that book.'[15]

Haushofer was asked about Hitler's concept of *Lebensraum* – literally 'living space' – which appeared to have been derived from his own geopolitical teaching. The term had originated with the German geographer, Friedrich Ratzel; Haushofer had combined it with the doctrine of the British geopolitician, Sir Halford Mackinder, to propose that world mastery would pass to whoever controlled 'the heartland' of Eurasia, and to suggest that Germany expand eastward at the expense of Soviet Russia. Asked whether Hitler had received his ideas on *Lebensraum* from Hess, Haushofer replied, 'Those ideas came to Hitler from Hess, but he (Hitler) never really understood them, and he never really read about them from the original books. He never read those books.'[16]

Haushofer's disdain for Hitler was not a product of hindsight: in Landsberg Hess wrote beseeching him to re-examine his estimate of the 'Tribune', who held him (Haushofer) in extraordinarily high regard: 'Your calm and intellectual way of speaking have made a great impression on him.' In the same letter Hess tried to reassure Haushofer on the Jewish question: the Tribune had not reached his present standpoint on this matter without 'hard inner struggle,' he wrote. He had been beset by doubts about whether he was not doing the Jews an injustice.[17]

This hardly accords with the pathological anti-Semitism displayed in *Mein Kampf* – typed by Hess. A passage alleging that German defeat in 1918 had been caused by Marxists at home fomenting revolution behind the fighting front continues:

> If at the beginning of the war or during the war one had held twelve or fifteen thousand of these Hebrew *Volk*-corrupters under poison gas such as hundreds of thousands of our very best German work-ers ... had to endure in the field then the millionfold sacrifices of the front would not have been in vain.[18]

This can be matched to a letter Hess wrote to Ilse Pröhl from Landsberg two weeks after the letter to Haushofer. He had taken tea to Hitler in his room and stayed to hear the latest section of his memoirs describing his arrival on the front line in Flanders in 1914 and the fear he had felt, constricting his chest and making his legs weak. Gradually he had overcome it; by the winter of 1915/16 he had been completely free of fear. Hess ended:

> ... he spoke of his battles and injuries and then of the treachery at home – 'oh, I will take a merciless and fearful revenge on the day I can do so! I will avenge in the name of the dead I saw before me then!' We were silent when he stopped reading; but as I left we pressed our hands together for a long time – I am devoted to him more than ever! I love him.[19]

DEPUTY FÜHRER

Hitler was appointed Reich Chancellor on 30 January 1933, spon-sored by military, political and industrial power groups determined to launch Germany on a second bid for European and world mastery.

He was the tool needed to bring the masses on side. Hess – now married to Ilse Pröhl – had been his secretary and confidant throughout this improbable journey from fortress detention a decade earlier. Recently he had accompanied him to a vital meeting with the leading conservative politician, von Papen. The deal was clinched after Hitler expounded his simple policy to bring order to political life: remove all Social Democrats, Communists and Jews from leading positions.

The first two groups were suppressed in short time after he became Chancellor. An arson attempt in the Reichstag attributed to the Communists provided a pretext for rounding up and interning Communist and socialist leaders,[20] and in the atmosphere of terror created Hitler was able to gain the necessary majority in the Reichstag for a law enabling him to govern without further parliamentary restraint.

The following month, April, he appointed Hess his *Stellvertreter*, or deputy. Hess had no ministerial portfolio but ran the *Verbindungsstab,* a liaison office co-ordinating policy between Nazi Party headquarters in Munich and government and state ministries – insofar as policy was not simply handed down from the Führer. His offices in the Wilhelmstrasse, Berlin, also served as nerve centre for a bewildering network of intelligence agencies, overt and covert. Besides the internal secret state police services and the central security service, military intelligence and counter-intelligence, telephone and signals intercept services and agents from organisations of Germans living abroad, who reported to his office, he had his own diplomatic intelligence service, which, according to its chief, Captain Franz Pfeffer von Salomon, had penetrated the British, French, US and Russian embassies in London, Paris and Moscow.[21] In addition to mediation and surveillance, Hess acted as a super ombudsman to whom every German had the right to appeal with his concerns.[22]

Hitler had neutered parliament, but his control of the country could not be complete until he had either gained the loyalty of the military standing behind the elite groups which had sponsored him as Chancellor or, on the other hand, replaced them with his own paramilitary street-fighting force, the SA, under its chief, Ernst Röhm. The army leaders feared Röhm, with reason; consequently Hitler had to choose between them and his long-time ally. He chose the established military, and on 30 June 1934 – known afterwards as 'the night of the long knives' – Röhm and senior colleagues and other enemies of the party were rounded up and thrown into jail, where many were shot. It was done in collusion with the military, on the understanding that on the death of the ailing President, von Hindenburg, Hitler would be appointed President – while retaining his position as Chancellor.

Von Hindenburg died in August. The army chiefs kept their side of the bargain and the loyal oath, bedrock of military commitment, was reaffirmed as 'unconditional obedience to Adolf Hitler, Führer of the Reich and of the German people, Supreme Commander of the Armed Forces ...' He had achieved total power.

Hess had a central role in the deception campaign preceding the coup and afterwards; closeted alone with Hitler at party headquarters, he argued long and passionately for clemency for many on the 'death list' of those to be executed. According to his adjutant, who heard the altercation from an adjacent room, he refused to be intimidated by Hitler's strongest outbursts and several men were spared – although not Röhm. When his name came up, Hess insisted he be shot: he was prepared to shoot the man himself.[23]

Nonetheless, the purge of the SA leadership took a toll on his psychological resources. His adjutant testified after the war that the example of Hitler's personal brutality 'deeply wounded his marked, almost feminine sensitivities', ageing him by years.[24] It is significant that the way he signed his name changed about this time. What had been a flowing signature rising confidently in a straight line now drooped at the end to form an arc. Even the shortened version, 'R. Hess', dipped despondently at the end.

Although in theory he was second only to Hitler in the councils of both state and party, formal structures counted for little in the Führer system of government by decree, and Hess, lacking the qualities of vivid showmanship or aptitude for faction of other paladins vying for Hitler's favour, appears almost to have exaggerated his natural tendencies in the opposite direction towards reticence, humility, asceticism and mysticism, and to offset the ostentation of so many in the new elite he seems to have made a virtue of idealism and incorruptibility, turning himself into 'the conscience of the party'. At the same time his goal remained, in the words of his adjutant, 'to be the most loyal interpreter of Hitler'.[25] These were impossible positions to straddle, especially in the chaotic system of parallel responsibilities that passed for government in Hitler's administration. As a result his health suffered. He was subject to sleeplessness and griping stomach pains which confined him to bed for days at a time. Conventional doctors failed to find a cause, and he turned increasingly to herbalists, nature healers, mesmerists and astrologers.

One problem that caused him particular concern at this time was the necessity to deal with ever more frequent outrages committed by Nazi Party rank and file against Jews.

CHAPTER FOUR

The Jewish question

THE JEWISH QUESTION was at the core of Nazi ideology. Jews were seen as a parasitic and impure race which had to be eliminated from the national body. For Hitler it was an emotional imperative. His hatred of Jews was all-consuming, and from the early 1920s he had given vent in public and private to the most blood-curdling promises to eradicate them root and branch – '*mit Stumpf und Stiel aus[zu]rotten*'.[1] Albert Speer, who observed Hitler closely during his years of power, reflected after the war on his 'insane hatred of Jews', concluding that this had been his central conviction, and everything else had been mere camouflage for this 'real motivating factor'.[2]

Speculation that Hitler's obsession stemmed from a suspicion that his grandmother had been seduced by a Jew before she gave birth to his father – and that consequently his own blood was suspect – has not been validated. Prodigious research has failed to reveal the Jew supposed to have employed and seduced her. Nonetheless, Professor Robert Waite has produced telling indications from Hitler's recorded speeches and conversations that he did indeed suspect he had Jewish blood from his father. In *Mein Kampf* he wrote – and Hess presumably typed – 'the black-haired Jew-boy lurks for hours, his face set in a satanic leer, waiting for the blissfully innocent girl whom he defiles with his blood.'[3] Jewish lust for pure German maidenhood was, of course, a cliché of popular anti-Semitic tracts.

Whatever the root of Hitler's phobia, he had given it open expression in speeches and conversation. He had talked of having gallows erected in Munich directly he had power: 'Then the Jews will be hanged one after another, and they will stay hanging until they stink';[4] the same procedure would be adopted in other cities 'until Germany is cleansed of the last Jew'. The word 'cleansed' is psychologically revealing, in terms of both his own blood and that of the 'Aryans' idealised by German nationalists as the 'master race' which was to inherit the earth, and which must be kept pure. Such a vision of eugenics on a national scale was recorded in *Mein Kampf*: 'The *völkisch* state has to perform the most gigantic rearing task here. One day, however, it will appear as a deed greater than the most victorious wars of our present bourgeois era.'[5] This was the task Hitler would lay on Heinrich Himmler.

Two key works elaborating the theme were published in Munich in 1930, Alfred Rosenberg's *The Myth of the Twentieth Century*, and Walther Darré's *New Nobility from Blood and Soil*. Both stressed the need for laws to protect endangered Nordic Aryan blood by culling inferior-value specimens and promoting the selective breeding of the 'ideal type' inside a 'closed blood source'. Himmler had made a start before Hitler attained power by selecting the tall, slender, fair-haired 'ideal type' for his praetorian guard, the SS.

Rosenberg was the most influential exponent of the Nazi Party's racial theories. An Estonian with German forbears and a romantic attachment to all things German, he had been a student in Moscow at the time of the Russian Revolution, and had come to Munich at about the same time as Hess convinced that Bolshevism was one arm of an international Jewish conspiracy to dominate the world. Events in Munich at this period might have been designed to prove the point. Rosenberg had become Hitler's intellectual mentor, editor of the Nazi newspaper, the *Völkischer Beobachter*, and pre-eminent party philosopher.

The Jewish issue, the purity of the German bloodstock and the struggle against Bolshevism were thus linked at the heart of Nazi ideology. Hess believed it uncritically; his numerous speeches on the Jewish question over the years leave no room for doubt. He told a mass

rally in 1934 that National Socialism was 'nothing but applied biol-
ogy',[6] and among the party chief executives reporting to him was the
Reichsärzteführer – the Reich Doctors' Leader – Dr Gerhard Wagner,
a vociferous advocate of anti-Jewish race laws, whose Head Office for
Volks Health in Munich dealt with such matters as 'Race Policy' and
'Kinship Investigation'.[7]

Yet a precise answer to the Jewish question had not been formulated. Hitler's accession to power had led to spontaneous action by
party members against Jews and Jewish shops. The violence had provoked Jewish organisations abroad to call for a worldwide boycott of
German goods, to which Nazi Party activists had responded by initiating a counter-boycott of Jewish shops and businesses in Germany. To
placate the party and quell lawlessness on the streets, legal measures
had been adopted to force Jews out of German life, beginning with a
decree removing their right to sue for damages caused by pogroms
and followed by laws excluding Jews from the Civil Service and the
legal and medical professions. Many Jews with money and the skills
to emigrate did so. Most remained, isolated within their communities.

Fresh waves of violence battered them in 1935, inspired by Joseph
Goebbels' official propaganda machine and popular newspapers dis-
pensing hatred and alarm at 'racial defilement'. The scale of lawlessness
and economic disruption became so damaging to the standing of the
regime that in August Hitler called for the end of 'individual actions';
Hess circulated the message to the party, insisting on the prosecution
of anyone causing criminal damage or bodily harm to Jews. Since the
activists to be disciplined were carrying out the central aim of the party
– to eradicate Jewish influence and 'contamination' by Jewish blood
– the situation was untenable. Pressure to achieve the party's racial
goal by legislation, making street action unnecessary, grew in leading government and party circles; the doctors' leader Gerhard Wagner
particularly called for a legal prohibition on sexual relations between
Germans and Jews, and at the annual party rally in Nuremberg that
September Hitler responded by announcing a 'Law for the Protection
of German Blood and German Honour', which prohibited marriage or
extra-marital relations between Jews and Germans, as well as a 'Reich
Citizenship Law' depriving Jews of German citizenship.[8]

What came to be known as the 'Nuremberg Laws' were followed by others reducing Jews to outcasts lacking any legal rights and enforcing their separation from Germans. Hess was an active participant in the process. He knew Hitler was determined to solve the 'Jewish problem' by removing them from the country, root and branch, but not how. And despite the brutal threats he had heard from him over the years, it is improbable he foresaw what was to become the 'final solution'.

THE ENGLISH QUESTION

At the opposite pole to the Jewish-Bolshevik question stood the English question. The English were kinsmen, respected as much for their Aryan blood as for their control of a world empire. In Hitler's strategic vision from the beginning they were necessary allies, or at least benevolent non-belligerents, so neutralising French hostility and securing the western borders while German armies thrust east to extirpate Jewish Bolshevism at source and gain *Lebensraum* for the *Volk*. He was determined not to repeat the Kaiser's mistake of antagonising Britain by building a fleet to challenge the Royal Navy. Hess held these views as fervently: if only the British could be persuaded Hitler had no designs on their empire, they would welcome an agreement to remove the Russian-Bolshevik threat to India and the Middle East. He took English lessons to enable him to play his part in winning over influential Englishmen.

One of the first of these was Geoffrey Shakespeare, a junior minister, who in 1933 took his son for treatment to a Bavarian Dr Gerl, with whom Hess was close. Hess invited Shakespeare on stalking expeditions after chamois and over the following years the Englishman came to know him quite well. Later, he reported on him as 'a man of some charm and a likeable creature' of 'superb personal courage' but 'no great intellectual gifts'; indeed, 'he is the simplest of souls and incapable of acting a part.' Shakespeare recognised Hess's complete devotion to Hitler, 'who is his god'; he also perceived a 'queer streak of mysticism in his make-up, and his glance and countenance gave me the impression of an unbalanced mind'.[9] After the war Karl Haushofer was to make similar comments about his former student's lack of mental balance. He recalled having once sent him to his family physician, Dr Bock, 'who discovered traces of infantilism'.[10]

As for political and diplomatic skills, Shakespeare found Hess 'a complete amateur' with 'no knowledge of government':

> His fixed idea when I met him was that there was no reason why Germany could not exercise supreme power in Europe without lessening the power of the British Empire in the world. England and Germany between them could govern the world. I do not think he liked England, but he admired the English in many ways ... He hated Russia and all it stood for.[11]

Hess never altered these views.

* * *

England *Politik* reached its high point in 1935 when Joachim von Ribbentrop, Hitler's improbably titled Commissioner for Disarmament Questions, brought home a bilateral naval agreement with Britain, limiting the *Kriegsmarine* to 35 per cent of the size of the Royal Navy. For Britain it was a shameful deal, in effect abandoning her former ally, France, and the aspirations for preserving peace through 'collective security' agreed at Versailles, gaining in return only an empty pledge. There was a failure in Britain to understand the nature and dynamic of Hitler's Reich; there was also much sympathy for Germany in the highest circles. The Royal family, landed and banking interests especially saw Russia and Communism as the greater threat to the Empire and their established position, and subscribed to Goebbels' line that Nazi Germany formed a barrier against the spread of international Communism. In extreme form, as expressed by the Governor of the Bank of England, Hitler and the President of the Reichsbank were 'the bulwarks of civilisation ... fighting the war of our system of society against Communism'.[12]

Senior officers of the armed forces held similar views. In the aftermath of the first war public feeling had run strongly against armaments as a cause of war, and all three services had been starved of funds. The naval staff knew they could not defend the eastern Empire against the rising power of Japan while engaged against Germany and Italy in the West, and hankered after a 'blue ocean' policy without European entanglements. Neither had the army general staff any wish to repeat the appalling bloodbath on the Continent, while the air staff recognised that the advent of bombing aircraft had altered traditional British strategy by removing the sea-bound invulnerability of the homeland. Aerial bombing was feared by all who thought seriously on defence matters.

The air staff had been an early target of Hitler's campaign of amity. In 1934 Rosenberg had invited the head of British Air Intelligence, Group Captain Frederick Winterbotham, to Germany and introduced him to Hitler, Hess and officers of the general staff, who had openly explained their plans for the conquest of Russian space by tank columns supported from the air.[13] The courtship continued, intensifying in summer 1936 at the time of the Berlin Olympic Games. The capital was transformed for the occasion. Swastika banners 45 feet tall were planted down Unter den Linden, in place of the lime trees from which this main thoroughfare took its name. Anti-Semitic notices and graffiti were removed from buildings and shop fronts; the chief Jew-baiting paper, *Der Stürmer*, disappeared from reading boxes at street corners; political prisoners on forced labour were kept from the vicinity of roads where they might be seen.[14]

Hess was at Hitler's right hand at the grand opening ceremony on 1 August. Among the British guests of honour was a distinguished young aviator, the Marquis of Clydesdale, MP, heir to the dukedoms of Hamilton and Brandon. Hess himself was an enthusiastic flyer – in 1934 he had won the 'Round the Zugspitze' air race – while Clydesdale had been the first pilot to overfly Mount Everest. There were ample opportunities for the two to meet at official functions during the following days, and Clydesdale was precisely the sort of 'influential Englishman' Hess hoped to win round, but whether they did much more than exchange pleasantries seems doubtful.[15] What is not in doubt is that Clydesdale had a long talk with Karl Haushofer's son, Albrecht. For both men it was a fateful meeting.

CLYDESDALE

Douglas Douglas-Hamilton, Marquis of Clydesdale, was an uncomplicated sporting aristocrat. As a schoolboy he had boxed for Eton, and as an undergraduate for Oxford University; he had subsequently become amateur middleweight boxing champion of Scotland and toured the world, taking part in exhibition bouts to raise money for charity. He had taken up flying early, attaining the rank of squadron leader in the Royal Auxiliary Air Force, reserve for the Royal Air Force, and commanded 602, City of Glasgow, Squadron.

His flight over Mount Everest in 1933 had brought him worldwide fame; for readers of the popular press he was now 'the Flying Marquis'. In a book written with his co-pilot on the expedition, and lifelong friend, David McIntyre, *The Pilots' Book of Everest*, he ascribed their pioneering feat to the development of the super-charger and the large propeller.

Clydesdale was Unionist Member of Parliament for East Renfrew, and it was as a member of a group of Parliamentarians observing the Olympics that he flew to Berlin in the summer of 1936. His real purpose was to see how the Luftwaffe was developing. He was accompanied by his brother, George – or 'Geordie' – who was also a squadron leader in the Auxiliary Air Force and commanded 603, City of Edinburgh, Squadron. Geordie had gained a Bachelor of Law degree from Edinburgh University after coming down from Oxford, and subsequently attended the Universities of Bonn and Vienna and the Sorbonne. Recently he had been admitted to the Scottish Bar (Faculty of Advocates). He spoke German, and since he later became the wartime chief of intelligence at RAF Fighter Command it is reasonable to assume that he, too, was keen to see something of the Luftwaffe.

Clydesdale had two other brothers, Lords David and Malcolm Douglas-Hamilton. Both were officers in the Auxiliary Air Force and, like Clydesdale himself, both belonged to the Anglo-German Fellowship, one of several British societies dedicated to promoting trade and good relations between the two countries. David had a special interest in German social policies – although he abhorred Nazi methods – and had gained practical experience working in German labour camps. He spoke the language enthusiastically, if not always grammatically, and among his many German contacts, one whom he found especially interesting, and talked about to Clydesdale, was Karl Haushofer's eldest son, Albrecht. When, at one of the official functions during the Olympics, Clydesdale and Albrecht found themselves at the same dinner, each already knew much about the other.[16]

Albrecht was a fluent English speaker. Like his father he combined powerful intellect with personal, if somewhat heavy charm. External brilliance hid a tortured soul. He was, after all, through his mother a quarter Jew, legally excluded from any part in German life. That he was, nonetheless, attending a state banquet was entirely due to Hess. Under Hess's protection he held a post teaching geography and geopolitics at the High School for Politics in Berlin, and travelled extensively, reporting particularly on attitudes in Great Britain and the United States for his father's journal, *Zeitschrift für Geopolitik*, and to Hess. He was Hess's principal expert on England and the Anglo-Saxon world. In a letter he wrote to Hess late in 1933 to express his gratitude that he and his brother, Heinz, had 'not been swept on to the rubbish heap as Germans of inferior value', he assured him of his 'full personal commitment to him as a person'.[17]

The words were carefully chosen. For while both he and his father were agreed on the general direction of German foreign policy – indeed, as has been seen, the policy was inspired in large part by Karl Haushofer's geopolitical theory – both had strong reservations about Hitler and the NSDAP. Albrecht was a poet and playwright as well as a formidable scholar, and was far too sensitive and intelligent not to be acutely aware of the moral knife-edge on which he and his father were balancing. In July 1934, after the Austrian Chancellor had been murdered by local Nazis supported by Hitler and his own patron, he had written to his parents wondering 'how long we can continue to carry the responsibility which we bear, and which starts little by little to turn into historic guilt or at least complicity'.[18] And a month later, on his father's birthday, he had expressed his doubts to his mother in even more pessimistic and prophetic vein, suggesting he should not wish his father 'something which no one may wish a man, before he has to experience things which are best left unspoken. That says basically all that I expect and do not expect of the future.'[19]

That autumn, less than a year after his letter of gratitude and commitment to Hess, he told a trusted student in Berlin about a small, close circle who were watching developments with a view to overthrowing the regime.[20] Among the conspirators he named were the Prussian Minister of Finance, Johannes Popitz; the chief of the general staff, General Ludwig Beck; and later the diplomat, Ulrich von Hassell, a lynchpin in the undercover opposition to Hitler. Nonetheless, Albrecht continued to work for Hess in the belief that he could do more for the opposition while close to the centre of power. At the same time he knew his patron was completely devoted to the tyrant they sought to depose. It was an irreconcilable dilemma. 'We are all indeed in the position of "conflicting obligations",' he had written to his parents in 1934, 'and must carry on even if the task has become completely hopeless.'[21]

He could hardly reveal his inner conflicts to Clydesdale and other British politicians at their first meeting during the Olympics. He gave them the party line: in return for modifications to the Versailles Treaty, Hitler would moderate German armaments and foreign policy. For his part, he had access to Hess and would do everything he could to persuade the Deputy Führer to use his influence in this direction. Albrecht knew this accorded with current policy in London. British politicians were bent on bringing Germany back into the comity of nations by 'appeasing' her demands for an end to the 'unjust' terms of the Versailles Treaty. This policy, dictated by weakness and the failure of 'Collective Security' under the League of Nations, was argued on high moral grounds as a search for 'just solutions by negotiation in the light of higher reason instead of resort to force'.[22] The Anglo-German Naval Agreement had been just such. For Hitler, the next stage was to convert the agreement into a tacit alliance that would free him to strike east against the Jewish-Bolshevik enemy. Albrecht was playing his part in this diplomatic drive, which agreed entirely with his own geopolitical convictions.

Accordingly, when Clydesdale told him he would like to see something of the German Air Force, Albrecht introduced him to its chief, Hermann Göring, at an extravagant party laid on by the great man at his Karinhall estate outside Berlin. Göring called over his chief lieutenant in the covert development of the Luftwaffe, General Erhard Milch, and told him to give Clydesdale a tour of aerodromes. Interestingly, Milch's genealogical table showed him as half Jew; his mother, however, had sworn his real father was Aryan. He offered to show Clydesdale anything he would like to see, adding with emphasis, 'I feel we have a common enemy in Bolshevism.'[23]

This was, of course, precisely the line Hitler, Hess and the officers of the general staff had taken two years earlier with the head of British Air Intelligence, Group Captain Winterbotham. Clydesdale was taken to see three Luftwaffe airfields that August, and in October, at Milch's invitation, he visited the Junkers factory at Dessau producing bomber aircraft, and a plant making diesel aero engines. He was left in no doubt about the pace with which the Luftwaffe was being expanded or the importance it was accorded in German military planning.

Both Clydesdale and Albrecht Haushofer made sure that their acquaintance begun at the Berlin Olympics was refreshed. Thus at the end of 1936 Albrecht sent seasonal greetings to Clydesdale in Scotland, while Clydesdale, on a skiing holiday in Austria at the time, called on Albrecht in Bavaria on his way home. Albrecht drove him to see his parents at their estate. Geopolitics was not discussed. Afterwards Clydesdale sent Karl Haushofer a copy of *The Pilot's Book of Everest*, and wrote to Albrecht to say that he had put his name before the Royal Institute of International Affairs, Chatham House.[24] Albrecht replied that he would be happy to speak at the Institute; he would, in any case, be in London in March (1937) and hoped to see Clydesdale then.

To judge by the way Albrecht was introduced to the Chatham House audience before he spoke on 'Raw Materials and Colonies: A German Point of View', 'appeasement' was very much alive at that august institution. It somehow survived even the crass analogy he used during his talk, likening the world war, a cosmic catastrophe, to a schoolyard brawl in which one of the bigger boys was set upon and kicked down by more numerous opponents, who then punished him, took his exotic toys – colonies – for themselves and forced him to sign a declaration that he was not fit to play with them – a ponderous

allusion to German humiliation at Versailles. In his refusal to accept
Berlin's responsibility for the outbreak of the war, hence the essential justice of her punishment at Versailles,[25] Albrecht revealed that
beneath his genial exterior he nursed the malign prejudices of German
nationalism. Clydesdale no doubt accepted his attitude in the interests of fair play or 'appeasement', to which he and his brothers and
all members of the Anglo-German Fellowship were dedicated; in any
event, Albrecht stayed at Clydesdale's home after the talk, and in later
correspondence and meetings they used Christian names, 'Douglo'
and Albrecht, in place of formal address.

It is not clear whether they became real friends or whether their
continuing association was chiefly political. Both were working for
amity between their two countries; each had the highest-level contacts
in his own country. Albrecht assumed that Clydesdale was formally
or informally an agent for the British Secret Service, and presumably
Air Intelligence; Clydesdale knew that Albrecht was working for the
Deputy Führer. They had to keep in touch. Towards the end of that
year, 1937, when Clydesdale was about to marry, Albrecht wrote to
send him his thoughts 'and a very strong feeling of friendship' as he
stepped to the altar.[26] Perhaps he meant it.

Clydesdale married Lady Elizabeth Percy at St Giles Cathedral,
Edinburgh, in November. She was the daughter of the Duke of
Northumberland, an aristocrat at the extreme end of the anti-Bolshevik
spectrum. He had served as a Guards officer in the Boer War and the
Great War, and since the early 1920s had financed and produced a
radical weekly journal, *The Patriot*, promoting anti-Communism and
anti-Semitism. One of his leading writers, Nesta Webster, an occultist
and conspiracy theorist, believed as fervently as Alfred Rosenberg in
the Jewish plot to subvert civilisation. In one article for *The Patriot*
she suggested that Hitler had successfully halted the Jewish attempt to
control the world.[27] Lady Elizabeth was too intelligent to swallow such
views; there is no doubt, however, that they had a place in the circles
in which she and Clydesdale moved.

In April 1938 Albrecht stayed with Clydesdale at his Scottish
home, Dungavel House, south of Glasgow. Hitler had recently seized
control of Austria, and Albrecht expressed such concern about his

further intentions that Clydesdale wrote to the Foreign Secretary, Lord Halifax, informing him that Dr Albrecht Haushofer would be in London the following week and might have interesting information. Halifax was not able to see him, but Albrecht did speak at length to two of his colleagues at the Foreign Office, leaving them in no doubt about Hitler's intentions for further advance in Czechoslovakia.[28]

HALIFAX

Hitler recognised before the British government that his hand of friendship would be spurned. From the beginning he had concentrated on armaments at the expense of exports; by summer 1936 a predictable foreign exchange crisis was threatening the import of food and vital raw materials. Rather than retreat, characteristically Hitler had advanced, decreeing increased arms production within a four-year plan for a self-sufficient war economy. Instead of trading in the world market, he would seize what was needed by force from Austria and Czechoslovakia as staging posts for his drive east for *Lebensraum* – hence Albrecht Haushofer's warning to Clydesdale and the Foreign Office.

Hitler knew that Britain and France must oppose Germany's forceful expansion; yet he was frustrated by Britain's cool response to his proposal for allowing her to keep her worldwide empire if she would only allow him his way on the continent of Europe, and he now viewed Italy under the dictatorship of Benito Mussolini as a more satisfactory friend. In November 1937, he revealed his strategy to his Foreign Minister, War Minister and service chiefs at a conference usually called by the name of his adjutant, Colonel Hossbach, who took notes. He left them in no doubt that he regarded Britain and France as 'two hate enemies' whom they would have to confront.[29]

The British Prime Minister, Neville Chamberlain, and Foreign Secretary Lord Halifax, had yet to take his full measure. The clues were abundant, but both were too rational to comprehend the hate and opportunism driving his conduct. Halifax was halfway there. He had met the Führer for the first time early that November, afterwards recording in his diary, 'we had a different set of values and were speaking a different language.'[30] This had not prevented Halifax from hinting at the possibility of territorial 'alterations' in the cases of Austria, Czechoslovakia and the Polish port of Danzig – precisely what realists in the Foreign Office had warned him not to do. It was full-blown 'appeasement' for the injustices Germany was supposed to have suffered at Versailles.

The next day, Halifax had met Göring at his Karinhall estate. The great man was dressed in a green hunting costume with a chamois tuft in his hat and a dagger sheathed in red leather at his waist. His manner was equally extravagant, but Halifax was attracted by his personality and completely taken in by his assurances that Germany had no aggressive intentions.[31]

This was disproved the following year. In the spring Hitler seized control of Austria with a mixture of internal subversion and military menaces, and in the autumn threatened to march on Czechoslovakia. Halifax at last saw the cloven hoof, and although Chamberlain, in collusion with the French, bought Hitler off at a conference in Munich by persuading the Czech government to hand over parts of their territory – returning home waving a peace pact he had persuaded Hitler to sign – Halifax knew there could be no more appeasement to Hitler or Nazism.

Vindication of his about turn, if any were needed, came little over a month later, on the night of 9/10 November, when the terror subsequently known as *Reichskristallnacht* – or 'night of broken glass' – was unleashed in supposedly spontaneous mob actions against Jews throughout Germany; some 7,500 Jewish businesses were destroyed, 267 synagogues burned down or damaged, hundreds of Jews beaten – many to death – and 25,000 male Jews confined in concentration camps. A British diplomat in Berlin wrote of the forces of medieval barbarism let loose. Halifax was revolted. A patrician of deep religious conviction – nicknamed 'the Holy Fox' for his Anglicanism and love of fox hunting, and scorned by Hitler after their meeting as 'the English parson' – he was moved to initiate a discussion in cabinet about action to help German Jews. Mass emigration to Palestine, which Britain administered under a Mandate of the League of Nations, could not be contemplated because of the hostility it would arouse in the Arab world, but Western Australia and British Guiana were considered briefly as possible Jewish homelands.[32]

Reichskristallnacht had an equally profound effect on Hess. The oppositionist von Hassell recorded in his diary how Hess's old Munich friends, the Bruckmanns, had told him of Hess's despair at the nation-wide pogrom; he had been depressed 'as never before' and beseeched the Führer to stop the outrages, without success.[33] Certainly Hess was suffering frequent bouts of illness and sleeplessness at this period.

The internal German opposition had gained impetus to act against Hitler after he outlined his war strategy at the 'Hossbach' conference. Emissaries had been despatched to London and New York urging the Western powers to stand firm in the face of Hitler's demands, arguing that this would bring on a crisis of confidence within Germany that would allow the army to stage a coup. However, Hitler had taken steps to cripple the centre of resistance. He had caused the resignations through scandal of the War Minister and Commander-in-Chief of the Army, appointed himself Supreme Commander of the Armed Forces, promoted a more malleable officer, von Brauchitsch, as Army Commander-in-Chief and, crucially, bypassed the army general staff by raising a co-ordinating department of younger, Nazified officers in the War Ministry to the status of Armed Services High Command.

These changes made it virtually impossible for the traditional army and aristocratic elite, termed the *Reaktion*, to mount a successful coup. Nonetheless, figures from the opposition continued to nourish representatives of the Foreign Office in London with prospects of a 'generals' revolt'. Halifax, while treating their reports with caution, seems to have clung to his opinion of Göring as a rational leader who might be encouraged to take Germany on a peaceable course. Meanwhile he attempted by all diplomatic and economic means to ensure Hitler could not penetrate further into south-eastern Europe.[34]

THE PALESTINE QUESTION

Official British policy towards Palestine had its origins in the 'Balfour Declaration' of 1917, a pledge made by the British Foreign Secretary, Arthur Balfour, in a letter to Lord Rothschild, head of the British branch of the Jewish banking dynasty, that Britain would aid Zionists in their efforts to establish a home for world Jewry in Palestine, traditionally the land promised to the Jews by God. It was believed to have mobilised powerful Jewish support for the Western Allies in the United States; Winston Churchill even believed that Jewish pressure had been partly responsible for America's entry into the war on the Allied side.[35]

After the war Britain was granted a temporary mandate over Palestine; Balfour's pledge came with it. Yet it was evident that if Britain were to impose a Jewish state on the Arabs of Palestine it would alienate the Arab world, whose friendship was needed to secure Middle Eastern oil and the vital passage through the Suez Canal to the eastern Empire. In the event, the volume of post-war Jewish immigration to Palestine led to clashes between Jews and Arabs, and in 1936 to a Palestinian Arab revolt. The British government sent out a Royal Commission under Lord Robert Peel, which recommended partition: the Jews to have a state in the north of Palestine, the Arabs a larger state in the south and east, with necessary exchanges of population. The Arabs were particularly unhappy with the plan, and the government set up a second Royal Commission to examine it in detail before it finally dismissed partition as unworkable.

With the need to secure Arab goodwill in the European war in prospect, Chamberlain's government put forward its own solution in a White Paper in May 1939: Palestine to become an independent state within ten years, the population ratio regulated at two Arabs to every Jew; Jewish immigration to be limited to 75,000 in total over the next five years and, crucially, no further Jewish immigration after that without Arab consent. Churchill, who had been fighting a lonely battle against Chamberlain's appeasement policy in Europe, denounced this blatant propitiation of the Arabs as a repudiation of Balfour's pledge to the Zionists, which it was. Nonetheless, it was approved by Parliament.

It is interesting that Adolf Eichmann, the expert on Jewish emigration and Zionism in Himmler's Security Service Main Office, visited Palestine in November 1937, four months after publication of the Peel Commission report. He found the 'Jewish Nationalist' – or Zionist

– leaders in confident mood, looking forward to the establishment of the Jewish state proposed by Peel as soon as possible, and expecting to be able to expand from it southwards into the territory marked out for the Arabs. They told Eichmann that if the English showed an inclination to postpone partition, the Jewish defence organisation would open hostilities against them. They further said they were delighted by the 'radical' German Jewish policy which would drive more Jews to emigrate to Palestine and give them a majority over the Arabs within foreseeable time.[36]

One of the aims of *Reichskristallnacht* the following November, 1938, was certainly to drive more Jews from Germany. By coincidence or design it took place a fortnight before the House of Commons debated the second Royal Commission report, which came down against Peel's partition plan for Palestine.

Time had run out for the Zionists; in May 1939, the day before Parliament approved the government plan for radically restricting Jewish immigration in what was to become the independent Arab state of Palestine, Hitler signed the 'Pact of Steel' with Mussolini. He was preparing to strike against Poland. European war would close down the Palestine issue for the duration.

CHAPTER FIVE

Struggle for peace

T HE BRITISH AND FRENCH governments, resolving to confront
Hitler's threatened advance on Poland, guaranteed support for
Polish independence. However, Chamberlain and Halifax still hoped
a negotiated settlement might be possible, and although the Polish
pledge had little strategic validity without Russian participation, both
shrank from an alliance with the Bolsheviks. Stalin suspected, with
reason, that at bottom they would prefer to leave Hitler a free hand
against the Soviet Union.

The British government's great landowning and business backers
were certainly of this persuasion. Two of the more committed, the
Duke of Buccleuch and Lord Brocket, demonstrated their feelings by
flying to Berlin to attend Hitler's 50th birthday celebrations that year.[1]
Brocket was on the pro-Nazi, anti-Semitic wing of Conservative opinion, Buccleuch, who deplored the Nazi persecution of the Jews, was
a mainstream imperialist, viewing Soviet Russia as a greater potential
danger to the Empire than Nazi Germany, and desiring detachment
from any European commitment.[2] Such was the stance taken by most
influential strategists of the time, their overriding consideration being
to avoid the carnage of the last war.

In July Halifax received warning from Albrecht Haushofer via
Clydesdale that the strike against Poland would be launched any
time after the middle of August. Hitler, Albrecht wrote in his letter

to 'Douglo', was still thinking in terms of British bluff. He wanted to avoid a 'big war' and hoped he might get away with an isolated local war; but Albrecht, fearing that 'the terrific forms of modern war' would make any reasonable peace impossible, argued they had to stop the explosion taking place: Britain should produce a peace plan for a long-term settlement between Germany and Poland 'based upon considerable territorial changes combined with population exchanges on the Greek–Turkish model'.[3]

Albrecht gave Clydesdale permission to show the letter personally to Halifax or his undersecretary, R.A. Butler. Significantly in view of later events, Clydesdale showed it to Churchill first, then to Halifax and Chamberlain, and instead of destroying it, as Albrecht had insisted he should, deposited it with his bank. Since the advice amounted to no more than a repeat 'Munich' over Poland, it is as likely to have been issued on Hess's behalf – the injunction to destroy it a ruse to conceal his patron's involvement – as to have been from Albrecht off his own bat as a friend or member of the German opposition.

At much the same time in July, one of Göring's chief economic advisers, Dr Wohltat, held talks in London with Sir Horace Wilson, Chamberlain's principal adviser on foreign affairs, who proposed an Anglo–German treaty of non-aggression and non-interference. A few days afterwards, another emissary from Göring, Birger Dahlerus, the Swedish managing director of a ball-bearing company in Luton who had personal connections to Göring, was introduced to Halifax for an off-the-record meeting. There were at least two subsequent deniable meetings between the two,[4] the upshot of which was a very secret conference from 7–10 August on the German North Sea island of Sylt between seven British businessmen, led by a director of the great shipbuilding company John Brown, and an extremely high-level German team led by Göring himself.[5] The British side, while insisting that the guarantee to Poland was firm, offered another four-power conference between Chamberlain, Hitler, Mussolini and the French premier, Daladier, to solve all outstanding European 'problems', with the Polish 'Corridor' and port of Danzig at the top of the agenda. They came away, like Halifax earlier, convinced of Göring's honesty: 'He impressed us all as being surprisingly trustworthy and straight.'[6]

These, and no doubt many other less formal contacts, reminiscent of Sir Edward Grey's desperate attempts to preserve peace in the dying days before the first war, failed to deter Hitler. They served only to convince him that, when tested, Britain and France would back out of their pledge to Poland. At the least it confirmed the strength and depth of British opposition to war. From the British side, it confirmed Göring as the acceptable face of the Nazi leadership. These impressions would persist.

THE NAZI–SOVIET PACT

British and French reluctance to enlist Soviet support forced Stalin to come to terms with Hitler. The announcement of the Nazi–Soviet non-aggression pact on 22 August 1939 came as a huge surprise to the Western powers, but it served the interests of both dictators. Hitler avoided the two-front war his generals refused to contemplate; Stalin bought time and acquired a buffer between him and his sworn foe – since it was agreed in a secret protocol that Poland and other intervening territories would be divided between them. He also gained a trade deal and the transfer of advanced military technology from Germany.

Hitler had been advised that the deal was secure a week earlier, and had immediately ordered preparations for the attack on Poland – termed 'Case White' – for the early hours of 26 August. Chamberlain only learned of the Soviet pact on the 22nd; he immediately wrote to Hitler to disabuse him of the idea that it would prevent Britain intervening on behalf of Poland. The French government took the same line. On the 25th Hitler nevertheless gave the executive order for Case White. That evening he learned that his friend Mussolini would not support him, and that a Polish–British defence pact had been signed as annex to a Franco–Polish military alliance, and he rescinded the order.

At about the time he backed down, Birger Dahlerus, who had flown to London to see Halifax on Göring's behalf to propose a Munich-style 'mediation', was shown in to the Foreign Secretary's grand room in the Foreign Office. Halifax refused the bait, but was flexible enough for Göring to continue negotiating via Dahlerus for many days, even offering to fly to London himself.[7]

Earlier that day, the 25th, Halifax had seen a prospective British peace envoy named James Lonsdale Bryans.[8] An Old Etonian, Bryans had recently been brought to the attention of MI5 by the police Special Branch in Malaya, where he had come to 'adverse notice' for saying 'he was in entire sympathy with Hitler' and trying, without success, to gate-crash the Penang Club on the strength of his old school tie.[9] Halifax, who would not have seen this report as Bryans had not been vetted, gave him his backing, according to Bryans' own account, 'to make contact with enemy groups opposed to Hitler'.[10] Why Halifax should have considered him suitable for this mission is a puzzle.

There is a possible clue in Bryans' MI5 file: a handwritten note on the minute sheet runs, 'H—y [or perhaps M—y] got his name from D of B as a potential contact with Germany.'[11] If 'H—y', this could have been Sir Maurice Hankey, the influential former cabinet secretary then serving on a committee overseeing the secret services, while 'D of B' probably referred to the Duke of Buccleuch. Many letters testify to the fact that Bryans was backed by Buccleuch and the pro-Nazi Lord Brocket.[12] As for his credentials as a 'contact with Germany', Bryans proclaimed his hatred for democracy and Jews, and was the author of a book on evolution called *The Curve of Fate* which so conformed to Nazi philosophy, it had recently been accepted for publication by a Leipzig publishing house.

Whatever the explanation, Bryans had already been granted an exit permit to travel to Venice. His stated purpose was to act as agent for the domestic affairs of Sir Hubert Miller, an elderly Hampshire landowner and former Guards officer who loved Venice and owned property in the city. Sir Hubert provided Bryans with a reference, as did Lord Rushcliffe, a Conservative politician and former government minister.[13]

However, according to Bryans' subsequent accounts, he made for Rome, arriving 'at the end of September'. There, after some weeks, he gained the confidence of a young Italian staying at the same hotel, who was engaged to be married to the daughter of the German 'conservative opposition' leader, Ulrich von Hassell.[14] It is interesting that this young man, Detalmo Pirzio-Biroli, was scion of an aristocratic family with estates in the department of Venezia, north-east of Venice. Could it be that Bryans went, or was sent, to Venice to meet him? There was ample time between his meeting with Halifax on 25 August and his arrival in Rome at the end of September. Yet if he went to Venice first, why should he have concealed it? There are several unanswered questions about his mission but the most significant remains why Halifax should have backed an unknown, inexperienced and, as it would prove, thoroughly unreliable agent.

The young Pirzio-Biroli was the son of General Allessandro Pirzio-Biroli and an American mother. He had been educated in the United States, and had visited England as a student in 1935, coming to the attention of Special Branch, who reported him stating that he was in London 'on a matter of policy'.[15] Later, in Rome, when von Hassell was the very popular German Ambassador in Mussolini's capital, Pirzio-Biroli had met and fallen in love with his daughter, Fey, and they had become engaged.

In the closing months of 1939 when Bryans 'gained his confidence', Pirzio had just come back from Germany, where he had been staying with von Hassell, who had given him a summary of the terms of peace which a new 'conservative' Germany, purged of Hitler, would be prepared to accept.[16] Bryans took the document for conveyance to Halifax.

WAR

Returning to the evening of 25 September 1939, the day Lonsdale Bryans had received his unofficial commission from Halifax, and Hitler had aborted the next day's planned attack on Poland, Hess, in Graz, Austria, addressed a congress of expatriate Germans on the Polish issue. Germany, he began, had shown immense forbearance in the face of Polish incitements to war and outrages against Germans living in Poland. It was England's responsibility for inciting the Poles; her reason for doing so was that Jews and Freemasons there wanted the war against Germany, 'this Germany in which they have lost their power.'[17]

He concluded with an affirmation of faith that providence had sent the Führer as their deliverance: 'In standing by the Führer we fulfil the will of that which sent us the Führer. We Germans, we stand by the colours of the Führer – come what may!'

He returned to Berlin, and there is a glimpse of him in Hitler's Chancellery in a surviving fragment of Himmler's diary for 28 August. It was evening. The British Ambassador had presented a note reiterating Britain's determination to honour her pledge to Poland. Hitler had said he would give his reply the next day. Afterwards, Himmler noted, he and Göring and Hess joined Hitler and his Foreign Minister, Joachim von Ribbentrop, in the conservatory. Hitler appeared to be in a very good mood, mimicking the ambassador's 'thick English accent'. He told them it was now necessary 'to aim a document at the British (or Poles) that is little less than a masterpiece of diplomacy'.[18]

The Poles refused to respond to the masterpiece, and at four in the afternoon of the 31st Hitler again gave the order for 'Case White'. This time he did not rescind it. The assault was preceded by carefully prepared and rehearsed 'provocations' in which Polish-speaking SS men in Polish uniforms took over German posts on the border in mock battles. Concentration camp inmates were brought to the scene, dressed in Polish uniforms, and then shot, the corpses being photographed *in situ* as evidence of the Polish 'invasion'. At 4.30 in the morning of 1 September German tank columns supported by aircraft crossed the border at multiple points. An hour later Hitler broadcast to his people: Poland had violated the frontier; he had had no option but to meet force with force.

Britain and France lacked military plans to give effect to the guarantee on which they were now hoist, but after vain protests found no option but to honour their pledge, and on 3 September both reluctantly declared war on Germany. So, finally, Hitler's England *Politik* had failed.

The British Ambassador, committed to appeasement to the very end, gained the impression that the mass of German people were horror-struck at the war thrust upon them.[19] The American journalist, William L. Shirer, looking at silent groups in the Wilhelmplatz, Berlin, had a similar perception of a people stunned by the outbreak of a second European war.[20]

German troops conducting the new *Blitzkrieg*, or lightning war tactics through Polish defences had few doubts; certainly the members of Himmler's special *Einsatzkommandos* following the advancing armies were executing orders to liquidate Jews, aristocrats, priests and the professional classes with savage conviction.[21] Himmler's chief executive, Reinhard Heydrich, explained the mission to his group commanders on 21 September: the aim was to expunge the Polish nation from the map; once the Polish leaders and educated classes had been annihilated, the Polish people would be incorporated in the German economy as migrant workers.

Just what Heydrich said about Polish Jews will never be known, as summarised in a secret circular he made a distinction between '1) the ultimate aim which requires a long period of time, and 2) the stages in the implementation of this ultimate aim, to be carried out on a short-term basis'. The preliminary stages included clearing Jews completely from the western areas of the occupied territory and concentrating them in the east in large cities at railway junctions or along railways 'so that future measures may be accomplished more easily'.[22] The nature of the future measures and 'ultimate aim' are subject to debate, of which more will be said.

The Western Allies, meanwhile, did nothing to ease the Poles' agony before the armoured onslaught that was crushing them. The Italian Ambassador in Paris told his British counterpart that he had seen several wars waged without being declared, but this was the first he had seen declared without being waged.[23]

In Britain those influential groups opposed to fighting Germany called for a negotiated peace. The Duke of Westminster hosted anti-war meetings at his London house attended by such grandees as the Duke of Buccleuch, the Marquis of Londonderry, the Marquis of Tavistock, heir to the Duke of Bedford, and numerous nobles of lesser pedigree, including Lord Brocket, Lord Noel-Buxton, who led a 'Peace Aims' group, and Lord Harmsworth, brother of the newspaper magnates, Lords Northcliffe and Rothermere.[24]

These aristocrats exercised great leverage in the Conservative Party through their wealth and palatial establishments, old school, family and club connections. Westminster himself, like Lord Brocket, was on the pro-Nazi wing of the peace campaigners; he was reported to the War Cabinet that September for saying the war was part of a Jewish plot to destroy Christian civilisation.[25] Lord Brocket had been reported to the internal security service, MI5, shortly before the outbreak as a result of a telephone interception revealing him making a secret assignation with an official of the German Embassy.[26] Others like Tavistock and Noel-Buxton were pacifists, but perhaps the majority were simply expressing the view held by military experts and many ordinary people – especially after an announcement on 17 September that the Russians were invading Poland from the east – that Britain should not be involved in the war, and that Bolshevism represented a greater danger than Nazism.

The Royal family needed no persuasion: the murder of Tsar Nicholas and his family by the Bolsheviks in 1917 was still raw in their memory. Banking and financial circles were equally concerned by the threat to the economy if the war continued, and the danger of becoming dependent on US finance. For politicians of many colours the potentially ruinous costs and the scale of state intervention war would bring threatened liberal democracy itself. On 20 September, David Lloyd George, Prime Minister during the first war, added his powerful voice to the doubters, telling a meeting of concerned MPs it was time to take stock of the military position; if the chances of victory were less than even, 'we should certainly make peace at the earliest opportunity.'[27]

This mood, which touched all classes, was not lost on German intelligence. After Warsaw fell on 27 September, peace feelers began reaching London from Hitler's ministers.

PEACE FEELERS

The majority of significant German peace probes – those deemed worthy of filing at the Foreign Office – came from Göring, the early ones through Dahlerus. Chamberlain, while wishing to negotiate an end to the unwanted war, refused to deal with a government led by Hitler, whom he could not trust; his private secretary suspected there was also an element of damaged vanity. In early October Hitler himself, in an impassioned speech to the Reichstag at the Kroll Opera, Berlin, called for Britain to come to an understanding.

It is no doubt a coincidence that a letter from Clydesdale, drafted with Halifax's advice, appeared in *The Times* on the day Hitler made his appeal. It began by recognising that if the German people really were 'behind Hitler in his cruelties and treacheries', the war had to be fought to the bitter end:

> But I believe that the moment the menace of aggression and bad faith has been removed, war against Germany becomes wrong and meaningless. This generation is conscious that injustices were done to the German people in the era after the last war. There must be no repetition of that ...[28]

He looked forward to 'a trusted Germany' again coming into her own, when 'a healing peace' could be negotiated – but a precondition had to be effective guarantees against any race being treated as Hitler had treated the Jews on 9 November the previous year. Noted in Berlin, the letter was broadcast on the German news that night.

A few days later Chamberlain delivered a blunt rejection of Hitler's appeal to reason. Hitler drew the conclusion that before he could bring Britain to terms he had to teach her a lesson: as Goebbels put it in his diary after a talk alone with him on 23 October, 'The Führer thinks no more of peace. He wants to put England to the sword';[29] and after another talk in early November, 'He is of opinion England must receive a K.O. blow ... or there will be no peace in the world ... The strike against the Western powers will not be long in coming.'[30]

For the moment, peace feelers continued to arrive in London, designed more to sow dissension and probe the strength of the various British peace movements than to initiate serious talks. Chamberlain and Halifax, who had been approached by genuine members of the German opposition and still hoped that Hitler might be toppled in a military coup and replaced by Göring, had their imaginations fanned by agents of the regime. That October Halifax's undersecretary at the Foreign Office, R.A. 'Rab' Butler, a thoroughgoing appeaser, was sent to meet one of these, the Sudeten German landowner, Prince Max zu

Hohenlohe, in Switzerland. Their meeting was very secret: so secret it has been expunged from the Foreign Office 'Peace feeler' files, if indeed it was ever recorded. At Lausanne Butler discussed possible peace terms should Hitler be replaced by Göring.[31]

Simultaneously Heydrich was playing a deception on the British Secret Intelligence Service, MI6, in western Europe. It was apparently designed to set the political conditions – or excuse – for the strike west, on which Hitler had set his mind. The details remain obscure. It may have started as a feeler from genuine opposition circles in the German Army, which leaked to MI6.[32] Directly Heydrich took control it became an intelligence game to entrap two senior MI6 officers in the Netherlands, Major Richard Stevens and Captain Sigismund Payne Best, who believed they were negotiating with a general leading a coup against Hitler. Stevens gained approval from London to continue talking, and was sent briefing notes on peace terms drafted in the Foreign Office and approved by Chamberlain.[33] These expressed a desire to treat with a 'reasonable' Germany – with Hitler removed – and to create a league of European states under the leadership of Great Britain to provide a front against militant Communism. The lead German agent, posing, with monocle, as Captain Schaemmel of the Transport Division – actually Walther Schellenberg, chief of Heydrich's foreign Counter-Intelligence Division – feigned satisfaction with the terms and promised to bring the general leading the revolt to Holland to meet the British officers on 8 November. At the last moment he postponed the meeting until the next day.

There are reasons to suppose that a rigged assassination attempt on Hitler on 8 November formed a part of the plan. On that evening every year the 'old fighters' of the Nazi Party gathered in the Bürgerbräukeller in Munich to celebrate the 1923 'Beerhall Putsch'. This year was no exception. Hitler was received with storms of applause when he entered with Hess, Goebbels, Himmler and other leaders, and the speech, in which he made cutting attacks on England and promised to settle accounts with her, was received, as Goebbels recorded it, with 'mad enthusiasm'.[34] Afterwards, instead of staying to reminisce with the old comrades, as he had always done in the past, he left in some haste with his retinue of ministers to catch a scheduled express train for Berlin. Minutes later an explosion in a pillar behind the podium from which he had been speaking brought down part of the ceiling, killing eight of those beneath and injuring dozens more.

Hitler received the news when his train stopped at Nuremberg. Goebbels noted in his diary that if the programme followed in all previous years had been adhered to, none of those in their party would now be alive. 'The Führer began [his speech] half an hour earlier than in previous times and ended in good time,' he wrote. 'He stood under the protection of the Almighty. He will only die when his mission is fulfilled.'[35] In directives to Press and radio Goebbels pursued the theme of Providence protecting the Führer, and Heydrich targeted a whispering campaign at parish priests to persuade them to spread from their pulpits the idea of Divine intervention to preserve the Führer.

Goebbels' diary entry for that night continued with a phrase that surely gives the lie to the authenticity of the *Attentat*: 'When we catch the perpetrator there will be vengeance that conforms to the magnitude of the crime.'[36] For, unlike the later conspirators in the failed 1944 bomb plot to kill Hitler, who were hanged with piano wire, there was no vengeance. A joiner named Georg Elser was caught on the German–Swiss border on the night of the explosion trying to flee the country. He had a Communist badge inside his lapel – he was indeed a former Communist – and in his pocket a picture postcard of the Bürgerbräukeller with the pillar in which the bomb had been concealed marked with a red cross. After interrogation by the Gestapo he was neither tortured nor executed, but locked away in solitary confinement in Sachsenhausen concentration camp in a cell converted from two single cells and fitted out as a carpenter's workshop. In the dying months of the war he was transferred to Dachau, and on 29 April, the day before Hitler committed suicide in Berlin, he was executed with a shot to the neck on orders from Himmler's Security Service headquarters.

Given Hitler's pitiless nature it seems inconceivable that Elser would have survived to serve a sentence, let alone been treated as a privileged prisoner if it was thought he was guilty of a real attempt on his life. Captain Payne Best, who was also to find himself in Sachsenhausen – as will appear – claimed that Elser had smuggled notes to him which told a rather different story: early in the war the joiner had been plucked from Dachau, where he had been sentenced for being antisocial and workshy, and offered freedom and a new life in Switzerland if he would build the bomb into the Bürgerbräu pillar. Naturally he had accepted.[37] During his time in the camps after the deed, Elser was isolated from other inmates; finally he was silenced for ever.

In his notes to Payne Best Elser said that he was being kept as principal witness in a show trial to be held when Britain had been defeated; he had been coached in a story implicating the two British agents (Payne Best and Stevens) in the bomb attempt on Hitler's life. Nevertheless, a transcript of Elser's Gestapo interrogation revealing him as the sole perpetrator of the bomb attempt has convinced German historians that he was indeed acting on his own and intended to assassinate the Führer.[38] If so he was a truly remarkable man, fully deserving the memorials erected to him as a hero of the German resistance to Nazism.

At all events, the German newspapers on the morning of 9 November led with the sensational story of Hitler's providential escape, leading Stevens and Best to wonder whether the opposition general they were going to meet had been involved. Their rendezvous with 'Schaemmel' was in the Café Backus at Venlo, some 50 yards from the Dutch–German border. As their car approached the café, an SS squad in an armoured car crashed the border barrier, in reverse in order to make a smart getaway afterwards. There was a brief exchange of gunfire, in which a Dutch intelligence officer accompanying the two British officers was mortally wounded, and before the border guards could react both Britons were snatched and driven into Germany.

There is no proof, but Heydrich's biographer, Eduard Calic, is in no doubt that the Bürgerbräu *Attentat* and the 'Venlo incident' were engineered by Heydrich to provide the pretext for the assault on the Western powers through neutral Holland which Hitler hoped to launch in mid-November. Stevens and Best were accused by Goebbels' propaganda agencies of having commissioned and paid for the attempt on Hitler's life from British Secret Service European headquarters in the Hague. In the event the assault on the West was postponed, apparently because of the weather, but when it was launched the following spring, accusations of British and Dutch involvement in the Bürgerbräu bomb were resurrected by Ribbentrop as pretexts. In the meantime the German people, who had been showing dissatisfaction and unhappiness at shortages in the shops and the prospect of war with the Western powers, had become, according to an internal Security Service report, united behind the Führer in gratitude for his escape, and spoke bitterly about England and the Jews.[39]

The German Security Service gleaned sufficient from Stevens and Best to roll up virtually the entire British intelligence operation in western Europe.[40] Moreover, the generals who were contemplating action against Hitler took fright when they heard that the two British officers were being interrogated about just such a plot at Gestapo headquarters. This was, perhaps, the most significant effect of Heydrich's coup. After questioning, Stevens and Best were sent to concentration camps. Both survived the war, which again would not have been the case had Hitler believed they were in any way implicated in a plot to kill him.

LONSDALE BRYANS

The 'Venlo incident' served to ensure that MI6 and the Foreign Office treated further approaches from the German military opposition with utmost scepticism. Nonetheless, peace feelers continued to arrive from Göring via Dahlerus and another Swedish emissary, Baron Knut Bonde, a diplomat serving in the Swedish Legation in the Swiss capital, Berne, married to the daughter of a Scottish former Guards officer and on the Swedish side close to Count Eric Rosen, brother of Göring's first wife, Karin – after whom Göring had named his estate. His approach was based on the unlikely premise that Göring would take over from Hitler.

In early January 1940 Lord Brocket's agent, Lonsdale Bryans, arrived in London from Rome with von Hassell's proposed 'peace terms', again for a Germany without Hitler, and took them, together with an introductory letter from Pirzio, to Halifax at the Foreign Office on the 8th. Halifax found them so encouraging he had the Passport

Office grant Bryans 'all possible facilities' to return to Rome,[41] while Cadogan, Permanent Undersecretary at the Foreign Office, arranged with the Treasury to fund him. Bryans' cover this time was to see his publishers in Rome about a possible Italian translation of his book, but he told the passport officer it might be assumed that he was 'undertaking some special work for the Foreign Office'.

On Bryans' return to Rome, Pirzio, who was now married to Fey von Hassell, began a code correspondence with his father-in-law to set up a face-to-face meeting between him and Bryans. This was eventually accomplished by von Hassell's wife taking their eldest son, who was asthmatic, to Zurich. From there she was able to telephone to Rome without fear of Gestapo interception, and it was arranged that she and her son would travel to Arosa, near St Moritz. Her husband (code name Charles) would join her; Bryans (code name the Doctor – i.e. attending their son) would meet him there.[42]

They met as planned on 22 February when they had three conversations: before lunch, in the afternoon and in the evening. Bryans made a favourable impression on the German diplomat and they met again the following morning when von Hassell gave Bryans a handwritten statement in English to take to Halifax stipulating terms for a lasting European peace. So far as territory was concerned, the union of Austria and the Sudeten with Germany, and the eastern frontiers of the Reich were not for discussion – in other words Hitler's conquests were to be rewarded. The final section, evidently intended to convince the British government they would be dealing with a thoroughly de-Nazified Germany, stipulated certain political and moral principles to be accepted in the reconstruction of Europe; these included Christian ethics, justice and law, and liberty of thought, conscience and intellectual activity.[43]

Von Hassell's diary entries make it clear that Bryans was following Halifax's intentions to the letter:

B's [Bryans'] aim is: to get a Statement from Halifax that, on the approximate basis of my Statement, he would do all in his power to ensure that a possible regime-change in Germany would in no way be exploited by the other side, but on the contrary would be used to arrive at a lasting peace. Especially in this case the English side would attempt to arrange an immediate armistice. On the other hand B maintained that a peace agreement with the present German government was totally out of the question ...[44]

Von Hassell told Bryans he was not in a position to reveal the names of the men behind him, but could assure him that a statement from Halifax would get to the right people. He stressed that his own statement was valid only before the start of major military operations, commenting in his diary, 'Mr B himself urged very great haste in view of a possible German offensive.'[45]

After their talk on the 23rd Bryans left for Zürich, thence flew via Paris to London, arriving on the 24th. He gave the statement he had received in Arosa to Cadogan to pass on to Halifax with a note stressing that von Hassell could not initiate any action against Hitler without clear documentary proof that Britain would not take advantage of the consequent internal disruption.[46] Such a note was refused since, he was told, something similar had been given to another group in Germany a week before.[47] There were two other channels to German opposition groups, one running through the Vatican, another also through Switzerland; both groups had indeed received assurances that favourable peace terms would be offered to a non-Nazi Germany.

The fastidiousness of Chamberlain's government was not shared by all: the grandees of the peace movement – Buccleuch, Brocket, Londonderry, Tavistock – wrote constantly to Chamberlain or Halifax calling for negotiations with Germany before the bombing and destruction started. A similar campaign was mounted by a small Labour group led by the MP for Ipswich, R.R. 'Dick' Stokes. Lord Beaverbrook, owner of the *Express* newspaper group, backed Stokes and published articles by the distinguished military historian Basil Liddell Hart, whose views on Britain's strategic position could not have been more pessimistic. Asked in private by one editor what could be done, he replied, 'Come to the best possible terms [with Germany] as soon as possible.'[48]

In February the US Assistant Secretary of State, Sumner Welles, sailed from New York on an official 'fact-finding' mission to Europe.

It was hailed in the Press as Roosevelt's peace mission. If Welles had such expectations they evaporated when he met Hitler, Hess and other Nazi leaders in early March: he was left in no doubt that Hitler was securely in control and that he and his entourage felt themselves masters of the future of Europe – or as Goebbels put it more bluntly in his diary: 'Victory and not a rotten compromise must be the result of this war';[49] and after a talk with Hitler at the end of the month, 'one way or another he [the Führer] will strike England to the ground. Of which I am also firmly convinced.'[50]

In this atmosphere the German generals on whom von Hassell, Chamberlain and Halifax had to depend for any coup against Hitler found themselves, for practical, cultural, historical and psychological reasons, unable to act. By the time Pirzio had managed to arrange another meeting between 'Charles' and 'the Doctor', again in Arosa, Hitler had unleashed his campaign in the west.[51] The moment, if it had ever existed, had passed.

CHAPTER SIX

Churchill – and the Jews

HITLER'S ASSAULT in the west began in April with amphibious strikes on Denmark and Norway. British expeditionary forces landed in Norway were unable to stem the German advance. On 21 April Goebbels noted:

> England recognises the seriousness of her position. The Führer intends to remove her with a KO blow. Despite it he would make peace today. Conditions: England out of Europe and our colonies ... returned ... He will certainly not destroy England nor destroy her empire ...[1]

On the 25th, after another talk with Hitler, Goebbels noted that the Führer was determined to smash France, thereby removing London's mainland sword, but 'England can have peace if it keeps out of Europe and gives back our colonies.'[2]

On 10 May Hitler launched the strike against France with a feint by Army Group B through the Netherlands. Coincidentally, on the same day, the British government fell, rocked by failures in Norway. Churchill replaced Chamberlain as Prime Minister and formed a coalition administration with Labour.

In Churchill Great Britain found a leader guided, like Hitler, by instinct, emotion and imagination. Like Hitler, he lacked formal academic training and tended to oversimplify complex issues and extemporise solutions – 'a mind not judicial in any sense, not logical, not analytical,' his doctor, Lord Moran, diagnosed,[3] and Jock Colville, who now became his private secretary, observed that 'his mind did not operate in predetermined grooves ... a sudden whim or unexpected judgement caught his family or staff unawares no less frequently than the Cabinet or Defence Committee.'[4]

Yet he was a student of war and his intuition was informed by the long series of conflicts in which Great Britain had thrown her navy and her trading power and finance against the pretensions of Continental tyrants. His historical vision thus transcended the present balance which hypnotised Liddell Hart and most military men, and Lloyd George and the high Tory grandees. He divined that Hitler and Stalin must in the long or short term fight for mastery in Europe, and his priority was to hold on until he could somehow draw the United States actively into the war on Britain's side.

Here the Jewish question assumed significance. Churchill was convinced, as noted earlier, that the Balfour Declaration of 1917 promising the Jews a permanent home in Palestine had been instrumental in mobilising American-Jewish support for US entry into the First World War. Since 1933 Nazi treatment of Jews had made the American-Jewish lobby a committed ally in his struggle against Hitler from the back benches. In this sense Hitler and Hess had grounds for their paranoia about an international Jewish conspiracy against Germany: they had called it down upon themselves.

Churchill had close family connections with the British line of the international Jewish banking house of Rothschild: the first Baron Rothschild had been his father's intimate adviser at the Treasury, and Churchill knew the family socially as a guest at their country seat at Tring in Hertfordshire. In 1936 he had lent his backing to an association formed by Jews and Trade Unions called the 'World Anti-Nazi Non-Sectarian Council', soon renamed 'The Focus'. The chief financial support came from British Jews, the main sources of intelligence from Jewish banking connections and the huge number of German-Jewish émigrés who fled from Hitler. In 1938, when Churchill found himself in such financial straits he was forced to put his beloved home,

Chartwell, on the market, he was rescued by Sir Henry Strakosch, born a Moravian Jew, who paid the then substantial sum of £18,162 to clear his debts, after which Churchill withdrew Chartwell from sale.[5]

It would be a mistake to conclude that Churchill felt beholden to or was bribed by the Jewish interest, or on the other hand used the Zionists cynically for his own ends. He felt genuine compassion for the Jews in Germany and Poland. The Labour leader, Clement Attlee, described him one day in the Commons with tears pouring down his cheeks as he described what was being done to Jews in Germany.[6] That he played the Zionist card for all it was worth in his attempt to tip the United States into the war is not, however, in doubt.

Churchill's second card was Soviet Russia. Long before the war he had foreseen that the only way to counter German military expansionism was to weld the European nations, including Russia, into a ring around Germany. It was the failure of successive Conservative governments even to contemplate bringing the Soviet Union into a defensive alliance that had finally projected Stalin into Hitler's arms. Churchill had no sympathy with Communism. He was an imperialist, as dedicated as high Tory and service circles to the maintenance and glory of the British Empire; unlike them, he saw Hitler as the greater threat.

It was a judgement he had made before the war. In power he followed it through ruthlessly to its logical conclusion. He had a boyish spirit and a strong heart, schooled in adversity. Aspects of his childhood had been shaped, like Hitler's, by trauma, in his case parental neglect. He had known despair and continued to be subject to that dark malady, which he called his 'black dog'. Probably only such a man, neither analytical nor stable, but touched with the spark of folly necessary to overcome the highest obstacles could have pulled the country through the crisis which now unfolded as tanks of General Gerd von Rundstedt's Army Group A burst unexpectedly through the Ardennes, sliced through the French armies and divided them from the British Expeditionary Force in the north.

The British, trapped between von Rundstedt and Army Group B advancing through the Low Countries, fell back towards the coast. That substantial numbers were able to make good their escape was due to Hitler's intervention. At von Rundstedt's headquarters on 24 May he ordered the tanks to halt and not cross the canal line Lens–Bethune–St Omer.[7] The order was not rescinded until late on the 26th, allowing the British time to establish a defensive perimeter around the beaches at Dunkirk, from where over the following days large numbers were rescued by Royal Navy destroyers and innumerable small craft.

The reasons for Hitler's order remain subject to dispute. Probably the consensus view is that it was made on military grounds:[8] the terrain towards the coast was unsuitable for tanks, and it was necessary to concentrate the armour for a strike against the main French force to the south; in any case the Luftwaffe was ordered to destroy the trapped enemy.

Hitler always maintained it was a political decision: he told Hess it would have been easy with the mass employment of their tanks, artillery and aircraft to destroy the British force and some 100,000 French troops with them, or compel their surrender in quick time: 'But that was just what I did not want. I did not want to humiliate the British with a crushing military defeat, but on the contrary finally to bring them to an armistice and peace negotiations.'[9]

Senior staff officers present at a meeting between Hitler and von Rundstedt at the latter's headquarters that day came to suspect that this was indeed the case: Hitler had deliberately spared the British. One of them, General Blumentritt, told Liddell Hart after the war that Hitler had been in best humour when he visited their headquarters and expressed the view that the war would be over in six weeks. He wished to conclude a reasonable peace with France, after which the way would be open for an agreement with Britain:

> He then astonished us by speaking with admiration of the British Empire, of the necessity for its existence, and of the civilisation that Britain had brought into the world ... He compared the British Empire to the Roman Catholic Church – saying they were both essential elements of stability in the world. He said that all he wanted from Britain was that she should acknowledge Germany's position on the Continent.[10]

Hitler went on to say that the return of Germany's colonies would be desirable, but not essential, and that he would even support Britain militarily were she to become involved in problems anywhere. This is virtually what Hitler had said to Goebbels the previous month. At the very least it is clear that Hitler's priority was to force France out of the war, not to destroy the British Army.

As it was, the successful evacuation of the greater part of the British Expeditionary Force, the essential nucleus from which to rebuild the army, allowed Churchill to rally the country and send a message of defiance to Hitler:

> We shall go on to the end ... We shall defend our island, whatever the cost may be. We shall fight on the beaches. We shall fight on the landing grounds, we shall fight in the fields and in the streets, we shall fight in the hills; we shall never surrender ...[11]

He made his long-term strategy equally clear: the British Empire would carry on the struggle 'until, in God's good time, the new world, with all its power and might, steps forth to the rescue and the liberation of the old.'

THE 'FIFTH COLUMN'

Those circles in Britain seeking a negotiated peace with Germany had already received rough warning of Churchill's resolve. On 22 May Regulation 18b of the Emergency Powers (Defence) Act had been strengthened to allow the internment without trial of anyone showing sympathy to an enemy power; habeas corpus was suspended and no appeal allowed. It was an affront to the principles of freedom under the rule of law for which Britain stood.

The first victims, rounded up the next day, were Oswald Mosley, leader of the British Union of Fascists (BUF), some 30 of his leading adherents, and Captain Archibald Maule Ramsay MP, founder of the pro-Fascist Right Club. Hundreds more members of the BUF and other anti-Jewish or pacifist societies dedicated to a negotiated peace with Germany were to follow over the next weeks and months.[12]

Interestingly the real grandees calling for an accommodation with Germany, such as the Dukes of Buccleuch and Westminster and the Marquis of Tavistock, heir to the Duke of Bedford, were not interned.

Buccleuch was, however, removed from the high office he held in the Royal Household. This was apparently at the request of King George VI himself. In a note from Buckingham Palace dated 14 May Churchill had been informed that the King wished to change the Lord Steward 'for reasons which are probably known to you but which I could, if required, explain.'[13] No explanation accompanies this document in the file held at The National Archives. On 22 May, as the decision was taken to strengthen Regulation 18b, Churchill was informed by the Lord Chamberlain that Buccleuch had tendered his resignation as Lord Steward, and in his place the King desired to appoint the Duke of Hamilton.

This was Douglas Douglas-Hamilton, former Marquis of Clydesdale, whose father, the 13th Duke of Hamilton, had died recently. Churchill was advised in a brief note that the procedure now was for him to inform the Lord Chamberlain that he would have no objection to submitting the Duke of Hamilton's name to the Palace. Across the top of the note, someone in Churchill's office wrote in pencil, 'PM says do whatever is necessary.'[14] This note, dated 24 May, was withheld from the file released in the normal way to the National Archives, and was only restored to its place in the file in February 2005. Why it should have been withheld is a mystery. Undoubtedly Hamilton's appointment as Lord Steward in the Royal Household with direct access to the King had a major bearing on Hess's decision to target him in his peace mission the following year, but at the time of this note Hess had not even conceived the idea of intervening personally to stop the war.

Some of the circumstances that had led to the amendment to Regulation 18b and the internment of Fascist sympathisers appear similarly opaque. The swift German victories in Norway and the Low Countries were believed to have been aided by a 'fifth column' of pro-Nazis in each country overrun, and the possibility of a German invasion of Britain had raised fears of a British 'fifth column'. Members of Mosley's BUF seemed to fit this category. Guy Liddell, head of counter-intelligence in the internal security service, MI5, had no doubt about it, and had pressed for 500 selected BUF members to be interned.[15] The submission had been rejected by the Home Secretary for lack of evidence; indeed Mosley had publicly exhorted his BUF members in the event of invasion to throw themselves into the national effort to drive the enemy from British soil.[16]

Liddell had finally gained his desired outcome on the back of a separate investigation. His section head in charge of countering political subversion, Maxwell Knight, had learned from undercover agents he had planted in Captain Ramsay's Right Club that a key member, Anna Wolkoff, was associating with a cipher clerk at the US Embassy named Tyler Kent, and that he had shown her documents he had stolen from the embassy. Several were messages between President Roosevelt and Churchill when First Lord of the Admiralty, revealing Roosevelt's strong support for Britain. Apparently Kent, a committed isolationist, hoped that by publishing the messages he could expose what he saw as a plot to bring America into the war.

Anna Wolkoff had introduced Kent to Captain Ramsay, who had also inspected the documents, and she had copied several and passed them to an attaché at the Italian Embassy.[17] Italy was still neutral, but decrypts of intercepted Italian diplomatic traffic revealed that Rome was passing the documents to Berlin. In addition it appears that Knight's agents had induced Wolkoff to send a message in code to William Joyce,[18] a former member of the Right Club who had fled to Germany on the eve of war and was now broadcasting enemy propaganda to Britain from Berlin as 'Lord Haw-Haw'.

For Churchill the leaked correspondence threatened his strategy for winning the war by drawing America in; for Roosevelt, fighting isolationist sentiment in the United States, Kent's activities threatened his intended campaign for an unprecedented third term. There is no doubt he had already extended co-operation with Britain far beyond America's formal neutrality, and according to the later testimony of both Kent and Knight some of the messages Kent had collected introduced the concept of 'Lend-Lease',[19] the vital measure which was to turn America into the 'arsenal of democracy', but which would not be announced publicly until December that year after Roosevelt had secured his third term.

Kent and Anna Wolkoff had been arrested on 20 May. The following evening Liddell, accompanied by Maxwell Knight, attended a meeting with the Home Secretary, Sir John Anderson, regarding the BUF. Anderson opened by saying he found it difficult to believe that BUF members would assist the enemy, and pointed to Mosley's recent appeal to their patriotism. Knight, whom Liddell allowed to do most of the talking, replied that this was merely an example of how insincere Mosley really was; then, according to Liddell's diary, he went on to describe

> something of the underground activities of the BUF and also of the recent case against Tyler Kent involving Maude Ramsay. Anderson agreed that the case against Ramsay was rather serious but he did not seem to think that it involved the BUF. Max [Knight] explained to him that Ramsay and Mosley were in constant touch with one another and that many members of the Right Club were also members of the BUF.[20]

Anderson was still not convinced that he should lock up British subjects without firm evidence. Next day, 22 May, he reported to the War Cabinet that MI5 officers who had studied the BUF were unable to produce evidence against them, but were of opinion that some 25 to 30 per cent would be willing to go to any lengths on behalf of Germany.[21] This was enough: with huge pressure for action against the 'fifth column', and Clement Attlee and his Labour members of Churchill's coalition government wanting measures against the far right, and Churchill himself particularly alarmed by the Kent–Wolkoff case, the decision was taken to amend Defence Regulation 18b in the direction Guy Liddell required: the internment of anyone showing sympathy to an enemy power. So, as noted, orders were signed for the detention of Mosley, Ramsay and the first tranche of BUF members.

These measures were, above all, an indication of Churchill's absolute resolve within his first fortnight in office to pursue his policy of wooing and supporting Roosevelt in his bid for a third term and to stamp on calls for a compromise peace with Hitler. Of equal or possibly greater relevance in view of Hess's later mission was a parallel case of subversion under investigation at this time by Guy Liddell, which also involved the US Embassy in London.

In early February, some weeks before Tyler Kent met Anna Wolkoff, Liddell had received information that the German Secret Service had been and was possibly still receiving American Embassy documents including Ambassador Joseph Kennedy's despatches to President Roosevelt. Kennedy was on sick leave at the time. In his absence Liddell wrote to the Counsellor at the US Embassy, Herschel Johnson, to report this.[22] He made no mention of it in his diary, but five days later, on 12 February, recorded that he had 'passed a report to Herschel Johnson which I received from SIS [MI6] regarding leakage of information relating to despatches between Kennedy and Roosevelt.'[23] Then on the 14th he recorded Felix Cowgill, head of MI6 Section V – counter-intelligence – coming to see him 'about a certain Kurt Jahnke, with whom he [Cowgill] had been indirectly in touch'.[24]

Jahnke was a Prussian who had emigrated to the United States before the First World War and become a naturalised American citizen. When America entered the war he had worked as a German intelligence and sabotage agent there. After the war he had built up contacts in intelligence circles in China, Japan and Russia, where he had worked for Soviet Military Intelligence; later he set up his own intelligence agency in Berlin and worked for Admiral Canaris, head of Military Counter-Intelligence (*Abwehr*). After Hitler's accession to power he and his agency had been absorbed into Hess's intelligence operation under Pfeffer von Salomon – known variously as the *Abteilung* (Department) von Pfeffer, the *Büro* Jahnke or *Büro* 1. In line with Hess's mission to strengthen Anglo–German ties, he had cultivated British intelligence circles, and during the Polish crisis in 1939 had used his British contacts in the vain effort to prevent war with Britain and France.

Cowgill told Liddell that before the war Jahnke had been getting copies of MI6 reports, also the contents of Ambassador Kennedy's despatches to Washington; his (Jahnke's) informant was said to be a clerk in the Foreign Office, or the wife of a clerk. Liddell recorded that Cowgill was 'anxious to know whether this Jahnke was identical with a man of the same name who had before Locarno [Treaty of

1925] been acting as an agent of the Russian 4th Department [Military Intelligence]'.[25]

They were one and the same. Liddell's officers soon tracked down a Foreign Office man named Harold Fletcher, now working at the Government Code and Cipher School at Bletchley Park, who admitted having visited Berlin in 1935 and meeting both Pfeffer von Salomon and Jahnke. He was investigated, but it appears that nothing was proved against him.[26]

The significance of this case in relation to Hess's flight to Britain arises from comments made much later by Sir Maurice Oldfield, head of MI6, or 'C' during the Cold War. Interviewed about Hess by the journalist Phillip Knightley, Oldfield asked if Knightley knew that the head of Hess's intelligence service had been an agent of the KGB, and followed this up by suggesting that he consider whether this KGB man had, perhaps, been behind Hess's flight to Britain.[27] Oldfield's information appears to have come from a file on Hess he had removed from the MI6 registry to save it from destruction at a time when many files were being weeded.

Jahnke, although not the head, was certainly the brains of Hess's intelligence service, and fits Oldfield's story better than the actual head, Pfeffer von Salomon, one of Hitler's original 'old fighters'. Reports in the recently released MI5 file on Jahnke reveal that both he and his secretary and agent-runner Dr Carl Marcus were opposed to Hitler and National Socialism, and probably had contacts with Communist circles;[28] a report by Himmler's counter-intelligence chief, Walter Schellenberg, who employed Jahnke later, stated that 'he hated Hitler and nearly all Nazis';[29] and Schellenberg revealed in his post-war *Memoirs* that he once received a 'detailed compilation of evidence proving that Jahnke was a top-level British agent', who travelled to Switzerland to meet his British contacts.[30]

It is clear from Liddell's diary entry that Cowgill of MI6 'had been indirectly in touch' with Jahnke in February 1940; and the index of documents in the MI5 file on Jahnke shows that correspondence about him with MI6 continued in March and April, July and December 1940, and picked up again on 2 May 1941,[31] a week before Hess's flight, although the documents themselves have been weeded from the file.

THE 'MADAGASCAR PLAN'

Hitler's field headquarters for his western campaign was in the Eifel massif west of the Rhine, close to both the Dutch and Belgian frontiers. Here on 25 May 1940 Himmler reported to him. After the conquest of Poland the previous year, Hitler had appointed him Commissar for the Consolidation of German Nationhood, with responsibility for settlement and population policy in the occupied east; he now presented Hitler with a memorandum containing his latest thoughts on the treatment of the Poles, Jews, Ukrainians, White Russians and other non-German ethnic groups in the newly acquired territory. His stated aim was to extinguish their national consciousness, deprive the young of education above primary school level and create 'a leaderless work-*Volk* of annual itinerant labourers' for their German masters.[32]

Exceptions were to be made for children of good racial appearance: their parents would be notified that their child should attend school in Germany and remain in Germany permanently; thus 'genetically valuable' blood would be captured for the Reich: 'Cruel and tragic as this may be in each individual case, if one rejects the Bolshevik method of physical extermination [*Ausrottung*] of a people from inner conviction as unGermanic and impossible, then this method is really the most lenient ...'

The sentence has drawn much attention. It suggests that at this date, May 1940, Himmler was not considering and had not yet been charged with the task of physically exterminating the Jews, an interpretation reinforced by the only detailed reference to Jews in the memorandum. It came in the context of removing all national consciousness from the different racial groups: 'The concept "Jews" will be completely eliminated, I hope, through the possibility of a great exodus of all the Jews to Africa or otherwise into a colony.'[33]

Hitler approved the memorandum and copies went to the governors of the provinces, or *Gaus*, into which the German half of Poland had been divided, to Hess's secretary, Martin Bormann, and to other high officials, no doubt reinvigorating discussion of the 'Jewish problem'. At all events, in early June a new young head of the Jewish department of the Foreign Ministry, Franz Rademacher, proposed a scheme for deporting Jews to the French Indian Ocean island of Madagascar. It was not a new idea. It had been mooted and investigated from long before the war. Rademacher updated it in the light of Hitler's impending victory over France, suggesting that in the treaty ending the war France should be required to cede Madagascar to Germany under mandate. That the Royal Navy might prevent the shipment of Jews overseas was not considered a problem as England was expected to sue for peace after the defeat of her Continental ally.

German troops entered Paris on 14 June; the armistice was signed eight days later. Hess, who was being treated by a masseur, Felix Kersten, for stomach cramps, accompanied Hitler to the signing ceremony. Returning afterwards to Kersten, he told him he was certain they would make peace with Britain as they had with France; the Führer had told him only a few weeks ago about the great value of the British Empire in the world. Germany and France had to stand together with Great Britain against Bolshevism, the enemy of Europe.[34]

Kersten also treated Himmler, who had told him much the same thing in February. When Kersten asked why Britain should give up her traditional policy of preserving the balance of power on the continent, Himmler had said it was only the small ruling group backed by the Jews who wished to preserve the old policy; when the Führer made peace with England he would demand the expulsion of her Jews.[35]

Churchill had, of course, resolved not to make peace. When this finally came home to the German leadership the 'Madagascar Plan' died a natural death. In the meantime, it appeared to gain brief approval. It was taken up by Eichmann, now heading the Department of Jewish Evacuation in Himmler's Security Service Main Office, and the deportation of Jews to Poland was halted. Hitler mentioned the plan to Mussolini and others, including Goebbels, who noted it in his diary on 17 August: 'The Jews we want to transport to Madagascar later. There they can build their own state.'[36] In Eichmann's project this was to be a police state controlled by the SS.

To judge by Himmler's memorandum of May 1940 and the subsequent detailed plans to deport European Jewry to Madagascar, it appears that the 'final solution' to the 'Jewish problem' – physical extermination – was chosen only after expulsion overseas was rendered impossible by Britain's refusal to make peace, that is, some time after the 'Battle of Britain' in autumn 1940. This is perhaps the consensus view of historians.

An alternative view is that the Madagascar Plan was a deliberate deception fed the Jews and the outside world, particularly the United States with its influential Jewish lobby – for physical extermination had started with the war. Jews had been rounded up and slaughtered in local actions from the beginning of the Polish campaign; they had since been deliberately frozen to death in railway carriages, worked to death in labour camps, and many were dying of starvation in the ghettos into which they had been herded in major towns in Poland in the course of what Heydrich had termed in his September 1939 directive the preliminary stages of the 'ultimate aim' for the Jews. It is hard to understand why he had found it necessary to shroud the 'ultimate aim' in the strictest secrecy if it merely meant deportation out of Europe.

When confronted with this directive of Heydrich's at his trial long after the war, Eichmann could think of no other explanation for the term 'ultimate aim' than physical extermination, and had to agree that 'this, call it basic, conception was already firmly established at this date, 21 September 1939.'[37] His Israeli prosecutor had come to the same conclusion by studying Eichmann's pre-trial police interrogation.[38] And the most exhaustive recent study of Nazi Jewish policy concludes that behind the Madagascar project lay 'the intention of bringing about the physical annihilation of the Jews under German rule'.[39]

The same intention is also implicit in the first 'General Plan East' of May 1940, prepared in Himmler's Head Office for the Consolidation of German Nationhood. This called for the deportation of all Jews in German-occupied Poland to the south-eastern province named the General Government, together with 3.4 million Poles, so freeing up settlement space for the introduction of 3.4 million ethnic Germans from the Reich and elsewhere.[40] There can be no doubt that, as in the updated General Plan East the following year, known as 'the Hunger Plan', those Jews and Poles crowded into the General Government were to be worked and starved to death.[41]

* * *

Ultimately the answer to the question of just when the physical anni-hilation of the Jews was decided depends on the pathology of the Führer. It is apparent from *Mein Kampf* and his speeches that he was a visceral anti-Semite. One speech stands out. It was made before the Reichstag on 30 January 1939, the sixth anniversary of his accession to power. He asserted that during his struggle for power the Jewish people had laughed at his prophecies that he would one day assume the leadership of the state and bring the 'Jewish problem' to a solution.

> Today I will be a prophet once more. If international finance-Jewry in Europe and outside should succeed in once more plunging the nations into a world war, then the consequences will not be the Bolshevisation of the world and thereby a victory for Jewry; but, on the contrary, the annihilation of the Jewish race in Europe.[42]

Significantly, he was later to remind the world of this prophetic speech at the very time industrial methods were being applied to physical extermination of the Jews. No order or decree has been found to link him with this 'ultimate' or 'final' solution. Yet the gassing methods used were developed from 'euthanasia' programmes for the men-tally ill or incurable – defined as 'life unworthy of life' – which he had demonstrably ordered in summer and autumn 1939. The first experi-mental group gassing had taken place in a disused prison in January 1940, and it was apparently the head of his Chancellery who suggested the ruse that came to be adopted to decoy the victims to their death: camouflaging gas chambers as shower rooms.[43]

There are reasons for believing that the killing experiments con-ducted in the 'euthanasia' programmes were not only intended to devise an efficient method of mass killing, but also to act as a psycho-logical selection process for those suited to administer the procedure. It was especially valuable in turning doctors into killers. In his study, *The Nazi Doctors*, Robert Jay Lifton points to the involvement of doc-tors in every stage of the systematised genocide of the Jews, and he concludes that the 'euthanasia' programmes were crucial for breaking down the barriers between healing and killing, conditioning doctors for mass killing in the name of healing, or purifying the race.[44]

If this was the intention and the physical liquidation of German and European Jews was on Hitler's agenda before the outbreak of war – because certainly his primary goal was the purification of German blood – the Madagascar Plan was a deception of the kind Heydrich and Himmler used regularly against their enemies. In this light the reference Himmler made in his memorandum to 'a great exodus of all the Jews to Africa or otherwise into a colony' was at that time the agreed euphemism for physical extermination; and his rejection of extermination as 'unGermanic' applied to the Poles and other ethnic groups but not to Jews, whom he classed as *Untermenschen*, or sub-humans.

The work of converting the general public, insofar as it still needed converting, to official anti-Jewish policy had also begun early in the war. Goebbels read the script for the film *Jud Suss* in November 1939, noting in his diary that it was 'the first really anti-Semitic film'.[45] Its effect, when released in the summer of 1940 about the time of the Madagascar Plan, was such that people coming out of the cinemas felt they wanted to wash their hands, and street demonstrators called for ridding Germany of the last Jew. Hess wrote Goebbels 'a hymn of praise' for the film.[46]

PEACE OFFENSIVE

Halifax and his undersecretary, 'Rab' Butler, shared Hitler's expectation that Britain had to make peace after the fall of France. Since the demonstration of German armed might in the Norwegian campaign Butler had been working through Carl Burckhardt of the International Red Cross in Geneva for further contact with Prince Hohenlohe. The Prince, after sounding out Burckhardt and the British Ambassador in Berne in early May, had reported to Berlin that those in Britain who had opposed Churchill and his circle about intervention on the Continent were pointing out how right they had been: 'Butler, in particular belongs to this group, [and] is overflowing with pessimism and feverishly seeking a way out.'[47]

One path Butler was pursuing led through the Vatican. On 7 June he called in Kenneth de Courcy for his opinion on terms that might be acceptable. De Courcy had been secretary and intelligence officer of the Imperial Policy Group of high Tory and service circles – dissolved on the outbreak of war – which had lobbied against intervention on the Continent. De Courcy suggested that the US Ambassador, Kennedy, noted for his extreme pessimism about British prospects, be asked to press Roosevelt for an American peace initiative; Butler authorised him to put it to Kennedy, which he did, and found him surprisingly receptive.[48]

Next day Butler told de Courcy Kennedy liked the idea and had already spoken to Halifax, who was delighted. He asked de Courcy to see Kennedy again. Before de Courcy could do so he received an urgent telephone call instructing him to meet Butler's private secretary, 'Chips' Channon, on the bridge in St James's Park. Both he and Channon were to express surprise at seeing each other.

When they met Channon said to him, 'My master is in deep trouble over this Kennedy business. I want you to go back to your office and destroy your file of letters with my master, then go up to Scotland for a couple of weeks and do not see any diplomats.'[49] De Courcy assumed that Churchill had got wind of the proposal, and lay low for a while.

On 17 June Butler himself, returning from lunch across St James' Park, 'chanced' upon the Swedish Minister to London, Björn Prytz, and asked him to his room for a talk. It is probable that the encounter was arranged much as de Courcy's had been,[50] since the Swedish government was under pressure from Germany, particularly with regard to German troop movements through Sweden, and urgently needed to know London's position after the fall of France. Butler told Prytz that Britain's official attitude continued to be that the war must go on, but assured him that 'no opportunity would be neglected for concluding a compromise peace if the chance was offered on reasonable conditions', and added that 'no diehards would be allowed to stand in the way.'[51]

Butler then received an urgent summons from Halifax and left the room. He returned with a message from his master: 'Common sense and not bravado would dictate the British government's policy', with the proviso that this should not be interpreted as 'peace at any price'. Obviously Halifax had been aware of the meeting. Prytz reported his conversation by wire to Stockholm, where the Swedish Foreign

Minister interpreted it as an indirect British approach to Berlin to pave the way for peace talks, and passed the contents to the Swedish ministers in Berlin and Moscow.[52]

Churchill learned of the Butler–Prytz talk on the 26th and wrote to Halifax saying it was clear the Swede had derived a strong impression of defeatism; 'would it not be well for you to find out from Butler what he did say.' It was put to Butler the same day, and he wrote Halifax a letter denying he had given an impression of defeatism and omitting any mention of Halifax's own input; whereupon Halifax assured Churchill he was completely satisfied with Butler's discretion and loyalty to government policy.[53] These incidents and the records of cabinet meetings of the period make it clear that Halifax and Butler were still running an appeasement policy in direct contravention of Churchill and behind his back.

This was noticed in Berlin. Goebbels entered in his diary, 'There are two parties [in the British government]: one thoroughgoing war party and one peace party. They wrestle for the upper hand.'[54] And he noted that peace feelers had been extended via Sweden and Spain.

On the 30th the head of the personal staff of the German Foreign Minister, Joachim von Ribbentrop, wrote to Prince Hohenlohe asking him to let him know if he heard of any approaches from the English. Hohenlohe visited Switzerland in early July, reporting afterwards that he had been told by Carl Burckhardt and others that the British Ambassador in Berne, Sir David Kelly, wanted to see him. Kelly had found an opportunity at a diplomatic reception they both attended. Lady Kelly had found Hohenlohe first, urging him to lose no time in telling her husband what he thought about the possibilities for peace. Kelly then drew him into a side room and said he would like to discuss the situation and the future. Hohenlohe replied that if he were a postman for Churchill there was no more to be said. Kelly's response was that their mutual friends in England, Butler, Vansittart and Halifax, had a following.[55]

The meaning was clear: a strong opposition to Churchill existed. Yet it is inconceivable that Sir Robert Vansittart belonged in it. As Permanent Undersecretary or head of the Foreign Office before the war, 'Van' had been as dedicated as Churchill in warning of the danger of trying to appease Hitler.[56] He had studied in Germany before the first war and saw Nazism not as an aberration but as the inevitable outcome of the militarism, hate and sense of racial superiority he had observed then.[57] His unrelenting opposition to Chamberlain's policy had led to his removal in 1938 into a specially created post outside active involvement in policy, titled, with exquisite irony, Chief Diplomatic Adviser to the Government.[58] He retained sources of intelligence within Germany and western Europe though, and became active head of disinformation.[59] His influence rose with Churchill's accession to power, and for Kelly to link his name with Halifax and Butler is surely evidence of a deception campaign he was running for the Prime Minister. A poem Vansittart published in *The Times* that month indicates the clear water between him and those in Britain who sought a compromise peace:

> Can one green defended knoll [Britain]
> Make the spreading desert whole [Europe]?
> Can those locusts of the soul
> Fail? Can God Almighty trust
> *Us* to save his work from dust?
> Yes. He can because we must.[60]

Continuing their conversation, Kelly had agreed with Hohenlohe that Britain's position was serious and scarcely any other choice remained to her but to continue fighting for the honour of the Empire until in a position to conclude a reasonable peace. The conversation turned to inner political divisions in Britain; Hohenlohe said he could not believe that such an unserious person as Churchill, so often under the influence of alcohol, embodied the English people. Kelly agreed, Hohenlohe reported, insomuch as to say, 'Churchill was a bull running his head into a wall, but the attitude of Butler and Halifax and also Vansittart was not the same.'[61]

Hohenlohe soon ended the conversation, he reported, because of the obvious suspicion that Kelly was merely trying to gain time with talks – which is exactly how Kelly described it in his post-war memoirs: Hohenlohe, he wrote, brought the message that the Führer had no desire to harm Britain or the British Empire; his sole condition was that we should leave him a completely free hand in Europe. 'Knowing the vital importance of gaining time, I made a show of interest.'[62]

Gaining time was the obvious strategy for Churchill. If Hitler could be convinced that behind the government's belligerent façade cooler heads were prepared to make peace, the less importance he would attach to invading England; and if invasion were deferred past the present summer and Roosevelt were to succeed in winning a third term, he would surely bring America into the war. Harold Nicolson, Parliamentary Secretary to the Ministry of Information and man about town, wrote to his wife on 19 June, 'I think it practically certain that the Americans will enter the war in November, and if we can last till then, all is well.'[63]

Churchill's other presumption was that Hitler would turn against his real enemy, Soviet Russia. 'Should he [Hitler] be repulsed here or not try invasion,' he wrote in a memorandum on 8 July, 'he will recoil eastward.'[64] This was three weeks before a Führer conference on plans for the invasion of Britain during which Hitler expressed extreme pessimism about the chances of success and mooted the idea of smashing Russia instead.[65]

* * *

While Churchill played for time, Hitler and Göring launched a serious peace offensive. One message came through Squadron Leader Carl Aschan, assistant Air Attaché at the British Legation in Stockholm. He was a Swede with British nationality whose post was a cover for intelligence work in enemy-occupied Norway and Denmark. That July he was visited by a Swedish friend, Carl-Gustav von Rosen, whose late aunt on his mother's side had been Göring's first wife, Karin. Carl-Gustav had an urgent mission. His uncle, Göring, had given him a vitally important message for the British government. It was long and detailed but Göring had not been prepared to commit it to paper; Carl-Gustav had memorised it. He dictated the message to Aschan, who then took it to the British Minister in Stockholm, Victor Mallet. A summary was sent to London by radio, followed by the complete text in the diplomatic bag.[66]

The gist of it was hardly new: if Britain would allow Germany a free hand on the European continent, Germany would guarantee and if necessary help to defend the British Empire against Russia or Japan.[67] As Aschan recalled, there were no penalties for Britain – except, of course, for her pride and influence. Nevertheless, under the circumstances, with Hitler master of western Europe – and Mussolini had thrown in his lot with the Führer the previous month when he saw France collapsing – it appeared to be a generous offer. Similar offers were received through Berne, Lisbon, Dublin and Washington, where the British Ambassador was Lord Lothian, one of Albrecht Haushofer's contacts before the war and a prominent supporter of appeasement.

On 19 July Hitler made a long-awaited triumphal speech to the Reichstag in the Kroll Opera House, listing the achievements of his military commanders, conferring the title of *Reichsmarschall* on Göring, praising Hess, Ribbentrop and Goebbels for their political work, and finally appealing to 'reason and commonsense in Great Britain' to end the war.[68] He left this public appeal deliberately vague. His terms had been spelled out through countless clandestine channels; it was up to Britain to respond. A flat rejection came within the hour. This was amplified in a speech by Halifax three days later – despite frantic calls from Lothian in Washington begging him not to say anything which might close the door to peace. Goebbels noted: 'Halifax's speech is a much sharper rebuff than one could assume from the shorter version ... The Führer sees it as England's final rejection. The die is cast ... Now the great attack on England will not long be delayed.'[69]

Yet Hitler still hesitated. A report had come in via Berne from the Swiss Ambassador in London that Churchill's cabinet was running into increasing opposition from court and financial circles and a section of the Conservative Party. 'These circles are no longer willing to follow Churchill and Eden [Secretary of State for War] unconditionally,' read the report. 'The Prime Minister sees his following limited to Conservative diehards and the Labour Party, who desire to continue the war on ideological grounds.'[70] Goebbels had also noted in his diary 'some voices of reason' reported via the neutrals, 'above all the Duke of Windsor and Lloyd George.'[71] Earlier, on 17 July, Goebbels had entered, 'Duke of Windsor ... lets us know if he were King he would immediately conclude peace.'[72]

THE DUKE OF WINDSOR

After the death of King George V in 1936 his eldest son reigned briefly as Edward VIII before being forced to renounce the throne. Ostensibly this was because of his determination to marry Mrs Wallis Simpson, a divorcee; a deeper underlying cause was government alarm about his openly pro-Fascist views and belief that the peace of Europe depended on an Anglo–German alliance. It was feared, with reason, that he might precipitate a constitutional crisis.

On abdicating he had become His Royal Highness the Duke of Windsor. He had married Mrs Simpson the following year, 1937, but the Royal family had refused to grant her the style of Royal Highness, a rejection which cut them both deeply. Later that year he had advertised his admiration for Nazism by accepting an invitation to visit Germany, during which he and his Duchess had been received by Hitler and other leading figures of the regime.

Hess had entertained them at his Munich-Harlaching home. Ilse Hess, hugely apprehensive beforehand about playing hostess to 'the most elegant and *mondaine* woman of the century', found her fears groundless, and described the Duchess afterwards as 'a very lovable, charming, warm and clever person' whose affection for the Duke had captivated them all.[73] Hess himself, despite his natural reticence, engaged in animated discussion with the Duke about their shared vision of an Anglo–German understanding;[74] at one point he had taken him up to the attic to show him his collection of model warships and re-fight the Battle of Jutland.

The Duke had hoped to balance his German tour with a visit to the United States afterwards, but his public approval of Nazism – a movement which had smashed German Trade Unions and rendered Jews non-persons – raised so much hostility from American Labour and Jewish organisations the tour had been called off.

On the outbreak of war he had accepted a post in the British Military Mission to French Headquarters, designed principally to keep him out of Britain. His subsequent reports from across the Channel had pointed to defects in French defensive strategy and morale, and when in May 1940 these had proved all too accurate the Military Mission became one of the casualties of the rapid German breakthrough. He had retired with the Duchess to their villa, La Croë on Cap d'Antibes, thence after the French armistice and Mussolini's entry to the war, the couple had made a hurried evacuation in a convoy with other British evacuees across the Pyrenees into neutral Spain. They had arrived in Madrid on 23 June and booked into the Ritz Hotel. The British Ambassador, Sir Samuel Hoare, called on them that evening.[75]

Hoare, a distinguished politician who had occupied all the great government offices apart from that of Prime Minister, had been on the 'appeasement' wing of Chamberlain's War Cabinet and a particular critic of Churchill's stance. Churchill, on becoming Prime Minister, had dismissed him, and subsequently appointed him Ambassador Extraordinary and Plenipotentiary on Special Mission to Spain. The special mission was to keep the Spanish dictator, Generalissimo Francisco Franco, from entering the war on the side of his perceived natural allies, Hitler and Mussolini. With consummate diplomatic and social skills – combined with financial inducements for Spanish generals and officials, and the pressure of the British naval blockade – Hoare was ultimately successful.

In the meantime, his reputation as an appeaser and the appearance of the Windsors in Madrid had been exploited by German propaganda. Rumours spread that Hoare and the Duke were conspiring for a negotiated peace. The Duke did nothing to dispel the notion, openly expressing his conviction, even to pro-Nazi Spaniards, that the war should be ended without delay before thousands more lives were lost to save politicians' faces.[76] Thus on 2 July, as he was about to leave for Lisbon, where he and the Duchess were supposed to board a flying boat for return to England, the German Ambassador in Madrid, Eberhard von Stohrer, was able to wire his Foreign Minister, von Ribbentrop:

[Spanish] Foreign Minister communicated that Duke of Windsor travels to Portugal today or tomorrow ... Windsor has told the Foreign

Minister that he will only return to England if his wife is recognised as a member of the Royal family and if he receives an influential post of military or civil type. Fulfilment of these conditions is as good as out of the question. He intends, therefore, to return to Spain, where the Spanish government has offered him the Palais des Kalifen in Ronda as a residence. Windsor has spoken out to the Foreign Minister and also to other local acquaintances sharply against Churchill and against this war ...[77]

Stohrer's information about the conditions on which the Duke was insisting before he would return to England was accurate;[78] it can be assumed, therefore, that the Duke was indeed intending to disregard his instructions and return to Spain. Hoare had reported his demands to Churchill, and on arrival in Lisbon the Duke found a telegram from Churchill reminding him that he had taken active military rank and refusal to obey orders 'would create a serious situation'.[79] He hardly had time to digest this court martial threat before another telegram arrived from Churchill offering him a post as Governor of the Bahamas. It was an extraordinary appointment for a former king: the Bahamas was among the least important of Britain's colonial territories, but like his original posting to France, it was a way of avoiding the embarrassment he might cause if he were to return to England. On the other hand he had to be removed from the Iberian peninsula, where he was a focus for German intrigue.[80]

While apparently accepting the Bahamas post, it was not long before Windsor sent a message to the Spanish Foreign Minister asking for a confidential agent to come to him in Lisbon, and repeating his earlier intention to return to Spain.[81] Learning of this, Ribbentrop wired instructions for the confidential agent to invite the Duke and Duchess for a short one- or two-week visit to Spain; once there, they were to be persuaded or forced to stay, the intention being that

the Duke must then be told at a given time in Spain that Germany desires peace with the English people, that the Churchill-clique stands in the way and that it would be advantageous if the Duke held himself ready for the further development. Germany is resolved to compel Britain to peace with all means of force and would in this case be prepared to meet the Duke's every expressed wish, especially in regard to smoothing the Duke's and Duchess's path to the English throne.[82]

The idea of ascending the throne astonished the Duke and Duchess when it was put to them, since it would be impossible under the English constitution. When told that the course of the war might bring about a change in the constitution they became very thoughtful, especially the Duchess, so the confidential agent reported. Meanwhile, they again expressed themselves very happy to return to Spain.[83]

The couple were staying at the villa of a wealthy Portuguese banker just outside Lisbon, under the closest surveillance by the British authorities. Churchill was kept fully informed of German machinations, and while Ribbentrop had a second confidential emissary sent to the Windsors and despatched Himmler's counter-intelligence chief, Walter Schellenberg, on a special mission to return them to Spain, Churchill engaged the Duke's legal adviser during the abdication crisis, Sir Walter Monckton, to fly to Lisbon to persuade the Duke to take up his post. Churchill eventually won the contest. The pair sailed on S.S. *Excalibur* for the Bahamas on 1 August.

The next day, the German Ambassador to Portugal sent Ribbentrop a report on the reasons the Duke had given his host, the banker – also a German agent – for this choice:

> First of all the Duke praised the Führer's desire for peace, which fully accorded with his own feelings. He is firmly convinced that if he had been King it would never have come to war. To the appeal made to him to co-operate on the peace-work at a given time, he concurred. To be sure, he asked for it to be understood that at present he had to follow his government's instructions: insubordination would uncover his intentions prematurely, provoke a scandal and rob him of prestige in England. Also he is convinced that at present his engagement would be premature since as yet there is no inclination in England for approaches to Germany. As soon as this mentality changes, however, he is ready to return immediately. He

gave two possibilities for this. Either that England called him, which he believed absolutely possible, or that Germany declared a desire to negotiate with him. In both cases he was prepared for any personal sacrifice and would make himself completely available without the least personal ambition. He would remain in constant touch with his former host [the banker] and had agreed with him the key word on which he would immediately come over ...[84]

The previous day Goebbels had noted in his diary, '[Peace] Feelers from here to England fruitless. Also via Spain. London wants the catastrophe. Duke of Windsor visibly distances himself from the London clique. The Führer now sees no possibilities apart from war.'[85]

CHAPTER SEVEN

Clandestine approaches

O N 1 AUGUST, as the Windsors sailed for the Bahamas, King Gustav V of Sweden sent a telegram to King George VI offering to act as a channel of communication for peace discussions with Germany. Churchill drafted an uncompromising rejection detailing some of the 'hideous crimes' committed by Germany against the countries on her borders: 'His Majesty's Government see in them not the slightest cause to recede in any way from ... their intention to prosecute the war against Germany ... until Hitlerism is finally broken, and the world relieved from the curse which a wicked man has brought upon it.'[1] Before any proposals for peace could even be considered, he concluded, they needed guarantees 'by deeds not words' that Czechoslovakia, Poland, Norway, Denmark, Holland, Belgium and France would be restored to independent life. Halifax toned down the more colourful phrases and, after consultation with the Dominion governments, sent Gustav a formal rejection.

This did not prevent further approaches. The Foreign Office assumed they were co-ordinated in Berlin, but German Foreign Ministry files suggest they were actively encouraged by the British Minister in Stockholm, Victor Mallet. Thus a report from Himmler's Security Service stated, 'It was learned through our Swedish connections that the English Minister in Stockholm has declared in the closest circles in unmistakeable terms that his government would possibly be prepared to ascertain unofficially whether Germany is prepared for peace negotiations.'[2] On the strength of this Dr Ludwig Weissauer, a top Security Service *V-Mann* (confidential agent) with high-level contacts in Sweden and Finland was sent to Stockholm to test the reports. He had previously held talks about Swedish foreign and economic policy with the president of the Swedish High Court of Appeal, Dr Birger Ekeberg, a confidant of King Gustav,[3] and he now told Ekeberg of his wish to meet the British Minister.

Ekeberg accordingly saw Mallet, who reported the approach to the Foreign Office the same day, 5 September, adding, 'Weissauer is understood to be a direct secret emissary of Hitler'. He had, he went on, told Ekeberg that in view of His Majesty's Government's views on continuing the war he could see no useful purpose in meeting Weissauer, but requested instructions 'most immediately' as to whether or not he should.[4]

Weissauer's account in the German Foreign Ministry archives gives a different slant on the conversation. Ekeberg, Weissauer reported, had learned from Mallet that the British government was divided on peace negotiations. Churchill strove to continue the war with all means, but was hard pressed by his cabinet colleagues. Churchill had expressed himself prepared to consider negotiations provided England's prestige was not compromised, the starting point for which had to be cultural autonomy for Poland and the other occupied countries.[5]

The Foreign Office wired Mallet the following day, 6 September, instructing him not to meet Weissauer: 'Attitude of His Majesty's Government has been made quite plain in reply to King of Sweden ... in which we emphasised necessity of words being effectively guaranteed by deeds.'[6] The same day, Sir Robert Vansittart sent Halifax a memorandum on this latest approach. Besides indicating Vansittart's continuing involvement in the highest level of British foreign policy, the note mirrors Churchill's views, and its extreme language appears designed to stiffen Halifax's backbone:

URGENT
Secretary of State.
I hope that you will instruct Mr. Mallet that he is on no account to meet Dr. Weissauer. The future of civilisation is at stake. It is a

question of we or they now, and either the German *Reich* or this country has to go under, and not only under, but right under. I believe it will be the German *Reich*. This is a very different thing from saying that *Germany* has got to go under; but the German *Reich* and the Reich idea have been the curse of the world for 75 years, and if we do not stop it this time, we never shall, and they will stop us. The enemy is the German Reich and not merely Nazism, and those who have not yet learned this lesson have learned nothing whatever, and would let us in for a sixth war even if we survive the fifth. I would far sooner take my chance of surviving the fifth. All possibility of compromise has now gone by, and it has got to be a fight to a finish, and a *real* finish.

I trust that Mr. Mallet will get the most categorical instructions. We have had much more than enough of Dahlerus, Goerdeler, Weissauer and company.[7]

Halifax himself was, of course, one of those who, not having yet learned this lesson, had in Vansittart's estimation 'learned nothing whatever'.

Mallet saw Ekeberg on the 7th, and told him he could not see Weissauer, but if the German wished to tell him, Ekeberg, more about his mission, he would be interested to hear what he said. The Swede, evidently believing Mallet's interest indicated a significant move on the part of the British government, returned that afternoon in 'a state of considerable excitement' to tell him that Weissauer had been sent by Hitler, who felt responsible for the future of the white race, and consequently wished for 'sincere friendship with England'. The ground had to be prepared first, after which official discussions could begin; until then conversations should be unofficial and secret.[8]

Hitler's basic idea, Ekeberg went on, was that economies now had to be calculated over wide areas; continental Europe had to be considered as a single economic unit. On a previous visit Weissauer had discussed with Ekeberg how Sweden should fit into this German-dominated continental economy; in fact planning for a continent-wide economy under German leadership taking in all the peoples 'from Gibraltar to the Urals and from the North Cape to Cyprus, with their natural colonial extensions"[9] had been proceeding at euphoric pace in Berlin since the fall of France.

Mallet reported back to the Foreign Office after his interview with Ekeberg that Hitler's concept was:

> For the white race there must be two great economic units – Germany, the continental unit, and the British Empire and America as the centre of the world economy. England and America now have ... the biggest navies and they need the oceans for their maintenance, Germany has the continent. As for Russia Weissauer gave the impression that she should be considered as a potential enemy. The two great groups could resist the encroachment of the Yellow Race.[10]

Weissauer had gone on to sketch peace terms comprising the permanence of the British Empire, the continental supremacy of Germany, restoration of a 'Polish' state, Czechoslovakia to remain German and sovereignty restored to other occupied countries. He suggested this would be the last chance for peace and, as Hess was to do later, warned of the terrible things that would happen if it were neglected.

Mallet's report to the Foreign Office stressed that he had been 'careful to rub in that I have absolutely no authority from you to discuss such high matters of state', but he added that if they wanted any more questions asked he could easily get Ekeberg to put them to Weissauer 'as though coming from me alone'.

The directive he received from Alexander Cadogan, Permanent Undersecretary at the Foreign Office, and agreed by the War Cabinet was as defiantly Churchillian as his original instructions; he was to reply to Ekeberg:

> His Majesty's Government did not enter this war for selfish aims, but for large and general purposes affecting the freedom and independence of many states in Europe ... the intention of all the peoples of the British Empire to prosecute the war has been strengthened by the many horrible crimes committed by the rulers of Nazi Germany against the smaller states on her borders, and by the indiscriminate bombing of London without the slightest relation to military objectives ...[11]

And it was repeated that before any peace proposals could be considered, freedom must be restored to France and the other occupied countries.

VIOLET ROBERTS

Hess conceived the idea of his peace mission in June 1940 while with Hitler during the French campaign, so he told Lord Simon in June 1941, a month after his flight to Scotland.[12] The Führer had expressed the view then that the war could perhaps be the means for finally coming to the agreement with England that he had been striving for all his political life. When England subsequently rejected Hitler's peace offer, Hess formed the impression that she had done so for reasons of prestige: 'Therefore, I said to myself, I must more than ever realise my plan because if I were over there in England, she could use this as grounds for negotiations without losing prestige.'[13] Whether he let Hitler into his idea at this early stage is unclear. At the time he told Lord Simon about it he was claiming that his flight was his own idea entirely; Hitler knew nothing about it.

The idea of flying on a personal peace mission to Britain would undoubtedly have appealed to Hess's romantic idealism. It is remarkable, and no doubt a sign of his dissatisfaction with his party-political activities, that on the outbreak of war he had applied to Hitler for permission to join the Luftwaffe to fly as a front-line pilot. Hitler responded by making him promise to give up flying for the duration; Hess had managed to limit the prohibition to one year.

Directly the ban ended that September, 1940, he began seeking an aeroplane to fly. Göring, head of the Luftwaffe, refused him, as did individual aircraft factories, but finally Professor Willi Messerschmitt, designer of Germany's front-line fighter aircraft, agreed to him having an Me Bf 110 two-seater fighter-bomber and his chief test pilot as instructor for practice flying from his factory and airstrip at Augsburg, little over 40 miles from Hess's Munich-Harlaching home.[14]

Although Hess knew Messerschmitt it is unlikely that he told him at this early stage why he wanted an aeroplane. It is clear, however, from the post-war testimony of Hess's secretaries that he had already formed the intention of flying to Britain. Thus his Berlin secretary stated that from 'the late summer of 1940' she had been ordered to obtain weather reports over the Channel, North Sea and British Isles;[15] and his Munich secretary stated, 'Beginning in summer 1940 ... by order of Hess I had to procure secret weather reports about climatic conditions over the British Isles and over the North Sea, and forward them to Hess.'[16]

Their testimony is confirmed by a meteorologist working at that time at the *Zentrale Wetterdienst Gruppe*, or Central Weather Service, at Potsdam-Wildpark. Writing in 1993 as 'Dr F.S.' to conceal his identity, he stated, 'Every day round 10.0 am, we received a call from Rudolf Hess's secretary asking for the weather forecasts for the triangle formed by the cities Oslo–Kiel–Edinburgh.'[17] Naturally, the meteorologist on duty complied and provided the information in comprehensible form. This went on for several months, Dr F.S. wrote, until one day the secretary said, 'Thank you very much, gentlemen, from tomorrow my boss no longer needs your information.' The next day they heard that Hess had flown to Scotland.[18] In fact the announcement of Hess's flight had been delayed two days; but Dr F.S.'s minor slip of memory is understandable after 50 years.

Meanwhile, at the beginning of August Hess had summoned Albrecht Haushofer and asked him about the possibility of approaching influential people in Britain opposed to the war; on the 15th he instructed him to prepare for the 'special task' of opening a way to such people,[19] and on the 31st he drove to Karl Haushofer's country estate, Hartschimmelhof, apparently expecting to see him again. Albrecht was not there, but Hess discussed the project with his old friend and mentor during a three-hour walk in the Grünwalder Forest and afterwards until 2.00 the next morning.

Karl Haushofer described their discussion in a letter to Albrecht three days later:

> All is prepared, as you well know, for a very hard and sharp action against the island in question so that the top man only needs to press a button and it all goes off. However, before this unavoidable decision the thought again arises whether there is really no way of

preventing the infinitely grave consequences. In this context there is a line of thought which I simply must pass on to you since it was obviously communicated to me with this intention. Can you see no way in which one could talk about such possibilities at a third place with a middleman such as the old Ian Hamilton or the other Hamilton?[20]

The phrasing here suggests that Albrecht had been pessimistic about the possibilities in his earlier talks with Hess. The 'old Ian Hamilton' was General Sir Ian Hamilton, certainly a friend of peace, who had invited Hess to stay with him in Scotland in the summer of 1939. The 'other Hamilton' was, of course, Albrecht's friend, 'Douglo' Clydesdale, now – since the death of his father – Wing Commander the Duke of Hamilton and Brandon.

Haushofer had suggested to Hess that centenary celebrations soon to be held in Lisbon would provide especially good cover for such a meeting on neutral ground, 'in which connection', he continued in his letter to Albrecht:

> it seems to me a sign of fate that our old friend Missis [*sic*] V R evidently found a way, even after a long delay, of sending a card with kind and cordial good wishes not only for your mother but also for Heinz [Albrecht's brother] and me, and added the address: [in English] Address your reply to:- Miss V. Roberts, c/o Postbox 506, Lisbon, Portugal. [reverting to German] I have the feeling that no good possibility should be passed up, at least it should be considered.[21]

The old friend was Mrs Mary Violet Roberts, a 76-year-old widow living in Cambridge. She and her late husband had known the Haushofers since before the First World War and had refreshed their acquaintanceship between the wars, visiting them at Hartschimmelhof at least twice in the 1920s.[22] She had now taken advantage of a postal service provided by Thomas Cook which allowed friends to communicate across hostile borders via neutral Portugal; hence the Lisbon return address. Why she had done so is a mystery, which will be addressed later.

On 8 September Hess summoned Albrecht and quizzed him again about the possibilities of making Hitler's serious desire for peace known to important persons in England. Albrecht, according to the summary of the discussion he sent his father a week later, suggested several diplomats, including Hoare in Madrid and Lothian in Washington. Then:

> As the final possibility I mentioned a personal meeting on neutral ground with the closest of my English friends: the young Duke of Hamilton, who has access at all times to all important personalities in London, even to Churchill and the King. I stressed in this case the unavoidable difficulty of resuming contact, and again repeated my conviction of the unlikelihood of success – whichever course one followed.[23]

He added that he had had the strong impression the discussion was conducted with the prior knowledge of the Führer, and that he would hear no more about it unless Hess came to a further agreement with Hitler.

However, Hess wrote to Karl Haushofer on the 10th, just two days after the discussion – five days before Albrecht wrote his account of it – to say that on no account must the contact with the old lady friend of his family be disregarded or allowed to fizzle out.[24] He considered it best if Karl or Albrecht were to write to her to ask whether she could enquire if Albrecht's friend would be prepared to come to the neutral country in which she lived or had her forwarding address in order to talk to Albrecht.

Albrecht's friend was, of course, Hamilton, the neutral country Portugal. By choosing Hamilton rather than one of the ambassadors Albrecht had suggested, Hess was seeking to bypass the diplomatic circles serving Churchill's government which had proved impervious to all previous peace feelers; and, as will appear, it was Hamilton's privileged access to the King which weighed as much in his calculations as Albrecht's friendship with him or Hamilton's published desire for 'a healing peace ... with a trusted Germany' in his letter to *The Times*.

Karl forwarded Hess's letter to Albrecht, who replied to Hess on the 19th – claiming that postal delays had prevented him receiving the letter until the day before. He agreed to write to Mrs Roberts, enclosing a letter for her to forward to Hamilton,[25] and began drafting both the same day. On the 23rd he sent them by hand of Hess's brother, Alfred, to the Lisbon postbox number.[26]

LETTERS TO HAMILTON

While Hess had been laying the groundwork for his peace mission, Hitler ordered Göring to destroy the defensive capability of the Royal Air Force to create the conditions for an invasion of Britain, code-named *Seelöwe* – 'Sealion'. The resulting aerial contest known as the Battle of Britain reached a climax at the end of August; then pressure on airfields and aircraft factories eased as Hitler, responding to RAF raids on Berlin, shifted the focus of attack to the civilian population.

British cities suffered frightful destruction and loss of life, particularly London; on 10 September Goebbels noted reports from neutral observers representing 'an apocalyptic picture' of the city,[27] and on the 17th Harold Nicolson, Parliamentary Secretary to the Ministry of Information, recorded such bitterness at the devastation in the East End of London 'that even the King and Queen were booed the other day when they visited the destroyed areas.'[28]

Hess was particularly distressed by the two Nordic races slaughtering each other. In his later interview with Lord Simon he explained that before his flight he had had ever before his eyes 'not only on the German side, but also on the English side endless rows of children's coffins with the weeping mothers behind them.'[29] There is no reason to doubt this: there is ample testimony from his wife and adjutants of his health suffering, for whatever reasons. Goebbels noted on 15 October having to talk him out of his worries about the situation,[30] and in November recorded: 'Hess ... appears very bad and is certainly not healthy. He is so decent a chap. It is a shame that his work energy is consumed in continual illness.'[31]

Ill health had not stopped his preparations for his mission. Cleared by Messerschmitt's test pilot to fly solo on the Me 110, he had made numerous practice flights on his own. He had also started drafting a personal letter to the Duke of Hamilton, and on 9 October called in Ernst Bohle, the English-born, South African-educated head of his 'Foreign Organisation', for Germans living abroad, to translate the letter into English.

After the war Bohle told Dr Robert Kempner of the US legal team at the Nuremberg war crimes trials that Hess had explained to him that he wanted to write to the Duke, whom he had met at the Olympic Games and who had great influence, to suggest a meeting in Switzerland. He had sworn him to the strictest secrecy; above all the Foreign Minister, von Ribbentrop, was not to hear even a whisper of this intention as he would sabotage it immediately. Hess had then handed him the first part of the letter and asked him to translate it right away in an adjacent office.[32]

Subsequently Bohle was summoned every few weeks to translate further parts of the letter. By 4 November – according to Bohle's testimony before the letter was completed – Hess evidently felt he was ready, for he wrote from Berlin to his wife and small son:

> My dears
> I firmly believe I will return from the flight I am about to undertake in the next few days and that the flight will be crowned with success. If not, however, the goal I set myself was worth going all out for. I know that you know me: you know I could not do otherwise.[33]

It is a curious note, particularly as there had been no reply to Albrecht's 23 September letter to Hamilton via Mrs Roberts; indeed Hamilton had not received it. The letter had been retained at the Censorship department in London after arriving on 2 November on the desk of examiner 1021, who had reported:

> Writer probably a German & possibly writing from Berlin ['B'] requests addressee to forward a letter to the Duke of Hamilton, whom he knew as Lord Clydesdale & M.P. & intimates that it may be of significance for him and his friends in high office. Writer states

he is sincerely convinced that it can do no harm & it is conceivable it may be 'useful for all of us'.[34]

The examiner had copied out a part of the enclosed letter to Hamilton on the reverse side of his report:

If you remember some of my last communications in July 1939 you – and your friends in high places – may find some significance in the fact that I am able to ask you wether [*sic*] you could find time to have a talk with me somewhere on the outskirts of Europe, perhaps in Portugal. I could reach Lisbon any time (and without any kind of difficulties) within four days after receiving news from you. Of course I do not, know wether [*sic*] you can make your athorities [*sic*] understand so much, that they give you leave.

But at least you may be able to answer my question. Letters will reach me (fairly quickly; they would take some four or five days from Lisbon at the utmost) in the following way. Double closed envelope. Inside adress [*sic*]: Dr A.H." Nothing more! Outside adress [*sic*]

Minero Silricola Ltd.
Rua do Cais de Santarem 32/I
Lisbon. Portugal.[35]

This was the cover address for the German Military Counter-Intelligence (*Abwehr*) station in Portugal.

Censorship first intended to send the letter to the Foreign Office and a photostat copy to MI12 for MI5, but on 6 November it was decided for some reason to send the original letter to MI12 for MI5 with photostats to the Foreign Office and the Interservices Research Bureau (IRB), a cover name for the Special Operations Executive (SOE).[36]

Since the public release of the diaries of Guy Liddell, head of the counter-espionage, 'B', branch of MI5, it is clear that receipt of Albrecht's letter prompted an investigation into Hamilton's loyalty, or as Liddell put it: 'enquiries were started on the assumption that the Duke's bona fides might be in question ... these led to nothing ...'[37]

Since July that year Wing Commander the Duke of Hamilton had been serving as station commander at RAF Turnhouse, outside Edinburgh. On 12 November, just six days after Albrecht's letter went to MI5, he handed over to his second in command and took ten days leave.[38] Whether this was connected with MI5's enquiries is not known; nor is it known where he spent his leave, since his diary for 1940 is missing.

On 22 November, coincidentally or otherwise the day after he resumed command at Turnhouse, MI5 informed Henry Hopkinson, private secretary to Sir Alexander Cadogan, Permanent Undersecretary at the Foreign Office, that they proposed to forward the letter to Hamilton 'provided you do not object'.[39] Hopkinson, who acted as Foreign Office liaison to the head of MI6, replied on 7 December that they had done nothing about the letter and had no objection to it going on to Hamilton.[40]

Meanwhile, on 12 November, by coincidence the day Hamilton had started his leave, Albrecht had written to his mother, Martha Haushofer: 'From L [Lisbon] nothing. It will doubtless come to nothing.'[41]

MI5

Hess made his first attempt to fly to Britain on 10 January 1941, so he told Lord Simon in June 1941.[42] His adjutant, Karl-Heinz Pintsch, who accompanied him on all visits to Messerschmitt's Augsburg airfield, when interviewed by the author James Leasor in the 1950s, also named 10 January as the date of his chief's first attempt to fly to Britain.[43] The mission was abandoned, Pintsch said, when a fault developed in one of the plane's ailerons. Ernst Bohle, who translated sections of Hess's letter to Hamilton intermittently from October 1940 until early January 1941, told his interrogators after the war that he had heard Hess made his first attempt in mid-January.[44]

The date cannot be verified from the Augsburg control tower logs since most were destroyed during Allied air raids in 1944,[45] but weather conditions on 10 January were favourable. After a bitterly cold week with snow and mist throughout Europe, the skies cleared on the 9th, allowing RAF Bomber Command to raid German naval bases in ideal conditions: *The Times* reported, 'the moon shone brightly and there was no cloud or even ground haze.'[46] Clear weather persisted through the 10th with bright sunshine and good visibility. Given reasonably accurate *Wetterdienst* reports Hess could have anticipated this.

It is, nonetheless, difficult to accept that he made a serious attempt to reach Britain in January. His experimental long-distance flights had shown him the need for more technical preparation if he was to be his own navigator, and he requested modifications to equipment throughout the following months. Helmut Kaden, his mentor at the Messerschmitt works, began a series of test flights on his machine lasting from 29 March to 6 May.[47] Hess was thorough in everything he undertook. He would not have attempted such a demanding solo flight until both he and Kaden were completely satisfied with his machine and fittings. Besides, as will appear, he admitted later while in captivity in England that he made his first attempt to fly to Britain on 10 May.[48]

* * *

Two documents discovered recently in the Moscow State Archives suggest that his flight to Britain was preceded by months of negotiation with the British.[49] One, the testimony of Karl-Heinz Pintsch, who accompanied him to the Messerschmitt airfield from where he took off for Scotland, even states that the flight was made 'by prior arrangement with the English'.[50] Historians are sceptical since both documents were based on statements made by Germans close to Hitler or Hess under duress in Soviet captivity, who subsequently denied them when freed. Yet the statements, made separately, do corroborate each other in many respects – as will become clear. Besides, it defies common sense to suppose that the Deputy Führer flew off into enemy territory on the off chance of meeting someone sympathetic to his views and powerful enough to conduct meaningful talks. There must have been prior negotiations. Perhaps the most widely held view is that on the British side the negotiations were bogus – that he was lured across by an arm of British intelligence.

If there was a trap, it was not prepared by the internal security service, MI5. This is demonstrated by Guy Liddell's diary – as will be seen. On 11 January 1941 John Maude of 'B' division, MI5, approached the chief of Air Intelligence, Air Commodore Archie Boyle, about the possibility of providing the Duke of Hamilton with cover for a journey to Lisbon to contact Albrecht Haushofer. Boyle's response was positive, and Maude wrote to Major T.A. 'Tar' Robertson, the head of section B1a, which ran double agents:[51]

> This goes to you now because it seems likely that the Duke of Hamilton (formerly the boxing Lord Clydesdale) is going to make an interesting double agent ...
>
> Boyle is perfectly prepared to send the Duke to Lisbon and can give him perfect cover, a real Air Force job.
>
> Boyle wants SIS [MI6] and us to run him, and he is *most* keen to help ...
>
> It is impossible to say that the Duke never received the original [letter from Albrecht Haushofer] since we have lost it. Also we cannot say whether or not he has received any other communication from Haushofer ...

Guy Liddell noted in his diary, 'The whole case looks like a peace offer.'[52]

Discussing it with colleagues, Robertson concluded that not enough was known about Hamilton or Mrs Roberts to take the matter on. Instead, on the 20th, he saw Boyle and suggested the Duke be sent for, questioned about the letter and asked if he would be prepared to write a reply to Haushofer. 'In the event of Hamilton agreeing to this we might then take up the case.'[53]

However, it was not until nearly the end of February that Hamilton received a letter from Air Intelligence inviting him to a meeting in London; not until mid-March that the meeting took place and the Duke was asked if he would like to go to Lisbon to meet Haushofer and 'see what it's all about'.[54] His response was not enthusiastic. Meanwhile Thomas Cook had provided Mrs Violet Roberts' address in Cambridge, but she had still not been questioned.[55]

MI5 had been in disarray for some time. Its veteran director at the outbreak of war, Sir Vernon Kell, had been in post since the service was founded before the first war. In poor health, he seems not to have coped with the vast expansion of staff required to deal with the wartime threats posed by aliens, enemy agents and home-grown extremists of right and left. By the time Hitler launched his western campaign in May 1940 the increased demands placed on the service had, in the words of its authorised historian, 'brought its administration close to collapse'.[56] In June 1940 Kell was replaced by his deputy, and in July the head of a recently formed Home Defence Security Executive was given executive control. The dual leadership proved ineffectual and it was not until February 1941, when Sir David Petrie, a former head of intelligence in India, was appointed Director General, that effective leadership was restored.

In the meantime, to escape the bombing on London, the majority of staff and the Registry had been transferred from Wormwood Scrubs prison – where they had occupied cells vacated by prisoners – to Blenheim Palace, near Oxford. The move had taken place in October, just before Albrecht's letter to Hamilton was picked up by Censorship; this may have accounted for the loss of the original. Certainly administrative difficulties had increased, as the senior officers and Guy Liddell's 'B' Division remained in London and files had to be transferred between Oxford and London.[57]

Any possibility that MI5 was directly involved in Hess's flight is ruled out by Guy Liddell's diary entry for 13 May 1941, after learning that Hess had flown to Scotland three days before: 'Today's sensational news is the arrival of the deputy Führer Rudolf Hess in a Messerschmitt-110 ... He seems to have been carrying some sort of message to the Duke of Hamilton from Professor Karl Haushofer ...'[58] Had his division been implicated he would scarcely have named the wrong Haushofer. Liddell also speculated on Hess's motive: 'He has probably fallen out with his party ... alternatively he may have come over with some kind of peace offer ...'

Indirectly, however, MI5 was undoubtedly involved through misinformation planted by the double agents run by 'Tar' Robertson, in conjunction with MI6 and other agencies, as will appear.

MI6

Unlike MI5, the Secret Intelligence Service, MI6, was, to quote one of its serving officers at the time of Hess's flight, 'in the Hess thing up to their necks'; but, he went on, contrary to stories put out later for public consumption, 'there was never any conspiracy to lure Hess to Great Britain'.[59]

MI6's chief had died in 1939 shortly before the 'Venlo incident' which had resulted in the destruction of much of the agent network in western Europe. His deputy, Colonel Sir Stewart Menzies, succeeded him as 'C' – as the chief was known – against the wishes of Churchill, who was at that time First Lord of the Admiralty and a member of the War Cabinet.

Apart from Menzies' involvement in the disaster at Venlo, Churchill's chief objection was that he belonged in those high Tory, court, City and service circles who viewed *rapprochement* with Germany and even a tacit alliance with her against Communism as the sole means of preserving the British Empire. He and his close circle, which included the Duke of Buccleuch, a fellow member of White's Club in St James, had been known as 'terrific anti-Bolshevists'. In the lead-up to the war, while MI5 had consistently advised standing up to Hitler, MI6 had backed Chamberlain's policy of seeking to rectify what it termed 'Germany's legitimate grievances'[60] – since characterised as 'appeasement'.

Menzies had been born at the centre of British power, in all probability the illegitimate son of Sir George Holford, a court grandee, who married Menzies' mother, a great beauty and favourite at the court of Edward VII, the year after her husband, John Menzies, died; in *Who's Who* Stewart Menzies described himself as the son of Lady Holford. He had served with distinction in the first war, while inwardly detesting the slaughter that cut down all his year group from Eton. Posted to the intelligence section of the staff in France at the end of 1915 he had found his true métier.

On confirmation as 'C' in November 1940 Menzies exerted himself to overcome Churchill's distrust and they eventually formed a close bond. His control of the ultra-secret decrypts of intercepted German code messages produced by the Government Code and Cipher School at Bletchley Park helped after Churchill became Prime Minister. The more important decrypts, code-named 'Boniface' – known later as 'Ultra' – he brought to Churchill every day in ancient buff-orange boxes to which the Prime Minister alone had the key. Throughout his career Churchill had had a passion for secret intelligence.

Together with 'Boniface' in the boxes, Menzies delivered intelligence derived from his enemy opposite number, Admiral Wilhelm Canaris, chief of the *Abwehr*. Once a committed supporter of Hitler and National Socialism, Canaris had been profoundly shocked by the abominations committed by SS *Einsatzkommandos* in Poland and had turned against the regime. Lamenting in private that 'Our children's children will have to bear the blame for this',[61] he had become convinced that the future of Western civilisation depended on Britain's survival; and besides sheltering officers opposed to Hitler, he conveyed information to Menzies through several covert channels.[62]

One agent sent to Britain in December 1940, a young Yugoslav banker named Dusan 'Dusko' Popov, was probably not sent by Canaris personally; after recruitment into the *Abwehr* he had contacted the MI6 station in Belgrade on his own initiative and offered his services to the British as a double agent. The *Abwehr* officer who briefed him for his mission in Britain was a former university friend, Johann Jebsen, who was, Popov told his MI5 interrogators later, 'very pro-British, and I think if he was sure he would be safe he would come over here.'[63]

According to Popov's post-war memoirs Jebsen told him, among other things, that Rudolf Hess had been saying that high personalities in Britain were seeking contact with Germany; also that the *Abwehr* was in touch with Welsh nationalist circles in which there was talk of Lloyd George becoming Prime Minister and negotiating peace.[64]

It is interesting that Jebsen should have singled out Hess: he was practically the only top Nazi leader not so far implicated in putting out peace feelers; doubly interesting that he should link this with talk of Lloyd George coming back as Prime Minister and negotiating peace. For that was precisely Hess's aim – if not Lloyd George, then Halifax or Sir Samuel Hoare or some other figure on the appeasement wing.

On arrival in London Popov was met by Major 'Tar' Robertson, head of MI5's B1a division running double agents, whom he described as 'like Hollywood's concept of a dashing British military type.'[65] Appearances apart, Robertson was an exceptionally able officer and shrewd judge of character. His first double agent, who had been caught writing to his Hamburg controller even before the war and 'turned' to work for the British was a Welsh electrical engineer code-named SNOW. Shortly after the outbreak of war Robertson had sent him on a mission to his *Abwehr* case officer in company with a retired Swansea police inspector, code-named GW, who had posed as a Welsh nationalist explosives expert.[66] These two no doubt accounted for Jebsen's reference to Welsh nationalist circles.

After Popov had been appraised by Robertson over a drink at the Savoy bar, he was subjected to intense interrogation for some days by MI5, MI6 and service intelligence officers. Finally inducted into Robertson's double-agent system under the code name SCOUT – changed later to TRICYCLE – he was introduced to Sir Stewart Menzies, who invited him to spend the New Year weekend with him at his brother's place in Surrey. There Menzies talked to him alone about Admiral Canaris, and said he wanted information about anyone closely connected with him. It was apparent to Popov that Menzies and Churchill viewed the *Abwehr* chief as a catalyst for anti-Hitler elements in Germany, and he gained the impression that Menzies was 'contemplating a dialogue with Canaris with a view to ousting Hitler.'[67]

Popov's memoirs do not reveal whether he said anything to Menzies about Hess's belief that high personalities in Britain sought contact with Germany; nor is it known whether he said anything about this in his initial interrogations, since the record of these is missing from his recently released MI5 file. It would be surprising, however, if he failed to mention it, particularly in view of the impressions he was instructed to convey to the *Abwehr* when he was flown out to Lisbon on 3 January: on the one hand he was to emphasise the strength of British defences against invasion, on the other to suggest that British morale was being so undermined by bombing 'that many politicians thought it was time to overthrow Churchill and his "clique" and negotiate a peace.'[68]

The aim was, of course, to persuade Hitler that an invasion of England would be too costly and was in any case unnecessary since the British would shortly come to terms, so encouraging him to turn east against his real enemy without invading first. Within this overall aim it is easy to imagine Popov's inside information on Hess giving Menzies the idea that he might target the Deputy Führer with disinformation about the prospects for a negotiated peace.

That is speculation. What is not in doubt is that two weeks later one of Menzies' top experts on Germany flew to Lisbon. Frank Foley had been head of the MI6 station in Berlin before the war under the customary guise of Passport Control Officer at the British Embassy, where he had used his position to help thousands of Jews flee the country, sometimes sheltering them in his own home at great personal risk. He was well acquainted with the Nazi leadership.

His journey to Lisbon has only recently come to light with the emergence of his wife's diary. A brief entry records his departure for Lisbon from Whitchurch aerodrome, near Bristol, on Friday 17 January 1941.[69] This was six days after 'Tar' Robertson had been alerted to the possibility of sending Hamilton to Lisbon – and it will be recalled that Air Commodore Archie Boyle had wanted MI5 and SIS (MI6) to run him in tandem.[70]

After a fortnight in Lisbon with his secretary as cover Foley returned to Britain on Saturday 1 February. What he had been doing there is not recorded in the diary. The service's files have not been released to the public, but an MI6 historian told a *Daily Telegraph* reporter that while much of the Hess material has been destroyed, a single more recent reference reveals plans for a 'sting' operation in response to Albrecht Haushofer's letter to Hamilton – a copy of which had been sent to MI6 on 6 November, over two months before. According to the recollections of old MI6 hands, Foley on his return reported that a 'sting' would be too risky.[71]

There, it is assumed, the matter was allowed to drop. Yet, as noted, it was taken up with Hamilton himself towards the end of that month by Air Intelligence. In the meantime, on 2 February, the day after Foley had left Lisbon, Albrecht Haushofer had flown to Sweden, returning on the 5th. What he was doing there and whom he saw is unknown, but he must have gained clearance to go from Hess, who summoned him on the 21st for three days of talks.[72]

It is interesting in this connection that the King of Sweden's offer to mediate a peace settlement was the subject of a letter from Menzies to Henry Hopkinson, his liaison at the Foreign Office, on 19 February. He wrote that he had just learned via their Dutch intelligence link that Franz von Papen, German Ambassador in Angora (Ankara), had urged the King of Sweden to try to bring the war to an end in collaboration with the Pope, but the King 'did not think that the time was yet opportune for a [peace] move of this sort'.[73] The bottom half of this letter has been torn off neatly in a straight line just below 'Yours ever', so removing the 'C' in green ink with which Menzies signed his correspondence – continuing a tradition set by the first head of the Secret Service.

The question is what, beside his 'C', had Menzies written below the typed message that was so sensitive it had to be torn off before this file was released to the public in 2007?

SOE

The Special Operations Executive, SOE, was formed in July 1940 to take the war behind enemy lines with sabotage, subversion and propaganda. Churchill intended it to 'set Europe ablaze', or as an officer recruited in November 1940 recalled being told, 'to do to [German-occupied] Europe what Pitt had done to France before 1807.'[74] The organisation was formed from the sabotage and propaganda Section D of MI6, the guerrilla warfare section of the War Office and the propaganda department of the Foreign Office, and placed under the Minister of Economic Warfare, Hugh Dalton.

It will be recalled that a copy of Albrecht Haushofer's 23 September letter to Hamilton via Mrs Violet Roberts had been sent to the IRB (code name for SOE) by Censorship on 6 November. It is now known from John Harris's researches that Mrs Roberts was the aunt of Walter Stewart Roberts, a contemporary of Stewart Menzies at Eton, and with him in the prefectorial society 'Pop', who was recruited into SOE as 'Establishment and Finance Officer' in November 1940.[75]

Violet Roberts was evidently close to him since after the tragic death of her only son, Patrick, in a car crash in 1938 she lived for a time in Walter's London house – that at least was the address she gave on the probate papers for Patrick's estate.[76] Her husband had died some years before.

By 1940 she had moved back to Cambridge. MI5, besides finding her Cambridge address from Thomas Cook & Sons on 29 November 1940, had established that her letter had been addressed to Martha Haushofer, Munich, and sent on 26 July.[77] Yet no further action appears to have been taken until almost four months later on 22 March 1941 when Robertson's deputy in B1a, John Marriott, sent a letter to the Regional Security Officer in Cambridge, Captain C.M. Hughes, asking him to check up on Mrs Roberts.[78] Police enquiries turned up nothing, and Hughes appears to have forgotten the matter until 14 May when, accompanied by an inspector from the Cambridge force, he visited her at her home, 10 Wilberforce Road.[79] It is hard to imagine this was not prompted by the news of Hess's arrival in Scotland three nights before.

Hughes and the inspector were ushered into a drawing room hung with religious pictures. Soon afterwards Mrs Roberts came in, a small, very thin woman in her early seventies with grey hair and grey eyes. 'As soon as she began to talk,' Hughes reported, 'I realised that she was a well-educated, intelligent and very alive woman.'[80]

She told him she had known the Haushofers for a long time and had stayed with them in Germany. Their son Patrick had been very friendly with Albrecht Haushofer and had brought him to stay with her and her husband in Cambridge on occasions when Albrecht was in England. She had never written to Albrecht, nor he to her. He was a friend of Hess, and she added that she had met Hess, who agreed with Professor Haushofer's geopolitical principles.

As to her July 1940 letter, she had been in constant communication with Martha Haushofer before the war, and when, after the outbreak of war, a German-born friend of hers, a Mrs Stephenson, told her about Thomas Cook's facilities for communicating across enemy frontiers, she had decided to use them to continue her correspondence with Martha.

113

Hughes concluded his report of the interview by stating that he had established at least two important facts: the letter from Albrecht was unusual since he had never written to her before; secondly, she did not know the Duke of Hamilton.[81]

If Hughes asked to see examples of her pre-war correspondence with Martha Haushofer he did not mention it. He was evidently struck by her intelligence, and accepted all she told him. There the matter should, perhaps, rest – except that there is a curious postscript. She had written another letter to Martha some five weeks before this interview, on 6 April. Again, if she told Hughes about it he did not allude to it in his report.

This second letter was until recently in the German Federal Archives in Koblenz. One scholar who saw it in the 1990s describes it as a reply to a postcard from Martha Haushofer about family affairs, not a reply to Albrecht Haushofer's September 1940 letter, which she did not mention.[82] Evidently that had never reached her. Her reply to Martha dealt with mundane matters such as reading and gardening; 'a real letter' was impossible, she wrote – since she was obviously aware of censorship – but she wanted to send her old friend and her family a message of love and friendship. It was a testament to the warm relationship between the two women.

It was picked up by German Censorship, passed to the Gestapo and Martha was summoned for interview on 29 August 1941. She evidently gave satisfactory explanations for they released the letter to her.[83] It has now disappeared from the archive, but there is nothing to connect it with Hess's mission; indeed she did not receive it until three months after his flight.

Nor is Violet Roberts' original July 1940 letter in the Haushofer papers in the Federal Archives; this is not surprising, perhaps, since it was addressed to Martha and was probably regarded as ephemeral. Moreover, there is nothing to connect it with her nephew, Walter, and she sent it some months before he joined SOE. There is nothing, therefore, to support a conjecture that he or a colleague in intelligence prompted her to re-establish contact with the Haushofers because they were known to be close to Hess. Nonetheless, in view of her close relationship with Walter, who had known Stewart Menzies at Eton and was inducted into SOE later that year, and in view of Hess's subsequent flight to visit Albrecht Haushofer's friend the Duke of Hamilton, her decision to write to Martha Haushofer in July 1940 after the fall of France, if a personal whim, was a remarkable coincidence.

AIR INTELLIGENCE

As noted previously, It was not until 11 January 1941 that Archie Boyle, head of Air Intelligence, was alerted to Albrecht Haushofer's 23 September letter to Hamilton.[84] Long after the war Colonel 'Tar' Robertson ascribed the delay since receipt of the letter partly to the disruption of MI5's move to Blenheim Palace, chiefly to the fact that the letter was not considered especially important.[85]

Boyle gave it no higher priority, for it was over a month later, on 26 February, that Group Captain F.G. Stammers of Air Intelligence wrote to Hamilton asking if he would be in London in the near future as he was anxious to have a chat with him on a certain matter.[86] The Duke, it will be recalled, had taken ten days leave from 12 to 21 November the previous year, possibly in connection with MI5's investigation into his 'bona fides'. He had taken another ten days leave from 26 January to 4 February 1941. His diary for that period has the single word 'Lesbury'[87] – his brother-in-law's estate near Alnwick, seat of the Dukes of Northumberland. It is evident he had no further leave due. Yet he took a third period of ten days from 8 to 17 March, presumably in response to Stammers' letter.[88]

During this time he made a statement to the Provost Marshal's department at the Air Ministry about his relationship with Albrecht Haushofer, and was asked if he would be prepared to meet him in Lisbon. His answer, recorded in the Provost Marshal's report was:

> if it would be of any service to my country I would naturally go and meet this man but I would like to suggest that a better man to go would be my brother, David Douglas-Hamilton, who is a flying instructor at Netheravon and who has a considerable intimate knowledge of Germany.[89]

When Guy Liddell came to describe the case later in his diary he wrote, 'eventually the Air Ministry produced his [Hamilton's] brother. After further delay they got hold of the Duke himself ...',[90] suggesting that Air Intelligence had talked to one of the Duke's brothers before the Duke was interviewed. Whether this was David or George 'Geordie' Douglas-Hamilton, then chief of intelligence at RAF Fighter Command, is unclear since there is no record of either brother in the MI5 files on this case. However, Guy Liddell was never intimately concerned with the project – he believed, as noted earlier, that Karl Haushofer had written to Hamilton – and it is likely that the actual sequence of interviews was Hamilton first, then his brother and after further delay Hamilton again, as will appear.

On 15 March, a few days after making his statement to the Provost Marshal, Hamilton reported to Group Captain Stammers at the Air Ministry. Stammers asked him what he had done with the letter from Haushofer. Hamilton assumed he meant Albrecht's last letter before the war and replied that he had lodged it with his bank.

'The one you have just received,' Stammers said, and pushed a photostat copy of Albrecht's 23 September letter across to him.[91]

Hamilton had not received the original and never would. He read the copy with amazement, as he told the author James Leasor after the war.[92] This indicates that his brother, whichever one it was, had not been interviewed yet, otherwise Hamilton would undoubtedly have been alerted. Stammers then explained that Haushofer was believed to be a significant figure and asked if Hamilton would go to Lisbon to meet him. The Duke had, of course, already told the Provost Marshal that he would go, while suggesting his brother David as a better choice.

Stammers sent Hamilton's statement to Robertson on 19 March. Probably David, or possibly 'Geordie' was approached about this time, but there is no record in the MI5 file. The next paper is an internal note to Robertson from his deputy, J.H. Marriott, dated 24 March: 'The case seems to have been allowed to go to sleep for no particular reason, but the position now is that HAMILTON is prepared to go to Lisbon, and I suggest that he do it forthwith.'[93] Robertson wrote to Stammers the next day: 'My own personal view is that the Duke should make a trip to Lisbon and get in touch with Haushofer. However, I will arrange to have this done through Air Commodore Boyle who has expressed his willingness to help us in this direction.'[94]

Twelve days later, on 6 April, he saw Boyle, and followed it up on the 7th with a letter asking Boyle to send Hamilton to Lisbon on an official mission that would make his presence 'unsuspected by anyone'. In order to cover the long delay since receipt of Albrecht's letter, he proposed that Hamilton should take the line, 'he wrote almost immediately but ... the letter must have been lost in transit.'[95]

Boyle replied two days later, on 9 April, that before he attempted to find a posting for Hamilton it would be necessary to get the story 'absolutely tidied up and clean'; he would wait, therefore, until Robertson had seen the Duke himself.[96]

The meeting took place a fortnight later on 25 April in Group Captain D.L. Blackford's room at the Air Ministry. In the course of a long talk Robertson suggested to Hamilton that he would be given the necessary cover to go to Lisbon for about three weeks; when he arrived he should write to Albrecht to tell him he had managed to get there at last, and would be glad to see him again.

'Hamilton seemed to get quite pleased with the plan,' Robertson reported, 'and in general quite willing to carry it out', but found difficulty in seeing what would be gained. 'A good deal of information about how Germany is weathering the war,' Robertson replied, and offered to write a script for him.[97] His report continued:

> Hamilton at the beginning of the war and still is a member of the community which sincerely believes that Great Britain will be willing to make peace with Germany provided the present regime in Germany were superseded by some reasonable form of government.
>
> This view, however, is tempered by the fact that he now considers that the only thing that this country can do is to fight the war to the finish, no matter what disaster and destruction befalls both countries ...
>
> He is a slow-witted man, but at the same time he gets there in the end, and I feel that if he is properly schooled before leaving for Lisbon he could do a very useful job of work.

Hamilton had flown a Hurricane down to Northolt aerodrome for the interview.[98] Afterwards he flew north to Acklington aerodrome, Northumberland, and on the 26th sought advice on Robertson's project from his wife's uncle, Lord Eustace Percy, a former Tory cabinet minister,[99] before flying back via his RAF Group headquarters at Ouston to Turnhouse, and resuming command.

Two days later he wrote to Blackford at Air Intelligence agreeing to go to Lisbon so long as the British Ambassador there was told of his mission, and provided he was authorised to explain the position to Sir Alexander Cadogan at the Foreign Office. Also, he was concerned that he should be able to explain to Haushofer why he was answering his letter after a delay of seven months; and he asked for an explanation of the circumstances in which the letter had been withheld from him last autumn.[100]

Blackford replied on 3 May, saying he had discussed his letter with Air Commodore Boyle and both agreed that 'this may not be the right time to open up a discussion, the nature of which might well be misinterpreted'. The delay since receipt of the letter – due to 'another department' mislaying it – made it 'extremely difficult to find a watertight excuse for action at the present time'; he therefore asked Hamilton to regard the matter as in abeyance.[101]

He sent copies of the correspondence to Robertson, who replied on 6 May that he thought Hamilton's two 'objections' – presumably the two conditions he had stipulated – were 'reasonable'; he would take up the questions raised immediately and let Blackford 'know the result of our deliberations as soon as possible'.[102]

The final decision was taken on 11 May. An internal note to Robertson states, 'we discussed the case today and decided that in all the circumstances it would be better not to press the matter and that the project of angling for the Duke to go to Lisbon could therefore be dropped.'[103] There is no explanation of 'all the circumstances' that led to the case being aborted. Long after the war Robertson told Hamilton's son, Lord James Douglas-Hamilton, that he had advised dropping the matter because of the loss of the letter and the consequent long delay.[104]

This had not been his view only a fortnight before. What had changed his mind will probably never be known. The two conditions Hamilton had imposed would hardly have hampered the operation – although they might have made it more difficult to deny had anything gone wrong. It is possible that MI6 intervened. Air Commodore Boyle had originally wanted the case run by both MI6 and MI5, and officers from these two and other intelligence services met every week on a committee set up in January 1941 – the Twenty or XX ('Double-Cross') Committee – to run double agents.[105]

In the meantime, on 10 May, the day before MI5 dropped the case, Hamilton wrote to Group Captain Blackford agreeing to 'regard the matter as in abeyance'[106] until he heard from him again; and that evening Rudolf Hess took off from Messerschmitt's Augsburg airstrip to fly to Scotland.

CHAPTER EIGHT

Deception operations

WHILE ENGAGED INTERMITTENTLY with Albrecht Haushofer's letter to Hamilton, Air Intelligence was confronted with an extraordinary proposal said to have come from Hitler's personal pilot, General Hans Baur. It originated in Sofia, Bulgaria, in late December 1940. A peasant farmer named Kiroff approached the British Military Attaché claiming that his daughter was married to Baur. As proof he produced family photographs. Baur, he said, had lost two brothers in the war and had become 'fed up' with continuous duty for Hitler. He was prepared to aid world peace by attempting a forced landing in England with the Führer and entourage aboard his plane.[1]

The Military Attaché passed the matter to the Air Attaché, who reported it to the Air Ministry and the Foreign Office. No one could be found to identify the 'Baur family' photographs; nonetheless the contact was approved by Cadogan; Kiroff was handed instructions detailing signals Baur should fire when approaching the English coast, and special instructions for receiving him in Hitler's four-engined Focke-Wulf Kondor were sent to Lympne aerodrome in Kent. On 9 February Air Vice Marshal Trafford Leigh Mallory visited Lympne to inspect.[2]

Subsequently Kiroff failed to arrive at an arranged meeting and dis-appeared, but Baur or someone acting in his name maintained contact with the Air Ministry, since on 7 March Archie Boyle wrote to the chief of Fighter Command, Air Marshal Sir W.S. 'Sholto' Douglas, describing changes Baur had made in the recognition signals he intended to make on his approach to Lympne, and giving the expected date of his arrival as 25 March or after, between 5.00 and 8.00 p.m.[3]

Fantastic as it seemed that Hitler's private aircraft with fighter escort should stray into British airspace and land at Lympne, the Air Ministry took it seriously. This was demonstrated on 17 March when the aerodrome was put on full alert for the arrival and a Ford V8 box-body touring car and two motorcycle escorts were sent down to collect the prisoners. The instructions were to bring 'the booty' straight up to the Air Ministry in London 'from the scene of the "accident"'. Should there be 'a large bag only the biggest birds need to be sent in the Ford'.[4]

In the event Baur's Kondor did not arrive. The special arrangements for receiving him were nonetheless kept in force. They were about to be called off in May, but Hess's arrival in Scotland caused the Air Ministry to continue them until the end of the month.[5] Finally on 1 June they were annulled and the box-body Ford and motorcycles were returned to London.

It is possible that this curious plot had some connection with Hess's mission. The historian Rainer Schmidt has pointed out that the Deputy Führer was the only person at that time with a motive for opening a channel to the British Air Ministry[6] and perhaps probing aspects of British air defences. It is interesting that Baur was spelled 'Bauer' in the Air Ministry papers, possibly a mistake in the original transcription of his name from Sofia, but suggesting that later communications were verbal, not written, since both spellings sound the same.

Baur himself was devoted to Hitler throughout his life and would never have contemplated betraying him.[7] He did assist Hess with his flight by providing him with a map of forbidden air zones over the Reich,[8] but no doubt unwittingly since Hess would not have told him his intended destination. The real significance of the extraordinary episode lies in the fact that Baur, or someone acting in his name, established a clandestine channel of communication with British Air Intelligence. Nowhere in the open files is there a hint of the method or persons involved after the Bulgarian, Kiroff, left the scene; yet the change in recognition signals notified on 7 March and the reception organised on 17 March could only have been prompted by communications from the enemy.

THE BRITISH DECEPTION

Hitler's idea of ending Britain's resistance by smashing Russia had hardened over the late summer and autumn of 1940. It would remove Churchill's last hope on the European continent before America could intervene. In any case, he dared not risk invading England without naval and air superiority; as Goebbels put it, 'The Führer will not cross over. He dreads the water.'[9]

He maintained the pretence of preparing to invade England, but in December 1940 issued Directive No. 21 for the armed forces to be prepared by spring 1941 for a rapid campaign to crush Soviet Russia. It would bring on the two-front war his generals feared, but he was confident in the superiority of German leadership and materiel over those of the Red Army, and thought in any case the British might crack under the relentless bombing of their cities.[10]

British intelligence had, of course, attempted to foster this belief. Major 'Tar' Robertson's double agents and prominent political and social figures selected to spread disinformation, together with British diplomats in neutral capitals had contributed to a picture of growing disaffection against Churchill's government.

Traces of this subterranean campaign appear in reports to Ribbentrop's Foreign Ministry from late summer 1940 on: a telegram of 19 August from Madrid recorded the Spanish Foreign Minister having stated, after a talk with the British Minister, that he had the impression England was possibly ready for negotiations.[11] At the end of the month it was reported from Lisbon that the Duke of Buccleuch had been confined in his castle, and his imprisonment for spreading pacifist propaganda would ensue.[12] Neither assertion was true.[13] From Madrid at the beginning of September had come a report that the Spanish Ambassador in London had described British capitalists wanting an end to the war, and the City of London as 'the stronghold of pacifism and pessimism'.[14] A few days later Lisbon had reported that since the start of the air attacks the opposition to Churchill had come to life again.[15] A more dramatic report from Lisbon on 17 September described 'the organisation of London as completely destroyed by the air raids, accompanied by looting, sabotage and social tension'. 'Anxious capitalists fear internal disorder,' it ran. 'Growth of opposition against cabinet is plain. Churchill, Halifax are blamed for sacrificing England to destruction instead of seeking a compromise with Germany, for which it is still not too late.'[16]

There were elements of truth in these reports, but also exaggeration; just how much is as difficult to judge now as it must have been for German intelligence then. At the beginning of September British postal censorship had reported the morale of the country as 'extremely high'.[17] Later in the month, after ten days of bombing on the capital, Harold Nicolson, Parliamentary Secretary to the Ministry of Information, had, as noted earlier, entered in his diary that everyone was worried about the feeling in the East End of London, where there was much bitterness.[18]

Towards the end of the month Joseph Kennedy, the notoriously defeatist US Ambassador in London, had sent a message to President Roosevelt in a wire whose contents were revealed to the German Ambassador in Washington, thence reported to Ribbentrop, that England was completely finished.[19] He meant financially. This was true. However, a despatch reaching the Foreign Ministry from the German Ambassador in Lisbon cited the Portuguese Military Attaché in London reporting the mood of the people good 'in consequence of the English character and propaganda'.[20]

The difficulty of distinguishing between disinformation and genuine approaches to Germany by the British 'peace' faction is exemplified by the case of Sir William Wiseman in America. MI6 head of station in New York during the first war, Wiseman is described in the authorised history of the service as 'the most successful "agent of influence" in the service's first 40 years';[21] he was also, for some unstated reason, deeply distrusted by Menzies.[22] Travelling to San Francisco in November 1940, Wiseman came to the attention of the FBI when he met the suspected German spy, Princess Stephanie von Hohenlohe – once married to a distant relation of Prince Max von Hohenlohe.

The FBI bugged Wiseman's hotel room and heard him telling the Princess he represented a group of Englishmen who believed peace was possible, and asking her to sound out the German Consul General in the city, Captain Fritz Wiedemann, about possible terms acceptable to Hitler.[23]

Wiedemann had served as adjutant to Hitler and Hess successively before the war, and represented Hess's Foreign Organisation. He met Wiseman the following evening and again the FBI bugged their conversation. Wiseman was heard to say that he spoke for a very influential political group led by Lord Halifax, which hoped to bring about lasting peace between Britain and Germany. The problem was how far any British government could trust Hitler – which led to a discussion about restoring the German monarchy.[24]

When Wiseman's remarks were reported to the British authorities, they disowned him.[25] It is indeed hard to believe that Halifax, a member of Churchill's War Cabinet, would have authorised Wiseman to use his name as leader of a political grouping in opposition to government policy. Wiseman's activities remain mysterious.

An equally puzzling incident occurred that December 1940 in neutral Switzerland. Sir David Kelly, British Ambassador in Berne, hinted to Ribbentrop's agent, Prince Hohenlohe, that 'an understanding between England and the National-Socialist [Nazi] regime was not outside the realms of possibility.'[26] Significantly, Hohenlohe reported his impression that Kelly himself now inclined towards a compromise with Germany. At about the same time Göring's earlier peace envoy, Baron Knut Bonde, serving at the Swedish legation in Berne, received a telegram from one of his closest British friends, Lady Barlow, which impelled him to set up another meeting with Göring.[27] The wording of Lady Barlow's wire, like that of Violet Roberts' earlier message to Martha Haushofer, is not known, nor whether it was a genuine appeal or a strand of the British deception.

Bonde saw Göring on 14 January 1941. The interview convinced him that negotiations were possible if the British made positive proposals, and he wrote to Lady Barlow proposing a visit to London in order to meet Lloyd George and persuade him to try to move the government in this direction. His letter was forwarded to Cadogan at the

Foreign Office by a mutual friend.[28] By this time Cadogan had received a report on the Bonde–Göring meeting from Kelly,[29] and also two messages from Samuel Hoare in Madrid suggesting from information received that Göring might be willing to separate from the Nazi Party and negotiate peace.[30] Cadogan minuted on the Bonde file: 'Note that Göring would welcome any possible message from our side. I have no doubt he would. He wants us to sue for peace. It is just what he won't get ...'[31]

Halifax had by this date been removed from the War Cabinet. Lord Lothian, British Ambassador in Washington, had died suddenly in December. Churchill had asked Lloyd George to go to Washington in his place, but he had declined, pleading doctor's advice. In reality he believed Churchill was heading for disaster and intended holding himself in readiness to take over and negotiate a compromise peace.[32] Churchill had turned to Halifax, who very reluctantly agreed to go to Washington. Churchill replaced him as Foreign Secretary with his liegeman, Anthony Eden.

Churchill now wrote to Eden saying he trusted he was keeping an eye on all the peace feelers: 'Your predecessor [Halifax] was entirely misled in December 1939. Our attitude towards all such enquiries and suggestions should be absolute silence ...'[33] On 6 February instructions to this effect were wired to the British Ambassadors in Berne, Stockholm and Madrid,[34] the three neutral capitals through which most German approaches had come. Meanwhile British intelligence continued to encourage the Germans to believe in the possibility of negotiations.

This is shown most vividly in a wire from the German Ambassador in Lisbon to the Foreign Ministry in Berlin dated 23 January 1941, enclosing a report from an 'agent of the *Abwehr* about the present position in England'.[35] The agent was undoubtedly the double agent Dusko Popov. Everything in the report matches the account he gave in his memoirs about his time in England and subsequent flight to Lisbon, where he passed on false information to his *Abwehr* handler, greatly exaggerating the strength of the coastal defences, the number of army divisions available, and the effects of bombing on London. The final section is especially interesting:

As friendly towards peace the agent described:

1) Lord Brocket
2) Lord Londonderry
3) Lord Lymington

If one gave these three men the power they strive for, they would agree to any conditions.[36]

These were well-known as appeasers or, in Brocket's case, pro-Nazi. Londonderry was hugely wealthy and influential, socially and politically – the King called him 'Charley'. A former Secretary of State for Air, he had been dismissed when it was finally recognised that Britain had fallen behind German aerial re-armament. Nonetheless, believing the horrors of the first war must not be repeated, he had continued to court the Nazis, inviting von Ribbentrop – subsequently dubbed 'the Londonderry Herr' – to his palatial seat, Mount Stewart; going shooting with Göring at Karinhall; and taking his family to visit Hitler.[37]

Lymington was a more eccentric figure. One of the founders of a ruralist society called the English Mistery, much in tune with Nazi ideas of 'blood and soil', he had broken away later to form a more specifically racial group, the English Array. Just before the war he had founded the British Council against European Commitments with William Joyce, notorious after the outbreak as the Nazi radio propagandist 'Lord Haw-Haw'.

Popov's message about these men would have been readily accepted by German intelligence.

LONSDALE BRYANS – AGAIN

Lord Halifax's erstwhile envoy, Lonsdale Bryans, had met the German oppositionist, Ulrich von Hassell, for a second time in Arosa in mid-April 1940. As noted earlier, their talks had come to nothing since by then Hitler had launched his assault in the west.[38] Shortly afterwards Mussolini joined the war on Hitler's side and Bryans had to leave Italy. He went to France and requested assistance from Cadogan. As France fell he moved to Lisbon, from where he wired his young friend, Pirzio, in Rome about the possibility of a further meeting with 'Charles' – von Hassell – in Spain. The reply was discouraging: 'Charles not returning Spain. Impossible publish book at present. Write to me after the war.'[39] The reference to publishing possibly referred to toppling Hitler, but probably did refer to Bryans' book. Despite the apparent finality of the message, and silence from the Foreign Office, Bryans elected not to come home, but took ship to the Portuguese Atlantic island of Madeira, where he could live more cheaply than in Lisbon. His motives are open to question.

He had from his earliest days in Rome established what he subsequently explained as a 'dual identity' or 'camouflage' by writing to his pre-war publishers in Leipzig as if he were 'an Englishman politically of pro-Nazi sympathies, deploring the war between our two countries as a "fratricide of fellow Nordics"'.[40] He claimed his purpose was to 'screen' himself from possible Gestapo curiosity if he managed to enter Germany. To the same end he had had many talks with the Counsellor at the German Embassy about flying to visit Hitler in the private aeroplane of Prince Philipp of Hesse, who, he claimed, 'seemed keen enough at first'.[41]

For an undistinguished visitor to Rome he had made extraordinarily high-level contacts. Prince Philipp was on personal terms with both Hitler and Göring and was married to the daughter of King Emmanuel III of Italy. As such he had often served as an intermediary between Hitler and Mussolini; he had also acted as an art agent for Hitler in Italy, having studied art history at University. He had many English contacts, including King George VI's younger brother, the Duke of Kent.

The connections Bryans was able to make in Rome suggest channels previously opened to him by the grandees who backed him. Or perhaps Halifax's name had been sufficient to prise open these lofty Roman doors?

Having arrived in Funchal, Madeira, Bryans wrote to Brocket for funds, but received no reply, due possibly to the circuitous route via Gibraltar taken by all mail from the island. Subsequently, on 22 October 1940, he wrote again to his former Leipzig publisher, a bombastic screed in which he deplored the outbreak of war between Britain and Germany as a folly caused by 'the false slogans of democracy and machinations of a Jew-led "Front Populaire"', and maintained that while he had not arrived back in England in August 1939 in time to prevent the course of events, he had established a 'counter-influence' with Lord Halifax in the direction of sanity; if he were able, with the publisher's help, to enter Germany and have an audience with the Führer he could arrange everything 'to the mutual satisfaction and future prosperity of our two countries.'[42] He based his claim on the effect his book would have on Hitler.

He had evidently lost any hold on reality – as a reading of his book confirms – but his letter did contain a core of truth: 'There are many who feel as I do in England and in USA, and some of them are people of supreme influence.'

Because of the length of time taken by post from Madeira, he entrusted this letter and another, to Brocket, to a Danish wine merchant named Ole Erik Andersen who was travelling to Germany via Lisbon. He had met him at his hotel in Funchal and found they had a common admiration for Nazi Germany and hatred of Jews.[43] It proved Bryans' undoing. Andersen was suspected of being a German agent and was removed from his ship on the way to Lisbon by a British naval patrol. Bryans' letters to Brocket and the *Herrn Direktor*, Schwarzhaupter Verlag, Leipzig, were delivered to MI6, thence MI5 and a copy to the Foreign Office.

Tipped off by the British, the Portuguese authorities refused to renew Bryans' Madeira permit and he too took ship for Lisbon, arriving in mid-December. From there he attempted to re-establish contact with Pirzio in Rome by sending him a 'Happy New Year' telegram. The response was immediate and enthusiastic: 'Happy New Year; write; Charles sends greetings; writing. PIRZI.'[44]

Von Hassell was in Paris when he received a telegram from Pirzio to say that 'the Doctor' was in Lisbon requesting news of Wolf-Ulli – his asthmatic son. During his visit to the French capital von Hassell had noted increasing economic distress among the people, and he sensed that with Hitler's failure to invade England, and Italian defeats by the British Eighth Army in north Africa, the mood was changing rapidly from a 'not unfriendly' attitude towards the conquerors to 'masked hostility'.[45] It was perhaps these impressions that led him to respond positively to Pirzio. He wired back that he would be in Arosa until Saturday 1 February, and made arrangements to meet Wolf-Ulli there in case Bryans should appear, commenting in his diary, 'Above all it is interesting that the "Doctor" sends word. But the one who gave him his commission [Halifax] is no longer at the helm!'[46]

By remarkable coincidence, when von Hassell arrived in Geneva he was approached by Carl Burckhardt, acting president of the International Red Cross, with news of a recent approach from influential British circles wanting a negotiated peace[47] – as will appear.

Bryans, meanwhile, failed to make the rendezvous in Arosa. He pestered the British Embassy in Lisbon, claiming that he had the ear of Lord Halifax, wrote to Brocket and sent urgent wires to Buccleuch pleading for funds – 'Delay disastrous if forced home abandoning work.'[48] Buccleuch arranged to see R.A. Butler – still Undersecretary of State for Foreign Affairs – on his behalf.[49] To no avail. Any credit Bryans may have had was blown by the evidence of treachery in his letter to Schwarzhaupter Verlag found with Andersen, and further damning disclosures about his intentions from the Dane under interrogation. Cadogan minuted, 'He is a wash-out and a crook and he never had any "roving commission" from Halifax'[50] – a questionable assertion in view of the extraordinarily lenient treatment he was to receive on his return to England.

Andersen had been interrogated on 17 December 1940, around the time Bryans returned to Lisbon from Madeira. He had revealed that Bryans told him of his attempt to fly with the Prince of Hesse from Rome for an audience with Hitler, and that it remained Bryans' intention to travel into Germany to see Hitler or von Ribbentrop. One of Andersen's business connections was a wine merchant, Carl Henkel, whose niece was married to Ribbentrop; Bryans had asked him if he could arrange an interview with Ribbentrop for him through Henkel.[51] Bryans had also wanted him to seek out a certain Stahmer in Berlin and solicit his aid in getting him into Germany. Andersen was to tell Stahmer that the Duke of Buccleuch would vouch for him – Bryans had also listed others who would do the same.[52] The list was short,

Bryans' spelling erratic: 'Lord and Lady Brockett' (correctly Brocket), 'Captain Fitzroy Viers G.V.o' (Fyers), 'H. Drummond Wolffe' (Wolff), 'Lord Limington' (Lymington).[53]

It will be recalled that the two peers, Brocket and Lymington, had been described in 'Dusko' Popov's deliberately suggestive report to his *Abwehr* handlers as agreeable to 'any conditions' for peace.[54] Popov had been briefed by Stewart Menzies and MI6 officers over the New Year period a fortnight after Andersen's interrogation. It is likely then that these names were picked from Bryans' list. In any event, Bryans' unauthorised activities and loose talk in Rome and Lisbon was fostering just the impression of an influential British peace party that Menzies and the Double-Cross Committee were seeking to promote. Significantly, Bryans' really big backer was not mentioned in Popov's report: Walter Buccleuch had long been in Menzies' close circle of friends.

Initially during his interrogation Andersen had said that the Stahmer he had been asked to approach was the translator for Bryans' book, *The Curve of Fate*. Yet he had been given no address, and when pressed as to how he was to find him eventually said he had been told to go to the Foreign Office in Berlin and ask for him.

'What makes you think that any official in the Foreign Office would know the name of Stahmer?'

'Well, Bryans told me that Stahmer was a big noise.'[55]

In that case, Andersen had to concede, he was not a translator.

Heinrich Stahmer was a not inconsiderable noise in Ribbentrop's Foreign Ministry. There was also a lesser noise, one Herbert Stahmer, a former pupil of Albrecht Haushofer, presently serving as Legation Secretary in the Madrid Embassy, who was commissioned by Albrecht around this time to open a channel for peace negotiations to the British Ambassador in Madrid, Sir Samuel Hoare – as will appear. Which Stahmer Bryans was seeking to contact remains a mystery, although it is likely, perhaps, that it was the senior of the two.

Bryans was returned to London in early March, his flight and debts paid off by the Lisbon Embassy. Cadogan and MI5 would have liked him locked up[56] – he had committed an offence under the Defence Regulations by attempting to communicate with the enemy – but it

131

was realised that if treated severely he would make public his contacts with Lord Halifax and the travel facilities granted him by the Foreign Office, to the considerable embarrassment of both. Consequently no action was taken against him, and he was dealt with gently when questioned. He was not asked about Stahmer.

MI5 kept Bryans under strict observation. MI6 had graver concerns. In early May, a week before Hess's flight to Scotland, Menzies wrote to Cadogan to say the time had come to take off the kid gloves and 'interrogate him [Bryans] thoroughly about matters that seriously affect the safety of our organisation abroad'.[57] Menzies knew by this time that 'Charles' was von Hassell.[58] Did he suspect that Bryans had been used by German intelligence through his contact with von Hassell? At all events, it is difficult to understand how Bryans could have 'affected the safety' of Menzies' agents – unless, of course, MI6 was in touch with Albrecht Haushofer's former pupil and believed he might be the Stahmer Bryans was trying to contact.

Menzies' concern also prompts questions about Frank Foley's arrival in Lisbon with his secretary as cover on 17 January – as described earlier[59] – at the time Bryans was making a nuisance of himself there. It has been assumed that Foley's mission was connected with Albrecht Haushofer's 23 September letter to Hamilton. It now seems at least possible that he went with the more immediate task of investigating Bryans as he sought to enter Germany claiming he had a commission from Lord Halifax.

CLAUDE DANSEY

Albrecht Haushofer's bid to open a channel to Hoare through Herbert Stahmer in Madrid coincided with a significant escalation in British approaches to Germany, although whether in continuation of the deception campaign or as genuine offers from the British peace faction is unclear. Several strands have been noted: in November Sir William Wiseman had approached Fritz Wiedemann in San Francisco;[60] in December Sir David Kelly in Berne had given Prince Hohenlohe the impression that he inclined towards a compromise peace,[61] and Lady Barlow had wired Baron Bonde, encouraging him to seek another meeting with Göring.[62] Now, in January 1941, Carl Burckhardt in Geneva was approached by an emissary purporting to represent influential British circles seeking a negotiated peace.

This was Tancred Borenius, a Finnish-born art historian who had settled in London before the First World War. After lecturing in the history of art at University College London he had been appointed Professor in the faculty in 1922. Besides building an international reputation as a scholar, he was an accomplished raconteur and had established himself in the highest circles of British society.

He was art adviser to Henry Lascelles, 6th Earl of Harewood, who was married to King George VI's younger sister, Mary. Borenius was also well acquainted with the King's younger brother, the Duke of Kent, and his wife, Marina. He was also involved in Polish affairs as Hon. Secretary General to the Polish Relief Fund, through which charity he had come to know General Wladyslaw Sikorski, Prime Minister of the Polish government in exile in London.[63] Sikorski was naturally concerned for a peace restoring Polish independence, although there is no evidence linking him to Borenius' Swiss mission.

When von Hassell travelled to Switzerland in January 1941 hoping to meet Lonsdale Bryans – who failed to show up – he was contacted by Carl Burckhardt who told him of a recent approach by Professor Borenius on behalf of English circles who believed a reasonable peace could still be concluded. Borenius had claimed close connections with Buckingham Palace, 'above all the Queen'. The British royal connection was blanked out in the original, Swiss, publication of von Hassell's diaries, but appears in the more recent German edition. Borenius also told Burckhardt he was convinced there was a mood for compromise in the English cabinet, although Eden's entry in place of Halifax was a handicap; however, there was much opposition to Eden's appointment.[64]

Burckhardt had questioned him on terms, to which Borenius replied:

> Holland and Belgium must be restored; Denmark could remain an area of German influence; some kind of Poland (without the former German provinces) must be established for reasons of prestige

"because the Poles have struck out so bravely for England". Otherwise in the east no special interest (not even for Czechoslovakia). Former German colonies to Germany. The British Empire otherwise unshorn. For France no special enthusiasm in England.[65]

These were weak and impractical terms that would not have been contemplated by any British cabinet led by Churchill supported by Eden and Labour realists like Attlee and Bevin. On the question of who the British would be prepared to deal with, Borenius had expressed himself very cautiously, but had given the clear impression they would be extremely unwilling to conclude peace with Hitler. 'Chief argument: one cannot believe a word he says.'[66]

It is now possible, since the researches of John Harris, to say with all the certainty possible without documentary evidence that Borenius was sent by MI6. Harris interviewed his son, Lars Ulrich – known as 'Peter' – Borenius, who has since died, and was told that Tancred had been briefed for his journey to Switzerland by Claude Dansey, and had been given a book to take out – believed to have been a code book – and a poison pill 'the size of a golf ball'.[67] It was a family joke that he would have choked to death on the pill before the cyanide could have taken effect. Peter also told Harris that after Switzerland his father had moved on to Italy. Presumably this was possible because he travelled on his Finnish passport. It is surprising nonetheless, since it was well known that he was based in London. Perhaps the poison pill was supplied for the Italian leg of his journey.

The significance of Peter Borenius's story is that Claude Dansey was at the time Stewart Menzies' second in command in MI6 with the title Assistant Chief of Secret Service (ACSS). A formidable operator with wide experience in many countries, his specific role since 1936 had been the establishment of an intelligence-gathering network for Germany and Italy entirely separate from the existing structure of MI6 officers working as passport control officers at British embassies and consulates – a wholly transparent cover known to every foreign intelligence service. Dansey set up his parallel system under cover of commercial enterprises; his headquarters at Bush House in central London was ostensibly the export department of Geoffrey Duveen &

Co., international fine art dealers.[68] A connection with Borenius seems very likely.

Since Dansey's code name was 'Z', his network was known as the 'Z' organisation. On the outbreak of war he had moved his operation to Switzerland, but after the fiasco at Venlo and Menzies' appointment as 'C' he had been posted back to London, where he established himself as, in effect, chief executive under Menzies of the agent-running departments of the service, excluding his nominal equal, the Deputy Chief (DCSS), Colonel Valentine Vivian, whose responsibilities were confined to the code and cipher establishment at Bletchley Park, security and counter-espionage, which included liaison with MI5.[69] Dansey could exert much charm, but was better known for malevolence. He hated Vivian;[70] the two did not speak to each other. This could help to explain why MI5 was left in the dark about actions MI6 took to follow up Albrecht Haushofer's letter to Hamilton, although, of course, MI5 and MI6 officers did work together on the Double-Cross Committee.

On return to London Dansey had left a substantial staff in Switzerland running agents in Germany and occupied Europe. Among them was Halina Szymanska, wife of the former Polish military attaché in Berlin whom Canaris had helped across the border. She supplied information from within Germany, provided by an official connected to the opposition circle within Canaris's *Abwehr*, and from Canaris himself, whose MI6 code name was 'THEODOR'.[71] There were difficulties communicating with London since the Swiss only allowed enciphered messages to be sent through the Swiss Post Office – lending credence to Peter Borenius's account of his father being given a code book to take out to Geneva.

A clear trace of an MI6 campaign to persuade German intelligence of influential figures in the British establishment looking for a negotiated way out of the war can thus be seen variously in the stories of Sir William Wiseman – a friend of Claude Dansey – in San Francisco; of Dusko Popov, briefed by Menzies himself over the New Year; and of Professor Borenius, briefed by Dansey.

It will be recalled that in September Dr Ludwig Weissauer had conveyed Hitler's peace terms to the British government through the president of the Swedish High Court of Appeal, Dr Ekeberg, who had transmitted them to the British Minister in Stockholm. These terms, which included restoring a Polish state and returning sovereignty to the western occupied countries, but not to Czechoslovakia, were remarkably similar to the conditions Borenius had brought to Switzerland.[72]

Curiously, Borenius was not the only Finnish peace emissary that January. The previous November Dr Weissauer had enlisted the help of the Finnish Ambassador in Berlin to ascertain how British business and financial circles judged the prospects for peace. The Ambassador commissioned for the purpose a Finnish businessman, Dr Henrik Ramsay, who was due to go to London for talks on British nickel concessions in Finland. Ramsay travelled to Stockholm in December, meeting Dr Ekeberg at the end of the month, thence via Berlin and Lisbon to London, where he stayed from 18 to 26 January 1941.[73] He returned, again via Berlin. Whatever his findings, his report has been lost.

Meanwhile, the questions hanging over the peace soundings in Sweden and Switzerland were matched by those surrounding Sir Samuel Hoare in Spain.

SAM HOARE

Sir Samuel Hoare had been posted to Madrid in summer 1940 as His Majesty's Ambassador Extraordinary and Plenipotentiary on Special Mission. His task was to prevent the Spanish dictator, General Franco, from entering the war on Hitler's side. Beyond that role in early spring 1941 his activities were extraordinary and opaque.

Hoare came from the wealthy banking family of that name. His early career in Parliament had been interrupted by the First World War; ill health had prevented him serving at the front, but as a result of learning Russian he had been recruited by the chief of the Secret Service and posted to MI6's Petrograd station. Resuming his Parliamentary career after the war he had risen rapidly and held a succession of the highest cabinet posts during the 1930s, latterly on the extreme 'appeasement' wing of the government as a sharp critic of Churchill. On coming to power in May 1940 Churchill had dropped him from the cabinet, but soon found him this special mission to Spain, which suited his exceptional negotiating talents.

At the same time Churchill had one of his own friends, Captain Alan Hillgarth, posted to the Madrid Embassy as Naval Attaché with the clandestine mission, co-ordinated with Stewart Menzies, of subverting Spanish generals and officials to the British cause. For this he was provided with an initial US$10 million from contingency funds. His other special responsibilities were countering enemy intelligence operations and reporting U-boats in Spanish waters. He was permitted to communicate directly with Menzies.[74]

In the vital spheres of financial aid to Spain and trade through the British naval blockade Hoare was advised by David Eccles, a perceptive politician and businessman recruited by the Ministry of Economic Warfare. Eccles came to know Hoare well and to admire him for his superb intellect and knowledge of the world, his social gifts and powers of negotiation. The Spaniards, Eccles wrote to his wife, liked Hoare very much, 'quite undisturbed by that element of Jesuitism in his character, which is so often found in their own.'[75] Churchill's private secretary, Jock Colville, described it as a 'natural bent for intrigue ... It was not without justification that he was called "Slippery Sam".'[76]

Of Herbert Stahmer's approaches to Hoare on behalf of Albrecht Haushofer, we only have Stahmer's brief account in an unpublished manuscript. There is no corroborating evidence. Hoare did not report them to the Foreign Office and in his memoirs denied responding to overtures.[77]

Stahmer's story is that Albrecht called him to Berlin late in 1940, briefed him fully on Hess's desire for peace and his letter to Hamilton, and asked him to make contact with Hoare to discuss a basis for negotiations and 'arrange a conference in Spain or Portugal as soon as possible between both Ambassadors [British and German] and Haushofer, to which Hess might also find opportunity to take part'.[78]

Albrecht was playing a double game: while this approach to Hoare had Hess's approval and authorisation, Stahmer was clear that his commission to open a line to the British Ambassador came from 'the group Popitz, Hassell, Haushofer' – in other words the anti-Hitler opposition – 'for the eventuality of a coup against Hitler.'[79]

Some time during the winter of 1940/41 Stahmer opened conversations with Hoare through the secretary at the Swedish Embassy in Madrid and, according to his own account, soon established that a change in both British and German governments was a precondition for an armistice leading to peace negotiations. He went on to arrange a secret conference between Hoare and Lord Halifax on one side, Hess and Haushofer on the other, for February or March 1941, in Lisbon or another suitable place.[80] This is puzzling, for while it is known that Albrecht Haushofer regarded Hoare as 'half shelved [by Churchill] half lying in wait [to replace him]',[81] it is impossible to imagine Hess taking part in conversations predicated on a coup to remove Hitler.

It is also puzzling that Albrecht never mentioned Stahmer's negotiations with Hoare. He did not include them in a report he made to Hitler on his British connections immediately after Hess's flight,[82] an omission which could have had fatal consequences for him had Hitler known of the talks from discussions with Hess. It must be assumed, therefore, that Albrecht did not tell Hess the whole story of Stahmer's progress with Hoare: the inference is that he intended to conduct the negotiations with Hoare and Halifax himself on behalf of von Hassell's opposition circle.

In view of the premise of the proposed negotiations that both Hitler and Churchill would be removed, it is interesting that this proposition had come up in a New Year address by Franz von Papen, German Ambassador in Angora (Ankara), Turkey. The British Ambassador to Turkey reported on von Papen's speech in a letter to Eden and added that 'one of his cherished ideas is that Herr Hitler and Mr Churchill should be bartered against each other.'[83]

It was a period of mounting tension in Spain. Franco had replaced his Anglophile Foreign Minister with an aggressively pro-German relative, Serrano Suñer, who had stepped up the pressure on him, if not to join Hitler, at least to allow German troops through Spain to take Gibraltar, the British citadel holding the western Meditarranean. There were constant rumours of German troops on the border. While Hoare had won a superlative reputation among the Spaniards,[84] he lacked physical courage: David Eccles had observed this on several occasions and noted the resulting 'bouts of hesitation and compromise'.[85]

The panics were particularly evident in the early months of 1941, betrayed by long, repetitive wires for Churchill's immediate attention, which annoyed Cadogan and struck Foreign Office officials as 'both excitable and confused'.[86]

His actions were similarly erratic. On 5 March he talked with Ribbentrop's envoy, Prince Hohenlohe, against the explicit instructions of the Foreign Office – as will appear. On 15–17 March he travelled to Lisbon, not for the conference with Halifax, Haushofer and Hess that Stahmer had allegedly prepared, but to see President Roosevelt's special envoy, Colonel William Donovan. The following month he left Madrid for Seville, thence travelled to Gibraltar, stirring a barrage of speculation. It was noted at the Foreign Office:

> It should be on the record that the Ambassador went to Gibraltar in spite of categorical instructions that he was not to do so. He did not inform us of his movements, nor has he given any explanation why it was necessary for him to spend a week at Gibraltar ...[87]

If Hoare subsequently gave an explanation it does not appear in the files.

Haushofer's activities during this period in early 1941 are also undocumented. Between 2 and 5 February he travelled to Sweden, no doubt for Hess, but what he discussed with whom is not known.[88] It was probably in connection with the King of Sweden's offer to mediate between Britain and Germany. It was a fortnight later, on the 19th, that Menzies wrote to Henry Hopkinson telling him of a letter von Papen had written to the King of Sweden encouraging him to try to bring the war to an end in collaboration with the Pope; the King did not consider the time opportune. As noted earlier, the bottom half of this letter is missing from the file.[89]

Between 21 and 24 February Albrecht was again with Hess, but the content of their talks is not known. He appears in von Hassell's diary on 10 March, saying in a discussion at Popitz's residence in Berlin that there was an 'urgent desire from above' for making peace. 'He [Haushofer] himself now thinks as we do,' von Hassell noted, 'and recognises the "qualities" of the regime in the shape of the whole world's distrust of Hitler and his insufferableness as the obstacle to any reliable peace.' They then discussed how von Hassell's connections in Switzerland could be exploited to allow Albrecht to obtain authentic confirmation of this view of 'the possibility of negotiations with a regime change'.[90]

Albrecht was with Hess again from 12 to 15 April.[91] On the latter day Martha Haushofer recorded in her diary an extended discussion between her husband Karl, Albrecht and Hess in connection with some 'remarkable news' – undisclosed – that they had received.[92] On the 26th, Hess's birthday, Albrecht was again in discussion with him, this time at his house in Harlaching. The talk was of the 'important mission' to Switzerland on which Albrecht was about to embark.[93]

There is no trace of Albrecht ever meeting Hoare or even travelling to Spain.[94] The envoy who did succeed in gaining Hoare's ear during this period was Prince Hohenlohe; he came on behalf of Ribbentrop, for whom Hess had nothing but scorn.

HOARE AND HOHENLOHE

Churchill's instruction to Eden that all German peace feelers should be met with 'absolute silence' had been passed to Hoare by wire on 7 February 1941:

> In order to avoid all possibility of misapprehension as to the attitude of His Majesty's Government, your attitude towards all such enquiries and suggestions should be absolute silence. Nevertheless since these approaches sometimes afford useful information, you should continue to report fully any indication of German inclinations to negotiate that you may receive.[95]

The silence was soon broken by Churchill himself. The Japanese proposed to mediate between the belligerents. Declining the offer, Churchill composed a formal statement of British war aims and handed it to the Japanese Ambassador. On 28 February Cadogan forwarded the text to the British Ambassadors in Berne, Stockholm and Madrid:

the battle which this country is waging is for the overthrow of the system of lawlessness and violence abroad and cold, cruel tyranny at home which constitutes the German Nazi regime.

It is this system that the peoples of the British Empire, with the sympathy and support of the whole English-speaking world, are resolved to extirpate from the continent of Europe.[96]

In his covering letter Cadogan indicated that this memo provided the latest statement of the government's attitude towards negotiations with Germany, but pointed out that the instructions contained in the previous 'absolute silence' telegram still held good.[97]

Whether or not Hoare had received this latest notification by the time Prince Hohenlohe arrived in Madrid and asked to speak to him, the line he should have taken was absolutely clear from the original telegram. Still, Hoare granted Hohenlohe an interview. It took place on the 5 March, and it is apparent from his subsequent explanation to Cadogan that he knew he ought not to have talked to him: 'In the ordinary course of things I would have telegraphed to you before seeing him. As, however, he may be leaving Madrid at any moment it was a case of seeing him yesterday or not at all.'[98]

At the Foreign Office it was noted that Hoare's action was 'certainly contrary to the spirit if not the letter of our telegram',[99] and Cadogan sent Hoare a mild reproof: 'as a general rule we are not much in favour of meetings of this sort, which run a risk of disclosure and misinterpretation.'[100]

In his report of the meeting Hoare stated that he had seen Hohenlohe in the flat of the British Military Attaché with the attaché present 'in order that there should be no subsequent misrepresentation of the talk'.[101] Hohenlohe's message had been that the war was a calamity; Hitler had been prepared to make peace the previous July after his great success in the west; why was Great Britain not prepared to make peace after her successes in north Africa? The only result of continuing the war would be the end of European civilisation and the 'Communisation' or 'Americanisation' of the world. Hitler had never wanted to fight Great Britain and if peace were made now she should find him very reasonable.

I pressed him as to what he meant by Hitler's reasonableness. The answer was that Hitler wanted eastern Europe and China. As to western Europe and the rest of the world he wanted little or nothing. He must however have Poland and Czechoslovakia and the predominant influence in the Balkans. Having obtained this answer, I said to him as definitely as I could that for two reasons I could see no possibility of any peace. In the first place no one in England believed Hitler's word ... In the second place the specific terms that he had suggested meant the German domination of Europe, and we were not prepared to accept any European dictatorship ...[102]

Hohenlohe replied that if Britain would not make peace with Hitler, she would not be able to make peace at all: Hitler was the only man who counted in Germany – after which the discussion stalled, although Hohenlohe was frank about Hitler's intentions towards Russia: 'sooner or later, in his view the sooner the better, Germany would have to absorb the Ukraine and the Russian oilfields.' This passage of Hoare's report was scored in pencil in the margin, presumably at the Foreign Office.

Finally Hoare reported that on parting he had made it clear to Hohenlohe that he saw 'not the least chance of finding any basis for a peace discussion.'

The despatch Hohenlohe must have sent to the German Foreign Ministry is missing from the archives. However, the Italian Ambassador in Madrid sent a report of a conversation between Hoare and Hohenlohe of about this date, which has been published in the Italian diplomatic documents. It presents a very different picture. By this account Hoare stated that the position of the British government could not remain secure; Churchill could no longer rely on a majority, and sooner or later he, Hoare, would be 'called back to London to take over the government with the precise task of concluding a compromise peace'.[103] He would have to remove Eden as Foreign Secretary and replace him with R.A. Butler.

This was sent on 14 March, thus nine days after the meeting described by Hoare, but its general tenor is echoed by a despatch, also of the 14th, from the German Ambassador in Madrid which has Hoare saying that 'sooner or later he had to reckon on Churchill's resignation and assume that he himself would then be called upon to form a government'.[104] However, he would only accept 'if given a free hand to liquidate the war'. Similar remarks by Hoare were reported from Lisbon on 29 March.[105] Both these despatches are missing from the captured German Foreign Ministry documents stored in the Foreign and Colonial Office, London.

Possible explanations for the opposing accounts of Hoare's conversation with Hohenlohe are: that the meeting gave rise to rumours, which mushroomed in the feverish atmosphere of Madrid at this time of German pressure on Franco; or that the Germans used the rumours deliberately to spread disinformation, or British intelligence put out stories along the lines of the deception the Double-Cross Committee had long been pursuing. However, it is also possible that Hoare did say these things on behalf of the British peace faction, or even to establish his credentials with the Germans as a future leader of a pro-Nazi Britain behind Churchill's back.

It is interesting that the remarks the German and Italian Ambassadors credited him with were not so far removed from reality in the circumstances of that spring. Thus Harold Nicolson at the Ministry of Information noted on 2 March that while he felt the country could resist the worst Hitler could throw at them, the people would become so exhausted it would be difficult to reject a compromise peace if one were offered. When things got very bad there might be 'a movement to attribute the whole disaster to the "war mongers", and to replace Churchill by Sam Hoare or some appeaser. That will be the end of England.'[106]

Hoare continued to irritate Foreign Office officials with long, excitable and repetitive reports, particularly on the propaganda battle in Spain; and in April he again disobeyed instructions, as noted previously, by spending a week in Gibraltar after travelling to Seville for 'Holy Week', and offering no explanation.[107]

His stay in Gibraltar coincided with the time from 12 to 15 April when Albrecht Haushofer was in discussions with Hess, and Martha Haushofer recorded in her diary the receipt of 'remarkable news'.[108] The following week it was reported from Vichy France that Hess had flown to Madrid with a personal letter from Hitler to Franco.[109] Asked about this, Hoare replied that all his information inclined him to discredit the story.[110] He added that the German Ambassador had been away at Barcelona since the 22nd, the date Hess had reportedly flown to Spain. Further reports had Hess meeting the German Ambassador in Barcelona, but Hoare's agent in Barcelona could not confirm it: 'If Hess came here his arrival has been kept remarkably secret and his presence in town is not even rumoured yet,' Hoare stated.[111]

CHAPTER NINE

Two-front war

T HE ASSAULT ON RUSSIA was scheduled for the latter half of May 1941. A deception operation would be prepared against England, Goebbels noted in his diary on 29 March, 'and then back like lightning and go straight for it [Russia] … Great victory is imminent.'[1] If Hess was to succeed in preventing a two-front war he would have to launch his peace mission to Great Britain before then.

The United States was another consideration. Albrecht Haushofer had warned Hess the previous September that the British and Americans were on the point of concluding an alliance.[2] Secret Anglo American staff talks initiated by Roosevelt's administration were indeed held in Washington from January until the end of March 1941, resulting in what was termed the 'ABC-1' agreement: in the event of the two powers being engaged in war in the Far East and Europe, the principal effort would be made in Europe. The Japanese Embassy in Washington had learned of the 'Germany-first' strategy and informed Berlin.[3]

Even more provocatively, in the battle German submarines were waging against British shipping in the Atlantic, Roosevelt had thrown off all pretence of neutrality and moved a so-called 'US Security Zone' patrolled by the United States Navy progressively further east into mid-ocean some 2,000 miles from America's eastern seaboard. He seemed to be angling for an incident whereby the United States might be drawn into the war. Meanwhile American industry was supplying Britain with ever increasing quantities of war materials.

Behind the anticipation of war against Russia in the east and an Anglo–American alliance in the west lay the shadow of the final solution to the Jewish problem in Europe. On 30 January 1941 Hitler, in his annual speech commemorating the Nazi seizure of power, had repeated the public warning he had given the Jews in January 1939: should they succeed in plunging the nations into war – as meanwhile they had – it would not mean their victory, 'but on the contrary the annihilation of the Jewish race in Europe.'[4]

Why had he recycled his prophecy at this time? The simplest explanation is that he now intended to fulfil it with physical extermination. This, after all, was his deepest psychological war aim; in triumph, as master of Europe, he needed to proclaim it.

It is abundantly clear that extermination was being prepared. The Madagascar Plan, if ever anything more than a deception, was impossible while Britain remained an enemy and the Royal Navy controlled at least the surface of the seas. The plan now, as perhaps it always had been, was to liquidate the ideological and racial enemy behind the armies advancing into the east.[5] Himmler had been given this task, and on 13 March the Armed Forces High Command (*Oberkommando der Wehrmacht* or OKW) issued additional instructions to accommodate his units in the Russian campaign: 'In the Army's area of operations the Reichsführer-SS [Himmler] has been given special tasks ... resulting from the necessity finally to settle the conflict between two opposing political systems.'[6] The nature of these special tasks is revealed in the orders his chief lieutenant, Heydrich, gave to the commanders of the SS and police *Einsatzgruppen* who were to carry them out behind the fighting front: all Communist Party officials, Jews in the service of state or party, and all extremist elements were to be executed. It is clear, however, from the testimony of those involved and the massacres that subsequently took place that Heydrich gave oral instructions to execute all Jews whether members of the Communist Party or not, since Judaism was the source of Bolshevism 'and must therefore be wiped out in accordance with the Führer's orders'.[7]

Beyond this, methods of mass extermination for those Jews already assembled in ghettoes adjacent to railway lines in Poland or about to be sent there were at an experimental stage, but the fundamentals had been worked out and the executives sifted during the so-called 'euthanasia' programmes for the mentally ill and 'unworthy of life'. As for the rank and file who would carry out the lethal work, they and the public at large had been psychologically prepared by Goebbels' latest and vilest anti-Semitic film, *Der ewige Jude* ('The Eternal Jew'), premiered the previous November. In official pronouncements the ultimate fate of the Jews was masked as the *Endlösung*, or 'final solution', to the Jewish question. In May instructions issued under Göring's authority banned Jewish emigration because of 'the doubtless approaching *Endlösung*'.[8]

Hess was fully in the picture. As super ombudsman and 'conscience of the party' to whom every German had the right to voice his concerns, he was more aware than most of the human consequences of existing anti-Jewish policy in the conquered territories, especially Poland.[9] It is significant that at the beginning of March 1941 the party's racial ideologist, Alfred Rosenberg, had turned to Martin Bormann, Hess's chief of staff and personal secretary, when he wanted to know whether to include a reference to the Madagascar Plan in a speech he was due to make at the opening of a new anti-Semitic research institute in Frankfurt. Bormann evidently advised against, for when Rosenberg spoke at the end of the month he made no mention of Madagascar, simply stating, 'The Jewish question will only be solved for Europe when the last Jew has left the continent.'[10] Hitler had given Rosenberg responsibility for Central Planning for Questions of the East European Area, where the Jewish problem would be solved.

Hess was to summon Rosenberg for a last-minute talk hours before he took off on his peace mission to Britain, as will appear. It is not known what they discussed, but Rosenberg's diary has recently been discovered and when released to the public may well yield clues. Until then all that can be said is that Rosenberg, like Hess, was dedicated to an understanding with the British, their racial brothers, and was also deeply involved in the strategy for the conquest of Russia and the 'final solution' of the Jewish problem. After the war Karl Haushofer was to suggest that Hess flew to Britain because of 'his own sense of honour and his desperation about the murders going on in Germany'.[11] Hess was on trial as a major war criminal at Nuremberg at this time and Haushofer had to watch what he said. It is possible, therefore, that his reference to 'murders in Germany' was a euphemism either for the murders in Poland or for the slaughter planned for European Jews.

BURCKHARDT

20 April 1941 was Hitler's 52nd birthday. Hess delivered his customary eulogy, broadcast on all German stations, as he put it, 'conveying the thoughts of the entire German people in reverent love' for the leader under whom they had accomplished the greatest deeds in German history, ending, 'The German people unites all its wishes for you, my Führer, in the prayer: Lord God, protect our Führer!'[12]

It was two days later, according to reports, that Hess flew to Spain. 'Authoritative German sources' took the unusual step of denying this in broadcasts the following day,[13] while Sir Samuel Hoare, as noted earlier, used a form of words short of denial in replies to the Foreign Office.[14]

On the 26th Hess celebrated his own 47th birthday at his home in Munich-Harlaching. Karl and Albrecht Haushofer joined him, and they discussed a visit Albrecht was about to make to Geneva to meet Carl Burckhardt.[15] Here again, as with Stahmer's approaches to Hoare, Albrecht was playing a double game. Ostensibly he was acting for Hess, clandestinely for von Hassell's opposition circle. The meeting had been arranged by von Hassell's wife, Ilse, who had told Burckhardt that Albrecht would be coming with 'a double face', outwardly for Hess but *de facto* for the resistance movement.[16]

In the report Albrecht was later commanded to write for Hitler, he stated that Burckhardt had contacted him from Geneva with greetings from his (Albrecht's) old English circle of friends. Believing this message might be connected with his letter to Hamilton the previous September, he had referred it to Hess, who had decided he should go to Geneva. There Burckhardt told him he had been visited some weeks before by a distinguished person well known in London and close to leading Conservative and city circles – Professor Borenius – who wished to examine the possibilities for peace; in discussing possible channels, Albrecht's name had come up.[17]

After the war Burckhardt denied this completely, as of course he had to; at the time he had been a member of the Committee of the International Red Cross and so bound not to engage in inter-national politics. However, he asserted that he did not know any of Albrecht's 'old English circle of friends'.[18] While this is doubtful, the 'English greetings' were almost certainly cooked up by von Hassell and Albrecht at the 10 March meeting in Popitz's apartment as a way of getting Hess to authorise Albrecht's journey to Geneva.

After meeting Burckhardt on 28 April, Albrecht travelled to Arosa to see Ilse von Hassell – something he naturally omitted from his report to Hitler. He told her that Burckhardt, on the grounds of his discussion with the art historian, Borenius, and further talks with English diplomats, still believed England was prepared to make peace on a reasonable basis, but not with the present regime in Germany and perhaps not for much longer. The air raids on Westminster Abbey, Parliament and so on naturally bred increasing hatred.[19]

Von Hassell recorded in his diary that Burckhardt had agreed to make further contact with the British and would meet Albrecht again in a few weeks' time; they would then be better able to evaluate the prospects. Interrogated after the war, Karl Haushofer also stated that a second meeting had been arranged, at which, he added, Albrecht would be flown to Madrid for a conference with Hoare.[20] He repeated this with more detail in another interview: Burckhardt had agreed to act as contact man between Hess and the British at some time during the second half of May. Hess was to meet Hoare on an abandoned ten-nis court near Madrid. Albrecht had reported this to Hess, who had seemed pleased with the success of the meeting, but 'feeling utterly unhappy about much that happened in Germany and from a mixture of depression, romanticism and impatience' he had decided to fly to Britain instead.[21]

Whether Karl Haushofer had perhaps confused his son's twin channels, through Stahmer in Spain and Burckhardt in Switzerland, or whether he was embellishing his testimony at a time his former pupil and friend was on trial for his life for war crimes cannot be known. Terse entries from Martha Haushofer's diary for the beginning of May tend not to support such a positive outcome from Albrecht's meeting in Geneva:

> 3.5 ... Afternoon ... call from Albrecht from Hödingen [by Lake Constance, where his brother's parents-in-law lived] on the return from his – not completely abortive – diplomatic mission. If one dares to hope –

> 5.5 ... 4 afternoon K[arl] collected Alb[recht]. His discussion with —— in —— was not completely fruitless, which is more than we had expected ...'[22]

In his report to Hitler Albrecht made no mention of a suggested conference with Hoare in Madrid. It is difficult to see why, if this had been proposed, he should have omitted it, particularly as he could not have known what Hitler had learned from Hess.

THE ASTROLOGERS

Looking back to spring 1941 some years later, Hess acknowledged that he had probably not been quite normal. His life had revolved around test flights, instruments, fuel tanks, auxiliary oil pumps and radio direction beams.[23] At night he fixed a map of southern Scotland to the wall of his separate bedroom, the highest peaks circled in red, and memorised his planned route across the border country to Hamilton's home, Dungavel.

Driven by the imminence of Hitler's planned assault on Russia, despair at the senselessness of the two related Nordic nations meanwhile tearing themselves apart, and according to Karl Haushofer burdened with guilt at his idol's murderous course, he was also in thrall to astrology and the occult. In January he had asked Ernst Schulte-Strathaus, a personal friend who headed one of his cultural departments and also served as his 'astrological adviser', to predict a favourable day for a journey in the interests of peace. Schulte-Strathaus had come up with 10 May on the basis of an unusual constellation of six planets in the sign of Taurus on that day, together with a full moon.[24]

In March Hess asked a prominent Munich astrologer, Maria Nagengast, to name a promising day for a foreign journey; she also identified 10 May, afterwards receiving 50 Deutschmarks for her trouble.[25] It has been suggested that British intelligence somehow infiltrated Hess's astrological circle, which included the Swiss, Grete Sutter, who had given him a prediction at Christmas; but there is no firm evidence of this[26] and, of course, there was no need. Hess had been planning his flight since the previous year; the evidence suggests he was obsessed by his mission and determined to go.

One omen to which he attached particular importance was a dream Karl Haushofer had recounted on one of their last walks in Munich. Haushofer had got wind of Hess's intention to fly to Britain and was apparently trying to find out if it were true in order to confront and dissuade him. He invented a dream in which he saw Hess walking through the tapestried halls of English castles bringing peace to two great nations.[27] Hess refused to be drawn, but took it as a remarkable portent. Apparently, it was not the only one: a report on Hess after his arrival in Britain stated, 'Recently the Professor [Haushofer] told Hess that he had seen him in his dreams, on three separate occasions piloting an aeroplane, but he knew not where.'[28]

The significance Hess accorded these metaphysical intimations is demonstrated in a letter he wrote to his wife from England nine months after his flight. He told her that in the folder he had given his adjutant before flying he had included:

1. A note on the momentous dream of the General [Haushofer]
2. The horoscope drawn up by Schulte-Strathaus
3. The prophecy that Grete Sutter made ...

He asked her to copy these and deposit them with a notary, adding, 'I am interested in the matter from a scientific point of view',[29] by which he meant he wanted to test their reliability in the light of events as they turned out.

THE LAST TALK WITH THE FÜHRER

On 30 April, before Albrecht Haushofer had returned from his interview with Burckhardt in Geneva, Hess received the leader of the
Spanish Falange syndicates – Spain's fascist organisation – at party
headquarters, the Brown House, Munich. Afterwards he drove to
Messerschmitt's Augsburg works. His instructions to prepare his personal aircraft and fill the auxiliary fuel tanks had been phoned through
earlier. Arriving at the airfield, he changed into flying gear, climbed
into the cockpit of the Me 110 and was ready to take off when an adjutant ran across from the management building signalling him to shut
off the engines.[30] The Führer had phoned: he was unable to give his
customary May Day address the following day and wanted Hess to
stand in for him.

Hitler had just returned to Berlin from improvised field headquarters in south-east Austria after directing operations to punish
Yugoslavia for not complying with his plans for the Balkans. That day,
the 30th, he was discussing with the army high command the launch
date for the coming Russian offensive[31] – fixed finally for 22 June – no
doubt the reason he asked Hess to give the speech the following day.

Messerschmitt's Augsburg works had been selected as the 'National
Socialist Model Enterprise' that year for its outstanding contribution
to armaments, and it was there that Hess returned on 1 May to lead the
celebrations and inspire the nation on the Labour Day holiday.[32] After
his speech, which was broadcast nationally, he bestowed gold medals as Pioneers of Labour on two ministers, then on Professor Willi
Messerschmitt, praising him as 'the designer of the best fighter aircraft
in the world ... thanks to which the German Luftwaffe enjoys its present undisputed superiority in aerial combat.'[33]

Finally he awarded the 'golden flag' to Messerschmitt's factory as
a model enterprise, and the ceremony ended with a roll of drums and
the singing of '*Brüder in Zechen und Gruben*' – loosely, 'drinking companions'. Afterwards he took Willi Messerschmitt aside and discussed
additional modifications to his personal Me 110, including 'the second
seat's oxygen bottles [to be] fed into those of the pilot'. He needed
them by the following Monday, 5 May.[34]

Whether or not Hess had originally told Messerschmitt why he wanted an aeroplane, it is scarcely possible the designer was not by this time fully in the know, indeed a collaborator. At the end of the war Göring's chief executive, Field Marshal Erhard Milch, was adamant that Messerschmitt knew precisely what was going on;[35] the plane he gave Hess had been specially equipped for the purpose. It must be assumed that Messerschmitt approved of Hess's aim. It is equally difficult to believe that Göring was ignorant of Hess's plan. The majority of German peace feelers had come directly or indirectly from him.

It is almost certain, however, that the flight Hess had had to abort on 30 April was to have been another test run, not the real thing.

On 3 May Hess flew to Berlin, and the following day, at six in the evening, with Göring, Himmler and the Interior Minister, Wilhelm Frick, he accompanied Hitler to the Kroll Opera House, still serving as the Reichstag. Deputies rose and roared approval as the party entered. Hitler stepped to the rostrum. His carefully prepared speech was aimed at an international, especially American audience – hence the late hour – and he focused his attack on Churchill as a warmonger aided by the Jewish financial interests standing behind him. He himself had striven only for peace. He detailed the many times he had publicly extended offers to end the war, but all his efforts for an understanding had come to nothing, wrecked by Churchill and his small clique resolved on war whatever the consequences. After turning to recent German military successes in Greece and the Balkans, he ended by taunting Churchill on a record of defeats which would have cost any other leader his job.[36] Stepping down to clamorous applause, he took his usual seat beside Hess.

Afterwards the two conferred on the English question. This is certain, since there are contemporary statements to this effect from both Hitler at the Berghof on 13 May while attempting to explain Hess's flight to Britain to senior party members,[37] and from Hess on the same day in Scotland when explaining the reasons for his flight to a Foreign Office official, Ivone Kirkpatrick.[38]

A third testimony to their discussion was allegedly found by the French war correspondent and author, André Guerber, at the end of the war, among documents in the ruins of the Reich Chancellery in

Berlin.[39] It must be treated with great caution since the documents themselves have disappeared. According to Guerber's report, one of these documents showed that Hess, a month before his flight to Britain, flew to Madrid, where in talks with Franco and British agents he formed the impression that Britain was interested in negotiating peace.

This, according to another of Guerber's documents, he reported at a conference with Hitler and Göring at Berchtesgaden on 4 May. The problem here is that on 4 May all three were, as noted, in Berlin for Hitler's speech at the Reichstag, not at Berchtesgaden. Guerber claimed that he read the notes of this discussion written up by Hitler's secretary, Rolf Inliger. It may be that Inliger did not record the venue or that Guerber mis-stated it.

Later that day, 4 May, according to Guerber, Inliger recorded a further meeting between Hitler and Hess. As noted, such a meeting can be proved to have taken place after Hitler's Reichstag speech. Inliger had Hess saying, 'We must show the British we are sincere. If we do that the British people will rise up and compel Churchill to make peace.'

According to Guerber, Hitler then commissioned Hess to carry 'Plan ABCD Nr S 274K' to Britain. Guerber found a copy of the plan in the Reich Chancellery archives – 'ABCD' apparently referring to its four parts:

a) To demonstrate to the British Government by means of documents that it was useless to continue the war ...

b) To promise Britain that if she would withdraw from the war she would preserve her full independence and retain her colonial possessions, but would have to undertake not to 'meddle in any way' with internal or external affairs of any European country.

c) An offer to Britain of an alliance of 25 years with the Reich ...

d) A demand that Britain should ... maintain an attitude of benevolent neutrality towards Germany during the German–Russian war.[40]

This find in the Chancellery archives seems altogether too convenient, yet when Hess arrived in Britain he did carry out a), b) and d) in precisely that order, apparently omitting only c), the 25-year alliance.

Guerber could not have known this in 1945 when he filed his report. According to the British government's only detailed statement on Hess, published in September 1943, the Deputy Führer had indeed 'emphasised ... the certainty of England's defeat in two to three years', and the terms he offered had certainly been based on clause 'b)', Britain having a free hand in her empire if she allowed Germany a free hand in Europe;[41] but the statement made no mention of 'benevolent neutrality' or a 'German–Russian war' and stipulated that negotiations could not be held with the present, Churchill, government.

Guerber could have invented the documents he claimed to have found in the ruins of the Berlin Chancellery, for it is certain that Hitler, Hess and Göring were not at the Berghof above Bechtesgaden on 4 May when he alleged Inliger recorded their first conference there; yet why should an experienced and respected war correspondent stoop to such a device?

Hess's meeting with Hitler after the Reichstag speech was confirmed by one of Hess's security officers, Josef Portner. Some time after Hess flew to Britain Portner told Ilse Hess of a discussion between Hitler and Hess at the Reich Chancellery, Berlin, that had lasted four hours. Stationed in an anteroom outside the conference chamber, he had heard their voices raised frequently, but not what they said. When at length the two emerged, Hitler put an arm around Hess's shoulders and they parted 'almost cheerfully'. Hitler's last words were, 'Hess, you are and always were thoroughly pig-headed (*ein entsetzlicher Dickkopf*)!'[42]

It will be recalled that the two had had a similar marathon discussion or argument with raised voices over the 'death list' of those to be executed after the Röhm purge in 1934.[43] Since Portner's account was almost contemporary and certainly neutral it seems eminently credible. However, he gave the wrong date. He believed the meeting took place on 5 May, but that is not possible since both Hitler and Hess left Berlin by train on the evening of the 4th following their discussion after the Reichstag speech. The meeting he heard must have taken place on the 4th.

Whatever was said between Hitler and Hess on this last occasion they spoke on the evening of 4 May, the object of their frustration,

Winston Churchill, was sitting in spring sunshine on the lawn of the Prime Minister's country house, Chequers, working on Menzies' special buff-orange boxes and glancing up suspiciously from time to time to make sure that his private secretary, Jock Colville, was not trying to read the secret papers. The rest of the house party was inside, among them Churchill's friend, Captain Alan Hillgarth, then serving as naval attaché and intelligence officer at Hoare's Madrid Embassy. Colville's diary entry for that evening describes Hillgarth as 'a fervent disciple of Sam Hoare'.[44]

This is hugely significant. If anyone knew what Hoare had been up to the previous month when the German and Italian Ambassadors in Madrid had reported him suggesting the imminent collapse of Churchill's government and his own recall to form a new government to liquidate the war, it was the intelligence officer, Hillgarth. And if, as Churchill's loyal confidant and guest on the weekend before Hess's flight, Hillgarth was expressing 'fervent' devotion to Hoare it surely means that Hoare, far from being a defeatist and potential traitor, had been conducting a deliberate campaign of disinformation. Further, if, as Guerber asserted, Hess had flown to Madrid in April, he had evidently fallen for the ploy.

On 5 May Hess was again at Augsburg checking on the modifications he had ordered for his aircraft. There he summoned Albrecht Haushofer to report on his talk with Burckhardt in Geneva.[45] It is not known what Albrecht told him; no doubt it was on the lines of his later report to Hitler, that Burckhardt had said that leading circles in London were still interested in peace negotiations, and had agreed to arrange for a British representative to meet him (Albrecht) if he would return to Geneva. Whether Hess agreed to Albrecht making a second trip to Geneva, as Karl Haushofer asserted after the war, is immaterial since by this time he had evidently made up his mind to launch his own mission on the coming Saturday, 10 May – both a weekend, as favoured by Hitler for surprises, and the date recommended by his astrologers.

The next day, Tuesday 6 May, he went again to the Messerschmitt works at Augsburg and took a final brief test flight with Helmut Kaden at 11.20 a.m.[46]

CHAPTER TEN

Take off!

IN THE FINAL DAYS before he flew off Hess spent an extraordinary amount of time with his three-and-a-half-year-old son, Wolf Rüdiger, nicknamed 'Buz'. Ilse hardly knew what to make of it as her husband took Buz for lengthy walks along the river Isar, which flowed past the rear of their garden, or spent hours with him at the zoo nearby or indulged in private games with the boy behind the closed doors of his study.[1] It was only afterwards she understood: he had needed the simple companionship of the child to distract his mind and calm his nerves before the venture; and he must always have known he might not return.

In England, meanwhile, opposition to Churchill's direction of the war increased. The recent defeats for British armed forces, which Hitler had mocked in the Reichstag, led to withering criticism from Lloyd George and others in the House of Commons. Churchill knew things his critics could not. From secret sources and the 'Boniface' ('Ultra') decrypts in his buff boxes he knew Hitler was about to attack Russia and that the German Army in North Africa was short of supplies and had been instructed not to advance into Egypt. He replied with spirit, as Harold Nicolson described it in his diary: 'He stands there in his black conventional suit with the huge watch chain. He is very amusing. He is very frank. At moments I have a nasty feeling that he is being a trifle too optimistic. He is very strong, for instance, about

Egypt.'[2] He assured the House that Hitler had his problems too; and looking back on all the perils Britain had already overcome, 'upon the great mountain waves in which the gallant ship has driven', he felt sure they need not fear the tempest. 'Let it roar, and let it rage. We shall come through.'[3]

He was rewarded in the division that followed by a vote of confidence of 447 to three, and as he left the chamber cheering broke out spontaneously and was taken up outside. Later Jock Colville recorded, 'He went early to bed elated by his forensic success.'[4]

To Goebbels this signified nothing. His reports from London indicated a deep mood of pessimism, above all because of the shipping losses to U-boats. 'If the blow [against Russia] succeeds,' he noted in his diary, 'and it will succeed ... with what plausible goal will England then continue fighting?'[5] It was true that behind the defiance shown in the Commons there were many doubters. Harold Nicolson feared that people would jump at any escape that made cowardice appear respectable. 'Morale is good,' he wrote in his diary, 'but it is rather like the Emperor's clothes.'[6]

The next day, 8 May, Hitler returned to Berlin. Goebbels saw him at midday, finding him in brilliant form. He told Goebbels that England had lost the war the previous May. What could she do now? In the end it would be the ruin of the Empire. Roosevelt was only interested in prolonging the war so that he and his people would inherit England's world position. And assuming imminent triumph in Russia and a consequent struggle with America for global mastery, he told Goebbels that the United States could never produce as much as they could with the whole economic capacity of Europe at their disposal.[7] It was a gross miscalculation.

On the 9th Hitler went by train to Munich, where he was met by Göring, not Hess.[8] After spending the day there, he moved up to his Alpine retreat, the Berghof. He and Hess were never to meet again.

That day, a Friday, Hess was making final preparations. He had already written a long letter to Hitler explaining his scheme and his reasons, which his adjutant, Karl-Heinz Pintsch, was to deliver personally after he had taken off. This was either a genuine explanation – if it is assumed that Hitler did not know already – or more probably a necessary measure to ensure that his peace mission could not be attributed to the Führer. He had also written letters he would leave for Ilse, for his parents and brother Alfred, for Karl and Albrecht Haushofer, and one for Himmler stating that none of his staff knew what he intended and requesting that no action be taken against them.

Before he set off, he had to see Alfred Rosenberg. His reasons have yet to be explained. Rosenberg was in Berlin. Hess summoned him to Munich. Impossible, Rosenberg replied, but Hess insisted, and told him he would lay on a plane to get him to Munich the next morning.[9] He also called a legal officer on Martin Bormann's staff to ask the position of the King of England,[10] an odd request at this late stage. At the time of his alleged first attempt in January he had told his adjutant that when he arrived in Scotland he expected the Duke of Hamilton to arrange an audience for him with the King;[11] probably he now wanted to know the extent of the King's power to remove Churchill. The lawyer did not know the answer and said he would call back.

Hess also tried to phone the Minister of Agriculture to postpone a conference that month. Failing to reach him, he wrote a note instead, saying that he was making a long trip and didn't know when he would be back; he would be in touch again on his return.[12]

* * *

Saturday morning, 10 May, dawned fine and sunny. Hess phoned his adjutant, Pintsch, who lived a short distance away, and told him to report at 2.30 that afternoon. It was perfect flying weather; he was sure this was the day. The weather reports from Potsdam confirmed it. He intended taking off at about six that evening.[13]

After breakfast he took Buz and the family's four German Shepherd dogs for a last walk along the river path. Ilse was feeling ill and stayed in bed.

At noon Rosenberg arrived in a car Hess had sent to collect him from the airport. He showed him into the dining room, where a light lunch of cold meats, German sausage and salad had been laid out on the sideboard. The staff had been told they were not to be disturbed, and they ate alone. No record was made of their discussion, and after the war both men were careful to reveal nothing. Nor were they probed. Apparently the only thing that struck Rosenberg as odd was that after they finished their lunch young Buz was taken up to bed, but Hess went up and fetched him down again.[14]

Rosenberg stayed a while after lunch, talking, and left at some time between one and two o'clock. According to his adjutant who had accompanied him to Munich, they then drove straight to the Berghof.[15] The distance from Munich to Berchtesgaden is little over 150 kilometres (110 miles), much of it along a fast autobahn, so it is probable that Rosenberg arrived at Hitler's mountain eyrie before Hess took off on his flight.

Hess, meanwhile, had a short rest until about 2.30 when he changed into a Luftwaffe blue shirt, blue tie and breeches and high flying boots and went into Ilse's bedroom to take tea with her. Ilse always maintained that she knew nothing of her husband's purpose or destination when he left her that day, and this seems to be borne out by one of Hess's letters from captivity recalling how he had gone 'hot and cold' when he thought she had divined his real intention at this last leave-taking.[16] He never discussed official business with her, and on this occasion especially it can be imagined he would have wanted to spare her anxiety.

On the other hand she had seen the chart on his bedroom wall, and on this day she was, according to her own account, reading *The Pilot's Book of Everest* by the Marquis of Clydesdale – as the Duke of Hamilton had been – and his co-pilot, Group Captain D.F. McIntyre. The book had been given to them by English friends two years before the war and was inscribed on the flyleaf, 'With all good wishes and the hope that out of personal friendships a real and lasting understanding may grow between our two countries.'[17] Hess had looked at this inscription that morning after asking her what she was reading. He had then turned to a picture of Hamilton, remarking as he handed the book back open at this page, 'He's very good-looking.' Ilse agreed, puzzled.[18]

If this occurred and she really had no idea of where he was going it was a truly remarkable coincidence. As for his recollection of going 'hot and cold' when he thought she had guessed his destination, that was written in a letter from Nuremberg when he was still maintaining

– as he continued to do for the rest of his life – that no one else had known his purpose. Probably it was to tell her to maintain the pretence. Nothing in Nazi Germany can be taken at face value.

Ilse asked him when he would be back.

'I don't know exactly, perhaps tomorrow, but I'll certainly be home by Monday evening.'[19]

She did not believe him.

He left quickly to take leave of his sleeping son. Afterwards he pulled on a trench coat and went out to where his adjutant, Pintsch, his security officer and the driver waited by his Mercedes. A small suitcase containing little but a flat box of homoeopathic medicines, Ilse's Leica camera, his letter to the Duke of Hamilton, charts of his route, flying calculations and a wallet containing family photographs and Karl and Albrecht Haushofer's visiting cards had already been stowed in the boot. He climbed into the front seat beside the driver, the other two in the back, and they drove off to the autobahn towards Augsburg.[20]

They were ahead of schedule, and coming to a wooded stretch shortly before the exit to Augsburg Hess told the driver to pull in to the side. He climbed out, followed by Pintsch, and they walked in sunlight through crocuses and spring shoots into the trees. Focused on the flight ahead, he asked Pintsch for the weather reports. He was handed two flimsy sheets on which his adjutant had typed the details received from the Potsdam Weather Service that morning, and tried to memorise them as they walked on before returning to the car.[21]

At the Messerschmitt works all was prepared. Hess's personal twin-engined Me 110 was standing, fuelled and ready on the apron before the hangar as they arrived, pale blue-grey on the underside, mottled grey-green camouflage above, the black Luftwaffe cross on the side of the fuselage flanked by the code letters 'VJ + OQ'. Hess entered the administration building where he put on a Luftwaffe captain's uniform jacket made for him by a Munich tailor, and over it a fur-lined flying suit. Pintsch, who had followed him in with the suitcase, helped transfer the contents of the case to his pockets. He strapped the charts to his thighs and slung Ilse's camera around his neck.

Pintsch escorted him out to the runway, where he shook hands with the works group assembled around his plane before climbing up into the cockpit and beginning the starting rituals. Shortly, one after the other, the engines roared into life, clouds of whitish smoke billowing from their exhausts. It was some time before six – a quarter to six according to a chart he annotated later – when he gave the thumbs-up sign for the chocks to be pulled from under the wheels, and taxied away up-wind.[22]

Among the works party watching his plane rise into the bright evening sky and swing away northerly was his friend and collaborator, Professor Willi Messerschmitt. This has come to light almost by chance in the recent memoirs of Lord Colyton,[23] formerly Henry Hopkinson, 'C's liaison at the Foreign Office. He was told it by Messerschmitt himself when lunching with him in Marbella years after the war. If this was so it is significant that neither Pintsch nor any other witness at the Messerschmitt airfield that evening ever revealed it, suggesting a conspiracy of silence about the extent of the circle with pre-knowledge of Hess's mission.

FLIGHT

Hess's flight from southern Germany to Scotland at the height of the war was an exploit in which he took huge pride, with every reason. Later, in captivity, he described it in some detail in a letter to his son.[24] By then he had accepted that his mission had failed, and he planned suicide, in which circumstances the account carries all the weight of a last testament of a man who believed he was close to death. It is generally accepted by historians.

Nonetheless, there are doubts. Hess's flying instructor at the Messerschmitt works, the late Helmut Kaden, suggested that Hess invented the route he described to his son in order to avoid revealing to his British captors the way he had been able to avoid German air defences.[25] There are many other reasons for questioning his account – as will appear.

Leaving these aside for the time being, the route he described took him from Augsburg north-westerly (320°) to Bonn, thence north-north-westerly (335°) over the heavily defended industrial region of the Ruhr to the Zuider Zee and the Texel, where he made a 90° turn to the right towards Heligoland Bight for 23 minutes before resuming his north-north-westerly course up the eastern side of the North Sea beyond detection by British radar.

Reaching what he termed the 'North Point' of his flight shortly before 9.00 p.m., he turned left to a west-south-westerly (245°) course towards a 'Point B' he had marked on his chart near Bamburgh on the coast of Northumberland, just south of the Farne Islands; but finding it still too light to enter British airspace, he turned back after 20 minutes to the reciprocal course (65°) and flew back and forth between 245° and 65° for 'a long time' before making his approach to the English coast.

In letters to Ilse after the war, he recalled overwhelming feelings of loneliness and awe at the 'fabulous beauty' of the evening light over the North Sea. 'The many small clouds far below me looked like pieces of ice on the sea, crystal clear, all tinged with red',[26] but as he flew on they disappeared, and instead of the 'dense cloud at 500 metres [height]' forecast by Potsdam he was left without cover in a completely clear sky. He considered turning back, but the consequences did not bear thinking about. 'Hold on!' he told himself, 'come what may!'

In another letter, written on the eve of the seventh anniversary of his flight, he described sighting England at sunset on his final approach.[27] He had planned to make for Mount Cheviot as the most easily recognisable landmark, but from the distance he was unable to distinguish it from several hills rising above a low haze over the land; all he could do was steer for the one that looked most likely. It proved the right choice for he soon made out Holy Island and the chain of Farne Islands to seaward of the distinctive outline of that part of the Northumbrian coast he had studied on the map a hundred times at home. A convoy escorted by three warships in line abreast was steering between the islands and the shore. He held his course for the Cheviot to avoid them.

From this point on his track can be followed from British radar and, over the land, Royal Observer Corps records. They corroborate his description of diving from 3,000 metres (c. 10,000 feet) practically to sea level as he crossed the coast in order to attain maximum speed in case of pursuit. At 10.24 p.m. he roared in over the little town of

Bamburgh scarcely above the roofs at a speed of 750 kilometres per hour (c. 470mph), both engines at full throttle. He continued towards the Cheviot, skimming trees and houses, cattle and men in the fields and, as he recalled it later for Ilse, 'literally climbed the slope a few metres above the ground'.[28] At the top he altered course a few degrees right to 280° and scorched onwards, still so low that by his own account he waved at people in the fields, towards his next point of aim, a small lake in the hills by the peak of Broad Law; here he made another slight alteration to take him over the Duke of Hamilton's seat, Dungavel House.

By the time he passed over the estate it was too dark to make out the house. He had planned for this contingency and flew on to the west coast, crossing at West Kilbride. The Firth of Clyde was like a mirror under the moon; ahead a hill rose sheer from the water glowing red with the last of the light – 'a fabulous picture,' he recalled[29] – it was no doubt Little Cumbrae Island. Turning south, he swung in over the land again at Ardrossan and picked up the pattern of railway lines he had memorised, following the silver threads to a bend near Dungavel. He made out a small lake he had noted on his map to the south of the estate, but not the house itself.

His fuel was now very low. He had released two wing drop tanks that had provided the extra fuel needed to reach this distance; no doubt white warning lights for both main fuel tanks were glowing on his instrument panel. He pulled the control column back and climbed until at 2,000 metres (over 6,000 feet) he felt he had sufficient height for a parachute jump.[30] Switching off the engines, he swung the cockpit roof back and tried to climb from his seat, but the plane was still moving at speed and he was unable to force himself out against the wind pressure.[31] He suddenly remembered being told that the way to escape from a modern aircraft was to turn it on its back and let gravity do the rest. He turned the plane over, but he had never practised bailing out and instinctively pulled back on the control column as though performing the second half of a loop. With the machine upside down the nose headed for the ground. The centrifugal force generated caused the blood to drain from his head and he blacked out, consequently releasing his backward pressure on the stick. Fortunately the

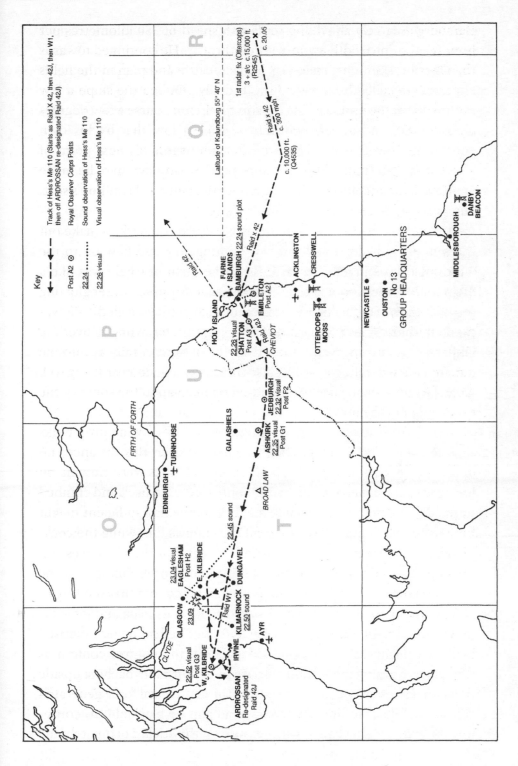

Key

--◄-- Track of Hess's Me 110 (Starts as Raid X 42, then 42J, then W1,
        then off ARDROSSAN re-designated Raid 42J)
⊙ Post A2   Royal Observer Corps Posts
22.24 ...... Sound observation of Hess's Me 110
22.26 visual Visual observation of Hess's Me 110

plane had now completed the bottom arc of the loop and was heading vertically upwards, the speed falling away rapidly. He came to again with the machine standing on its tail, stalled, the speed dial register-ing zero. He pushed out with both legs, propelling himself from the cockpit and falling, striking his right foot hard on a part of the tail as he plunged past.[32] At the same instant the aircraft itself began to fall. He pulled on the ripcord of his parachute. 'The harness tightened, I hung – an indescribably glorious and triumphant feeling in this situation!'[33]

He floated down on to a grassy field, white under the moon, stum-bling and falling as he hit the ground, and once again blacked out.

* * *

There are questions about what Hess omitted from his accounts of his flight for Buz and Ilse. They concern his radio navigation instruments, the operation of which he was determined to conceal from his British captors. There is also a question over whether he really intended a night landing at Dungavel. It would have been an extremely hazardous undertaking. In the letter telling Ilse how he considered turning back when he saw there was no cloud cover over England, he described his thoughts: 'Night landing with the plane – that cannot go well. And even if nothing should happen to me the Me[sserschmitt] would be smashed up, possibly irreparably.'[34] And years later, coming up to the ninth anniversary of his flight, he wrote to her about a compass he had worn on his wrist, 'intended to guide me after my jump, when I stepped out of the parachute to make my way to Dungavel. However ... in the struggle to get free of my plane ... I landed a couple of hours' march from Dungavel.'[35]

These excerpts surely suggest he had intended from the beginning to bail out over Dungavel, not to attempt a landing on Hamilton's grass strip. This is lent support by a note in the navigation calculations found on Hess and held for a time at the RAF navigators' school. Against 'Du', presumably Dungavel, since his starting point is designated 'Au' for Augsburg, is the note 'Kabine auf', meaning 'Cockpit open'.[36] For what purpose would he open the cockpit at 'Du' other than to bail out? Yet this was as inherently dangerous as a night landing, and hardly the way for such a high-ranking peace envoy to arrive. It is a great puzzle.

A far larger question is whether he made the flight on his own initiative, as he maintained to the end of his life, or whether he was sent on an unattributable mission for the Führer. If the latter, it is difficult to believe that Hitler would not have insisted on fighter cover for his deputy on the potentially hazardous daylight leg over the North Sea.

There are small clues that this might have been the case: Heydrich's widow, Lina, wrote a memoir after the war in which she claimed that her husband learned of Hess's flight 'while he was "residing" on the Channel [coast] and likewise piloting Me 109s [fighter aircraft] towards England'.[37] It is hard to imagine why Himmler's chief of security should be flying fighter missions to Britain at this period shortly before the great offensive against Russia in which his *Einsatz* groups were to play a key role exterminating Bolsheviks and Jews behind the lines unless he was involved in an equally vital task, such as protecting the Deputy Führer.

A further indication comes from Hans-Bernd Gisevius, the *Abwehr* representative in Zürich and informer for the German opposition through MI6's agent, Halina Szymańska. He was close to Heydrich's chief of criminal police, Arthur Nebe, who told him that Heydrich was flying over the North Sea on the day of Hess's flight. On his return to head office Nebe asked him whether he could by chance have shot down the Deputy Führer. Unusually Heydrich was lost for words; then he replied curtly that if he had done so it would have been a historic coincidence – so Gisevius told Heydrich's biographer after the war.[38]

Another mystery concerns Göring. It is difficult to imagine Hess flying through the heavily defended airspace over the Ruhr without Göring's knowledge or consent. The air ace Adolf Galland was commanding a fighter group on the Channel coast at this period and in his post-war memoirs recalled in the evening of 10 May receiving a very agitated telephone call from Göring ordering him to take off with his whole group. 'The Deputy Führer has gone mad and is flying to England in an Me 110,' Göring told him. 'He must be brought down.'[39]

Galland wondered who had gone mad: the light was failing; there were many Me 110s in the air on service trial flights; how were they to tell which one Hess was flying? As a token response he ordered each of his wing commanders to send up one or two planes; he did not tell them why. By his account there were about ten minutes left until dark. If he meant civil twilight this places Göring's call at about ten o'clock as Hess was making his final leg towards the Northumbrian coast. Why Göring should have given such a pointless order – indeed why the Reichsmarschall, who had extended so many peace feelers himself, should have wanted the envoy shot down – is hard to imagine; it is harder to conceive why Galland should have made the story up.

Karl-Heinz Pintsch in his post-war account to James Leasor said that after Hess had taken off he waited in the Messerschmitt administrative building until shortly after nine, then phoned the branch of the Air Ministry in Berlin responsible for the directional radio beams used by German bombers to find their targets. Speaking on behalf of the Deputy Führer, he asked for a beam from Augsburg to Dungavel Hill, 15km west of Glasgow. He was told this was difficult as they had a big raid over Britain that night, but a beam could be provided until 22.00.[40] If true, this would not have helped Hess, who did not reach the British coast until some twenty minutes later. However, Pintsch's call provides a possible explanation for Göring's knowledge.

BRITISH AIR DEFENCES

If a remarkable story printed in *The Yorkshire Post* in 1969 is to be believed – and there is no reason not to believe it – Hess was expected that night. The story came from Albert James Heal, who in 1941 had been Yorkshire Area Secretary of the Transport and General Workers' Union.[41] He claimed that at about midday on 9 May he had had a telephone call from Ernest Bevin, Minister of Labour in Churchill's government, who had asked him to go to the Civic Hall, Sheffield, that evening; Bevin was to address a regional conference there and needed to speak to him urgently.

When Heal arrived Bevin took him into a private room and produced a coded message, which, he said, he had just received from one of his industrial contacts inside Germany. The code was one that Heal had devised when secretary of the South Wales 'No More War' movement. He had taught it to a London girl, evidently now Bevin's 'industrial contact' inside Germany. Decoded, the message appeared to say that Rudolf Hess was to fly to Britain to meet the Duke of Hamilton. Heal asked for more time to check this. Meanwhile Bevin had to deliver a speech in Leeds. Heal drove him there, then went to work again on the code, and satisfied himself that his original interpretation was correct: Hess was about to fly to Hamilton with peace proposals. After his speech Bevin phoned Churchill. Heal, who overheard a part of the conversation, gained the impression that Churchill treated it as a joke.

The following morning at 9.30 Heal met Bevin again and was told that Hess had arrived in Scotland; he was under no circumstances to divulge the information. Of course, on Heal's chronology that morning was 10 May, and Hess was still at his home in Harlaching. Yet Heal was recalling events almost 30 years later; no doubt he had simply worked back one day from the 10th,[42] when Hess was known to have made his flight. In fact the conference in Leeds at which Bevin spoke was not on the 9th, but the 10th. The following morning was therefore the 11th, and Hess had indeed arrived. Heal's account thus becomes wholly plausible, the more so because it is hard to think why a trade union official should invent such a basically preposterous tale.

Testimony that Hess was known to be in the air even earlier in the evening of the 10th comes from James Douglas, then Duty Supervisor in the Mayfair, London, Information Bureau of the BBC Monitoring Service. Douglas recalls receiving what was termed a 'flash' message from the BBC Listening Centre at Evesham at some time around 8.00 p.m. Evesham had picked up a south German (Douglas thinks Munich) radio station announcement that the Deputy Führer had taken off on a flight and had not returned. Douglas asked Evesham to put it on the teleprinter, which they did, and he immediately sent it to the Air Ministry and Fighter Command Headquarters. Subsequently he received two further messages with additional details including the type of plane Hess was flying and the direction in which he was heading. When Douglas left the Bureau at 11.30 p.m. Hess was, so far as he knew, still missing in an aeroplane, and on reaching home he told his wife. She remembers this well.[43]

The difficulty with the story is that there is no trace either in the BBC digests of monitored enemy broadcasts or in the boxes of raw 'flash' forms retained in the Imperial War Museum archives of any message about Hess on 10 May. On the other hand both sources have what is regarded as the first announcement of Hess having taken an aeroplane and disappeared broadcast by the Deutschlandsender, Berlin, on 12 May.

The obvious inference is that after some 60 years Douglas's memory had slipped by two days. In order to test this, the 12 May Berlin announcement of Hess's disappearance was read out to Douglas, omitting the date. 'Hess started on Saturday 10 May at about 1800 from Augsburg on a flight from which he has not returned up to now. A letter which he left behind unfortunately showed in its confusion the traces of mental disturbance ...'[44] On hearing 'confusion' and 'mental disturbance' Douglas said this was quite definitely not one of the flash messages he had received that night. The 12 May announcement ended with the presumption that as nothing had been heard from Hess he must have 'crashed or met with a similar accident'. Douglas would hardly have alerted the Air Ministry and Fighter Command to a message about an aircraft that had taken off two days before and was presumed lost. Moreover, the 12 May announcement from Berlin was reported on the BBC nine o'clock news the same night. Therefore, if Douglas had received the messages on the 12th rather than the 10th his wife would have known that Hess was missing before he returned and told her after midnight. Yet she remembers being surprised.[45]

There are two possible explanations. The BBC Monitoring Service came under the Ministry of Information, whose Director General was Walter Monkton. He worked closely with the security services, and in view of the sensitivity of Hess's arrival, could have ordered the suppression of any mention of these broadcasts in the daily digests, and the physical removal or destruction of the flash forms.

Alternatively the messages were not broadcasts picked up by the BBC Monitoring Service but radio signals intercepted by the 'Y' Service, which monitored enemy signals traffic. As seen earlier, Adolf Galland had wondered at Göring giving him such an apparently pointless order with regard to Hess's flight; if we consider the possibility that Göring supplemented his telephone call with *en clair* radio messages then perhaps the communication was always intended to be picked up by the British and alert them to the fact Hess was coming. It is even possible that Willi Messerschmitt himself sent signals to alert the British to Hess's flight; some weeks later he sent Air Vice Marshal Trafford Leigh Mallory a coded warning that parachutists would be dropped under cover of a raid on Luton to assassinate the Deputy Führer – as will appear.

Whatever form of communication was used, Hess was expected that night. Apart from Albert Heal's testimony, there is too much confirmation from other sources to doubt it – as will become clear.

* * *

British air defence relied on a chain of radar installations known as Radio Direction Finding (RDF) stations around the coast, and, once the enemy had come in over land, on Royal Observer Corps (ROC) posts manned chiefly by over-fighting-age volunteers who monitored the onward movement of the intruders by sight or sound bearings. RDF posts reported to Fighter Command Headquarters at Bentley Priory, near Stanmore, Middlesex, where aircraftwomen 'tellers' at a plotting table in the 'Filter Room' placed markers to represent the position, estimated number, altitude and course of the aircraft on the table-top chart, updating it as further reports came in. When the ROC posts took over they reported to their respective sector centres.

Hess was picked up first at 10.10 p.m. some 70 miles from the coast by the RDF station at Ottercops Moss, north of Newcastle-upon-Tyne, and reported as 'three plus aircraft' at approximately 15,000 feet.[46] The report caused considerable scepticism since Ottercops Moss was situated in a hilly area and had a reputation for reporting false echoes from atmospherics. Nevertheless, as the reports continued the track was plotted under the designation 'Raid X (unidentified) 42', course due west, speed 'approximately 300mph'. Four more RDF stations picked up the echo as it neared the coast, but they all reported it as a single aircraft; a subsequent investigation by the Operational Research Section of Fighter Command accepted this majority estimate.[47]

Two Spitfires from RAF Acklington already on patrol over the Farne Islands were vectored on to the raid,[48] and at 10.21 another Spitfire was scrambled from Acklington;[49] two would have been unable to keep together in the gathering darkness. The pilot of this plane, Sergeant Maurice Pocock, a veteran of the Battle of Britain, was instructed to patrol the airfield at 15,000 feet, but as he reached 8,000 feet he was told on his radio telephone that the enemy was descending rapidly on a north-westerly course, and was an Me 110; he was directed on to the same heading, but saw nothing against the dark background of hills. Half an hour later he was recalled to base.[50]

The identification of an Me 110 flying at 50 feet had come from the ROC post at Chatton a few miles inland from Bamburgh at 10.25 p.m.[51] It was generally disbelieved even when confirmed by other ROC posts beneath Hess's westward flight track, because an Me 110 lacked the fuel endurance to get home again.[52]

Meanwhile the coastal RDF stations reported Raid 42 circling away north-easterly over the Farne Islands.[53] The lone aircraft flying west across country was assumed to have broken off from this formation and was consequently given the split-raid designation '42J'. The later Operational Research investigators concluded that the outgoing echo 'was not that of Raid 42 but a fighter aircraft despatched to intercept Raid 42'[54] – in short that the fighter was being vectored on to its own radar echo. It is not clear which fighter. It could not have been Pocock, who had been directed overland north-westerly.

Before the formal investigation it was assumed at RAF Ouston, headquarters of No. 13 Fighter Group responsible for this area, that the confusing echoes may have been from the two fighters on patrol over the Farne Islands: 'RDF plotted raid [42] as travelling towards Holy Island and turning E fading. This may have arisen from plots of 72 White [two Spitfires of 72 Squadron] who were detailed to raid and were searching off Farne and Holy Islands.'[55]

The operations record book (ORB) of No. 72 Squadron contains no record of these two Spitfires or any other fighters aloft at this time.[56] It is also curious that if the outgoing track was actually a Spitfire or Spitfires, the 'Identification Friend or Foe' (IFF) radio transponders with which they were equipped to mark them as friendly did not respond. Without the raw information on which the later investigators based their secret report it is idle to speculate on these apparent anomalies; an omission by the officer who wrote up No 72 Squadron's ORB and malfunctioning IFF are probably to blame.

It could, of course, be suggested that Raid 42 consisted of Hess's escort of Me 109 fighters led by Heydrich swinging back out to sea, leaving their charge to continue on his westerly course overland, but this is in the highest degree unlikely. Even if Heydrich did escort Hess some of the way up the North Sea, he would have lacked the fuel endurance to stay with him while he flew back and forth waiting for darkness before approaching the British coast.

Hess's plane was sighted by ROC posts at Jedburgh at 10.30 p.m.[57] and Ashkirk moments later; both reported it correctly as an Me 110. There were no further posts on his westerly track and it was not until 10.45, as he neared Dungavel, that his plane was detected again by sound from Glasgow ROC; the speed was estimated by sound bearings as 300mph, and on this data alone Glasgow reported the plane as probably an Me 110.[58]

Meanwhile, RAF Ayr on the Scottish west coast, some 30 miles south-west of Glasgow, 20 miles west of Dungavel House, had been alerted to a fast-moving bandit moving towards their sector; and at 10.35 p.m. Pilot Officer William 'Bill' Cuddie had been sent up in a Defiant night fighter to intercept.[59] He was instructed, 'Scramble Angels two five – zero nine degrees' (Climb to 2,500 feet, steer 009°), and when he had attained this height, 'Dive and buster – vector three five zero' (Dive at full throttle, enemy at 350°).[60] Defiants had a rear gunner behind the pilot; by flying below the enemy they were able to see it in silhouette against the night sky and were proving successful night fighters. However, Hess was also flying low. Cuddie did not see him.

There is no doubt that although Hess was expected in some quarters that night he was not deliberately allowed through British air defences: the two known pilots ordered to intercept him, Cuddie and Pocock would certainly have shot him down if they had seen him,[61] and it must be assumed the two unknown and unrecorded pilots of 72 White patrolling the Farne Islands would also have done so, since they were controlled by Acklington.

However, a recent book by a Czech military archivist, Jiri Rajlich,[62] claims that two Czech Hurricane pilots of 245 Squadron, RAF Aldergrove, Northern Ireland, were also vectored on to Hess's Me 110 that night and did sight him but were ordered to break off action just as they were going in for the kill. Rajlich based his account on the testimony of one of the two pilots, both of whom have since died, and his flying logs. There is no mention of times in the flying log,[63] certainly no mention of their patrol in the ORB of RAF Aldergrove, and the pilots are not recorded as being in the air at the time. That is understandable, for if such an extraordinary incident did occur it would have been kept out of the ORB and all parties would have been sworn to secrecy.[64]

Of more significance for any theory that Hess was allowed through British air defences – because it is documented – are the actions, or rather the inaction, of the Duke of Hamilton. He was on duty that night at the controller's desk at RAF Turnhouse. For the base commander to be on late night duty seems surprising in itself, especially since he had flown a Hurricane to RAF Drem that afternoon and practised a dog-fight over the Firth of Forth with his second in command.[65] However, it is not possible to study the Turnhouse duty rosters to discover how usual or unusual it was for the base commander to stand night duty.

Although Hess did not enter the Turnhouse sector until towards the end of his flight, Turnhouse and Drem, which came under control from Turnhouse, were the only two RAF bases in a position to scramble fighters that failed to do so. Moreover, as Hess moved towards Glasgow and into the Clyde (Anti-Aircraft) Gun Defended Area, which was controlled by Turnhouse, requests to open fire were refused, and no air-raid sirens were sounded.[66] This was extraordinary since the aircraft was heading towards a city that had been subjected to recent bombing raids.

An NCO at AA Brigade headquarters, Glagow, remembers the 'flap' that night as the unidentified aircraft that did not respond to challenge and ignored requests to show the colours of the day moved through the sights of at least two heavy AA batteries and Turnhouse refused permission to open fire.[67] An intelligence officer on duty in the gun operations room that night has explained that Turnhouse rejected the Observer Corps identification of an Me 110; Hess's plane was therefore 'unidentified' and it was the rule not to fire on 'unidentified' planes.[68] This is difficult to accept in view of the imminent danger to the inhabitants of Glasgow, and the very different reaction to 'Raid 42J' from RAF Ouston, Acklington and Ayr; indeed it is very hard to account for Hamilton's inaction unless he was expecting Hess.

ROC observers on a hill at West Kilbride on the coast of the Firth of Clyde were alerted to the approach of an Me 110 by ROC Glasgow, and heard the roar of the engines before they sighted Hess's plane speeding towards them very low. At 10.52 p.m. it shot past, actually below the level of their observation post, and so close they were able to make out every detail in the moonlight: the black crosses on wings and fuselage, the swastika on the distinctive twin tail fin, as it swung out over the firth and turned southwards.[69]

The next report came from the ROC post at Ardrossan, just south, as Hess headed inland again and began following the railway line to Kilmarnock. Finally, soon after 11.00 p.m. he was sighted almost overhead from the ROC post at the edge of Eaglesham Moor, some twelve miles north-west of Dungavel House. He baled out as they watched. They saw his parachute open and the aeroplane falling away and diving out of control. Moments later flames lit the sky and they heard the crash. It was nine minutes past eleven.[70]

HAUPTMANN ALFRED HORN

Hess was helped out of his parachute harness by David McLean, head ploughman at Floors Farm, Eaglesham, just south of Glasgow, where he had come down. McLean asked whether he was British or German. 'German,' Hess replied, and after introducing himself in English as *Hauptmann* (Captain) Alfred Horn, said he wanted to go to Dungavel House; he had an important message for the Duke of Hamilton.[71] No doubt McClean told him he was only some twelve miles from Dungavel.

He had difficulty putting his weight on the ankle he had struck while falling out of his plane, and McLean helped him limp from the field to the farm cottage in which he lived with his mother and sister. There Hess was made comfortable in a capacious armchair by the fireside

175

and McLean's mother offered him tea. He asked for water instead according to his own account, but a young private in the 3rd Battalion Renfrewshire Home Guard who had heard his plane overhead, seen him bale out and the plane crash and had made his way to the cottage, found him drinking tea in the kitchen when he arrived, watched closely by McLean. The private, Alan Starling, was particularly struck by his flying boots, which were of a quality he had never seen before. The airman reached into a pocket and showed them all photographs of his wife and family, saying 'in very good English' that his name was Horn and asking again if he was anywhere near the Duke of Hamilton's house. 'The Duke of Hamilton,' he kept repeating. 'Where is the Duke of Hamilton?'[72]

Shortly two sergeants from a secret signals unit nearby arrived at the cottage. They too had heard Hess's plane overhead and seen him descending by parachute. One, Daniel McBride, began questioning Hess, who again asked to be taken to Dungavel House; he was, he said, a friend of the Duke of Hamilton and had an important message for him.[73] At this point Alan Starling heard another plane overhead, and going outside saw it was a Boulton Paul Defiant[74] – evidently the plane that had been sent up from RAF Ayr to intercept the intruder.

It is extraordinary, and possibly significant, that in addition to signing 'Alfred Horn' on a scrap of paper McBride produced and again fetching out the photographs of Ilse and young Buz from his pocket to show him, Hess gave McBride the Iron Cross he had won in the First World War.[75] Perhaps he wanted him to show it to Hamilton as proof of his arrival. Whatever the reason, a bond seems to have formed between them. After the war McBride sent Hess Christmas cards every year, corresponded with Ilse and Wolf Rüdiger Hess and joined their campaign to free Hess from Spandau jail. It appears he believed Hess had been unfairly treated and it seems reasonable to ascribe this to what he had learned at his signals unit that night, for two years after the war, while working in the Far East, he wrote an article for the *Hong Kong Telegraph* stating 'with confidence' that high-ranking government officials were aware of Hess's coming.[76]

As noted earlier, Bevin had learned he was coming and had informed Churchill;[77] and it is claimed, although without documentary proof, that both the Air Ministry and RAF Fighter Command had been informed that Hess had taken off in an Me 110 and was heading northwards.[78] Knowledge of his mission in the highest quarters is surely the key to the otherwise baffling inaction of RAF intelligence officers from nearby bases that night. Although Hess told everyone he met, including Home Guard, RAF and ROC officers, that he wanted to talk to the Duke of Hamilton and had an important message for him, although the two nearest RAF bases, Ayr and Abbotsinch, were informed of this and Hamilton at RAF Turnhouse was rung at least four times and told that the German pilot had something important to tell him, no intelligence officer was sent to interview Hess until the following morning.

The official reports of the units involved are telling: thus at 00.36 on the 11th, almost an hour and a half after the first reports of the crashed plane, Clyde Sub-Area heard from the unit originally detailed to escort the enemy pilot into detention, 'airman injured, thought to be serious, wanting to talk.'[79] This was passed to the duty officer at Glasgow Area Command, Captain A.G. White:

> ... as the man had asked for the Duke of Hamilton I thought he might be a profitable subject for immediate interrogation by the RAF Interrogation Officer ... I accordingly rang TURNHOUSE aerodrome. I got through at once and asked for Ft. Lt. Benson [RAF Interrogation Officer]. I was told that Ft. Lt. Benson was not available but that I was speaking to Ops 'B' Turnhouse and that the Duty Pilot was actually speaking. I narrated the same story to him and was informed that they had the story already both from the Observer Corps and from Ayr Aerodrome. He added that Ft. Lt. Benson had already been informed of the story and that he would leave for Glasgow at 08.30 hs. the following morning.
>
> I told the Duty Pilot that it seems to me that this was not an ordinary case and again enquired if Ft. Lt. Benson was aware of the whole facts. The Duty Pilot replied that I had told him nothing new.[80]

This response from Turnhouse was contrary to normal procedure. Standing orders required enemy airmen to be interrogated as soon as possible, when they might still be in shock and sufficiently disori-entated to give something away. The sequence of contacts for enemy airmen was laid down in instructions as 'unit making capture – RAF Interrogation Officer – Command Cage'.[81] Captain White had done his best in this regard. Turnhouse had rebuffed him. Reviewing the case later, Colonel R. Firebrace of Scottish Area Intelligence commented:

> If it is true that the RAF authorities were informed before 0100/11 that an important prisoner was anxious to make a statement to them, their laxity is most unfortunate as the prisoner might have had urgent operational information to divulge. It can only be assumed that the decision to do nothing until the morning was taken by Wing Commander the Duke of Hamilton and that in consequence Flt/Lt Benson could not go post haste to the spot as he should nor-mally have done.[82]

Glasgow Area Headquarters, Scottish Command, took up the ques-tion of the interrogation officer's late arrival to interview the prisoner, but if a report was ever issued, it has not been released.[83]

* * *

After his remarkable flight and providential landing, the hospitable reception in the farm cottage and his expectation that McBride might take him or his message for Hamilton to Dungavel, Hess experienced only helpless frustration. A group from the local Home Guard with other men collected on the way burst into the cottage led by a lieu-tenant in civilian clothes who had evidently been drinking and was brandishing a large First World War Webley pistol. Hess, who assumed he was a civil official, asked to be taken to Hamilton at Dungavel. Instead the lieutenant marched him outside, as Hess described it later for Ilse, 'pushing his gigantic revolver into my back, his tense finger on the trigger as he stumbled, belching merrily and continuously.'[84]

He was bundled into a car and driven a few miles to a Girl Guides hut in the next village of Busby, which served as headquarters for 'C' Company, 3rd Battalion Renfrewshire Home Guard. Ordered into a side room by the pistol-waving lieutenant, he lay down on the bare floor in a yoga relaxation position he often practised. It was a quarter to midnight,[85] almost six hours since he had taken off from Augsburg, and he was weary. His spirits were revived when 'a really nice little Tommy'[86] offered him a bottle of milk he had brought for his own night watch.

After a wait due to jammed telephone lines he was driven to battalion headquarters in a Scout hut about a mile up the road in Giffnock, arriving at fourteen minutes past midnight.[87] Again he asked to see Hamilton; again, it seemed to him, his request fell on deaf ears – but the message was being passed up the command chain, often embellished. The RAF had been informed, and it was about this time that Captain White at Glasgow Area Command was told that the prisoner had called to see the Duke of Hamilton, whom he (the prisoner) knew very well.[88] Another report suggested the prisoner was so seriously injured he might not last the night.[89] White, as noted, rang RAF Turnhouse to alert the intelligence officer, Flight Lieutenant Benson.

Meanwhile two police officers arrived at the Giffnock Scout hut and assisted in searching Hess, placing everything found in his pockets on a small table and itemising it in a list.[90] According to James Leasor's pioneer study of Hess's mission, the contents included an envelope addressed to the Duke of Hamilton, a hypodermic syringe, a small, flat box of homeopathic drugs, a gold watch, the Leica camera he had borrowed from Ilse, photographs of himself and his son and Ilse and his son, and the visiting cards of Professor Karl Haushofer and Albrecht Haushofer, the latter sewn inside his uniform jacket.[91] To this list must be added ten 100 Reichsmark notes, a small electric torch and a safety razor blade, reported in later investigations,[92] and also the maps he had strapped to his thighs. However, it is not known exactly what he had with him because the inventory drawn up at Giffnock and another made as he was transferred between different units that night are missing from the reports to which they were originally attached.[93]

The absence of both inventories cannot be coincidence. They have been removed from the file, and it is hard to think of any reason other than that they bore testimony to a letter from Hess to Hamilton – as described by Leasor – for this too is missing from the open files. Since Hess is known from a variety of sources to have written one or more letters to Hamilton, rendered into good English by Ernst Bohle, and the letter or letters have never come to light, it is evidently the content rather than the existence of a letter that had to be suppressed.

Other arrivals at the Scout hut included a group captain from RAF Abbotsinch; a wing commander and a squadron leader from RAF Ayr; an RAF intelligence officer whose base was not recorded, and who seems to have taken no part in interrogating Hess;[94] the assistant group observer from Glasgow ROC Centre, Major Graham Donald, together with a young pilot home on leave, named Malcolm, whom Donald had met while viewing the wreckage of Hess's plane;[95] and a Pole named Roman Battaglia who worked at the Polish Consulate in Glasgow and was called in by the police as a German speaker to help with the interrogation of the prisoner.[96] Asked later about his interrogation, Battaglia gave a scathing account of conditions in the Scout hut:

> of the 15 or 20 persons present [Home Guards and others] there seemed to be no official interrogator ... he [Battaglia] was asked to put questions from all corners of the room, some of which he considered offensive and which he refused to ask. No accurate record ... was made of the interrogation, and people wandered round the room inspecting the prisoner and his belongings at their leisure.[97]

Despite this, Battaglia said, Hess remained completely calm throughout, only occasionally showing slight distress by leaning forward and sinking his head in his hands. Asked why he had come, Hess said once again that he had a message for the Duke of Hamilton.

'What is this message about?'

'It is in the highest interest of the British Air Force.' Hess refused to say more.[98]

At one point, Major Donald of the ROC took up the questioning. Hess told him he had landed deliberately with 'a vital secret message for the Duke of Hamilton', and showing him Dungavel House marked on his map, said he hoped he was close to it.[99] Donald had spent some time in Munich during the 1920s and as he scrutinised the prisoner he thought he recognised him. Hess recounted the incident afterwards in a letter to Ilse:

> A Major among them [RAF officers] stared at me for a long time and then said suddenly in faultless German that I looked exactly like Rudolf Hess ... I replied innocently it was no news to me that I looked like Hess – a fact which had embarrassed me often enough.[100]

Donald then produced a sheaf of small aircraft identification cards, selected one showing an Me 110 and asked Hess to sign his name. He obliged, writing, 'Alfred Horn 10.5.1941'. Donald was nevertheless confident he was looking at Hess, claiming afterwards that he had tried to convince the others around him, but only provoked shouts of incredulous laughter. This is not mentioned in either Battaglia's or Hess's accounts, and the Home Guard battalion commander took the suggestion sufficiently seriously to ask the prisoner for identification. Hess had already been searched but managed to produce from the breast pocket of his tunic an envelope addressed to Hauptmann Alfred Horn with a Munich postmark. This seemed to settle it. Nevertheless, the battalion commander recognised that this was no ordinary pilot, 'particularly as it was obvious that his uniform was new and of particularly good quality, and had not seen service.'[101]

Donald returned to his ROC Centre at about 2.00 a.m. by his own account, immediately rang RAF Turnhouse and told the duty officer to advise the Wing Commander (Hamilton) that the German pilot had an important message for him, and that he was none other than Rudolf Hess.[102] This is no doubt true, since Donald stated his conviction of the airman's real identity in his official report written later the same day, the 11th,[103] long before the country at large learned of the Deputy Führer's arrival in Scotland.

It was two hours from Hess's arrival at the Scout hut before a military unit arrived to escort him to Maryhill Barracks, Paisley,[104] where he was to be detained for the night. The reasons for the long wait are probably connected with the late hour and busy telephone lines. A senior Home Guard officer, Major Barrie, drove Hess, with his possessions and the lieutenant and two men of the escort, to Maryhill Barracks, arriving at 2.30 a.m. No preparations had been made. They found the duty officer sitting up in bed in pyjamas. After persuading him to dress, Barrie drove Hess to the barracks hospital where the medical officer attended to his ankle and provided a sleeping draught, which Hess had requested. An empty room was found, a bed moved in and Hess was left to sleep under guard.[105]

Returning to the duty officer, Barrie handed over Hess's personal possessions 'and obtained the accompanying receipt'[106] – no longer attached to his report in The National Archives. It was by then after 4.00 a.m. Before leaving, Barrie heard the duty officer take a call from Area Command to say that the intelligence officer would not see the prisoner until 09.00, 'which, in my opinion, Barrie wrote, 'was too late as it gave the prisoner time to collect himself and make up some story.'[107]

'ARE YOU REALLY HESS?'

On the morning of 10 May, it will be recalled, Hamilton had written to Group Captain D.L. Blackford of Air Intelligence agreeing to regard the proposal to send him to Lisbon to contact Albrecht Haushofer as in abeyance.[108] That afternoon he had flown a Hurricane to RAF Drem and practised a dogfight with his second in command over the Firth of Forth.[109] This does not appear in the ORB of No. 603 Squadron, but non-operational flights were not necessarily recorded.

That evening, as Hess's Me 110 was plotted in over the coast and across the country as 'Raid 42J', Hamilton was on duty at the controller's desk in the operations room at RAF Turnhouse. He rejected the ROC identification of an Me 110 because, as he put it in his subsequent report for Churchill, 'this fighter type of aircraft had only once before been seen as far north as Northumberland (on August 15), and without extra fuel tanks could not make return flight.'[110]

A young Wren named Nancy Mary Goodall on the naval liaison desk in the ops. room that night remembers the incident. Her father, Squadron Leader W. Geoffrey Moore, was Deputy Commandant of the Scottish Command of the ROC and when the ROC identification was dismissed she felt the honour of the Corps at stake and asked why the plane could not be an Me 110. 'Because it wouldn't have enough fuel to get home,' was the reply, as if to a child.[111]

The ROC reports were also disbelieved at Fighter Command headquarters, Bentley Priory, and for the same reason. It was assumed instead that the plane was a Dornier 17 light bomber,[112] which also had twin engines and tail fins, and the plot of Raid 42J was passed to No. 13 Group headquarters, from thence to sector operations rooms, including Turnhouse, as hostile. So it is a question, as noted earlier, why Hamilton treated the aircraft as unidentified and refused permission for anti-aircraft fire or air-raid warnings when it entered the Clyde area controlled by Turnhouse.

Some time after learning the plane had crashed, Hamilton handed over to the night duty officer and went to bed in his house near the base. Later he was recalled to the operations room to take a message about the German pilot. Nancy Goodall remembers this as being about half an hour to an hour after the report of the plane crashing, and recalls the general amazement: 'The Duke took the call from the telephone on the Controller's desk, and appeared to be wearing his uniform over his pyjamas. He looked a very worried man.'[113] She retains a distinct image of him 'standing up, hunched over the phone, holding it in his shoulder, and looking extremely horrified'. Everyone remarked on his evident worry. The word went around that he had been called to speak to the German pilot.

Hamilton had at least four calls about the German pilot that night, from the ROC, from the controller at RAF Ayr who had been notified by the local police, from Captain White at Area Command and finally from Major Donald, by his reckoning at about 2.00 a.m., to tell him that the prisoner was Rudolf Hess. It remains unclear which of these calls Nancy Goodall witnessed.

Years later Hamilton's wife, then the Dowager Duchess, remembered him being called from his bed twice by messages about the German pilot.[114] That Nancy Goodall remembered only one occasion may be because she had gone off duty by the time of the second call, or alternatively because the second call was a message passed to him in his house by the duty controller.

Nancy Goodall's watch probably ended at midnight; she cannot be certain, but afterwards she had a twenty-minute drive to her father's rented house at Cramond, near Turnhouse, and it was dark when she arrived. Her father was up and she told him about the German pilot who had asked to speak to the CO. He said he was going to breach confidence; swearing her to absolute secrecy, he told her that the pilot was Rudolf Hess.[115]

If her watch ended at midnight, as the details of her recollection suggest, this would have been about 00.30 on the 11th, long before Donald had recognised Hess and made his call to Hamilton. But even if it was later and Donald had also phoned Nancy's father, why should he have spoken to her of 'breaching confidence' on the unsupported word of one of his Observer Corps officers?

According to the Duchess's recollection, when Hamilton was woken for the second time 'in the middle of the night', he said to her, 'I'll have to go, it's to do with the crashed plane.' He left and she did not see him again until about four o'clock that afternoon.[116]

It is less than 50 miles from RAF Turnhouse to Maryhill Barracks in Paisley, where Hess was taken that morning at about 2.30. If Hamilton and his intelligence officer, Flight Lieutenant Benson, had driven straight there after the last call from Donald at about 2.00 a.m. they would have arrived before Major Barrie and the military escort had left. The roads would have been empty of traffic. Yet Major Barrie heard the duty officer taking a call to say that the interrogating officer would arrive at 9.00 a.m.[117]

It is impossible to know how Hamilton and Benson spent their time between about 2.00 a.m. and 9.00 a.m. when they were due to arrive at Maryhill – or 10.00 a.m. when by Hamilton's account they did arrive. On top of the mystery of why Hamilton did not send Benson immediately to interrogate this prisoner who wanted to talk, this is a further mystery.

John Harris has recently discovered that Hamilton's colleague and lifelong friend, Wing Commander David McIntyre, his co-pilot in the flight over Everest, was taken to meet Hess on his arrival in Scotland.[118] McIntyre was chief executive officer at RAF Ayr, and it will be recalled that a wing commander and a squadron leader from Ayr arrived at the

Scout hut in Giffnock while Hess was there. Perhaps Hamilton conferred with McIntyre during the missing hours. That is speculation.

Precisely what Hess told Hamilton when he arrived at Maryhill Barracks hospital with Benson at ten o'clock on the morning of the 11th is also subject to speculation. Hamilton's report states that after inspecting the prisoner's effects he entered the prisoner's room accompanied by the interrogating officer and the military officer on guard: 'The prisoner, who I had no recollection of ever having seen before, at once requested that I should speak to him alone. I then asked the other officers to withdraw, which they did.'[119]

This was hardly the normal response of a senior officer confronting a prisoner of war. The explanation is, surely, that Hamilton was aware already that this was the Deputy Führer. Yet that was not the impression he gave Hess, who in a subsequent letter to Ilse described Hamilton as not believing it could be him until, as they spoke, he gradually realised it must be, and said 'in complete astonishment, "Are you really Hess?"'.[120]

Hamilton's report goes on to state:

> The German opened by saying that he had seen me in Berlin at the Olympic Games in 1936, and that I had lunched in his house. He said, 'I do not know if you recognise me but I am Rudolph Hess ...'
>
> From Press photographs and Albrecht Haushofer's description of Hess, I believed that this prisoner was indeed Hess himself ...

Hess, his report continued, went on to state that he was 'on a mission of humanity'; the Führer did not wish to defeat England and wished to stop fighting. This was the fourth time he (Hess) had tried to fly to Dungavel; on the previous occasions he had been turned back by bad weather. The report continued:

> The fact that Reichminister, Hess, had come to this country in person would, he stated, show his sincerity and Germany's willingness for peace. He went on to say that the Führer was convinced that Germany would win the war, possibly soon but certainly in one, two or three years. He wanted to stop the unnecessary slaughter that

would otherwise inevitably take place. He asked me to get together leading members of my party to talk over things with a view to making peace proposals. I replied that there was now only one party in this country ...

Hess went on to tell him what the Fuhrer's peace terms would be, but Hamilton said, according to his report, that if a peace agreement were possible it would have been made before the war started; he could see no hope of a peace agreement now. Hess then requested that he ask the King to give him 'parole', as he had come unarmed and of his own free will.

Hess's version of this in a letter to Ilse on the ninth anniversary of his imprisonment in Scotland was:

Then [on the first day of his imprisonment] I believed that it would last seven hours: directly I made myself known to the Duke and stated my mission as a *Parlamentär* [bearing a flag of truce] – even if on my own authority – I would be treated as a *Parlamentär*.[121]

Hess also asked Hamilton to let his family know he was safe by sending a telegram to Rothacker, Herzog Strasse 17, Zürich.

In his report Hamilton made no mention of any letter addressed to him either among Hess's possessions or as a topic during their talk. And if Hess mentioned a document he had brought containing precisely worded peace proposals Hamilton's report was not only silent on the subject, but actually ruled it out by stating that Hess had asked him to get together the leading members of his party 'to talk over things with a view to making peace proposals'. Yet it is known that Hess had written him a letter and it is believed – as will appear – that he also brought over a draft peace treaty worded precisely by an official in Ribbentrop's Foreign Ministry.

It should be noted that the report quoted above was not Hamilton's original, but a revised version he prepared for Churchill.[122] The original has been destroyed or suppressed.

After his interview with Hess, Hamilton, according to 'additional notes' he made later, told the officer commanding at Maryhill that he believed the prisoner to be an important person who should be moved out of danger of bombing and placed under close guard;[123] later that day Hess was driven to Drymen Military Hospital in Buchanan Castle on the shores of Loch Lomond, and a 100-strong guard was mounted.

Whether these precautions were taken on the advice of an RAF Wing Commander – even if the premier Duke of Scotland – may be doubted. The presumption must be that higher authorities were in control. In a Commons statement Churchill drafted but never made, he observed that Hamilton had been ordered to go to Maryhill Hospital to receive any statement the 'unidentified German' might make.[124] And a summary of the case wired to Moscow from the Foreign Office in 1942 states, 'the Duke was ordered by his superior officer in the Royal Air Force to see Hess, then under confinement in Maryhill Barracks, Glasgow.'[125]

* * *

After leaving Maryhill that morning Hamilton, according to his 'additional notes', drove to Eaglesham with Benson to inspect the remains of Hess's plane, then returned to Turnhouse and reported to his commanding officer at No. 13 Group Headquarters that he had an important matter to communicate to the Foreign Office.[126]

Mrs Pyne, at that time ACW Iris Palmer, one of two female clerks in the orderly room at Turnhouse, remembers Hamilton returning that afternoon, 'shattered, extremely tense', in marked contrast to his normal relaxed manner.[127] She cannot recall the time, but he went straight into his office and his first words were 'Get me Group!' She got Group Headquarters on the line for him, but from the orderly room did not hear what he said. Shortly afterwards he called the other ACW, Pearl Hyatt, into his office and dictated a report, which Pearl typed after returning to her desk in the orderly room. Mrs Pyne did not see the report. Both girls were aware without being told that this was a matter of the highest urgency. They had known since reporting for work at 9.00 that morning that Hess had landed with a message for the Duke; the whole station buzzed with the story.

It is not clear whether Hamilton called in briefly to his house off base before going to his office and putting the call through to Group, but the Duchess's recollection of the time he did return home suggests he may have done. He came in and straight up to her bedroom – the first time she had seen him since he left in the middle of the night – and showed her a photograph he had taken from the prisoner's possessions, saying, 'I think it's Hess. I must go to London at once. I haven't told anyone. Don't say a word about it.'[128]

The bedroom windows overlooked the drive leading to the front door, and at that moment she saw Squadron Leader Cyril Longden, whom she had asked to tea, walking up the drive with his two children. In some irritation that they should appear just now, she exclaimed, 'There's Cyril!'

It was to become a family joke: shown a photograph of the Deputy Führer who had flown over to see her husband, all she could say was, 'There's Cyril!'

It serves, however, to pinpoint Hamilton's arrival home as four o'clock or thereabouts, which suggests that he called in at home briefly before his office, for there is no doubt that he made a call to the Foreign Office long after tea time, and this was presumably, although not necessarily, from his office on the base. If this is correct, it would suggest that he spent a considerable time at the site of the wrecked plane after his 10.00 a.m. meeting with Hess.

He called the Foreign Office to try to arrange a meeting with Sir Alexander Cadogan that evening at 10 Downing Street. A junior official, John Addis, answered. Hamilton felt he could not tell him over the open line why it was so urgent he see the Permanent Secretary at once; Addis could not summon Cadogan from his country cottage on a Sunday without good reason. The conversation became heated, when, as Hamilton put it in his 'additional notes':

Suddenly in the midst of this rather acrimonious discussion a strange voice said 'This is the Prime Minister's Secretary speaking. The Prime Minister sent me over to the Foreign Office as he is informed that you have some interesting information. I have just arrived and I would like to know what you propose to do.'

I asked that he should have a car at Northolt [aerodrome] within an hour and a half and I should meet it there.[129]

The Prime Minister's secretary was Jock Colville. This phone conversation can be accurately timed from Cadogan's diary, which he kept meticulously, as an outlet, it has been said, for a somewhat unfulfilling marriage.[130] On Sunday 11 May, after describing a morning walk and listening to the news at one o'clock – 'Heavy Blitz on London last night, but we got down *33*. This is *really* good' – he let off steam about his political chief, Anthony Eden, then noted:

> 5.30 Addis rang me up with this story: a German pilot landed near Glasgow, asked for the Duke of Hamilton. Latter so impressed that he is flying to London and wants to see me at No. 10 tonight. Said I shouldn't be in London before 8. Fixed meeting for 9.15. Half hour later, heard P.M. was sending to meet His Grace at airfield & wd. bring him to Chequers – so I needn't be tr-r-r-oubled!
>
> Left about 6. Home 7.50. London awfully knocked about last night. And I fear Westminster Hall and Abbey got it. Also Parliament tho' I didn't care about that. I wish it had got more of the Members.[131]

There is, of course, a minor discrepancy between this contemporary account and Hamilton's later notes insomuch as Hamilton evidently did succeed in persuading Addis to ring Cadogan and arrange a meeting at No. 10 that night, although this was later countermanded. There can be no doubt about the timing of the call, though. There are far more serious discrepancies in Colville's description of the incident.

CHAPTER ELEVEN

Reactions

'I WALKED OUT INTO Downing Street at 8.0 a.m. on my way to the early service at Westminster Abbey.' Thus Jock Colville began his diary entry for 11 May.[1]

Smoke from numerous fires hung over Westminster after the heaviest night raid yet on the capital. Flames rose from the roof of Westminster Hall. What remained of the House of Commons was burning. Fire engines were pumping water into Westminster Abbey. As he reached the doors Colville was told by a policeman, 'There will not be any services in the Abbey today, sir.'[2]

This entry, on 10 Downing Street headed paper, is pasted on page 157 – numbered by hand – of Colville's hard-bound diary. Later on there is another entry for 11 May. This is because he spent much of the following weekend indoors with a heavy cold, copying entries from a red pocket diary into the hard-bound volume.[3] He reached 11 May again on page 196. This time the entry began: 'Awoke thinking unaccountably of Peter Fleming's book "Flying Visit" and day-dreaming of what would happen if we captured Göring during one of his alleged flights over London.'[4]

The published edition of his diaries prints this version. It then reverts for the second paragraph to the beginning of his original, page 157 entry, 'I walked out into Downing Street at 8.0 a.m. ...',[5] but this is not in the page 196 account copied from his pocket diary, which has as the second paragraph: 'Went to Church early, but found Westminster Abbey running with water, part of the roof having collapsed. Westminster Hall on fire and the south bank of the river ablaze. The House of Commons was destroyed.'[6]

Although this follows on directly after the opening, 'day-dreaming', paragraph in this second version of 11 May it does not appear in the published version. Nor does the next paragraph copied from his pocket diary, which describes going to Church at St Martin-in-the-Fields instead. There then follows a paragraph common to both original and copied entries, which does appear in the published version: 'After breakfast I rang the P.M. at Ditchley and described what I had seen. He was very grieved that William Rufus's roof at Westminster Hall should have gone. He told me we had shot down 45 which, out of 380 operating, is a good result.'[7]

In the second, or copied entry there is a note that the number of enemy bombers destroyed had been exaggerated – 'it was finally established that we got 33' – then a description of lunching at the St James' Club, after which comes a paragraph which concludes the published account but does not appear in the original, page 157 entry: 'Great excitement over an E. Phillips Oppenheim story concerning the Duke of Hamilton and a crashed Nazi plane. The Duke flew to London and I had been going to Northolt to meet him; but he was switched straight through to Ditchley.'[8]

Colville seems usually to have written his diary late in the day: the entries for the previous week concluded successively with Churchill working until 2.00 a.m.; Colville dancing to a gramophone at an evening party; Churchill going to bed early; the biggest air raid on Germany; Churchill leaving for the weekend for Ditchley Park; and on the 10th the start of one of London's heaviest air raids as Colville went to bed. It is possible, however, that on Sunday 11 May Colville was so impressed by the sight of London burning he described his impressions that morning on his return from church. This could explain why he omitted any mention of Hess's arrival, surely one of the most sensational events of the war, from this first entry for the 11th on Downing Street writing paper. He was at Downing Street; the Prime Minister was at Ditchley Park, and Colville may not have heard of Hess's arrival until later that day.

It is more difficult to explain a retrospective account Colville added in his published diaries after his 11 May entry, according to which he had walked over to the Foreign Office that morning to chat with Nicolas Lawford, Anthony Eden's Second Private Secretary, who was on duty over the weekend. Lawford was on the telephone when he came in, but turned when he saw him and, with his hand over the receiver, explained that it was the Duke of Hamilton with a fantastic story, which he refused to reveal in detail, but he wanted the Prime Minister's secretary to meet him at Northolt aerodrome. Colville took the telephone. Hamilton refused to be specific but told him he could only compare what had happened to an E. Phillips Oppenheim novel, and it concerned a crashed German plane:

> At that moment I vividly remembered my early waking thoughts on Peter Fleming's book and I felt sure that either Hitler or Goering had arrived. In the event I was only one wrong in the Nazi hierarchy. I telephoned to Ditchley [where Churchill was staying] and the Prime Minister instructed me to have the Duke driven directly there.[9]

This is highly unlikely since Hamilton's call to the Foreign Office was in the afternoon, not the morning as Colville's account has it. Cadogan's diary times the call he received from Addis – not Lawford or Colville – about Hamilton at 5.30 in the afternoon.[10] And Lawford was not even at the Foreign Office that weekend, but at home on his parents' Hertfordshire estate breaking in a half-Arab colt.[11]

On 14 May, between Colville's original pasted-in entry on Downing Street writing paper and the weekend when he copied in the second entry for the 11th, a leader had appeared in *The Times* headed 'The Flying Visit'. It compared Hess's arrival to the 'literary flight of fancy' published the previous year by 'a well-known young member of the staff of *The Times*' – Peter Fleming – under the title of *The Flying Visit*. This had described the Führer descending by parachute into a lonely region of the English countryside. The article ended with an allusion to Oscar Wilde's thesis that 'nature always tends to imitate art'.[12]

This, then, probably supplied Colville with inspiration for his own flight of fancy; but why had he felt it necessary? The answer probably lies in what Colville told Hamilton's son, Lord James Douglas-Hamilton, in 1969 when Lord James was preparing a book about his father's unintended involvement in Hess's mission. When Hamilton had said on the telephone that an extraordinary thing had happened, and compared it to something out of an E. Phillips Oppenheim novel, Colville had asked, 'Has somebody arrived?'[13]

It was a strange question. It must be assumed that, in order to explain the context later to Hamilton or anyone else Hamilton may have told, he had invented his strange dream. And in order for the dream to have been in his mind the phone call had to have taken place in the morning. The question is, why had he resorted to invention? That is probably unanswerable now. His different diary entries and evidently misremembered or deliberately bogus additional explanation merely reinforce the conclusion that much that took place on the night and morning following Hess's arrival has been withheld from the official record. Perhaps the most likely explanation is that Hess was expected, a high secret which could not be revealed since the implication of prior negotiations might have fatally undermined Churchill's strategy of drawing the United States into the war.

DITCHLEY PARK

On weekends when the moon was full and the Prime Minister's country retreat, Chequers, made a conspicuous target for German bombers,[14] Churchill retired to Ditchley Park, home of Ronald and Nancy Tree, he a wealthy Conservative MP, she a celebrated hostess and interior designer, born a Virginian who was nonetheless chiefly responsible in the 1920s and 1930s for creating what came to be called the 'English country house look'.[15] The interior of Ditchley Park, a large 18th-century Palladian building north of Oxford on the road to Stratford, was one of her masterpieces.

On Sunday 11 May her guests, besides Churchill and his young confidant, Brendan Bracken, included Roosevelt's special envoy, Harry Hopkins, and the Secretary of State for Air, Sir Archibald Sinclair. Churchill surprised his hostess that morning with a request for the Duke of Hamilton to stay the night.[16] He gave no explanation.

It will be recalled that he had been told of Hess's expected arrival[17] by Bevin the night before; presumably he waited for a positive identification, perhaps Hamilton's at Maryhill Barracks hospital, before he approached his hostess about the Duke.

The instructions he gave when Colville rang from Downing Street have been obscured by Colville's diary fictions, but whatever the nature of any negotiations preceding Hess's flight, Cadogan's diary entry for that day makes it clear he knew nothing until he received the phone call from Addis that afternoon.[18] From this it follows that whatever negotations there may have been, the Foreign Office was not a party to them.

* * *

Churchill must have sent Colville over to the Foreign Office some time that afternoon, where he fielded Hamilton's call and agreed to meet him at Northolt aerodrome with a car. On reporting back to Churchill Colville was evidently told that the Duke was to go to Ditchley. Consequently, when Hamilton arrived at Northolt in a Hurricane he was instructed to fly on to Kidlington, a new aerodrome just north of Oxford. There a car was waiting, and he was driven to Ditchley Park:

> I got out on the doorstep ... and was met by a very pompous and smart butler. My appearance can be better imagined than described when I tell you that I had had no sleep, or practically no sleep, for four nights and had just finished a rather arduous journey from Scotland to southern England.[19]

After washing in one of the prettily furnished bathrooms Hamilton was ushered into the dining room, the walls a soft grey with a greenish tinge, famously described by Nancy Tree as 'the colour of elephants' breath'. Dinner was over; the ladies had retired; the men sat at tall-backed yellow dining chairs with brandy and cigars. Churchill was holding forth 'in tremendous form', Hamilton wrote, 'cracking jokes the whole time.'[20] Hamilton was served dinner, then all except Churchill and Sinclair left the room. He showed them the photographs the German airman had brought with him and assured them this was the man he had interviewed that morning, adding, by his own account, that 'whether the man was Hess or not was still very uncertain'.[21] The Prime Minister, he wrote, 'was rather taken aback' by what he had to tell him.

Churchill was anxious to see a Marx Brothers film about to be shown, so this first interview was brief; it was not until after the film that he and the Prime Minister and Sinclair met again in private and he was pressed on every detail. This session, which started about midnight, lasted some three hours.

The following morning Hamilton was driven at high speed in the Prime Minister's convoy to Downing Street, where he repeated his story to Anthony Eden, Cadogan and Stewart Menzies among others, while Churchill conducted a whirlwind of interviews and meetings on the weekend sensation. Cadogan's diary gives a flavour of the activity:

> I have never been so hard pressed. Mainly due to Hess, who has taken up *all* my time ... Talk with A [Eden] and Duke of Hamilton, who says it is Hess! Sent for 'C' & consulted him about sending IK [Ivone Kirkpatrick] up to 'vet' the airman. He approved. Got IK about 1.15 and gave him his instr. 3.15 meeting with A and IK. Duke came at 4. Packed them off in plane at 5.30 from Hendon.[22]

Ivone Kirkpatrick had served as First Secretary at the British Embassy in Berlin from 1933 to 1938 and knew all the Nazi leaders. He was now director of the foreign division of the Ministry of Information and a senior member of SOE. The plane provided for Hamilton to fly him north was a short-haul passenger airliner, the de Havilland Rapide. Hamilton had to put down at Linton aerodrome on the way to refuel, and it was over four hours before they reached Turnhouse. There they were told of a wireless announcement by the German government that Hess had taken off from Augsburg on a flight from which he had not returned.[23] It was assumed he had crashed or met with an accident.

They also received a phone call from Sir Archibald Sinclair instructing them to proceed without delay to identify the prisoner.[24]

THE BERGHOF

Alfred Rosenberg, it will be recalled, had been summoned to an urgent meeting with Hess at his Munich-Harlaching villa just before he flew to Scotland. They had talked earnestly in private over lunch and continued in the garden afterwards. At about two o'clock Rosenberg left and, according to his adjutant, drove straight to Hitler's mountain retreat, the Berghof above Berchtesgaden, probably arriving even before Hess took off from Augsburg.[25] If so it is scarcely conceivable he did not tell Hitler that his deputy was about to fly on his peace mission to Britain.

A few days later Hitler was to tell top party officials and service chiefs that he had received a packet that Saturday night but had put it aside unopened, thinking it was a memorandum. When later he opened it he found Hess's letter explaining his plan to fly to 'Lord Hamilton' in Glasgow, and his reasons.[26]

Perhaps he did not open the packet at the time; probably he did not need to. Rosenberg, hot foot from Harlaching, must surely have told him. Rosenberg was the ideologue of the party. He shared and had no doubt helped inform Hess's hatred of Bolshevism; he shared Hess's vision of forging an alliance with the British against the Bolsheviks; and, like Hess, he despaired at the fratricidal struggle with the island kingdom. Moreover, in April he had been given the responsibility for planning questions for the – to be conquered – east European area.[27] It is difficult to imagine why he should have driven to the Berghof from his meeting with Hess if not to inform Hitler that his deputy was flying to Britain that day to bring peace in the west – allowing full force to be deployed east.

Supposition is backed by the testimony of Hess's driver, Rudolf Lippert: after release from Soviet internment and torture long after the war, he told Hess's son, Wolf Rüdiger, that he and others who had escorted Hess to Messerschmitt's Augsburg airstrip had been arrested by the Gestapo at Gallspach, Austria, at 5.30 in the morning of Sunday 11 May.[28] This was several hours before staff and other witnesses at the Berghof recorded Hess's adjutant, Karl-Heinz Pintsch, arriving with a letter from Hess informing Hitler that he had flown to Britain.

This otherwise puzzling story finds support in Pintsch's equally strange post-war testimony: after Hess took off he had waited at the Augsburg works until nine o'clock when he had rung a department of the Air Ministry in Berlin to order a radio beam for Hess to Dungavel Hill. Returning to Munich afterwards with Lippert and the security officer, he told the two of them to get something to eat, pack a few things and drive to the home of a homeopath friend of Hess in the Austrian village of Gallspach. They were to go in the two-stroke DKW, not the Mercedes, which was too conspicuous, and wait in Gallspach until they heard how the flight had gone. Pintsch would do his best to get a message to them as soon as he could.[29]

He himself was dropped off at the railway station to catch the next train to Berchtesgaden. It left at midnight, arriving at 7.00 on Sunday morning. He rang the Berghof from the stationmaster's office and explained to the duty adjutant, Albert Bormann, brother of Martin Bormann, that he had a letter from Hess to deliver personally to the Führer. Bormann sent a car to fetch him. Pintsch then waited in the great hall of the Berghof until Hitler appeared coming down the central stairway. He stood, saluted and handed him Hess's sealed letter. Hitler told him to come into his study, and after opening the envelope and glancing at the first lines of the letter, asked, 'Where is Hess now?'

'Yesterday, *Mein Führer*, at 18.10 he took off from Ausgburg for Scotland to see the Duke of Hamilton.'[30]

Pintsch's account lacks any suggestion of the histrionics described by most who claimed afterwards to have witnessed Hitler receiving the letter, but his timing is consistent with most other accounts; it was some time before noon, for he described Hitler reading the letter through twice before having an adjutant summon Göring and Ribbentrop from their weekend retreats, after which Eva Braun appeared in the doorway in tweed skirt and woollen jumper to announce, 'Lunch is ready!'[31]

Hitler's army adjutant, Major Gerhard Engel, recalled Pintsch wishing to speak to Hitler on an urgent matter when Hitler came down at about 11.00;[32] and Bormann made an entry in his diary, 'Midday Pintsch brings the Deputy Führer's letters: latter took off for England on 10.5 at 17.40.'[33]

However, Engel's account has Hitler turning chalk white, grinding his teeth and telling him in an agitated manner to get hold of Göring at once.[34] Göring's adjutant, General Karl Bodenschatz, also claimed to be alone with Hitler when he was handed the letter, but described him reading the first few sentences, then sinking into a chair, exclaiming, '*Um Gottes Willen! Um Gottes Willen! Der ist darübergeflogen!*'[35] (For God's sake! He has flown over there!') Bodenschatz thought Hitler was putting on a performance, and remained convinced he was at least a party to Hess's mission.[36] Hitler's architect, Albert Speer, who also claimed to be at the Berghof that morning, recalled hearing Hitler's incoherent, 'almost animal cry'[37] after receiving the letter. The various accounts seem mutually exclusive.

Then there is the post-war memoir of Hitler's valet, Heinz Linge: Hitler, Linge wrote, had given him explicit instructions not to call him before noon that day, but when Pintsch arrived at 9.30 with news that Hess had flown, Linge went to the Führer's door and knocked. Hitler asked him what it was and, when Linge explained, opened the door, revealing himself fully dressed and shaved. Linge realised afterwards that he must have been waiting for the news, and the bemusement, anger and sense of betrayal he was to exhibit before others was play-acting. He too concluded that Hess had probably been sent to England.[38]

Admittedly, this was not what Linge told the Russians immediately after the war. He was held for four years and interrogated brutally on his time serving Hitler.[39] According to the account he gave then – preceding his published account above – Albert Bormann and Pintsch appeared at about 10.00 a.m. in the antechamber to Hitler's study. Bormann asked Linge to wake Hitler as he had an urgent letter from Hess. When Hitler emerged, unshaven, from his bedroom he took Hess's letter from Pintsch and hurried downstairs to the great hall, where he opened the envelope. He then called for Pintsch. A few minutes later he told Linge to fetch the chief of police on his staff, and Pintsch was summarily arrested.[40] Of course, this does not square with Pintsch's account of having lunch with Hitler, Eva Braun and guests.

Hitler could not afford to be associated with Hess's mission. Should it fail it would manifest weakness, even desperation before the coming reckoning with Stalin. It had to be deniable. Hess denied it persistently all his life. Apparently the final passage of his letter to Hitler ran: 'And should, *mein Führer*, my project, which I must admit has very little chance of success, end in failure, should fate decide against me, it can have no evil consequences for you or for Germany; you can always distance yourself from me – declare me mad.'[41]

This letter, like the longer explanation contained in the package Hitler had received the night before – indeed like so much else from both sides of the affair – has been lost, but Ilse Hess claimed after the war that she remembered these final words perfectly since her husband had enclosed a copy of the letter in a farewell note he left for her.

If it is accepted that Hess flew on a deniable mission for Hitler, then Pintsch's and Lippert's otherwise bizarre tales become fully comprehensible. Pintsch could not drive straight to the Berghof from the Augsburg airstrip in Hess's Mercedes without arousing suspicion that the enterprise had been ordered by the Führer. Ideally news of Hess's arrival in Scotland would be announced by the enemy before his own arrival at the Berghof with Hess's explanatory letter. Likewise the other two who had accompanied Hess to the airfield had to be kept out of the way until it was known how events would turn out, in case they talked or were arrested by the Gestapo for complicity in their master's escapade. Hess left a letter for Himmler asking him not to act against his people, but the *Reichsführer* was evidently leaving nothing to chance and had the two picked up in the early hours, long before anyone was supposed to know.

Pintsch sat down to lunch with Hitler and his entourage and several others with appointments to see the Führer that day. It was to be his last taste of life at the top table. He was arrested that afternoon on Hitler's orders, together with Hess's other adjutant, Alfred Leitgen.

Despite the post-war accounts of Pintsch and Rosenberg's adjutant, Hess's driver and Hitler's valet, despite the scepticism with which Bodenschatz regarded Hitler's displays of anger and bemusement at Hess's departure, there are serious historians, British and German, who believe Hitler knew nothing of his deputy's plans.[42] This is due partly to doubts about the testimony of witnesses like Pintsch, Lippert and Linge, who suffered torture in Soviet captivity and may have tailored their stories to what their jailers wished to hear, partly to overwhelming testimony to Hitler's grief over the subsequent days. During a meeting of high party officials called to explain Hess's flight on the 13th he broke down in tears;[43] one of those present said afterwards he had never seen him so completely shocked.[44]

The unanimity of contemporary eyewitness accounts leaves no doubt that Hitler was heartbroken over Hess's departure. This does not necessarily indicate prior ignorance of Hess's plans, only that, as the likelihood of Hess's death turned into near-certainty, he grieved for his beloved friend and devoted colleague. It was an entirely natural reaction considering the duration and closeness of their relationship. It can have no bearing on the question of whether or not Hess flew to Britain on his commission or with his approval. On the other hand Pintsch's and Lippert's accounts in particular are so outlandish they could not have been fabricated and co-ordinated. The presumption must be that Hitler, and no doubt Göring and Himmler too, were complicit.

Ilse Hess always said she believed her husband flew without Hitler's knowledge. In this she was following the guidance of her man and, especially at the time of the Nuremberg war crimes trials, helping to distance him from Hitler's attack on Russia. Whether she really believed it cannot be known.

* * *

Uncertainty about Hess's fate dominated discussion at the Berghof, where Hitler was joined by Ribbentrop that afternoon and Göring and his air armaments chief in the evening. At first, it seems, Hitler refused to accept that Hess might have failed to reach his objective. He knew his man and his technical and mathematical abilities; when he set his mind to something he achieved it;[45] he imagined him dining with the Duke of Hamilton even as they argued. But on Monday, the 12th, as the hours passed with no news from Britain or from Hess's aunt, Frau Rothacker, in Zürich, hope faded and he was forced to conclude that an announcement could be postponed no longer. He instructed his Press chief to draft a release and incorporate Hess's own suggestion to account for the flight: that he had gone crazy.[46] After numerous amendments an inept version was finally agreed. It was broadcast on all home stations at 8.00 that evening.

> Party Comrade Hess, who has been expressly forbidden by the Führer to use an aeroplane because of a disease which has been becoming worse for years, was, in contradiction to this order, able to get hold of a plane recently. Hess started on Saturday, 10th May, at about 1800 from Augsburg on a flight from which he has not yet returned. A letter which he left behind unfortunately showed traces of mental disturbance which justifies the fear that Hess was the victim of hallucinations. The Führer at once ordered the arrest of Hess's adjutants, who alone knew of his flights, and who in contradiction to the Führer's ban, of which they were aware, did not prevent the flight nor report it at once. The National-Socialist movement has unfortunately, in these circumstances, to assume that Party Comrade Hess has crashed or met with a similar accident.[47]

Albrecht Haushofer had been brought to the Berghof and placed under guard that morning. Karl Haushofer had been called the previous evening and asked for Albrecht's Berlin telephone number – 'which made us think,' Martha Haushofer noted in her diary.[48] Hitler had not received Albrecht but had ordered that he be set to write a full account of his part in Hess's mission. It was a complex task. Albrecht knew his life would depend on how he completed it. He could assume Hitler knew of the feelers he had put out for Hess, but could not know what Himmler might have learned of his activities on behalf of von Hassell and the opposition. He began:

> *English connections and the possibility of employing them*
> The circle of English people I have known personally for years, whose activity in favour of a German–English understanding in the years 1934–1938 was at the core of my work in England, comprised the following groups and personalities: ...[49]

The first group he cited comprised young Conservatives, many of them Scottish: the Duke of Hamilton, whom he had known as Lord

Clydesdale; Chamberlain's Parliamentary Private Secretary, Lord Dunglass; and two ministers in the present British government. He described the close connections this circle had with the court – strangely omitting Hamilton's own position as Lord Steward of the Royal Household with personal access to the King – and went on to list old landed families with whom this young circle had close ties, and whom he himself 'knew from close personal contact over years'. He did not include the big names in what might be called the 'peace movement': Londonderry, Buccleuch, Brocket, Tavistock. He did cite

> the present Under Secretary of State at the Foreign Office, [R.A.] Butler ... [who] despite his many official statements is no follower of Churchill or Eden. Numerous connections lead from most of those named to Lord Halifax, to whom I likewise had personal access ...

Albrecht added more influential names, indicating how indispensible he would be in any future attempt to negotiate with the British, after which he described his talks with Carl Burckhardt in Geneva. Although he mentioned Hoare among other ambassadors he had suggested Hess might approach, he wrote nothing of his own approaches to Hoare via Stahmer in Madrid, an interesting omission since on the night of 10/11 May, after Hess had flown, Stahmer had wired the Foreign Ministry in Berlin with an urgent message for Albrecht to the effect that he had to give his lecture to the Academy of Sciences in Madrid on 12 May.[50]

It has been assumed this could have been a coded message to inform Albrecht that a meeting had been fixed with Hoare for 12 May. Stahmer's own post-war explanation was that it was a warning he had sent Albrecht after hearing a Reuter's news flash that Hess had landed in England.[51] Since no news of Hess's flight broke until the German home stations broadcast of the 12th, this sounds like fabrication. On the other hand, if Hoare knew of or was party to negotiations preceding Hess's flight, he may have got word to Stahmer that Hess had flown, in which case Stahmer may indeed have tried to warn Albrecht that he was in danger. This is scarcely more far-fetched than Albert

Heal's story of the coded message to Bevin from his 'industrial contact' inside Germany to let him know Hess was on his way.[52]

Why Hitler did not call in Goebbels before sanctioning the crass announcement broadcast that Monday evening is a mystery. Goebbels was phoned later, and recorded:

> I was called from the Berghof. The Führer is completely shattered. What an insight for the world: a spiritually deranged second man after the Führer. Horrible and unimaginable ... At present I know no way out ... I was stormed with telephone calls from all sides, *Gauleiter*, *Reichsleiter* etc. None will believe this idiocy ... I must come to Obersalzberg. There I will learn details ... It is a frightful evening ...[53]

William Joyce, the Nazi propagandist known to the British public as 'Lord Haw-Haw', included an announcement of Hess's death in his 22.30 broadcast in English from Breslau that night.[54]

IVONE KIRKPATRICK

Hamilton and Kirkpatrick learned of the German broadcast announcing Hess's disappearance when they landed at Turnhouse; it had been picked up by the BBC monitoring service and reported on the nine o'clock news. Receiving telephone instructions to proceed without delay to identify the prisoner, they drove to Glasgow and northwards through blacked-out streets to the military hospital in Buchanan Castle, Drymen, where they arrived shortly after midnight. Hess was asleep. When woken, he failed to recognise Kirkpatrick, but the former First Secretary at the British Embassy in Berlin drew him out on incidents they had witnessed together, and it soon became clear this was indeed the Deputy Führer sitting up in bed before them.[55]

After the preliminaries Hess began reading from a long statement he had apparently been preparing since arriving at the hospital. The first part was a historical polemic charging England with responsibility for the outbreak of the First World War by allying with France, moving on to the iniquities of the Versailles Treaty and Britain's subsequent failure to make concessions to the democratic German government, leading to the rise of Hitler and National Socialism; Hitler had then been compelled to occupy Austria and Czechoslovakia and when the British encouraged the Poles to resist his proposals, to invade Poland. England was thus responsible for the present war, and when after the Polish collapse Hitler had made a peace offer, England had rejected it with scorn; and had done so again when Hitler repeated the offer after the collapse of France. There was nothing further Hitler could do but pursue the struggle. Hamilton, who evidently had enough German to understand some of this, described it as 'one long eulogy of Hitler'.[56]

At about 1.00 a.m., with Hess still in full flood, Kirkpatrick and Hamilton were called away to the telephone. It was Anthony Eden from the Cabinet War Room with Churchill wanting to know whether it had been established that the prisoner was Hess, and if so what he was saying. Kirkpatrick replied that his identity was not in doubt, but he had only got halfway through his speech – presumably the sheaf of notes he was reading – and so far there was no explanation of why he had come. They returned and Hess continued reading. Hamilton soon nodded off, exhausted.

The second part of Hess's discourse was designed to prove that Germany would inevitably win the war. German aircraft production was far larger than that of Great Britain and America combined, and as for the Battle of the Atlantic, U-boat parts were being constructed in large numbers all over Germany and occupied Europe for transport by waterway to the coast for assembly. Crews were being trained on a huge scale. England must shortly expect to see vastly increased numbers of U-boats working in co-operation with aircraft against shipping. Moreover, there was not the slightest hope of bringing about a revolution in Germany. Hitler possessed the blindest confidence of the German masses.

Finally Hess moved on to his reasons for coming to Britain and his proposals for peace. He said he had been horrified by the prospect of the continuation of the struggle and had come without Hitler's knowledge in order to convince responsible persons that 'since England could not win the war, the wisest course was to make peace now'[57] – as

Kirkpatrick summarised it. After warning them that the United States had designs on the British Empire and would certainly incorporate Canada, Hess then made the well-worn proposal that Great Britain should give Germany a free hand in Europe and Germany would give Britain a completely free hand in the Empire – apart from former German colonies, which should be returned as they were needed as sources for raw materials.

Kirkpatrick asked whether he included Russia in Europe. 'In Asia,' he replied, at which Kirkpatrick said that under the terms he had proposed, Germany would not be at liberty to attack her.

> Herr Hess reacted quickly by remarking that Germany had certain demands to make of Russia which would have to be satisfied either by negotiation or as the result of a war. He added, however, that there was no foundation for the rumours now being spread that Hitler was contemplating an early attack on Russia.[58]

By this time the interview had lasted some two and a quarter hours. Kirkpatrick had scarcely interrupted the flow. He had occasionally attempted to draw Hess on particular points, but had otherwise allowed even his most outrageous remarks to pass, realising that argument would be, as he put it, 'quite fruitless'. He rose after Hess reached the end of his speech and roused Hamilton. As they were leaving Hess said he had forgotten to emphasise that his proposal could only be considered on the understanding that it was negotiated with an English government other than the present one, and added that Mr Churchill and his colleagues who had planned the war since 1936 were not persons with whom the Führer could negotiate.[59]

Hamilton and Kirkpatrick were given breakfast at the hospital, then drove back to Hamilton's house off base and turned in. Kirkpatrick rose after a few hours and phoned Cadogan at the Foreign Office just before 11.00. He summarised Hess's statement, but said his impression was that Hess would not open up very far to anyone speaking for the government. On the other hand, 'if he could be put in touch with perhaps some member of the Conservative Party who would give him the impression that he was tempted by the idea of getting rid of the present administration, it might be that Hess would open up freely.'[60] Cadogan told Kirkpatrick to remain at Turnhouse.

Hamilton, returning to the base, had ACW Pearl Hyatt bring her typewriter into his office so that he could dictate a report in private; it was his second report. Mrs Pyne, formerly ACW Iris Palmer, remembers Pearl saying, 'Oh. I've got to take this darned thing in to the Old Man's office!'[61] Pearl Hyatt also typed Kirkpatrick's report of his interview with Hess, and subsequent reports of interviews over the following days.

Kirkpatrick's suggestion to Cadogan that someone who could give the impression of wanting to oust Churchill might be able to draw Hess out may have been followed up that day. Nothing in the open files even hints at it, but a retired squadron leader, Frank Day, has provided compelling testimony that Hess was visited by a senior RAF officer and a civilian that Tuesday, 13 May.[62]

Day was then a pilot officer training on Spitfires at Grangemouth, near Turnhouse. On 12 May he made his first solo flight in a Spitfire, recording it proudly in his flying log. The next day, thus the 13th, he and five other young pilots on the course were instructed to report to Turnhouse. On arrival they were told they were to stand guard duty, and were driven a short distance – no more than 20 minutes – to a large Victorian house. Inside, a curving flight of stairs led to a first floor landing with about three doors. Day and another young pilot officer found themselves stationed beside one of these. Presently a tall German officer in uniform with a leather flying jacket came up the stairs escorted by two soldiers. They approached the door Day was guarding and the German and one of the soldiers went through. Day had a glimpse of an anteroom leading into a large living room furnished with easy chairs and a sofa. The other soldier remained outside holding a paper bag, which, Day discovered, contained 'pills' the German had brought with him.

Five minutes or so afterwards a ranking RAF officer with gold-braided cap and an array of medals[63] arrived with a civilian. Both entered the room. Day learned from a manservant that the RAF officer was 'the Duke'; he assumed the Duke of Hamilton. If his recollection was correct it could not have been Hamilton who, as a wing commander, had no gold braid on his cap, nor many medal ribbons on his tunic. The description does, however, fit the King's younger brother, Prince George, Duke of Kent, a group captain in the RAF Training Command with the honorary rank of Air Commodore.

There is nothing in the open files to suggest Hess was moved from his room in the Drymen Military Hospital on this Tuesday 13th, and Kirkpatrick did not report seeing him, which is odd since his interview in the early hours of that morning had left so many unanswered questions. On the other hand the detail in the late Squadron Leader Day's story is compelling, especially Hess's escort carrying his pills. When Day's son – not he himself – alerted *The Times* to this incident, Day had no idea that Hess had homeopathic medicines with him when he parachuted into Scotland. Nor did he know of a rumour attached to Craigiehall House, some five and a half miles from central Edinburgh, that Hess had been brought there in 1941 after landing in Scotland.[64] Craigiehall, built in the 17th century, had been extended in the Victorian era and converted into a hotel and country club in the 1930s. Requisitioned for use as Army Headquarters, Scotland, at the beginning of the war, it was exactly the kind of venue needed for a top-secret meeting between Hess and a royal Duke. Had Kent visited the military hospital at Drymen he might have been recognised – if it was indeed Kent – by staff or some of the hundred soldiers guarding Hess.

The Duke of Kent was a younger brother of King George VI. He had been close to the King's elder brother, David, briefly King Edward VIII, now Duke of Windsor, and, like him, openly in favour of a pro-German policy. He and his wife, Marina, had seen much of von Ribbentrop when he had been German Ambassador in London, virtually serving as channels of communication between the German Foreign Ministry and the heir to the British throne.[65] The Kents had also cultivated their mutual cousin in Germany, Prince Philipp of Hesse,[66] Hitler's one-time liaison with Mussolini – in whose aeroplane, it will be recalled, Lonsdale Bryans had proposed flying to Berlin.[67] In July 1939 the Duke and Prince Philipp of Hesse had met and discussed ways of averting the coming war.

When war came, the Kents had given up their London home and bought Pitliver House in Scotland, between Dunfermline and Rosyth on the opposite bank of the river Forth from Edinburgh. Whether the Duke was at home during the weekend of Hess's arrival and the subsequent few days cannot be established. His papers remain closed. A recent book on the Hess affair, *Double Standards*, claims that on the evening of 10 May he was waiting with others – including Poles – in a small house known as The Kennels adjacent to the Duke of Hamilton's airstrip at Dungavel. This is based on the testimony of an elderly lady who had been stationed at Dungavel with one of the women's services during the war, who wished to remain anonymous.[68] Moreover, she and a former colleague, who also wished to remain anonymous, told the *Double Standards* authors that the landing strip lights had been turned on and off again as or just before they heard a plane fly low overhead.[69] This implies electric lights. There is some doubt about this, but the small Dungavel airstrip was rated as an emergency landing ground for RAF planes and may well have been equipped with electric lights.[70]

Another claim in *Double Standards*, based this time on the recollection of one Nicholas Sheetz, who had attended a dinner party given by the Dowager Duchess of Hamilton, was that the Duchess had reminisced about Hess visiting their house off base at Turnhouse.[71] From this it is surmised that Hess was brought to Hamilton's house on the 13th on the way to his meeting with the high-ranking RAF officer, probably the Duke of Kent, at nearby Craigiehall House. This appears highly likely. However, there is no contemporary evidence for the Duke of Kent's whereabouts that day, nor of Hess's temporary removal from the military hospital.

One firm fact about the weekend of Hess's arrival is that General Wladislaw Sikorski, Polish Prime Minister in exile, flew in to RAF Prestwick from North America on the morning of Sunday 11 May,[72] thus hours after Hess parachuted down at Eaglesham nearby. The Kents took a great interest in Poland. The Duke had actually been offered the Polish crown; and Sikorski had been a guest at Pitliver House on several occasions since moving to England after the fall of France.[73] Poland, the trigger and ostensible cause of the war, was of course an interested party in any negotiations to bring peace. Can it be coincidence that Sikorski arrived in Scotland at almost the same time as Hess on his peace mission, with, if one accepts the inference of Squadron Leader Day's recollections, the Duke of Kent also on hand?

* * *

On Wednesday 14 May, the day following what appears to have been an unrecorded meeting between Kent and Hess at Craigiehall House, Hamilton and Kirkpatrick again drove over to Drymen Military Hospital to see him. They opened the conversation, according to Kirkpatrick's subsequent report, by asking Hess how he was and listening to a number of his requests: for the loan of specific books, the return of his medicines and camera and for a piece of his aeroplane as a souvenir. Hamilton promised to attend to these things,[74] after which Hess described in detail his flight and, as Hamilton put it in a later report, 'his extreme difficulty in getting out of his aircraft when he discovered that he could not make the landing ground at Dungavel'.[75] Towards the end of the interview he apologised for omitting two points from his peace proposals: that Germany could not leave Iraq in the lurch, and that British and German citizens should be indemnified for property expropriated as a result of the war. Finally, he again stressed that Germany would inevitably win the war by U-boat and aircraft blockade.

Both Hamilton and Kirkpatrick recorded this interview as little more than a friendly chat, taken up to a large extent with Hess's description of his flight and his escape from the aircraft. It seems entirely disconnected from their previous interview with him in the early hours of the 13th. There was no attempt to elucidate questions raised by the outline peace terms he had proposed; nor was he probed about his reasons for coming at this time. Perhaps these issues had been addressed at Craigiehall House. At all events, it is evident that Hess still saw himself as a peace envoy and was being treated as such. Kirkpatrick recorded him saying as they parted that 'if conversations were initiated as he hoped, he trusted that a qualified interpreter would be provided and that the conversations would not be attended by a large number of persons ...'[76]

The books he had requested were *Sea Power* by Grenfell, *Dynamic Defence* by Liddell Hart and *Three Men in a Boat* by Jerome K. Jerome.[77]

The first two advocated British disengagement from Continental affairs, precisely in line with his and all former peace proposals; *Sea Power* concluded by quoting a former Continental enemy:

> 'England', said Napoleon at St. Helena, 'can never be a continental power, and in the attempt she must be ruined. Let her stick to the sovereignty of the seas, and she may send her ambassadors to the courts of Europe and demand what she pleases.'[78]

The book had been published in September 1940 under the pseudonym 'T-124'; that Hess knew the author was the serving naval officer, Commander Russell Grenfell, is testimony to his intimate up-to-date knowledge of British strategic dissent.

CHAPTER TWELVE

Conflicting statements

GOEBBELS DROVE TO the Berghof in the morning of Tuesday 13 May. He knew by then that Hess was in Scotland: Churchill had released the bare facts of his arrival late the previous night and the BBC had broadcast the news in the early hours before Goebbels set off. It was a world sensation. Hitler's only public reaction had been to announce that the office of the Deputy Führer would from now on be termed the Party Chancellery and come under his own personal jurisdiction; it would be headed as before [under Hess] by Martin Bormann.[1] Otherwise German broadcasting stations remained silent.

On arrival Goebbels found Hitler waiting for him with the letter Hess had left behind. He recorded his shock on reading it:

... a muddled confusion, prime dilettantism, he wanted to go to England to make clear their hopeless position through Lord Hamilton in Scotland to topple Churchill's government and then make peace which would save London's face. That Churchill would have him arrested, he unfortunately overlooked. It is too idiotic. So, a buffoon was next man to the Führer. It is scarcely conceivable. His letter bristles with undigested occultism. Professor Haushofer and his wife ... have been the evil spirits. They have worked their '*Grossen*' ['big one'] up to this role. He has also had visions, had his horoscope drawn up and all bunkum ... One wants his wife, his adjutants and his doctors beaten to pulp ... The Führer is finished with him. He is completely shattered ... He pronounces on him [Hess] in the harshest terms, granting him idealism, however ...[2]

Taken at face value this diary entry shows either that Hitler had no prior knowledge of Hess's mission, or that whatever he had known, the Minister for Propaganda and Enlightenment had been left out of the loop. It would have been odd if this were so. Goebbels was privy to Hitler's big secrets: the coming eastern campaign, the fate awaiting the Jews; why not Hess's peace negotiation?

Goebbels' interest in truth was relative. His whole life was an exercise in propaganda, whether to serve the present or the future Germany. Besides presenting the Führer and the regime to the German people as sent by Providence to save the nation and the blood, he saw himself as witness to this heroic Germanic age for future generations. This was to become very obvious in the final days of the Reich. It seems likely that his entry on Hess's flight was in the same vein, to distance Hitler from what now seemed a failed attempt; the vehemence of his contempt for his former colleague suggests it.

He set about composing a new communiqué to throw light on the background to Hess's escapade. It was broadcast on German home stations at 2.00 that afternoon:

On the basis of a preliminary examination of the papers Hess left behind, it would appear that Hess was living under the hallucination that by undertaking a personal step in connection with the Englishmen with whom he was formerly acquainted it might be possible to bring about an understanding between Germany and Britain. As has since been confirmed from London, Hess parachuted from his plane in Scotland near the place he had selected as his destination ... As is well known in Party circles, Hess has undergone severe physical suffering for many years. Recently he has sought relief to an increasing extent in various methods practised by mesmerists and astrologers etc. ...[3]

At 4.30 this was expanded with the suggestion that it was 'also conceivable that Hess was deliberately lured into a trap by a British party';[4] and that evening Goebbels' deputy and chief radio commentator, Hans Fritsche, echoed the theme:

> Unless he has been consciously trapped by England, he – being an idealist and moreover a sick man – no doubt suffered from the growing delusion that in spite of the numerous and, heaven knows, sincere and generous peace proposals by the Führer, he himself might possibly, by a personal sacrifice and by personal contact with former English acquaintances, convince responsible Englishmen of the futility and hopelessness of further struggle on their part, a struggle which, the longer it lasts, will only demand ever-growing and more vain sacrifices from Great Britain ...[5]

This virtual paraphrase of Hess's address to Kirkpatrick at his first interview, and the stress on the sincerity of the Führer's desire for peace, suggests that Hitler may not have entirely given up hope of a successful outcome for his deputy's mission, an implication supported by a curious reference Fritsche made later in his broadcast to the bombing of Westminster Abbey on the night of Hess's flight almost exactly four years after the Coronation of King George VI (12 May 1937). He pointed out that the King who was crowned then should not really have been on the throne, and described the one who should have been 'as a man with a heart for the poor and wishing for peace and collaboration with Germany'[6] – a reference to the Duke of Windsor, now in exile in the Bahamas.

* * *

Nearly all those close to Hess or implicated in any way with his flight were dealt with ruthlessly over the following days: his adjutants, Pintsch and Leitgen, and his driver, Lippert, were expelled from the party, reduced to the ranks, sent to concentration camps and later to the Russian front, where they were captured.[7] Hess's brother, Alfred, was removed from his post as deputy to Ernst Bohle in the *Auslands Organisation* (Foreign Organisation) and expelled from the party. His intelligence chief, Pfeffer von Salomon, was interrogated at Gestapo headquarters for some months and then, on Hitler's orders, expelled from the party.[8]

Karl Haushofer was also interrogated by the Gestapo and although released was kept under surveillance, and a ban was placed on his books, virtually ending his professional career. Albrecht was held at Gestapo headquarters for over two months and when released was also placed under surveillance and prohibited from publishing. Hess's secretaries, his Anglophile friend Professor Gerl, and his astrologers were sent to concentration camps; and in June *all* astrologers, clairvoyants, mesmerists and faith healers were rounded up in a co-ordinated action and imprisoned, their publications and all alternative medicine literature banned.[9]

There were three important exceptions to this anathema: Ernst Bohle, who had by his own admission translated Hess's letters to Hamilton, when interrogated by Heydrich pointed the finger at the Haushofers, especially Albrecht,[10] and retained his post and party membership; Willi Messerschmitt, who had provided Hess with the aeroplane, whose staff had given him training and made the technical modifications necessary for his flight to Scotland, also escaped punishment. He was, of course, vital to the German war effort. Finally, despite Bormann's best efforts to persecute her, Ilse Hess retained her large villa in Harlaching, a pension equivalent to that of a government minister, and her son, 'Buz', whose sponsor – or in Christian terms godfather – was Hitler himself.

Bormann spread vicious rumours about his former chief, suggesting that he had been impotent for years, that Buz had been conceived during an affair Ilse had with an assistant to Dr Gerl, and that Hess had only flown to Scotland to prove he was a real chap ('*ein Mannsbild*').[11] Yet Hitler stood by Ilse. When, two years later, there was a scheme to convert her Harlaching villa into a nursing home, he vetoed it and decreed she should retain the house and could claim for all costs necessary for its upkeep.[12] Given Hitler's merciless treatment of those who betrayed him – and their kin – the protection he extended to Ilse is, perhaps, the surest sign that her husband flew on his commission.

CHURCHILL'S STATEMENT

Goebbels was scathing about the British government's failure to exploit Hess's arrival in Scotland, accusing his opposite number, Alfred Duff Cooper – Minister of Information – of once again proving himself a 'true dilettante'. Goebbels recognised that Churchill did not want peace discussions, but was clear that if he himself had been 'English Propaganda Minister' he would have known what he had to do.[13]

In fact Churchill had been anxious to make a frank public statement from the start. After the first German announcement on the Monday evening, the 12th, that Hess was missing, presumed crashed, and before Kirkpatrick had even reached Hess in the Drymen Military Hospital, he had called Eden, Menzies and Cadogan to a meeting in the Cabinet War Room, and presented them with the text of an announcement he had drafted, including the statement that Hess had flown to Britain 'in the name of humanity'.[14] It will be recalled that Hess had told Hamilton when he first saw him at Maryhill Barracks hospital on Sunday morning, the 11th, that he had come 'on a mission of humanity'.[15]

Churchill was dissuaded from making this statement or announcing anything beyond the bare facts of Hess's arrival; for as Cadogan noted, to talk of his arrival 'in the name of humanity' would look like a peace offer.[16] Yet Churchill still wanted to give a full explanation.

Goebbels produced one first. On Wednesday the 14th Berlin radio announced that on the evidence of papers Hess left behind he had intended flying to the estate of the Duke of Hamilton, whose acquaintance he had made at the Olympic Games in Berlin in 1936:

> [He] believed that the Duke belonged to the British group in opposition to Churchill as representative of the clique of warmongers. Hess further believed that the Duke possessed sufficient influence to be able to wage an effective fight against the Churchill clique ... [He] flew to Britain in order to explain to the circles with which he hoped to get into touch the fully hopeless position of Great Britain in the long run and to show them the unassailably strong opposition of Germany ... Hess under no circumstances had the intention of getting

in touch with Winston Churchill. On the contrary, he wanted to address himself to the internal political opposition against Churchill, as becomes unmistakeably clear from his notes. Rudolf Hess indeed had the absurd idea that he could return again to Germany after a short while when he had fulfilled his mission of *rapprochement* ...[17]

The communiqué ended by stating that Hess's notes showed he was 'well-nigh 100 per cent certain of success'. The close correspondence between this announcement and Kirkpatrick's report after his first interview with Hess – phoned through before the broadcast – provides conclusive proof of Hess's intentions, since Goebbels could not have known what Kirkpatrick said.

The German announcement sharpened Churchill's desire to give a full explanation in the Commons. That evening, Eden, Cadogan, Menzies and Duff Cooper gathered in No. 10 to hear what he proposed to say. Eden left after a while; the others waited while Churchill dictated. 'How slow he is,' Cadogan noted. 'What he said was all wrong – explaining what Hess had said (peace proposals) corresponding exactly to what Germans put out this afternoon. I said that, on that Hitler would heave sigh of relief. *And the German people.*'[18] It is remarkable that Cadogan, like Churchill and indeed Duff Cooper, seems not to have cared about the effect on the home front of an announcement that Hess had flown over because Hitler wanted peace. His concern was for the effect on the Germans. It suggests that the 'peace party' Hess thought he could mobilise against the government was not perceived as such a threat; no doubt it was also felt that most British people took Churchill's view of Hitler as the personification of evil who had to be defeated. Churchill laid stress on this moral aspect as he dictated his statement:

It must not be forgotten that the Deputy Führer, Rudolf Hess, has been the confederate and accomplice of Herr Hitler in all the murders, treacheries and cruelties by which the Nazi regime imposed itself, first on Germany, and is now seeking to impose itself on Europe. The blood purge of June 30 1934 ... the horrors of the German concentration camps, the brutal persecution of the Jews, the perfidious inroad upon Czechoslovakia, the unspeakable, incredible brutalities and bestialities of the German invasion and conquest of Poland ... are all cases in point.

He is at present being held as a prisoner of war who baled out in this country in uniform during an air raid. He is also being held in the character of a war criminal whose ultimate fate must, together with that of other leaders of the Nazi movement, be reserved for the decision of the Allied nations when the victory has been won.[19]

For the rest Churchill was perfectly open about Hess's idea of negotiating with 'a strong peace or defeatist movement' in Britain and his proposal that Britain and the Empire would be left intact so long as Germany under Hitler was left unquestioned master of Europe – the essence of Hess's peace plan. He even listed Hess's reasons for asserting that Germany was bound to win and American help would arrive too late. 'He appears to hold these views sincerely and he represented himself as undertaking a (self imposed) mission to save the British nation from destruction while time remained.'[20]

Here he was virtually allying Hess with Lloyd George, Liddell Hart and the many others who saw compromise with Hitler as the only hope before the country was forced to submit. He went on to defend the conduct of the Duke of Hamilton – named in the German broadcast – as in every respect honourable and proper, before concluding that the House, the country and their friends all over the world would be entertained and cheered by this remarkable episode, while the German armed forces, the Nazi Party and the German people would experience deep-seated bewilderment and consternation – as was the case.

Cadogan was firmly against making the statement. Beaverbrook, who dined with Churchill that night, backed up Cadogan's arguments, and later Eden in a heated telephone conversation persuaded him to say nothing.[21]

One typed copy of this statement to Parliament that Churchill never made has a curious handwritten comment in the margin: 'He [Hess] has also made other statements which it would not be in the public interest to disclose.'[22] This is hard to interpret. Kirkpatrick had interviewed Hess twice by this time but there is nothing in the typed reports of these conversations that does not appear in Churchill's intended statement. It is possible that Kirkpatrick reported 'other statements' verbally; it is also possible they were made to MI6 officers appointed to Hess, in Churchill's words, as 'guardians', or to the Duke of Hamilton, or even perhaps to the Duke of Kent during an interview at Craigiehall House not recorded in the open files.[23]

* * *

The next day, Thursday 15th, Kirkpatrick made a third and final visit to the Drymen Military Hospital to interview Hess. His instructions were to probe him on German intentions towards America; Roosevelt had suggested he might let slip something that could be used to wake the American people to the Nazi threat.[24] Hess did not oblige: 'Germany had no designs on America.' Hitler reckoned on American intervention, but was not afraid of it since Germany could outbuild America and Great Britain combined in aircraft. America, he went on, would be furious if Britain were to make peace now since she wanted to inherit the British Empire. Hitler on the other hand wanted a permanent understanding with Britain on a basis that would preserve the Empire. His own flight was intended to provide a chance for opening such negotiations without loss of prestige. If Britain were to reject the chance Hitler would be entitled, indeed it would be his clear duty, to destroy her and keep her in permanent subjection.[25]

Hess was still expecting negotiations: he gave Kirkpatrick the names of two German internees he would like to assist him if talks were opened, also one German stenographer and a typist. Remarkably, he knew that the two German internees were held at Huyton camp, near Liverpool, and knew their internment numbers.[26] Even more remarkably, both men had been transferred to a camp at Lochgilphead on the Scottish west coast just north of Glasgow only days before Hess's flight, on 7 and 8 May.[27] This is surely beyond coincidence. It must be proof of prior negotiation. Finally Hess complained to Kirkpatrick about his close guard; having flown over at great risk to himself, he said, he had no intention of running away or committing suicide.

Kirkpatrick went to this meeting alone. Hamilton had handed over to his second-in-command and flown down to London. In view of the rumours linking him with Hess's arrival, it is not surprising that Turnhouse station orders that day carried a reminder, 'All personnel are forbidden to communicate any service information which might directly or indirectly assist the enemy';[28] and a notice instructed qualified barristers or solicitors to report to the adjutant.

In London, Hamilton called on Cadogan to deliver Kirkpatrick's reports of his first two interviews with Hess, typed up by Pearl Hyatt, and said he wanted to see the King; Cadogan advised him to see the Prime Minister first.[29] Later Hamilton saw Duff Cooper to tackle him on Press and BBC reports that he had met Hess during the Olympic Games in Berlin and had received a letter from him only the previous September.

The innuendo swirling around Hamilton's role in the Deputy Führer's arrival stemmed from Churchill's failure to clarify events with an official statement or even to give Duff Cooper a clear line to take. Lack of any authoritative information from the British side had caused the British and American press corps especially to work themselves into what Sir Walter Monckton, Director General of the Ministry of Information, described as 'a state of fury' such as he had never seen before.[30] In an effort to give direction, Beaverbrook had hosted a lunch for newspaper editors and lobby correspondents at Claridges earlier that day, the 15th, and undoubtedly with Churchill's and Duff Cooper's approval, called for 'as much speculation, rumour and discussion about Hess as possible'.[31] The Prime Minister would make no statement, he went on, as that would end discussion; would they do all they could to make the most of this episode to the detriment of Germany.

Duff Cooper himself appears to have set the ball rolling by leaking the inaccurate story that Hamilton had received a letter from Hess the previous September. When Hamilton saw him that evening about clearing his name Duff Cooper suggested either an official statement in the Commons by Churchill or a reply to an inspired question. Next day Hamilton lunched with the King, who preferred the second option, and this was accordingly set in motion.[32]

The following day Cadogan drafted a 'Most Secret' circular to explain government policy on Hess to ambassadors and other British representatives in neutral capitals:

> No indication of Hess's statements or views should on any account be given to anyone except your immediate diplomatic staff. Our intention is to remain in constant contact with him and try to draw him. We do not know what will emerge, but we might eventually obtain information from him. For the time being we propose to say nothing officially about any results of interrogation, but to try to keep the Germans guessing. It may be possible however that by way of 'whispers' or gently inspired speculation in the press we may be able to cause embarrassment to the Germans ...[33]

The last sentence was cut before the telegram was sent, and replaced by:

> Their own official statements show the confusion that has been caused by Hess's escapade and we hope to make the most of this, so as to instil doubt and fear into the German government and people. Hess will be branded a war criminal and any attempt to sentimentalise over him discouraged.[34]

THE MISSING DOCUMENTS

Arrangements to isolate Hess in quarters near London where he could be studied and drawn out by picked MI6 'guardians' were in hand. Churchill had decreed he should be treated as a prisoner of war – 'with dignity as if he were an important general who had fallen into our hands' – but was to have no contact with the outer world, see no newspapers, hear no wireless and receive no visitors.[35] The instruction had not lacked a moral dimension: 'This man, like other Nazi leaders, is potentially a war criminal, and he and his confederates may well be declared outlaws at the end of the war. In this case his repentance would stand him in good stead.' It was a curious comment. Hess had expressed no repentance to Kirkpatrick; on the contrary he had blamed Britain for the war and threatened the country with starvation by U-boat and aerial blockade unless peace terms were agreed. He might have said something else to Hamilton at his first interview at Maryhill Barracks Hospital, but it is hard to imagine him expressing contrition.

There may be a small clue in the recollections of Professor Robert Shaw. In 1941 Shaw was a lieutenant in the Highland Light Infantry and was detailed to guard Hess when he was first brought to the Drymen Military Hospital. He had talked to him for some three hours, finding him articulate and polite. Hess explained the cause of the war as the refusal of the Poles to allow Germany the use of their deep-water port, Danzig, but, remarkably, he also tried to convince Shaw that Germany and Britain together should defeat Russia, a proposition he does not appear to have put to Kirkpatrick – if Kirkpatrick's reports are to be believed. In the context of repentance, he told Shaw that the atrocities they were beginning to hear about were not typical of the German people.[36]

So it is possible he made a similar remark to Hamilton, whose original 'rough notes' on his first meeting with Hess have disappeared. His 'more detailed and accurate report compiled from these notes', which Churchill had requested, was sent to the Prime Minister's private office on 18 May;[37] this report is in the open files and contains no suggestion that Hess mentioned German atrocities in Poland.

While at the military hospital Hess talked fairly freely. A letter from a doctor serving there, which was intercepted by Censorship, described him as:

> surprisingly ordinary – neither so ruthless-looking nor so handsome nor so beetle-browed as the newspapers would have us believe. Quite sane, certainly not a drug-taker, a little concerned about his health and rather faddy about his diet, quite ready to chat (to one of our junior officers) even about the origin of the war in Poland and Czechoslovakia – on which he had orthodox Nazi views.[38]

A Major Sheppard sent to Scotland to supervise his removal to London found him 'conversing freely with the officers guarding him', and noted the pleasure he seemed to take in describing the details of his flight; although at times he simply lay in his bed 'deep in thought occasionally making a few notes'.[39]

At 6.15 in the evening of Friday 16 May Sheppard informed him that he was to leave at once. Hess 'seemed somewhat elated at the news,' Sheppard noted, 'and assumed an air of great importance. Was anxious to know his destination.'[40] He had the grace, however, to thank the commanding officer of the hospital for the kindness shown him, and the treatment for his ankle.[41]

At 7.00 he was removed by ambulance as a stretcher case to Glasgow Central Station, thence by night train to London, where he was taken by ambulance to the Tower. He was to stay there for three days until a house outside Aldershot selected for his permanent residence had been prepared, the quarters he was to occupy wired for sound recording by MI6. At the Tower a flavoured sleeping draught was made up to ease his nights.[42]

* * *

Meanwhile Giffnock Police, RAF and MI5 officers had been recovering souvenirs taken by locals from Hess's plane and searching for documents at the crash site.[43]

As noted previously MI5 had been taken completely unawares by Hess's arrival. Guy Liddell had not noted it in his diary until three days after Hess landed in Scotland, and then as 'sensational news ... he seems to have been carrying some sort of message to the Duke of Hamilton from Professor Karl Haushofer'.[44] If referring to the correspondence picked up by Censorship some months before, this was, of course, the wrong Haushofer, and surely rules out Liddell and MI5 from knowledge of any prior negotiations. Similarly 'Tar' Robertson of the Double-Cross Committee only learned of Hess's arrival from the newspapers on Tuesday the 13th.[45]

On the 14th Censorship intercepted photostat copies of a letter Hess had brought with him, and sent a copy to Group Captain Blackford of Air Intelligence, who advised MI5's Regional Security Officer in Edinburgh, Major Peter Perfect, that 'various pieces of paper, presumably belonging to Hess' were in the hands of unknown persons.[46] Perfect spent the next day with the Giffnock Police investigating the matter, but whatever conclusion was reached does not appear in the open files.

Perfect also sent an officer called Buyers to interview those who had taken part in Hess's arrest. Buyers did not talk to Hamilton, Benson or any RAF officers – his reasons are not recorded – and the last page or pages of his report are missing from the file. This is certain since there is no signature, address or date on the final page, numbered 3; instead, at the bottom left corner, the word 'As', which after the style of the time denotes the first word of the next, now missing, page.[47]

It is evident from the covering letter with the report that the missing page contained references to lost documents, thus:

> I had not heard of the picking up through Censorship of a Photostat of a letter which Hess had in his possession at the time of his landing, but as Buyers concludes in his report, there is the possibility that some articles may have fallen from the plane at some distance from where it crashed. I do not know whether you think the documents which were recovered from a ditch in the field where Hess had landed, could have got there in such a way, or were as you think, planted there by someone who had pilfered them earlier.[48]

There is a reference to these documents in a letter written to a friend by Margaret Baird, wife of the farmer in whose field Hess landed: '... the police was ordered to search for a valuable document which was missing, he found it over near the wee burn in the park. Davy found a kind of oxygen mask in the turnip field ...'[49]

These revelations are of extraordinary importance. Before the MI5 folder containing Major Perfect's correspondence with head office was released there was nothing in the open files even hinting at the possibility that Hess carried a letter or documents with him to Scotland. Now there is irrefutable proof that he did so; moreover, Margaret Baird's letter shows that the documents, which had either dropped from his plane or been taken by souvenir hunters, copied, then replaced in a ditch near the crash site, were recovered by the police.

That the documents Hess brought with him went astray when he parachuted out might explain why Hamilton did not phone the Foreign

Office before late afternoon on Sunday 11 May.[50] No doubt Hess told him during his visit to Maryhill Barracks Hospital that he had lost his peace proposals; he probably assumed that they had dropped from his plane; and possibly Hamilton and Benson spent the rest of the day looking for them.

Yet the true significance of the proofs that Hess carried documents to Scotland lies in the fact that they have disappeared from the open files in this country and elsewhere. And it can hardly be coincidence that the letter or documents themselves, the page or pages of Buyers' report referring to them and all inventories of Hess's possessions when he landed have disappeared.[51] The documents presumably concerned Hess's peace plan. It is no surprise that they were suppressed at the time: they would have encouraged all forces of appeasement in the country – for that, after all, was Hess's purpose – and endangered Churchill's coalition government. The question is why they continue to be suppressed so long after the end of the war, and why so many papers relating to them have been weeded.

Their content, as divulged by an informant who claimed to have read them, does not provide the whole answer.

THE INFORMANT

The key to understanding Hess's mission has been provided by an informant, yet he is in a sense the weakest link in the story, for he cannot be named; hence his testimony can neither be probed nor proved. He insisted on anonymity and although he has since died, the conditions he laid down have to be respected: neither his name, nationality nor his post at the time can be revealed.

It can be said that he was in a position and had the qualifications to play the part he described: moreover, like Squadron Leader Frank Day, who stood guard during Hess's visit to Craigiehall House, he did not volunteer the information himself. He told the story over a dinner table in Sussex, but when questioned realised it was not common knowledge and broke off. Afterwards his host and friend of long standing, John Howell, passed on the information.[52] The informant provided further detail, but then checked with his former masters

– presumably MI6 or the Foreign Office – and afterwards closed down all contact.

This is the story he told before he was silenced: the documents Hess brought with him consisted of a proposal for a peace treaty drawn up in official German in numbered clauses, typed on Chancellery paper, and a separate translation into English. The translation was stilted, as if made with the help of a dictionary, and as a fluent German speaker the informant was co-opted by Kirkpatrick into a small group to study the German text and render its convoluted phrases into accurate and comprehensible English.

The informant could not recall the date he was approached for this task, but Kirkpatrick returned to London from Scotland on Friday 16 May and probably brought the documents down with him – or possibly Hamilton had delivered them to Cadogan the previous day. There is no record of their receipt in any open file, nor indeed in Cadogan's diary. It was shortly afterwards, presumably, that Kirkpatrick invited the informant and a few other German-speakers to BBC headquarters at Portland Place. He gave them a brief talk on the vital importance of the documents they were about to see and the need for absolute secrecy; nothing whatever could be said. The Official Secrets Act was not mentioned; it was not necessary: these were all members of the network based on school, university or club and shared associations whose fictional counterparts are familiar from the stories of John Buchan. Each member of the group was then given a different section of the German treaty, which had been re-typed in parts, and asked to make a precise translation into English to clarify the terms and portmanteau German words. The work of this secret committee was supervised and administered by Jock Colville; no doubt the typing was done by one of Churchill's female secretaries.

The informant saw the complete treaty once. For the rest he worked on the section assigned to him. The first two pages detailed Hitler's aims in Russia, outlining the precise plan for conquest and the destruction of Bolshevism. Other sections stipulated that Great Britain keep out of all Continental entanglements, in return for which she would retain her independence, her Empire and her armed services. German forces would leave France, but since France and other

Western nations had colonies which provided potential sources of friction with the British Empire, detailed provisions were made for the strength of forces in these areas; the informant remembered that clause 12 dealt with troops in the Suez Canal theatre.

Compare this with the post-war testimony of Ernst Bohle, who translated Hess's letter to Hamilton into English:

> As to the content of the letter itself I can only say that Hess strove for a peace with England on the basis of the status quo, required discussions about the colonies and devoted page after page to downright prophetic portrayals of the reciprocal air war and the fearful consequences if the conflict continued.[53]

Bohle believed the letter was never sent, but served Hess well as an aide-memoire for his discussions in England, since Hess sent him greetings in 1942 stating that he had made good use of his (Bohle's) English-language proficiency. Bohle also insisted that throughout the time he worked for Hess he believed that Hitler knew of the mission and was in full agreement with it.[54]

What he did not reveal was that he received assistance in the translation; yet the post-war testimony of his half-brother, H. Bohle makes it clear that he did:

> In 1941 ... I was translator (German–English) in the *Sprachdienst* [language service] of the German Foreign Office. One day I was called to my brother's office and was thunderstruck to find that my help was solicited to translate certain passages of a letter or letters from Hess to the Duke of Hamilton. This I was called upon to do on more than one occasion. I was sworn to secrecy.[55]

Ernst Bohle had been born in Bradford, England. His parents had moved to South Africa when he was three years old and he had been to school in Cape Town, leaving with a first-class matriculation.[56] He was obviously completely fluent in English, so it is a puzzle why he sought his half-brother's assistance. It would not be a puzzle, though, if the 'letter or letters' to be rendered into English were actually passages in a draft treaty. Then his half-brother's expertise as an official Foreign Ministry translator would have been required. H. Bohle's testimony consequently provides strong support for the informant's account, especially perhaps as it continued:

> The parts of the letter or letters which I had to translate were some-what disconnected ... My own indelible impression, based on the work I was doing, was that Hess was endeavouring, via the Duke of Hamilton, to come to some sort of an understanding with Britain ...[57]

After 50 years the informant could not remember whether an alliance was proposed, as in part 'c)' of the document André Guerber found in 1945 in the ruins of the Reich Chancellery,[58] but he did remember one phrase which provoked debate: *wohlwollende Neutralität*, finally rendered as 'well-wishing neutrality'. It will be recalled that part 'd)' of the plan Guerber found called for Britain's 'benevolent neutrality' during the German–Russian war. As for the date of Hitler's coming attack in the east, the informant was quite clear that Hess did reveal it.

It seems equally clear from Kirkpatrick's reports of his interviews with Hess that he was not told; indeed he reported Hess as saying that, contrary to rumour, Hitler had no immediate plans to attack Russia. If so, this was perhaps because Hess regarded Kirkpatrick as a representative of the Churchill government; He thought of Hamilton as an opponent of Churchill, and it is possible or even probable that he told Hamilton during their initial talk in the morning of Sunday the 11th that Hitler was about to launch his attack in the east. Lord Beaverbrook, who was brought into the affair by Churchill from the start, certainly believed so. In 1961 he wrote to the author James Leasor: 'Hess must have made it clear in that interview [with Hamilton] that his object was – or probably made it clear – to negotiate with Britain concerning the impending attack by Germany on Soviet Russia.'[59]

Beaverbrook also told Leasor that he believed Hess was on a mission for Hitler: 'For my part I have always held the view that Hess was sent, that Hitler knew of his journey, and that he intended to negotiate a treaty of peace on most favourable terms if Germany could be given a free hand to attack Russia.'[60]

It is interesting in this connection that during the War Cabinet meeting on Thursday 15 May, Ernest Bevin, who had originally informed Churchill of Hess's imminent arrival, had said, 'I think Hitler sent him here.'[61] At the same meeting Churchill said, 'I think they'll attack Russia.'[62] Churchill had many sources and reasons for his belief, but it is probably significant that he made the comment during a discussion about Hess.

The circulation list for MI6's subsequent report on reactions to Hess's flight from sources around the world had 'Sir R. Vansittart' placed second after 'Mr. Hopkinson', Menzies' Foreign Office liaison, and before 'Major Morton',[63] Churchill's intelligence adviser, an indication that Vansittart, Cadogan's predecessor, who had been removed from his post before the war because of his strident anti-appeasement stance, was still engaged at the highest levels of intelligence.

Vansittart's views on the war were unchanged. He had recently aired them in a series of radio broadcasts which had been published in January 1941 as *Black Record*, probably the most influential propaganda instrument of the war. By May they had gone through nine editions. He argued that Nazism was 'not an aberration but an outcome' of German history,[64] and pointed out: 'in Poland, for example, the Brazen horde [Nazis] is carrying out a policy of racial extermination as systematically as Imperial Germany exterminated the Hererros [*sic*] [of German South West Africa (now Namibia) from 1904 to 1907] ...'[65] The implication is that the negotiations which had surely taken place in the lead up to Hess's mission were, on the British side, bogus. Yet the informant's description of the care taken in rendering the German text into precise English suggests that the proposed treaty was taken very seriously by Churchill – possibly as a fallback in case of necessity.

CHAPTER THIRTEEN

Negotiations?

O N 20 MAY, the day Hess was moved from the Tower of London to the new home prepared for him in the home counties near Aldershot, Sam Hoare at the British Embassy in Madrid wrote a letter to Eden headed 'Personal and Private'; it was couched in veiled terms:

> Dear Anthony
> I have just written Winston a short personal note in view of the fact that he took so much interest last year in agreeing to our secret plans. I thought that he would like to know that during the last 2 or 3 weeks they have worked out very much as we hoped.
>
> I am enclosing a curious and very secret note that has just been sent me from Beigbeder. The suggestions in it bear a remarkable resemblance to what I imagine Hess has been saying in England. You will therefore no doubt wish to take it into account in connexion with anything that you get out of Hess ...[1]

Juan Beigbeder was the former Spanish Foreign Minister, an Anglophile with an English mistress. His note, enclosed in Hoare's letter to Eden, concerned an agent of Ribbentrop named Gardemann who had approached him through a personal friend to ask if he would speak to Hoare to find out what ideas the English had about peace. Gardemann claimed that a German victory was certain but that 'the

Germans did not wish to destroy the British Empire because it was an essential element in the future reconstruction of the world ...'[2] – exactly what Hess had been saying more discursively to Hamilton and Kirkpatrick.

The question is, what 'secret plans' had Hoare and Eden hatched and Churchill agreed to? Hoare's 'short personal note' to Winston might provide the answer but is not in Churchill's files.

Hoare had met Eden on 15 February at Gibraltar, where Eden stopped en route to the eastern Mediterranean on a special mission.[3] It had been a time of increasing German pressure on Spain either to join the Axis or to allow German troops through the country to seize Gibraltar; and Juan Beigbeder had been replaced as Spanish Foreign Minister by the pro-German Serrano Suñer.[4] The policies Hoare and Eden developed to meet what appeared to be the imminent danger of Franco succumbing to the proposition of inevitable German victory consisted chiefly of financial and food aid – allowing wheat in through the British naval blockade of the peninsula.[5] Concerted with Roosevelt's special envoy, Colonel 'Bill' Donovan, the policies were detailed in despatches to Churchill and the Foreign Office, and debated in Parliament. They were not secret.

At about this time, it will be recalled, Albrecht Haushofer's former pupil, Herbert Stahmer, was in covert touch with Hoare through an official at the Swedish Embassy,[6] and after the war both he and Karl Haushofer were quite clear that a meeting between Hess, Hoare and Haushofer had been arranged for February or March. It will also be recalled that MI6's agents had been spreading stories of powerful British circles who desired an end to the war, and the Assistant Chief of MI6, Claude Dansey, had sent Tancred Borenius to Switzerland to reinforce this message.[7] Meanwhile Hitler had made public offers of peace, and numerous German feelers had given clear indications of the terms available. It would surely have been irresponsible and probably out of character for Hoare not to have considered playing on Hitler's desire for peace in the west to stave off the crisis he feared in Spain: he had begun his career in MI6 and was known for deviousness.

Eden was a committed disciple of Churchill. If he and Hoare devised secret plans evidently concerning Hess's mission, in which

Churchill took great interest, the assumption must be that they involved bogus negotiations to play for time. Hoare's pre-war reputation as an 'appeaser' fitted him perfectly for the role. It might explain how he was able to tell Eden that he could imagine what Hess was saying in England, and why, after Hess's flight, Ribbentrop's agent was trying to contact him about British attitudes to peace.

Hoare's actions following his 15 February meeting with Eden support the supposition: thus, on 5 March he met Ribbentrop's envoy, Prince Hohenlohe, against Churchill's explicit instruction for 'absolute silence' to enemy peace feelers.[8] Hohenlohe's report of their conversation is missing, but both the Italian and German Ambassadors in Madrid reported Hoare suggesting that Churchill's government could not last, and that he himself would soon be recalled to London to form a new government with the object of concluding a compromise peace; he would have to remove Eden as Foreign Secretary and replace him with R.A. Butler.[9]

Early in April he had again disobeyed instructions by leaving Madrid for Seville and Gibraltar. This had earned him another reproof at the Foreign Office: 'It should be on record that the Ambassador went to Gibraltar in spite of categorical instructions that he was not to do so ... nor has he given any explanation why it was necessary for him to spend a week in Gibraltar ...'[10] Later that month he had been asked about reports that Hess had flown to Spain. He had wired back that all his information inclined him to discredit the story, but added that the German Ambassador had been in Barcelona since the 22nd – the date of Hess's alleged flight – and sent a note by diplomatic bag to say it could not be confirmed that Hess had met the German Ambassador in Barcelona.[11]

Whatever irritation Hoare caused by unauthorised excursions and windy and repetitive messages to the Foreign Office, he had retained Churchill's full confidence. During a Commons debate on 22 April on the proposed loan to the Spanish government, Churchill had answered an inspired question with a tribute to his ambassador in Madrid: it was, he said, largely due to the brilliant discharge of his duties that relations with Spain had tended to improve and not deteriorate at a crucial time.[12]

MYTCHETT PLACE

After Kirkpatrick's return to London Churchill had sent Cadogan a memo asking him to 'make now a fairly full digest of the conversational parts of Hess's three interviews', which he could then send to Roosevelt.[13] His strategy was based on bringing America into the war and he needed to end any suspicion of peace talks arising from Hess's visit; but why stipulate 'the conversational parts' of the interviews? Churchill used language precisely. The implication is surely that Hess had brought documents with him – as described by the informant[14] – which Kirkpatrick or Hamilton had carried down to London.

Churchill still wanted to give Parliament an explanation of Hess's motives, but at cabinet on 19 May he was finally dissuaded from making what Cadogan referred to in his diary as 'his stupid statement'.[15] Afterwards, with Eden and Cadogan, Churchill agreed to Kirkpatrick's original suggestion of bringing in someone to conduct bogus negotiations with Hess; Cadogan noted: 'I.K. [Kirkpatrick] came in to report. P.M. agreed we ought to draw Hess by pretending to negotiate & he came out with my idea of J. Simon for the part. We'll wait and see what "C"['s] men report.'[16] Like Hoare, Lord Simon had been a noted 'appeaser' before the war. He was now Lord Chancellor in Churchill's government, not a member of the War Cabinet.

'C's men were MI6 Germany specialists posted as 'personal companions' to Hess to try to draw information from him about Hitler, his ministers, war plans and the German war machine. They were led by Major Frank Foley, MI6 head of station in Berlin for fifteen years before the war. As passport control officer he had concerned himself with the plight of Jews and assisted many thousands in escaping, often at personal risk to himself. Today he is remembered in Israel by a grove of trees planted in Kibbutz Harel.[17] After returning to England in the early part of the war he had been posted to MI6 Section V – counter-espionage – and because of his unrivalled knowledge of Gestapo and *Abwehr* methods, co-opted as senior adviser on the Double-Cross Committee. Early that year, it will be recalled, he had been sent to Lisbon, either in response to Albrecht Haushofer's letter to Hamilton[18] or to check on Lonsdale Bryans' actions there.

The other two 'companions' went under false names: 'Colonel Wallace' was actually Thomas Kendrick, before the war MI6 head of station and passport control officer in Vienna, who, like Foley, had been overwhelmed by the numbers of Jews desperate to escape the country;[19] while 'Captain Barnes' had been born Werner Gaunt von Blumenthal in Berlin, elder son of a Pomeranian aristocrat and an English mother; educated in England, he had changed his name on the approach of war to Richard Arnold-Baker. The surname was that of his mother's second husband, an Englishman.[20]

The three companions were introduced to Hess on 20 May shortly after his arrival at the home chosen and adapted for him near Aldershot. A substantial house called Mytchett Place, it had served previously as a residence for senior army officers. To accommodate Hess, code-named 'Z', it had been converted into a fortified site named 'Camp Z' surrounded by inner and outer lines of barbed wire and machine gun pits, overlooked by spotlights, hung with alarm bells and patrolled by sentries. These were necessary precautions, not least as Poles serving in the British Army were found to be plotting to seize Hess and murder him in retaliation for the German occupation of their country.[21]

In the house, on the first floor a suite of bedroom, sitting room and bathroom had been prepared for him, furnished as any country house guest would expect but secured by a metal grille like a prison cage on the landing outside the entrance via the bedroom, and with the windows barred. These rooms, and the dining and drawing rooms below, had been fitted with concealed microphones to catch every word he might utter, with hidden wires leading to a sound room where the companions could listen in on headphones.

The camp was run by picked Guards officers under Lieutenant Colonel Malcolm Scott of the Scots Guards. Besides the security of the camp, Scott's orders held him responsible for the health and comfort of his solitary prisoner:

> Food, books, writing materials, and recreation are to be provided for him. He is not to have newspapers nor wireless ... He is not to have any contacts with the outside world whatsoever ... He is not to have any visitors except those prescribed by the Foreign Office ...[22]

By the time he arrived at Mytchett Place Hess's expectations on his move to London had given way to fearful perceptions. Requests to see Hamilton and Kirkpatrick had been refused and he was convinced he was being hidden away by the Secret Service on behalf of Churchill's warmongers, who intended to liquidate him.[23] In an attempt to pre-empt their plans, he had written to Hamilton on the 19th stating that in the letter he had left behind for the Führer he had told him it was possible that his death would be announced from England, and that it might be ascribed to suicide. But even if his death were to occur in peculiar circumstances it would be right to make peace with those in England who wanted peace. This was his last wish: 'Moreover, I have given the Führer my word that I will not on any account commit suicide. He knows that I would keep my word.'[24] Hamilton never received the letter: Cadogan and Eden decided it was not right for Hess to communicate with the Duke, to his 'possible embarrassment'.[25]

The sight of the armed sentries at Camp Z and the grille before the entrance to his room did nothing to remove Hess's apprehensions or relieve the deep depression he felt at the failure of his mission. No sooner had he been escorted in than he changed into pyjamas laid out for him, hung his uniform in the wardrobe and went to bed. Sitting up against the pillows he was introduced by the Director of Prisoners of War to Colonel Scott and his future 'companions', Wallace, Foley and Barnes. He was told that any requests he had would be passed on by Colonel Scott, at which he asked to see Hamilton and Kirkpatrick.[26]

He ate dinner in his room that evening, but when the following morning breakfast was brought up for him, he barely touched it, explaining that the duty officer, Lieutenant William Malone of the Scots Guards, was a member of the secret police and might be trying to poison him.[27] The one man whom he appeared to trust was the doctor, Colonel Gibson Graham, who had treated him in Scotland and accompanied him since. He had a long talk with him that morning, the 20th, repeating what he had originally told Kirkpatrick about the certainty of Germany winning the war and the mission on which he had embarked – without the Führer's knowledge – to stop the senseless slaughter, but doubting his prospects of success now that he was in the hands of the warmongers' clique who were preventing his access to the King. He could only gain access through the Duke of Hamilton, and they were keeping him away.[28]

Nothing could assuage his suspicions. He was told that Gestapo practices were not employed in Britain, but his mistrust seemed only to deepen. At meals taken in the mess over the following days with the Guards officers and 'companions' he would swap his plate for another in order to avoid being poisoned or drugged; when passed a dish from which to help himself he would take a portion from the far side; and apparently fearing that a member of the Secret Service would creep into his room at night and cut an artery to fake his suicide, he told Dr Graham – as he had tried to inform Hamilton – that he had given the Führer his word that he would not take his own life.[29]

His moods swung from cheerfulness to extreme depression, and he made no attempt to disguise either. The Guards officers, brought up in a stiff school to shun displays of emotion as unbefitting an officer and gentleman, were unimpressed. Malone kept a diary in which he recorded finding it difficult to imagine how 'this rather broken man who slouches into his chair careless as to his dress' could have been the Deputy Führer. 'He is such a *second-rater*, with none of the dignity, the bearing of a great man.'[30] Dr Graham remarked on his daily decrease in stature (character), and took to rating him in terms of the wage he might command in Britain: by Saturday 24 May, he estimated his worth at no more than £2 a week;[31] by the 28th Colonel Wallace judged this had fallen to 35 shillings.[32]

It is not at all apparent whether the fears Hess expressed were real or play-acting of a type he was to indulge later with great success, intended perhaps to bear out the Führer when it became necessary for Hitler to distance himself from the mission by declaring his deputy insane. It is more likely, perhaps, that he suspected his companions of using drugs in their efforts to elicit information. Six weeks later he wrote a long deposition claiming that after arrival at Mytchett Place he had been 'given in food and medicines a substance which has a strong effect on brain and nerves'; he described the sensations produced as similar to headache, but not the same, followed by many hours when he experienced feelings of extraordinary well-being, mental energy and optimism, giving way after some time to 'pessimism bordering on a nervous breakdown without any cause and ... extraordinary fatigue of the brain'.[33]

The description fitted the effects of amphetamines. These drugs had been in medical use since 1938, and while Hess did not take drugs, Hitler almost certainly boosted himself with amphetamines during the day; it is likely that Hess would have observed the effects. He was certainly aware of the effects of drugs on the victims of Stalin's show trials of 1936–38; they had made a deep impression on him because of his visceral aversion to Bolshevism. In any case, the major powers were all experimenting with 'truth drugs' at this period, and it is likely that Hess, with his interest in alternative medicines, took an informed interest in developments. No doubt he knew that Himmler's doctors used mescalin on concentration camp inmates, and he may have known that the *Abwehr* employed sodium thiopental when they wanted to break a man's will and force him to confess or reveal secrets.[34]

It is possible, therefore, that when he realised he was in the hands of the Secret Service – as he was – he assumed that they would use drugs to break his will and make him reveal what he knew; and knowing the effects of such drugs, he imagined suffering them, as it were, psychosomatically. Or he may have pretended to feel the effects, as later he would pretend to lose his memory, in a struggle to combat efforts to break his will. It is also possible, or even likely, that he was indeed being fed drugs to Menzies' orders.[35] Or he may simply have been describing the ups and downs of his own nervously unstable character, exaggerated by his sense of impotence at the apparent failure of the mission on which he had set such hopes.

Years afterwards, in another prison, when he set down his recollections of Mytchett Place for Ilse, he made no mention of drugs in his food; what he recalled were the fragrant glycineas and rhododendrons in the garden where he walked with his 'companions', and evenings in his room when he heard Mozart played on the gramophone in the music room below by Colonel Scott, 'in peacetime a professional artist, with a true artist's nature; outside were warm summer nights, and my heart was aching so.'[36]

On the night of 28/29 May his frustrations overwhelmed him. Lieutenant Malone was on guard duty. He had managed to break through Hess's reserve the day before by raising the subject of skiing; and when he came on duty that night Hess had shown him pictures of young Buz, which he had admired. At 2.45 in the morning Hess came out to where he was sitting reading inside the grille by the bedroom door and said he couldn't sleep, then in a stage whisper he began running through the reasons he had come to Britain, just as he had explained them exhaustively to Hamilton, Kirkpatrick and others before. Malone reported to Scott:

> He then asked me to get in touch with the Duke of Hamilton to request that he arrange an audience for him with the King, saying that if I did this I would in due course receive the thanks of the Monarch for a great service to humanity. I told him that this was impossible and this sort of thing put the Duke of Hamilton in a most unfortunate position. He then went on to say that he believed that the secret service at the behest of a clique of warmongers had hidden him here so that the Duke could not find him, and were trying to drive him to insanity or suicide ...[37]

Malone told him this was nonsense, at which Hess described a 'devilish scheme' in operation over the past few days to prevent him sleeping at night or resting during the day: doors slammed, people running up and down uncarpeted stairs, motorbikes nearby with engines running, aeroplanes sent overhead to break his nerves. Malone explained that there was a large military training camp nearby and such noises were normal, but Hess only shook his head and flapped his arms about before going back to bed. Minutes later he was out again to apologise, saying he was in a very nervous condition and perhaps did not mean all he had said.[38]

Nonetheless, when he came down to breakfast the next morning he was obstinately silent, and remained so during the day. His 'companions' were unable to draw a word from him, and that afternoon Dr Graham told Scott he believed that 'Z' had definitely passed over the border between mental instability and insanity.[39] It is not clear how he came to this conclusion. Hess had been subject to mood swings and sulks since his first arrival in Scotland, and particularly at Camp Z. No one who had reported on him had suggested he was insane. Moreover, Gibson Graham's own report after first meeting him at the Drymen Military Hospital on the 13th, scarcely over a fortnight before, stated specifically, 'he did not strike me as being of unsound mind. Such information as he gave me ... with regard to his health was given in a rational and coherent manner.'[40] After accompanying him to the Tower of London and Mytchett Place, he summed up:

> one gets the impression, *in the absence of evidence to the contrary*, of an intelligent man of no great character or driving force who has been dominated and hypnotised by his master [the Führer] ... He is conceited, introspective, neurotic. In addition there is evidence of delusions and lack of judgement. He reasons at times logically on obviously unsound premises. One has the impression at times of a certain amount of posturing in his gait and manner ...[41]

No hint there of madness. The answer may be that a diagnosis of insanity was ordered from the top. Long after the war Lord Beaverbrook told the author James Leasor that he suggested the idea to Churchill during a walk in St James's Park while discussing how to prevent the spread of rumours that Hess had come to Britain with a genuine peace plan. Beaverbrook, a Canadian, said he believed that anyone in Britain who came under the care of a psychiatrist was written off as mad, and this might provide a quick way to discredit Hess.[42]

It is what happened. Colonel Scott reported Dr Graham's opinion that Hess had crossed over the border to insanity to the Prisoners of War Directorate that afternoon and received a call back later to say that Colonel Graham would be relieved over the weekend by a psychiatrist. He noted in his diary that this was 'all to the good', suggesting that he at least was not party to any plot.[43]

THE ASSASSINS

On the night of 27/28 May, the night before Hess revealed his anxieties to Lieutenant Malone, German parachutists landed in England, apparently on a mission to silence him. They came down near Luton on the assumption that he had been taken to the Air Intelligence Interrogation Centre less than 20 miles away at Trent Park, Cockfosters. There is no trace of the mission in German records, and it is difficult to imagine why it should have been launched on such inadequate intelligence; difficult to imagine how it could have been expected to succeed. Nevertheless, the story, disclosed in 1979 by Lieutenant Colonel John McCowen in the *Luton Herald*,[44] can now be supported by an equally strange entry from Guy Liddell's diary.[45]

The Double-Cross Committee was running a double agent named Wulf Schmidt, alias Harry Williamson, code-named TATE, and on the night of 26/27 May a message came through from the *Abwehr* that money would be dropped for TATE on the following night during the course of a bombing raid near Luton. It would be contained in the thick ends of 'four birch tree branches, each a metre long'.[46] The operation was later cancelled 'on the excuse that the plane was not available', but four MI5 men were in any case sent to the area to observe. Guy Liddell noted:

> in the middle of the night a certain Major McCallum [*sic*] turned up at the offices of the Superintendent of the Beds. police. He had an extraordinary story about a man who was going to be dropped by parachute in order that he should assassinate HESS. He said he came from some anti-aircraft brigade. In order to convince the police of his bona-fides he took them out to see his Brigadier who was surrounded by A.A. guns and searchlights. The Home Guard happened to be doing a night exercise and were roped in. Hundreds of men appear to have been walking about all night all over the country ...[47]

Colonel McCowen's post-war story was somewhat different: not just one assassin, but several German Commandos had been dropped; and two or three were captured.[48] Liddell's diary entry has nothing about parachutists being caught, and his summary of enemy agents arriving by parachute lists only one name for May 1941, and that long beforehand on the 12th.[49] As McCowen told the *Luton Herald*, the details of the parachutists' capture and what happened to them subsequently 'is one of the missing chapters'.[50]

The episode, beset as it is by problems of verification, would hardly be worth recounting were it not for the source of McCowen's information about the assassins: none other than Willi Messerschmitt. McCowen, in May 1941 a Major on Air Vice Marshal Trafford Leigh Mallory's staff, expanded on this in 1990:

> Messerschmitt was aware of the R.A.F.'s 'Y' service which listened in to traffic, and he sent a coded message to Leigh Mallory – whom he presumably knew before the war – saying that German parachutists would be dropped in the early hours of 28 May – about 2.0 am. – in a bombing raid at Luton – as they believed Hess might be at the prisoners' interrogation centre at Cockfosters – to eliminate Hess.[51]

Leigh Mallory sent for McCowen and told him about the parachutists: 'You're an army officer. Get cracking! We'll support you as much as we can with the R.A.F. Move a mixed brigade of guns and searchlights at short notice!' McCowen relayed the order to a colleague in command of a mixed brigade of guns and searchlights at Windsor, who moved his unit to Luton; he also told the commander of a Home Guard battalion exercising in the area that they were to be out and about all night. McCowen could not have seen Liddell's diary entry about the anti-aircraft brigade and the Home Guard 'walking about all night' at this time since the diaries were not open to the public until 2005, and the entry quoted for 28 May is not in any case in the published edition.[52]

McCowen believed that Churchill had been warned about Hess coming over, probably by Messerschmitt through Leigh Mallory; and it will be recalled that Messerschmitt told Lord Colyton after the war that he had been at the Augsburg airstrip when Hess took off for Scotland.[53] The full story of these communications must remain speculative since Leigh Mallory died in an air crash in 1944.

LORD SIMON

The psychiatrist chosen to look after Hess in place of Dr Graham was Major Henry V. Dicks of the Royal Army Medical Corps. He had been born in Estonia to English-German parents of Jewish blood – an insensitive choice perhaps, but he spoke fluent German and appears to have maintained professional objectivity with his Nazi patient. He arrived on 30 May with the head of British Army psychiatry, Colonel J.R. Rees, in time for lunch. Afterwards Rees had a long talk with Hess, finding him anxious, tense and depressed, but 'certainly not today insane in the sense that would make one consider certification'. Rees judged Hess's extreme depression adequately explained by his current situation and sense of failure.[54]

By this date Lord Simon had agreed, after much hesitation, to Eden's request to pose as a peace negotiator, and after dinner that evening Foley told Hess that a high representative of the Foreign Office was to visit him to open negotiations. Hess replied that he would not speak unless a German witness was present, and reminded Foley that he had already put forward the names of two German internees; and once again he asked to see the Duke of Hamilton and Ivone Kirkpatrick.[55] Foley reported to Menzies:

> In his confused way he seems to think that they [Hamilton and Kirkpatrick] are outside the political clique or Secret Service ring which is preventing him from meeting the proper peace people and the King. He reiterated that he had come here of his own free will, trusting in the chivalry of the King.[56]

The question of peace negotiations remained a matter of highest sensitivity and potential danger for Churchill. It is significant that even Eden's Undersecretary for Foreign Affairs, R.A. Butler, had been kept in ignorance of what Hess was saying; he was, of course, an appeaser. To a querulous request he sent for 'a little more information', Cadogan had replied that he (Butler) was in the happy position of being able to tell questioners he didn't know; but he agreed to let him see the Kirkpatrick interviews.[57] For the same reason, Eden enjoined Simon to the utmost secrecy about the forthcoming 'negotiation', and pointed out that while he had to tell Hess that he came with the government's approval, it was hoped he would not emphasise this, 'since the man dreams of a change of government'.[58]

Simon briefed himself on Kirkpatrick's and Foley's reports of their interviews with Hess. In addition Kirkpatrick sent him a short summary:

> The object of Hess's journey is solely to convince responsible British leaders that, since there is no fundamental divergence between British and German aims, and since he is satisfied that Germany must sooner or later win this war, a peace of understanding should obviously be concluded now.
>
> The only basis on which he is at present prepared to impart information is to convince his listener that Germany will win. The best line of attack is, therefore, to invite him to explain clearly why Germany will win and to cross-examine him closely on those points in particular on which the military wish information ...[59]

He then suggested lines of enquiry Simon might pursue. First was 'Russia: What is the use of our concluding a peace of understanding with Germany if Germany is going to sign up with Russia and bring Bolshevism into Europe?' This suggests that Hess had not revealed Hitler's plan to attack Russia either to Hamilton or Kirkpatrick; indeed Kirkpatrick's reports of his interviews make this plain. Yet nothing in the documents on Hess's mission can be taken at face value. Neither Hamilton nor Kirkpatrick had revealed the existence of the documents Hess undoubtedly brought with him – as the recently released MI5 papers prove – so their narratives cannot be taken as complete, and no conclusions can be drawn from them: either, as they imply, Hess did not reveal Hitler's imminent attack on Russia, or he did reveal it but it was judged that at this critical juncture Lord Simon, a former appeaser, could not be trusted with the information.

Kirkpatrick went on to list Italy, Spain and Portugal, Iraq and the German-occupied territories as subjects on which to probe Hess. This is strange, unless his memorandum was indeed a complete blind. Why had Kirkpatrick not questioned Hess on these areas of crucial importance himself? He had been forced to listen to an interminable harangue during his first interview, but could have used his subsequent visits to probe Hess on specifics. More than this, it seems scarcely credible that Hess had come to negotiate peace without giving any intimation – either in the documents he brought with him or 'conversationally' – of such significant areas of concern as the treatment of France and the Low Countries. Earlier German peace feelers had made it plain Hitler was only interested in eastern Europe and the Balkans and was prepared to evacuate occupied western Europe.[60]

Given that it was crucial for Churchill to write Hess off as a lone madman and squash any hint of a credible peace plan, the fact that both Simon and the known wobbler R.A. Butler were allowed to see Kirkpatrick's reports suggests that they were tailored to conceal much – as confirmed by their silence on the papers Hess brought with him.

Just before his visit to Camp Z Simon received a report from Hess's new medic, Dr Dicks. Noting his patient's abnormal preoccupation with his health and suspicions of being drugged and persecuted, his fatalistic and superstitious attitude to life and desire to be a 'saviour and bringer of peace', Dicks diagnosed a paranoid personality. More perceptively, perhaps, since it confirms all German sources close to Hess, he deduced that 'in Hitler Herr Hess had seen the perfect father authority who would make the bad world right. The moment he felt that Hitler was ruthless and destructive, he must have experienced great anxiety ...'[61] He could not admit this, Dicks continued, or even allow himself to know that he felt it; the Fuhrer was still perfect so he had to continue being loyal and, at least consciously, reject the bad qualities of his idol. Meanwhile he had begun instinctively to look for a new 'pure object of veneration', and found it in 'the gallant Duke of Hamilton, or the chivalrous King of England'.

* * *

Simon arrived at Mytchett Place at 1.00 p.m. on 9 June, accompanied by Kirkpatrick as his 'witness'. To preserve secrecy they carried passes countersigned by Cadogan in the names of 'Dr Guthrie' and 'Dr Mackenzie', although Hess ('Jonathan') had been told their real names. While they had lunch with Colonel Scott, Hess, who had dressed with care in his Luftwaffe uniform that morning, remained in his room with 'Captain Barnes', refusing any food in case of a last-minute attempt to poison him.

At 2.00 p.m. MI5 officers arrived with Kurt Maass, the German 'witness' Hess had requested, and at 2.30 Simon, Kirkpatrick, a stenographer and Maass walked upstairs and through the grille on the landing into Hess's bedroom, thence to his drawing room, where he and Barnes, who was to interpret, waited to receive them.[62]

'*Herr Reichsminister*!' Simon began after introductions, 'I was informed that you had come here charged with a mission and that you wished to speak of it to someone who would be able to receive it with government authority. You know I am "Dr Guthrie" and therefore I come with the authority of the government and I shall be very willing to listen and discuss with you as far as seems good anything you would wish to state for the information of the government.'[63]

'*Ich bin ausserordentlich dankbar, dass "Dr Guthrie" herausgekommen ist ...*' Hess began.

'He is extraordinarily grateful that Dr Guthrie has come out here,' Barnes translated when he had finished. 'He realises that his arrival here has not been understood by anyone – because it was such a very extraordinary step to take he can't expect us to.'

Hess then launched into an explanation of how the idea for his mission first came to him while with the Führer during the French campaign the previous year. The Führer had said to him he believed the war could perhaps be the cause of finally coming to the agreement with England for which he had striven all his political life; and when after the French campaign England had refused the Führer's offer of peace, he (Hess) had become all the more determined to realise his plan.

He paused for a long time after Barnes translated this, then spoke of the air war during which England had sustained heavier destruction and loss of life than Germany. In consequence he had the impression England could not give way without suffering great loss of prestige, and had said to himself he must realise his plan, because if he were over there in England the English could use his presence as grounds for negotiation. He was enabled to keep to his plan, he went on, by holding ever before his eyes endless rows of children's coffins followed by weeping mothers. No doubt he was sincere; he had been greatly disturbed by the scenes he had witnessed during the French campaign. It is interesting, nonetheless, that one of several propaganda leaflets the RAF had dropped over Augsburg in the days immediately preceding his flight had shown a picture of a badly wounded dead child with the caption, 'This is not your child, but one of the countless children caught by German air raids.'[64]

From the humanitarian angle Hess passed to political history, treating Simon to the lengthy review of Anglo–German relations since the turn of the century that Kirkpatrick had suffered at his first interview, eventually reaching the lesson that British policy was always to form a coalition against the strongest Continental power and in the short or long term attack it. It would have been more accurate had he said 'been attacked by it', but he was, of course, relaying the Nazi view of history.

Proceeding to the charge levelled against Germany of breaking treaties, he said he could match this with an endless series of broken treaties and violations of international law in British history: Germany had not treated any nations as England had treated the Boers, the Indians, the Irish; Germany had had no Amritsar [massacre], 'nor have we created concentration camps for women and children as was the case with the Boers'.

Simon apparently let this pass in silence. No doubt, like Kirkpatrick during his first interview, he felt argument would be useless. He did say later he hoped Hess understood that if he did not challenge his account it was not because he agreed, but because they must agree to differ; his real purpose in coming was to hear about his mission.

'Essentially my flight was influenced,' Hess responded, 'the decision to make this flight was because those around the Führer are absolutely convinced that England's position is hopeless – so much so we ask ourselves on what basis England can possibly continue the war.' This led him into an account of Germany's vast aircraft production and huge numbers of trained flying personnel. When Simon attempted to press him on actual numbers he replied that on military grounds he could not go into details, but it was hundreds of thousands. The air attack prepared for England was something frightful. 'The previous air raids on England were only a small foreplay ['*Vorspiel*'] in comparison to what will come,' he went on, 'and that is the reason – I should like to stress it – why I have come over here. And it is something unimaginably frightful, an air war on the scale this air war will take.

'I consider myself, so to speak, duty-bound as a human being to appear here to warn you and make this proposal ['*Vorschlag*'] that I am delivering.'

Simon asked what his proposal was. He would happily explain, Hess replied, after he had made one more point: the U-boat war. However, he first returned to the air war and civilian morale under bombing, which led him to the assertion that in the last war the German collapse had come not from the fighting front but from the home front. 'And this internal enemy we have basically eliminated ['*ausgeschaltet*'].'

'And this enemy behind the lines has been liquidated,' Barnes translated.

'Conversely love for the Führer has never been as great among the German *Volk* as it is now,' Hess concluded.

Simon, who had been questioning him about aircraft numbers and civilian losses caused by British bombing, apparently allowed his remark about the liquidation of the enemy within to pass without comment. This seems strange: before the war Simon, who liked to explain that despite his name he was not a Jew, had taken Alfred Rosenberg to task about the treatment of Jews in Germany. Perhaps he was merely impatient at the time Hess was taking to get to the point; and he had not been asked to probe the situation of the Jews.

Hess passed on to the extraordinarily large U-boat fleet under construction to attack British merchant shipping and so starve the country, as U-boats had almost succeeded in doing in 1917; and the idea that Britain could carry on the war from the Empire if the motherland had to capitulate for want of merchant tonnage was, he asserted, false. When Barnes had translated this Hess again brought up the concentration camps created by the British in the Boer War, saying they (Germany) would have equally little compunction, if the Empire had not capitulated, in putting pressure on the motherland.

Kirkpatrick drew the conclusion: 'Starving out the British Isles.'

'That is a very hard position to take,' Hess agreed, 'But it is in England's hands to make an end [to the war] under the most favourable conditions. I don't know whether Dr Guthrie has already been informed of these conditions.'

The question is: what conditions? Kirkpatrick had not reported Hess making any conditions apart from the general concept of Britain allowing Germany a free hand in Europe and handing back Germany's former colonies, in return for Britain being allowed a free hand in her Empire. The terms 'Europe' and 'Empire' had not been defined, nor what was to happen to occupied western Europe or Poland, on whose behalf Britain had originally gone to war. So far as the open files are concerned there is nothing in the official record even hinting at conditions for a negotiated peace. Conversely, if the anonymous informant is to be believed, precisely formulated conditions had been laid down in the proposal Hess had brought with him. It is evident from Lord Simon's line of questioning that if Hess had brought such a proposal, Simon had not seen it.[65]

Lord Simon again asked him to explain his mission.

'I have learned the conditions under which Germany would be prepared to come to an understanding with England during a great number of conversations with the Führer. I must emphasise these conditions have been the same since the outbreak of war.'

There followed a confused discussion of when he had made his first attempt to fly to Britain. After explaining the delays since he had first conceived his plan – in obtaining a plane, training on it and having special instruments fitted – he said he had attempted to execute it on 7 January. 'For a number of reasons, weather conditions etc., and difficulties with the work on the plane, I was not able to carry it out.'

Simon asked if he came with or without the Führer's knowledge.

'Without his knowledge,' Hess replied in English without waiting for the translation, '*Absolut!*' and laughed.

Simon pressed him on why he had come at this particular time. The flight had been possible in practical terms from December on, he replied, but he had waited for suitable conditions; either it was bad weather in southern Germany or over the coast or in Scotland; earlier he had mentioned British victories in North Africa and against the Italians in Greece as additional reasons for putting off his flight.

Kirkpatrick made a free translation for Simon, ending, 'so what with the postponement because of the weather and postponement because of Wavell's victories May really was –'

Hess broke in, 'On 10 May I made my first attempt.'[66]

In an 'Amended Version' of the Simon interview prepared later for the legal officers at the Nuremberg war crimes trials this phrase is rendered as 'On 10 January I made my first attempt'. Only a few minutes earlier in the interview Hess had told Simon he had made his first attempt on 7 January. And it will be recalled that his adjutant, Karl-Heinz Pintsch, gave 10 January 1941 as the date of his first attempt.[67]

After parrying more probes by Simon on whether he had really been sent by the Führer, Hess handed Kirkpatrick two half-pages of handwritten notes he had prepared for the meeting.[68] Kirkpatrick read them aloud in translation.

'Basis for an understanding. One. In order to hinder, to prevent future wars between England and Germany there should be a definition of spheres of interest. Germany's sphere of interest is Europe. England's sphere of interest is her Empire –'

Simon interrupted to ask if Russia was in Europe.

'European Russia interests us obviously if we, for example, conclude a treaty with Russia, then England should not intervene in any way.'

Simon asked again if Russia west of the Urals – 'Moscow and all that part' – was part of the European zone.

'No, not at all.'

After questions about Italy, which Hess confirmed was obviously part of Europe, they moved on to his further points, which hardly differed from what he had told Kirkpatrick at the first interview: return of German colonies, indemnity for war losses suffered by individuals, and, a new point, peace to be concluded simultaneously with Italy. Simon suggested there must be more than four conditions written on two half-sides of paper, and pressed him successively on what would happen to Holland, Norway and Greece. Hess replied that the Führer had not pronounced, and returned to his basic condition for an enduring peace: that England should interfere in Continental affairs as little as Germany should interfere in the Empire.

They were able to get no further. Simon had concluded, as he was to put it in his subsequent report to Churchill, that Hess was 'quite outside the inner circle which directs the war',[69] and wound up the interview.

As they rose to leave Hess asked him if he could have a word in private. Once they were alone he began speaking very earnestly in English. His words were picked up by the concealed microphones and transcribed by a stenographer in the secret recording room.

'I have come here, you know, and I appealed to the gallantry of the King of England and the gallantry of the British people here, and I thought that the King and the Duke of Hamilton would take me under their protection. I have been very well treated in the hospital and in the barracks [Tower] in London. I came here and I seemed also to be treated well. But not behind me. I have been asked things since I am here, if I am sensitive to noises. And I am ...'[70] He listed noises in the corridor outside his room and continually banging doors, motorcycles in the road and aeroplanes, which had prevented him from sleeping. Simon assured him that the noises were not intentional. They moved on to the question of substances added to his food and drink. Simon told him that whatever happened in Germany did not happen here; he was being childish, idiotic.

'If you will not believe me I will go off my head and be dead,' Hess said desperately, and after more dismissive remarks by Simon, 'Then I don't eat more in this house.'

'That is very silly of you.'

Hess's English became more excited and ungrammatical as he tried to convince Simon that if he was found with his veins cut, the German people would be convinced that he had been killed by the Secret Service and it would be the definite end of understanding. And taking out photographs of his wife and son, he handed them to Simon. 'Please save me for them. Save me for peace and save me for them.'

'That is a nice portrait.'

'And I have to ask you to go to your King and get me a leave by his order. It is only that what I have to ask him, an urgent ask for you.'

Simon explained that matters like that were decided by the government, not the King, and urged him to behave like a soldier and a brave man. Hess, who had been a brave soldier in the first war and risked his life flying to Scotland, answered very reasonably, 'I am a soldier and I have been a brave man, but I have my experiences ...'

He could make no impression, and after a further admonition to show courage, Simon left.

Dr Dicks found his patient totally exhausted.[71] Colonel Scott recorded that Hess seemed relieved: 'was somewhat arrogant and truculent and strutted about the lawn after dinner with Major Foley.'[72]

* * *

A significant postscript to this interview is that the German 'witness', Kurt Maass, was afterwards, at the request of MI6, returned to the interrogation centre, Camp 020 at Ham Common, Richmond, and held in isolation, as was the other German internee Hess had originally asked for, Dr E. Semmelbauer, although he had not been present. An internal MI5 note states: 'MAAS [*sic*] visited Camp Z [Mytchett Place] and has since, for special reasons, been kept apart from SEMMELBAUER. SEMMELBAUER has also been kept apart from other prisoners at Ham.'[73]

From 20 July Maass and Semmelbauer were allowed to 'associate' twice daily for an hour at a time under observation by 'special staff', obviously German speakers, who reported what the two discussed, particularly in regard to what Hess had said to Lord Simon. On the 25th a report passed to Guy Liddell noted an assertion by Maass that when Simon had asked about the fate of the occupied countries, 'Hess replied that on this matter he was unaware of the Führer's views.'[74]

What Hess had also said, according to the transcript of the Simon interview, was that the Führer had simply stated, 'There are people who believe we will hold on to all that we have taken – I will certainly not be insane ['*wahnsinnig*']',[75] a Delphic utterance meaning presumably that Hitler did not mean to hold all the territory he had occupied.

Semmelbauer in particular protested repeatedly against being held in isolation, and on 29 August MI5 was notified that both Germans could be returned to normal internment:

It has been decided by the Prime Minister and Foreign Secretary that they [Maass and Semmelbauer] may be returned to an internment camp, provided they sign a statement promising never to disclose their knowledge about Hess, and that they are made to understand that any leakage will lead to severe punishment ...[76]

That the decision had been taken at the very highest level is an indication of the supreme importance attached to keeping all aspects of Hess's mission from leaking. The Prime Minister and Foreign Secretary would not ordinarily have been consulted on individual internment issues. If it is accepted that the anonymous informant and other sources to be detailed were correct in stating that Hess's proposals included the German evacuation of occupied western Europe, it can be inferred that the Prime Minister must have been reassured by the report on the internees' belief that Hess was 'unaware of the Führer's views' on this subject – in other words that the two Germans did not know Hess's peace proposals included German evacuation of western Europe, and could not, therefore, leak this bombshell.

CHAPTER FOURTEEN

The story leaks

SIMON DRAFTED a preliminary report on his interview the follow-ing day. He believed Hess's assertions that he had come entirely on his own initiative: 'he has not flown over on the orders or with the permission or previous knowledge of Hitler,' he wrote on House of Lords paper. 'It is a venture of his own.'[1] However, unless passages have been excised from the transcript of the interview, Simon's subse-quent observations appear to have been derived mainly from his study of the previous reports:

> Hess arrived under the impression that the prospects of success of his mission were much greater than he now realises they are. He imag-ined that there was a strong peace party in this country and that he would have the opportunity of getting into touch with leading pol-iticians in this country who wanted the war to end now. At first he asked constantly to see leaders of opposition and even imagined himself as likely to negotiate with a new government.[2]

Nor did Simon's further conclusions add anything new. He contended that Hess was 'quite outside the inner circle which directs the war', knew nothing of strategic plans, and had embarked on the mission to boost his own standing after a decline in his position and authority in the regime.

Cadogan responded to Simon's interview with a memo to Eden suggesting points for discussion:

1) Is there any government reply or comment to be made on his ['Jonathan's'] proposals?
2) If so I suppose it should be on the regular lines on which we have replied to similar peace 'feelers'. That will put an end to our semi-official conversations with him ...[3]

Next he suggested how Hess might be exploited for propaganda, wondered whether Hess might be allowed to read *The Times* – 'it might be of interest and even of value to watch the impact of the news upon him' – and finally:

5) Shall we take a favourable opportunity of giving him a drug that will encourage communications?

This suggests that Hess's suspicions about being drugged were up to that point without foundation – this undated memo clearly having been written shortly after Simon's interview.

On 14 June Churchill read the transcript of the interview, and dictated a memo to Eden:

it seems to me to consist of the outpourings of a disordered mind. They are like a conversation with a defective child who has been guilty of murder or arson. Nevertheless I think it might be well to send them by air in a sure hand to President Roosevelt ...[4]

He added that he did not see any need for a public statement at present, and in the meantime 'Jonathan' should be kept in strict isolation where he was.

Hess, meanwhile, had received no response to the 'proposals' he had put to Simon. This confirmation of his failure had pushed him into black despair. Colonel Scott recorded him being in a 'difficult' mood all that day, the 14th, pacing the terrace 'like a caged lion, refusing to answer when spoken to'.[5] He relented after dinner and played dart bowls in the garden with 'Captain Barnes', but in the early hours of the following morning, the 15th, he got out of bed and demanded to see Lieutenant Malone. Malone was on outside guard duty and Dr Dicks went to see him instead. Hess met him with such a torrent of abuse that Dicks became convinced, as he reported to Scott, that their prisoner was definitely insane.[6] Scott's adjutant eventually managed to calm him and get him back to bed.

Later that morning Malone went up to see him. Hess rose and greeted him like a long-lost friend, then poured out his customary allegations about being poisoned to the instructions of a small clique around Churchill who wanted to prevent him from bringing about peace; his interview with Dr Guthrie had, he said, convinced him that the cabinet as a whole were anxious to negotiate. After detailing the symptoms he had experienced from substances added to his milk and other drinks, he finally produced two envelopes, one addressed to 'Mein Führer', one to his wife, Ilse, and asked Malone to despatch them through official channels as soon as he was dead. He assumed, he went on, that they would not be sent, so he gave Malone two duplicates, asking him to deliver them personally at the end of the war. Malone said he would have to report that he had duplicates, whereupon Hess begged him 'in the interests of humanity' to keep them secret. Malone insisted he could not do that and Hess eventually took all the envelopes back.[7]

Malone could not have known, but these were suicide notes, dated 14 June:

Mein Führer,

My last greeting to you, who have been my inspiration for the past two decades. After the collapse of 1918 you made my life worthwhile again. Since then I have been allowed to commit myself to you and thereby to Germany. Scarcely ever has it been granted to men to serve a man and his ideas with so much success as [granted] to those under you.

I thank you with my whole heart for all that you have given me and what you have been to me.

I write these lines in the clear understanding that there remains for me no other way out – as hard as *this* end is for me.

My family, including my elderly parents, I commend to your care.

In you, my Führer, I greet our *Gross-Deutschland* which is drawing towards an undreamed of greatness.

I die in the conviction that my last mission, even if it ends in death, will bear some fruit. Perhaps, despite my death or indeed precisely through my death, my flight will bring peace and understanding with England.

Heil, mein Führer!

Your devoted
Rudolf Hess[8]

He had added at the end of one copy a fragment of a poem by Goethe: 'According to great, eternal laws must we all complete the circle of our existence.'[9]

The letter addressed to Ilse was for all his family and friends:

My dear all,
Because I am forced to end my life, my last greeting to you all and thanks for all that you have been to me!

The final step is very hard for me with thoughts of you, but I am left with no other way out.

I committed myself fully to a great idea – fate has willed this end! I am convinced nonetheless that my mission will somehow or other bear fruit. Perhaps despite my death or precisely through it peace will result from my flight.[10]

After the war Professor Karl Haushofer said of his former student and devoted friend that he had shown suicidal tendencies and a lack of balance as early as 1919, and had never been normal. 'I recall having him sent to our family physician, Dr Bock, who discovered traces of infantilism.'[11]

Besides the two farewell notes, Hess had written a detailed account of his flight addressed to his son – as mentioned earlier. He had begun it on 10 June, the day after his interview with Simon, and he concluded it sometime on the 15th with a personal reflection:

> Buz! Take note, there are higher forces controlling our fate – if we wish to give them a name we call them divine powers ['*göttliche kräfte*'] – which intervene, at least when it is necessary, in a great event. I *had* to come to England and talk here of understanding and peace!
>
> Often we do not comprehend these hard decisions at once; later one will always recognise their significance.

15.6.41   R.H.[12]

On the same day he added a note to what appears to be an aide-memoire he had written for his meeting with Simon. It was headed 'Extraordinary meeting, no protocol provided, convened on the appearance of a *Parlementär*'[13] (an emissary under a flag of truce). Five numbered paragraphs followed: '1. Understanding: wish of F[ührer] (Headquarters)'. The second point dealt with British scepticism, but 'position alters if E[ngland] learns *authentic conditions.*' The remaining points amounted to little more than overcoming mistrust in England by representing the history of the past years correctly, as of course he had attempted to do at great length. Now, having failed, he signed off: 'To my son to remember the accomplishment of the life mission of his father.'

Finally he wrote a brief note requesting that his uniform be delivered to the Duke of Hamilton for transmission to his family after the war.[14]

* * *

In the early hours of the following morning, the 16th, shortly before four, he emerged briefly from his bedroom in pyjamas and told the duty officer he couldn't sleep and had taken some whisky. Returning to his room, he dressed quickly in full uniform and flying boots, then called out for the doctor. The duty officer outside ordered the Military Police warder to fetch Dicks, who arrived sleepily in pyjamas and dressing gown, holding a bottle of sleeping tablets. As the warder slid the bolts in the grille door and pulled it towards him to allow Dicks through, Hess burst out of his room, eyes staring wildly and hair dishevelled. Dicks thought he was going to be attacked. Instead Hess knocked him aside into the warder, rushed the short distance to the banister surrounding the stairwell and vaulted over.[15]

He landed with an audible thud on the stone floor of the hall below, but his left leg had struck the lower banister on the way down, partially absorbing the momentum of his fall, and he lay fully conscious, but groaning in extreme pain, pointing to his left thigh and calling for morphia as Dicks, warders and the duty officer dashed down the stairs, joined soon by Colonel Scott, the 'companions' and others woken by the commotion. Blankets, pillows and tea were brought for him while Foley telephoned Menzies in London and obtained permission for a surgeon from the military hospital nearby to be called in. Arriving almost an hour later, the surgeon diagnosed an uncomplicated fracture of the upper femur with no abdominal injury. Dicks recorded Hess's reaction as 'chagrin at having his beautiful breeches cut open with scissors' and 'docile, childlike trust in and co-operation with the surgeon'.[16] His leg was strapped into a temporary splint and he was carried back up the stairs to his bedroom and given an injection of morphia. Dicks had been reluctant to administer one earlier in case it masked signs of internal injury.

Lieutenant Malone came on duty at 10.00 a.m. to find him lying awake in semi-darkness with curtains drawn. After a short silence Hess said he had written to his family the day before telling them what he was about to do, and explained his reason: he could not be mad in England.

'Surely you did not intend to kill yourself?'

Hess replied that he certainly had and still intended to do so. Malone's subsequent report continued:

> In killing himself he would be acting like a man. He knew that recently he had been behaving like a woman. When he first came here he had behaved as a man. 'I got up at eight o'clock in the morning, but then came a period of no sleep, no sleep' and he had begun to go to pieces under the influence of wine and drugs ...[17]

Dicks's chief, Colonel Rees, visited Hess that evening and saw him again two days later, reporting afterwards that his condition had deteriorated markedly since his first visit on 30 May:

> The delusional tendency which I then noticed has become more marked and more definitely organised so that he now has a delusional idea of poisoning and of a plot against his life and against his sanity which no one can argue him out of. He told me that his suicidal attempt was because he would rather be dead than mad in this country.[18]

He was clear that Hess's condition had 'now declared itself as a true psychosis' – insanity. The regime at Mytchett Place was altered accordingly: medical orderlies with mental nursing qualifications took over in place of the young Guards officers looking after Hess, and 'Colonel Wallace' and 'Captain Barnes' were returned to their normal duties, leaving Foley as Menzies' only direct representative in the house. Also, Hess was allowed *The Times* every day – perhaps, as Cadogan had suggested, to watch his reactions to the news.[19]

All intelligence from Enigma decrypts, agents and German troop movements suggested that Hitler was about to attack Russia; and on 9 June, the day of Simon's interview, Göring had informed British and American representatives in Stockholm via his go-between, Birger Dahlerus, that Germany would attack Russia 'by about the 15th'.[20] Whether it was hoped that this might aid Hess in his talks with the British, whether the negotiations that must have prompted Hess to come to Britain were continuing through agents and middlemen, or whether Göring was playing a part in a great deception on Stalin – that the real target was Britain – is quite unclear.

In the early hours of Sunday 22 June, anniversary of the French armistice in the Forest of Compiègne, massive German armies and Luftwaffe fleets deployed on the eastern front from Poland to the Balkans launched the invasion of Russia. The Red Army was caught by surprise and overrun, Red Air Force planes destroyed on the ground. Stalin, who had ignored all warnings under the impression that Hitler must secure his western front by coming to an understanding with Britain before marching east, was paralysed by indecision.

Later that morning at Mytchett Place Major Dicks came into Hess's room to tell him the news.

'So,' Hess replied with an inscrutable smile, 'they have started after all.'[21]

Hitler was with Goebbels at this crucial moment in the war, pacing back and forth in the salon of the Reich Chancellery; Goebbels entered in his diary: 'The Führer rates the peace party in England very highly. Otherwise there would not have been such systematic silence [about Hess]. The Führer only has words of contempt for Hess ...'[22]

THE APPEASERS

On 19 June, three days before Hitler's assault on Russia, the government's stance on Hess's mission had been questioned during the adjournment debate in Parliament.[23] A Labour Member, Samuel Sydney Silverman, asked whether Hess had brought any proposals with him, and whether any reply was contemplated. Silverman was a Jew who had raised himself from humble circumstances. During the first war he had served over two years in jail as a conscientious objector, but Hitler's accession to power had caused him to rethink his pacifism and he had supported Britain's declaration of war in 1939. A campaigner on behalf of Jews worldwide, and especially in Palestine, he had recently been elected chairman of the British section of the Jewish World Congress.

His question was echoed by Richard 'Dick' Stokes, also Labour, but from a very different background and with an opposing viewpoint. Stokes had a public school and Cambridge education; he had served in the Royal Artillery in the first war, winning an MC and bar, since when he had become chairman and managing director of a successful engineering firm in Ipswich, whose voters he represented. He shared Liddell Hart's views on the war and led a campaign for a compromise peace which had been supported the previous year by Lord Beaverbrook's newspapers. On 10 May, the day Hess had flown to Scotland, the Duke of Bedford, formerly Lord Tavistock, the most outspoken aristocratic advocate of peace, had written to him suggesting that Lloyd George, 'so obviously the one man who could save the country', should make a public statement indicating peace terms to which Germany could respond.[24]

While Silverman was anxious lest the government were talking to or even negotiating with Hess, Stokes believed that they should. In answering both, Churchill said that he had no statement to make at this time, but the United States government had been kept informed on the subject of Hess's flight to Britain; to a supplementary question, he said he had nothing to add to his previous answer.

Continuing to press him, Silverman referred to a statement published by the Lord Provost of Glasgow, Sir Patrick Dollan, that Hess had arrived in this country expecting to make contact with certain individuals or groups – unnamed – and to be able to go back again in two days' time; and he asked, 'Did he or did he not propose peace?'

Stokes again supported his question: 'To ordinary persons like me it appears that this is the most sensational thing that has happened for many hundreds of years'; and he referred to rumours that Hess was living at the Prime Minister's country retreat, Chequers. This was rebutted by R.A. Butler. Before that Major Vyvyan Adams had taken up the case for the government, accusing Stokes of identifying himself with the opinions of Lord Londonderry. Adams continued:

> I believe that Hess came to this country under the fond delusion that he could debauch our aristocracy by saying to them join us or we join Russia. It seems that he came having in his pocket proposals which might attract the mentality which now wants peace at any cost. There is such a mentality and it is mainly to be found here and there in corners among the well-born and well-to-do. Those who have more money than sense, those who whisper the dangerous fallacy, better defeat with our possessions than victory with Bolshevism, which is exactly what Hitler wants them to say. Such an outlook is to be found, only half ashamed in the corners of another place [House of Lords]. Appeasement is not dead among those whom I may call for the purpose of rough convenience the Cliveden set, an expression as historically convenient and geographically inaccurate as the Holy

> Roman Empire. I have no doubt indeed that *The Times* newspaper
> would quickly make surrender or compromise appear respectable ...[25]

Whether Adams had learned Hess literally had proposals 'in his pocket', or whether he meant it in a general sense, there is no doubt the thrust of his rhetoric about the number of 'appeasers' and their high social standing was correct. Indeed the topic had been broached at a top-level meeting at SOE headquarters in Woburn Abbey – ironically the seat of the pacifist Duke of Bedford – on the very day Hess had taken off for Scotland. Most unusually, two cabinet ministers had been present: Hugh Dalton, Minister of Economic Warfare and head of SOE, and the Foreign Secretary, Eden.[26] The Director General of Political Warfare, Robert Bruce Lockhart, also there, had noted in his diary: 'Sat. 10th May. Back to Woburn Abbey for meeting with Eden ... [who] talked about appeasers in the Conservative Party, plenty of them ... Dalton nearly gave away one of our biggest secrets at luncheon.'[27]

Hess had, of course, come to talk with the appeasers; and it will be recalled that the whole thrust of the deception run by all arms of British intelligence in the effort to turn Hitler eastwards was that Britain could be neutralised by negotiation with the powerful 'peace party' in the country.

LIEUTENANT LOFTUS

Although Hess's daily supervision had been taken over by medical orderlies, the Guards officers remained at Camp Z and continued to visit him and share meals with him as he lay in bed with his left leg encased in plaster suspended from a Balkan frame. On 17 July a newcomer, Lieutenant Murrough Loftus of the Scots Guards, introduced himself. He was the son of the Conservative MP for Lowestoft, Pierse Loftus. Foley had briefed him for his meetings with Hess, suggesting he make much of a family visit to Germany before the war when his mother had met Hitler, implying they had been impressed by what they had seen there.[28] The aim, as with all officers at Mytchett Place, was to extract information by gaining Hess's confidence.

The scheme, or Loftus's natural charm, worked at once. Hess took to the young officer at their first meeting over lunch in his room, and talked freely for an hour on many topics.[29] To a question about his flight he replied that he had intended to come as long ago as Christmas and had made two separate attempts, but had been forced back by bad weather or faults in the steering gear or wireless. He was quite certain that if only he had been able to contact some influential person in Britain they could have stopped the war between them. When asked whether he was sure that Germany would accept his peace proposals, he replied that Germany was Hitler, and he had complete agreement with Hitler. Asked what exactly his proposals were, he was studiedly vague. Afterwards Loftus wrote a long report on the conversation and his own assessment of Hess:

> He is incredibly vain, and flattery about his flight, for instance, makes him talkative and in a good humour. I don't think he is a subtle man or a liar. I think he is one of the simplest people you could meet and I very much doubt whether he is at all intelligent, but he has what has lifted the whole mediocre bunch to power – that single-tracked blind and fanatical devotion to an ideal and to the man who is his leader. But he differs from the rest of Hitler's henchmen in that he is genuinely religious and sincerely humanitarian. He doesn't doubt for a moment that Germany will win the war and sees himself building a house in Scotland ...[30]

He was so obsessed with his mission, Loftus went on, that he could not see things as they were. His manners were courteous and he had a disarming smile, but his appearance was slightly spoilt by his upper teeth, which tended to protrude: 'He is chiefly remarkable for his eyes which are astonishingly deep-set under pronounced brows and of striking intensity.'

The following day, the 18th, Major Dicks, who had never gained Hess's trust, was replaced by another psychiatric doctor. Two days later Colonel Scott noted in his diary that Hess seemed to improve every day; 'one begins to wonder if Col. Rees & Major Dicks were right in their diagnosis that he is permanently insane.'[31]

On the 25th Lieutenant Malone left Mytchett Place, and two days later at lunch Hess told Loftus he was the only one in the house he could trust, and he had something of momentous importance concerning his flight which he was prepared to divulge provided Loftus would give his parole not to repeat it to anyone in the house. Loftus refused to do so until he had consulted his father, who as a Member of Parliament and 'a friend of Germany' was to act as go-between to the Prime Minister. Colonel Scott noted in his diary that Loftus had said this 'in order to gain information as instructed; he actually had no intention of approaching or informing his father'.[32]

Foley did not expect much from the promised revelation; he was proved right. When Hess handed Loftus the report on 1 August it turned out to be little more than an amplification of his previous complaints, demands and suspicions, including almost clinical descriptions of the sensations produced by the drugs he alleged he had been given, and names of witnesses to incidents he complained of. He asserted that if he had given the impression of suffering from a psychosis it was because he wanted peace – presumably from the persistent questioning to which he had been subjected.[33] It appeared to be an admission that he had been play-acting. Moreover, he went on, he had now made it more difficult to give him 'harmful substances' by sharing his food and drink with the young officers who lunched and dined with him. He added that they had behaved in exemplary fashion towards him.

The latter part of the report was a request for an enquiry on the basis of his statements, to be conducted on the authority of the King, not the War Office or the Prime Minister; and he asked that a translation of this report should be given to the Duke of Hamilton: 'That gentleman promised me when I landed that he would do everything to secure my safety. I know that in consequence the King of England has issued appropriate orders ...'

Having unburdened himself, Hess started on a second, this time political as opposed to personal, report. He handed it to Loftus a week later, on 7 August: 45 manuscript pages headed 'Germany–England from the angle of the German–Bolshevik War'.[34] Again he asked for a translation to be forwarded to the Duke of Hamilton.

It was a logical, rather prophetic document, by no means the rambling of a psychotic. It began by questioning British war aims and asking whether the difference between coming to an understanding with Germany now or fighting on to achieve eventual victory was so great it was worth the sacrifices in men, materials, destruction and indebtedness to foreign countries which must ensue: '... the longer the war lasts the more the power relation between England and America becomes weighted in favour of the latter', in support of which he cited the final chapter of Commander Russell Grenfell's *Sea Power*, 'published under the pseudonym T-124'. Further, all these sacrifices could be in vain since it was not at all certain that England would win. Which brought him to his second point, already elaborated endlessly to Hamilton and Kirkpatrick, Foley and the 'companions', the young Guards officers and Lord Simon, that Germany's victory was certain. It would be accomplished chiefly by the U-boat campaign against British shipping and overwhelming air attack. It was this conception of the 'frightful things to come' that had strengthened his decision to attempt the flight to England; and he repeated previous assertions that his presence in England could be the best excuse for negotiations without Britain losing face.

None of this was new, but he went on to develop a prophetic warning about the Soviet threat. Despite being certain of German victory, he posed the hypothesis for the sake of argument that Britain and Russia would win the war:

> A victory for England would equally be a victory for the Bolsheviks. The victory of the Bolsheviks would sooner or later mean their marching into Germany and into the rest of Europe. The military strength of the Bolsheviks is no doubt a surprise for the whole world ... But Soviet Russia is doubtless only at the beginning of her industrial development. Imagine what the military strength of the Bolsheviks will be in the near future if their industries are strongly developed ...

Pointing to the size and population of Russia and her mineral riches, he supplied the answer: Soviet Russia would become the strongest military power on earth, the future world power, inheriting the world position of the British Empire. 'Only a strong Germany supported by the whole of Europe and the confidence of England can avoid the danger.'

This was the familiar Nazi appeal to regard Germany as the bulwark of Western civilisation against Communism, an argument which appealed and was intended to appeal to significant strands of British imperial thinking.

This evidently worried Eden, for on 11 August, four days after Hess had handed the document to Loftus, Menzies alerted Foley to the Foreign Secretary's disquiet:

> You will observe from the attached that the S of S [Eden] and Sir A.C. [Cadogan] are somewhat concerned lest the Duty Officer [Loftus] should convey anything whatsoever that he may glean about Jonathan [Hess] to his parents. I feel sure there is no danger, but can you confirm.[35]

The implication is that Pierse Loftus was known to be on the 'compromise peace' wing of the Conservative Party. In his reply Foley referred to the 'special circumstances' of Loftus's case,[36] which might suggest that the young officer had been posted to Mytchett Place specifically because his father was a Conservative MP in order to encourage Hess to talk. Immediately after Lieutenant Loftus's arrival, Foley stated:

> to make quite certain that there could be no possible misunderstanding, Lt. Col. Scott, his superior officer, at my request, invited him to the orderly room and solemnly reminded him of his oath of secrecy and took from him a verbal assurance that he understood.
>
> I attach a minute which he has written today at my request. It will allay any anxiety.[37]

The attached note signed by Loftus stated that his instructions, in common with those of other junior officers, were to extract from 'Z' any information that might be of use to the government:

> To achieve this end I set out to gain his confidence by pretending a sympathy towards many things which I myself and those people I introduced into the conversation were, in fact, very far from feeling.

The Führer, Adolf Hitler, and his deputy, Rudolf Hess, at a Nazi rally in
Weimar in 1936.

Winston Churchill, the leading opponent of appeasing Hitler, walks to Whitehall with the arch 'appeaser', Viscount Halifax, in 1938.

TopFoto   © Ullsteinbild/TopFoto   National Archives

(above left) Douglas Douglas-Hamilton, the 'boxing Marquess' of Clydesdale.

(above middle) Clydesdale's German friend and Rudolf Hess's England expert, Albrecht Haushofer.

(above right) Lord Halifax's unofficial envoy to the German opposition to Hitler, the old Etonian James Lonsdale Bryans.

Getty Images

Sir Samuel Hoare, a leading 'appeaser' who had held all high offices of state except Prime Minister, with King George VI and Queen Elizabeth.

(right)
Colonel Stewart Menzies, later chief of MI6, with his second wife in 1932.

(far right)
Claude Dansey of MI6 in the 1930s; he became Assistant Chief of the service in the Second World War.

Getty Images   Crown Copyright

The Granger Collection/TopFoto   Author's collection   Getty Images

(above left) Admiral Wilhelm Canaris, chief of German Military Counter-Intelligence (*Abwehr*), who worked against Hitler and the Nazi regime.

(above middle) Kenneth de Courcy, secretary and intelligence officer of a powerful group opposing British involvement in continental Europe; friend of Stewart Menzies.

(above right) Carl Burckhardt of the International Committee of the Red Cross, who worked for peace between Britain and Germany.

The Prime Minister, Winston Churchill, and his Foreign Secretary,
Anthony Eden, in 1941.

Hitler, Goebbels and Hess celebrating the anniversary of the Nazi 'seizure of
power' at the Berlin Sportpalast, January 1941.

The wreckage of Hess's Me Bf 110 (code VJ+OQ) at Floors Farm, Eaglesham, Renfrewshire, guarded by Home Guard and military.

(*far left*) The Duke of Hamilton in flying kit.

(*left*) The Duke of Kent in RAF uniform; note the 'scrambled eggs' around the peak of his cap, and his medals.

(above) The 'summer house' in the garden of Spandau jail, where Hess died.

(right) The extension flex with which he hanged himself, attached to the window catch.

(below) The lower end of the flex unplugged; note overhand knot by the skirting.

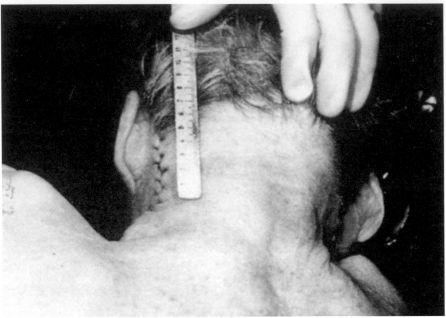

(above) The back of Hess's neck at the post-mortem, showing a horizontal mark more typical of strangulation than hanging.

(right) The 'suicide note' found in Hess's clothes, which reads:

'Request to the [prison] Directorate to send this home.

Written a couple of minutes before my death.

I thank you all, my loved ones, for all you have done for me out of love.

Tell Freiburg that, to my immense sorrow, since the Nuremberg Trial I had to act as if I didn't know her. There was nothing else I could do, otherwise all attempts to gain freedom would have been impossible.

I would have been so happy to see her again – I have received the pictures of her as of you all.

Euer Grosser [Your Big One]'

I reported my conversations to my Commanding Officer and to Major Foley who sanctioned me to continue along the lines I had chosen.

Nothing that has passed between Z and myself – either written or spoken – has been or ever will be mentioned to anyone but my Commanding Officer and Major Foley who are in possession of the full facts concerning my conversations with Z.[38]

On the 15th, three days after Loftus signed this affirmation, the officer commanding the Grenadier Guards at Windsor, Lieutenant Colonel W.S. Pilcher, was removed from his post, retired and forced into professional and social isolation in Scotland.[39] The reason for his abrupt disappearance has never been officially disclosed. His friend, Kenneth de Courcy, before the war secretary and intelligence officer of the Imperial Policy Group of powerful interests opposed to Britain's intervention on the continent of Europe, believed that he was removed because he had learned of Hess's peace proposals.

De Courcy gave no explanation of how Pilcher may have learned details of Hess's mission, but MI5 documents now reveal that de Courcy himself was briefed on Hess's proposals, and that the information came from Lieutenant Loftus.[40]

KENNETH DE COURCY

It was not until almost the end of 1942 that MI5 applied to the Director of Public Prosecutions for a charge against de Courcy for receiving information in contravention of the Official Secrets Act.[41] By this date Camp Z had been wound up, Hess had been moved to another location and Loftus had long ceased to have contact with him. Nonetheless, it is clear from the public prosecutor's notes that MI5 attempted to bring de Courcy to trial because of information about Hess he had received from Lieutenant Loftus:

In a charge against De Courcy of receiving information under Section 2 (2) of the [Official Secrets] Act it would be possible to rely upon the evidence of Loftus to prove his communication to De Courcy of the facts relating to Hess and the very character of the information might be relied upon in proving that De Courcy had reasonable grounds for believing at the time he received it that it was communicated to him in contravention of the Act by reason of the official position occupied by Loftus. I do not altogether like this suggested charge because it involves the necessity of, as it were, admitting that Loftus himself had committed an offence under Section 2 (1) of the Act ...[42]

From this it seems that Loftus had leaked what he knew of Hess's mission to de Courcy the previous year while serving at Mytchett Place under Colonel Scott.

De Courcy received confidential information from many sources, including service personnel, and recorded the details of what he had been told in a private diary dictated to his secretary. The public prosecutor recognised that it would be necessary to raid his office and seize this diary, but foresaw too many difficulties in proving that the entries had been communicated subsequently to other persons or were likely in themselves 'to prejudice the defence of the realm or the efficient prosecution of the war' to proceed against him. No action was taken.

The case is nonetheless significant as it shows that MI5 had reason to believe Loftus had supplied information on Hess to de Courcy. Guy Liddell himself wrote to Menzies at this time, 'There is no doubt that De Courcy has acquired a considerable knowledge of Hess's intended mission and of his behaviour since he arrived in this country.'[43] This throws an entirely new light on de Courcy's post-war statements on Hess. Heretofore it has been easy to dismiss them in light of his subsequently blackened reputation: besides being, in the words of *The Times*, 'a pro-Nazi friend of the Duke of Windsor ... fantasist and appeaser'[44] – in other words on the losing side in the war – de Courcy was jailed in the 1960s for alleged inability to return a million pounds put up by investors in a scheme for a garden city in Rhodesia – a charge and sentence against which he protested his innocence for the rest of his life. However that may be, the release of the public prosecutor's file on MI5's attempt to prosecute him for receiving information from Loftus elevates his disclosures on Hess's mission to insider information.

De Courcy had no doubt about the reason for Colonel Pilcher's liquidation from his command, his regiment and his friends. Long before the war Pilcher had predicted France's collapse, and had warned against Britain becoming involved on the Continent. Like his close White's Club companions Stewart Menzies and the Duke of Buccleuch, like many Tory grandees and members of the Royal family, like the military strategists Liddell Hart, General J.F.C. Fuller and Commander Russell Grenfell, he had believed Russia and the spread of Communism a greater danger for the British Empire than Nazi Germany.[45] These views had made him the object of deep suspicion to those supporting Britain's new alliance with Soviet Russia.

Chief among these, according to de Courcy, was Victor Rothschild of the banking dynasty. Rothschild was an extraordinarily gifted polymath: while still at Harrow School he had played first-class cricket for Northamptonshire. As an undergraduate at Trinity College, Cambridge he had played for the university, and despite many other enthusiasms and accomplishments, including playing Bach and jazz on the piano to a high standard, he gained a triple first-class degree; subsequently he was awarded a scientific research fellowship at his college.

Most significantly, during his time at Trinity he was initiated into the Apostles secret society. This small group of privileged young men was possessed by dissatisfaction with British society and enthusiasm for Communism; and Rothschild, a supreme rationalist, was drawn to the 'scientific' Marxism they professed.[46] He masked his views by committing to the Labour Party, but two of his friends in the Apostles, Anthony Blunt and Guy Burgess, like Kim Philby, were later recruited as Soviet agents. De Courcy had no doubt that Rothschild was their sponsor:

> He saw these brilliant young men at Cambridge, all of whom had a weakness, and he spotted it and put it to advantage, thinking they would get into higher levels of affairs. He saw the Nazis as the greatest threat to the Jewish race ever and was determined to back the Russians. He encouraged these men, helped them financially, succoured them and stood back.[47]

De Courcy himself was a prime target for the 'Russian group': a Soviet booklet entitled *Russia's Enemies in Britain* devoted 39 of its 70 pages to attacking him.[48] Conversely there is no doubt that he was in a position and had the contacts to know his own enemies in Britain. More recently his charges against Rothschild have been confirmed by the Australian author, Roland Perry, who has adduced compelling circumstantial evidence – admittedly no direct proof – to show that Rothschild was himself recruited by the KGB and was actively involved in passing information to the Russians, mainly through his friends, Blunt and Burgess – in short that he was not merely the sponsor, but was the 'fifth man' in the Cambridge spy ring of Blunt, Burgess, Philby and Donald Maclean.[49]

Perry lays the additional reproach that Rothschild was more loyal to his Jewish heritage than to the country of his birth. Certainly after the Nazis took power in Germany Rothschild advanced a great deal of money to the British Fascist leader, Sir Oswald Mosley, to extract Jews from Germany, Austria and Czechoslovakia.

In the late 1930s, as war approached, he attached himself particularly to the anti-appeasement set around Winston Churchill.[50] After the outbreak of war he leased a three-storey West End maisonette he owned at 5 Bentinck Street to two female friends from his time at Cambridge, who in turn sub-let a flat to Burgess and Blunt. They were often joined there by Rothschild.[51]

In April 1940 Rothschild joined MI5 at the invitation of Guy Liddell.[52] He was to head the counter-sabotage division, where he brought his scientific intellect and a quite exceptional courage to the task of defusing enemy bombs. His position also served as perfect cover for his spying activities, and he was soon instrumental in having Liddell take his great friend and fellow KGB agent Blunt into the service as his (Liddell's) personal assistant. Liddell recorded a discussion he had with Rothschild shortly before he took him on, observing, 'He [Rothschild] is quite ruthless where Germans are concerned, and would exterminate them by any and every means.'[53]

This was the man who, according to de Courcy, was responsible for Colonel Pilcher's professional exile:

Pilcher was removed under the influence of Rothschild, Blunt and others of that Russian party, and Churchill disgracefully went along with it.

Pilcher knew the secret of the Hess mission which was anti-Russian and with which the following sympathised:

Queen Mary [the Queen Mother], the Duke of Windsor, Aga Khan, Lord Londonderry, the Duke of Westminster, the Duke of Buccleuch, Lord Rushcliffe ...[54]

De Courcy was unwittingly involved in Pilcher's dismissal: a note Pilcher sent him detailing German military dispositions in Russia was intercepted by Censorship and photocopied before being allowed on its way, following which two Special Branch men visited de Courcy and had him sign a statement that he had received the note.[55] This infringement of the Official Secrets Act was the pretext on which Pilcher was ejected from his post. Subsequently, when he failed to appear at White's or respond to enquiries, de Courcy wrote to Menzies saying that something had gone wrong with Pilcher. He received a reply the next day warning him that any enquiries on this subject would be met with extreme displeasure from the very highest circles[56] – from which he concluded that Churchill had sanctioned Pilcher's exile.

He assumed the pressure had come from Rothschild, who had the backing of the immensely wealthy American Jewish lobby that Churchill was determined to keep onside. It is probable that Rothschild was also responsible for MI5's later attempt to prosecute de Courcy himself; Moscow exaggerated de Courcy's importance and was at this time in late 1942 urging his detention.[57]

* * *

De Courcy never disclosed the fact that Lieutenant Loftus had broken faith with Colonel Scott and Foley by briefing him on Hess. However, in one of his post-war *Special Office Brief* newsletters circulated some time after Pilcher's death in 1970 he claimed to have a note of what Pilcher had told him about the mission. The note was dated 28 May 1941,[58] thus before Loftus had come to Mytchett Place.

It suggested that Hess came over with the knowledge of the *Abwehr* chief, Admiral Canaris, and the real object was to topple Hitler. This runs counter to everything known about Hess's character and his blind loyalty to the Führer, and contradicts everything that Lieutenants Malone and Loftus reported after their conversations with Hess – of which more later. The note continued:

> Hess had become alarmed about the war and coming Nazi excesses. He believed a total reversal of strategy and policy to be essential. He had heard stories that Queen Mary, the Duke of Windsor, the Dukes of Westminster and Buccleuch, the Marquis of Londonderry, Lords Halifax and Rushcliffe, Basil Liddell Hart and R.A. Butler thought so too.
>
> His idea was the evacuation of France, Belgium, Holland, Norway and Denmark, peace with England and placement of the Jews to Palestine ...
>
> War with Russia would however be prosecuted.

The *Special Office Brief* piece went on:

> It was that factor which aroused the profound anxieties of the pro-Russian Party in Britain which brought vast pressure upon Churchill to stifle the whole project. One man threatened to leak the facts – Colonel W.S. Pilcher ... commanding the Grenadier Guards at Windsor. He was dealt with, relieved of his command ... and thereafter ordered to Scotland. He lived the rest of his life a virtual recluse until he died in 1970 ... His exit from a former social life was remarkable ...[59]

In a confidential memo headed 'Colonel W.S. Pilcher', de Courcy expanded on the aim of toppling Hitler:

> When Hess arrived Pilcher learned something at [*sic*] his mission which, to a limited extent, fitted into his opinions – at least it was clear that Germany could be turned East, would reduce in the West to a substantial extent and that as Germany became weaker

powerful elements within the armed forces and upper classes would turn against Hitler ...[60]

It is well known that Canaris sheltered anti-Hitler officers at his head-quarters; it is also known that throughout the war he provided MI6 with information via several of Menzies' agents[61] – and that he eventually paid a terrible price for his disloyalty. It is probable that he knew of Hess's mission, but the suggestion that Hess also aimed for Hitler's removal seems utterly improbable. What is interesting in de Courcy's account is that the terms Hess proposed included German evacuation of occupied western Europe – as the 'informant' later testified[62] – and the resettlement of the Jews in Palestine.

In another *Special Office Brief* newsletter, de Courcy stated, again like the 'informant' later, that Hess 'carried formal peace proposals for submission to wholly proper official channels ...'[63]

CHAPTER FIFTEEN

The 'final solution'

THE 'MADAGASCAR PLAN' for the resettlement of Europe's Jews on the French Indian Ocean island had been abandoned by the end of 1940, if not earlier. By 1941 the plan was for the wholesale massacre of European Jewry in the wake of the drive east. Probably Hitler had had this concept from the beginning: it will be recalled that Heydrich's orders to his commanders at the start of the Polish campaign in 1939 had distinguished between the short-term and the 'ultimate aim' for the Jews.[1]

It is probably significant that on 20 May 1941, ten days after Hess had taken off on his flight for peace, and still nothing having been heard from the British, the Reich Central Office of Emigration issued instructions on Göring's authority banning further emigration of Jews from the Reich; the reason given was the 'doubtless approaching final solution [*Endlösung*]'.[2] Later that same month Heydrich's head of Counter-espionage, Walter Schellenberg, circulated Security Police Departments with the same message: all Jewish emigration was banned because of the '*zweifellos kommende Endlösung*'[3] – the new euphemism for physical destruction.

If these orders are indeed linked to the apparent failure of Hess's mission they add credibility to de Courcy's claim that the peace proposals Hess brought included the resettlement of European Jews in Palestine. In reality the numbers involved virtually ruled this out since the storm such an influx would inevitably raise in the Arab world would threaten the stability of the region and its vital oil supplies. Nonetheless it is interesting, although probably coincidental, that on 19 May, the day before Göring's ban on Jewish emigration, Churchill raised the prospect with the War Cabinet of negotiating with Ibn Saud of Saudi Arabia on the creation of an autonomous Jewish state of 'Western Palestine'.[4]

It is inconceivable that Hess was unaware of the final solution planned for the Jews. It is true that the detailed scheme for industrial extermination camps had not been worked out before he flew to Scotland, but all special *Kommando* and police units who would liquidate Bolshevik commissars and Jews behind the lines of advance into Russia had been instructed and indoctrinated in their mission, and army commanders themselves had been fully briefed on the coming ideological battle to decide the future of the Reich.[5] Hess had been close to Rosenberg, appointed Reichsminister for the occupied east, who certainly knew the general plan for the Jews, and he was frequently with Goebbels, who demonstrably knew: on 20 June, two days before Operation 'Barbarossa' was launched, Goebbels made a comment in his diary on a report from Poland: 'The Jews in Poland gradually decay. A just punishment for inciting the people and engineering the war. The Führer has indeed prophesied that to the Jews.'[6] Hess had heard the prophecy as often as Goebbels, yet at Mytchett Place when challenged on Nazi Jewish policy he appears to have given nothing away. During a wide-ranging conversation with Lieutenant Malone in July he said that Hitler had decided to banish all Jews from Europe at the end of the war; their probable destination was Madagascar.[7]

When Foley asked Hess about the abuse and murder of Jews, Hess challenged him to produce evidence; and strenuously denied that cruelty or torture was practised in Germany.[8] At any mention of concentration camps he liked to quote the figure of 26,000 women and children who he alleged had lost their lives in British concentration camps during the Boer War.

On 11 August Colonel Scott recorded that Loftus had picked an argument with Hess over concentration camps and the persecution of Jews. This was four days after he had been handed Hess's second report questioning British war aims, which Hess hoped he would pass to his MP father and to Hamilton. Apparently Hess merely responded with the alleged 26,000 Boer women and children who had perished in British camps.[9]

On the 16th Foley reported to Menzies: 'We have been asking ourselves whether his [Hess's] expose [*sic*] was a pose which he had assumed for our benefit. We are inclined to think it was not and that he had been shocked by what he had seen in Poland and the West.'[10] There is no indication of what Hess had exposed. This must have formed the subject of a previous report, no longer in the file. The reference to his shock at what he had seen in Poland and the West suggests it concerned the brutalities of war, possibly even the treatment of Jews. Or it may have been an outburst about the senselessness of the war, since Foley was responding to a report from a journalist formerly resident in Berlin that before flying to Britain Hess had been 'amazingly open with his friends about the stupidity of this present war'.[11] If such was the case why should the actual report of his exposé be missing?

By this date Churchill had ample evidence of the early *wild* – defined in German–English dictionaries as 'wild, savage, fierce ...' – stages of the 'final solution'. It arrived every morning with Menzies' orange-buff boxes in the form of Bletchley Park decrypts of messages reporting mass shootings of 'Jews', 'Jewish plunderers', 'Jewish Bolshevists' or 'Russian soldiers' by police units behind the German advance into Russia. On 7 August the police commander, central sector, had reported 30,000 executions carried out since the start of the campaign.[12] Although the specific aim of liquidating Jewry, as opposed to shooting Jewish partisans and 'plunderers' had not yet been identified by British intelligence analysts, it is reasonable to assume that Menzies had briefed Foley on the mass killings for his conversations with Hess, and that Foley had put them to Hess, as he had earlier put allegations of Gestapo torture and cruelty. It is possible, therefore, that Hess's exposé was about the liquidation of Jews in the east. That is pure speculation.

By 24 August Churchill felt compelled to broadcast a speech on the atrocities, without, however, specifying the anti-Jewish nature of the campaign, and being careful to conceal the source of his information:

> As his [Hitler's] armies advance, whole districts are being exterminated. Scores of thousands – literally scores of thousands – of executions in cold blood are being perpetrated by the German police-troops upon the Russian patriots who defend their native soil. Since the Mongol invasions of Europe in the sixteenth century [sic] there has never been methodical, merciless butchery on such a scale, or approaching such a scale ...[13]

At the end of the month Churchill received decrypts reporting that the 1st SS Brigade had killed 283 Jews and Police Regiment South 1,342. Churchill circled the latter figure.[14] By this date he had received reports on seventeen occasions of groups of Jews being shot.[15] By 12 September when Police Regiment South reported disposing of 1,255 Jews, British intelligence had concluded that the figures were 'evidence of a policy of savage intimidation if not of ultimate extermination',[16] and it was decided not to include reports of this nature in future briefings for Churchill: 'The fact that the Police are killing all Jews that fall into their hands should by now be sufficiently well appreciated.'[17]

BEAVERBROOK AND STALIN

On 21 August Hess handed another 'political' deposition to Lieutenant Loftus, who gave it to Foley that evening. Unlike Hess's former reports, Colonel Scott did not include it in his diary.[18] It is impossible to say whether the omission is significant.

Early the following month Hess received a letter from Lord Beaverbrook dated 1 September reminding him of their last meeting in the Chancellery in Berlin and suggesting they have some further conversation.[19] Beaverbrook was due to fly to Russia for talks with Stalin about war materials, and knew that Hess would come up for discussion. Hess replied on the 4th that in recollection of the meeting in Berlin he would be happy to see him.[20]

He had sunk into deep depression after the failure of his latest attempts to use Lieutenant Loftus to get through to the groups he still felt certain would be sympathetic to his proposals. His medical orderlies felt that he was 'verging on the suicidal again',[21] and since his splint was due to be taken off a decision had been reached to refurbish his suite as a mental hospital ward with armoured glass in the windows.

He started writing another report for his meeting with Beaverbrook, but as the date of the visit neared he became more and more agitated, exactly as he had before his interview with Lord Simon. The day before the visit, he refused all food except biscuits and asked the doctor for morphia for a pain in his gall bladder.[22]

Beaverbrook arrived early in the evening of 9 September with a pass made out in the name of Dr Livingstone, and was shown up to Hess's bedroom at 7.30. In the secret recording room an MI6 officer and a stenographer listened as the two exchanged greetings.

'How well your English has improved,' Beaverbrook said.

'A little, not very much.'

'You remember the last time we talked in the Chancellery in Berlin?'[23]

The repeated reference to their last meeting in Berlin suggests Beaverbrook may have been covering up a more recent visit to Hess, possibly in the Tower of London. Perhaps it was merely small talk to break the ice.

After further discussion of Hess's understanding of English – there was no interpreter present – Beaverbrook said they had come to a bad pass. Hess agreed. Beaverbrook said he had been very much against the war; he had greatly regretted it, but it had all become extraordinarily complicated. He rambled on, attempting to draw Hess on what he knew. Hess pretended he knew nothing, but warned him that England was playing a very dangerous game with Bolshevism.

'Yes,' Beaverbrook replied, 'I can't myself tell why the Germans attacked Russia, I can't see why.'

'Because we know that one day the Russians will attack us.'

'Will attack Germany?'

'Yes ... and it will be good not only for Germany and the whole Europe. It will be good for England too if Russia will be defeated.'[24]

He was, of course, omitting the whole hinterground of Hitler's ideological, racial and colonising ambitions in eastern Europe. He continued stonewalling for the rest of their conversation, but took the opportunity to give Beaverbrook the report he had been writing. It was virtually a repeat of the political deposition he had given Loftus the previous month, questioning Britain's war aim in the light of the German–Russian war and warning against the danger Bolshevism would pose to Europe and the British Empire if Germany were defeated.[25]

He made the same point in his halting English during the conversation: of one thing he was sure, Bolshevism would emerge stronger as a result of the war.[26]

Beaverbrook left after an hour's meandering discussion, clutching the sheaf of manuscript notes Hess had given him, and promising to come and see him again after his return from Moscow – a promise he was not to fulfil. He admitted to Colonel Scott's adjutant he had got nothing new from the interview, 'but he found it very hard to believe that "Z" was insane'.[27]

Two years later he was to tell Bruce Lockhart, head of the Foreign Office's political intelligence department, that he thought Hess had probably been given drugs to make him talk. He also said he believed Hess had been sent by Hitler to gain a free hand against Russia, with the proviso that he would be disowned if anything went wrong; he had meant to land in Scotland unbeknown to anyone, burn his plane and find the Duke of Hamilton.[28] What Beaverbrook did not say, or what Bruce Lockhart omitted from his diary was why Hess and Hitler should have imagined the Duke of Hamilton would help. It is such an obvious question it suggests one or both held something back.

Years later, after the publication of James Leasor's groundbreaking book on Hess's mission, an MI6 officer with the rank of captain wrote to Leasor claiming he had been stationed in the recording room during Beaverbrook's conversation with Hess; afterwards he had made a copy of the transcript and taken it straight round to the British Communist Party headquarters. From the unrepentant tone of the letter it was evident the captain, whose name Leasor could not recall, believed he had done a good thing.[29] If his story is true Stalin would have known exactly what Hess had said long before Beaverbrook arrived in Moscow.

* * *

282

The original news of Hess's flight had caused alarm in the Kremlin in case he was carrying peace proposals to free Hitler for a strike east against Russia.[30] Initial reports from agents suggested this was exactly the purpose. The first such appears to have been from Kim Philby of the Cambridge spy ring, code-named 'Sohnchen'. A paraphrase of cryptogram No. 376 of 14 May from London ran 'Information received from "SOHNCHEN"' that Hess arrived in England to appeal to Hamilton, his friend and 'member of the so-called Cliveden clique'. It continued:

> KIRKPATRICK, the first person from the 'ZAKOYLKA' [Foreign Office] who identified HESS who announced that he had brought with him peace offers. The essence of his peace proposals we don't know yet.[31]

How Philby obtained his information is not clear. He would later be recruited into MI6, but at this date he was in SOE, training recruits in clandestine propaganda at a camp near Southampton. He produced further information on 18 May, and this time named his source as Tom Dupree, Deputy Chief of the Foreign Office Press Department. He stated that Beaverbrook and Eden had visited Hess, although it was officially denied – and there is still no hint in any open file that either minister had seen Hess by this date. The message went on to say that Hess believed there was 'a powerful anti-CHURCHILL party in Britain which stands for peace', which would receive a powerful stimulus from his arrival. It concluded:

> 'SOHNCHEN' considers the time for peace negotiations has not arrived yet. But in the course of further developments in the war HESS will be the center of intrigues for the conclusion of the compromise peace and will be useful for the peace party in England and for HITLER.[32]

Agents in Washington and Berlin passed similar information to Moscow: Hess had been sent by Hitler to propose peace. One, a particularly trusted informant in Berlin code-named 'EXTERN', reported in addition that if Britain agreed to the proposals Germany would immediately turn on the USSR.[33]

Stalin believed it: a British–German peace became in his mind the precondition for the German assault he knew he had to expect; thus, despite a spate of warnings of imminent attack in May and June, his forces were caught completely by surprise. As the Red Army was rolled back he fell into a state of shock, which, we are told, lasted several days.

In September Moscow received a rather more reassuring report on Hess from an agent in Vichy France; according to this Hess had been lured to Britain by MI6 in retaliation for their humiliation at the capture of their agents, Stevens and Payne-Best, at Venlo in 1939.[34] This time it was German intelligence that was fooled into believing in a fictitious conspiracy. Centred in Scotland and directed by 'Lord Hamilton', the conspirators had requested and arranged for the arrival of an important German representative to galvanise the movement. They had been astonished when this turned out to be the Deputy Führer. It is not known how much credence was placed in this report.

Nonetheless, Hess was still in Britain and still a cause of anxiety, particularly because of the veil of silence in which the British government had wrapped him; and when, towards the end of September, Beaverbrook and Roosevelt's envoy, W. Averell Harriman, arrived in Moscow at the head of an Anglo–American delegation to negotiate the war supplies Russia needed, Stalin asked Beaverbrook at dinner why Hess had not been shot.

'You just don't shoot a person in England,' Beaverbrook replied, 'he has to have a trial before a jury, but I can tell you why he is in Britain', at which, according to his account, he produced the transcript of his talk with Hess.[35]

It is more probable that he gave Stalin Hess's handwritten memorandum on the German–Russian war, for years later, writing to James Leasor, Beaverbrook said he showed Stalin 'a letter written to me by Hess in his own hand'.[36] Stalin sent the letter off for translation, and no doubt it was photocopied before being returned. The original can be seen today in the Beaverbrook Papers.

Towards the end of October Churchill's personal intelligence adviser, Major Desmond Morton, divulged aspects of Hess's mission at a lunch attended by a journalist from *Time* magazine named Laird. Some of the facts and remarks Morton attributed to Hess are so obviously false it is evident this was a disinformation lunch; to what end is not clear.

Laird duly passed on what Morton had said to the US Military Attaché, Captain Raymond E. Lee, who sent a full report to Washington.[37] The chief revelation was that Hess had flown to Scotland to tell Hamilton that Germany was about to fight Russia. Hess, Lee stated, had said, 'I knew the Duke would see immediately that it would be absurd and awful for England to continue to fight Germany any longer.'[38]

This conflicts with all the evidence from the open files. In June Lord Simon had been asked to probe Hess on Hitler's intentions towards Russia,[39] and after that interview Henry Hopkinson, Menzies' liaison with the Foreign Office, had written a memo concluding, 'We have no clear idea of Hitler's aspirations and intentions in Russia.'[40] While it is entirely possible that Hamilton and Kirkpatrick did not disclose all in their reports on their conversations with Hess – indeed it is clear they said nothing of the letter and documents he had brought – it is hard to believe that Menzies' right-hand man in the Foreign Office would have written a deliberately misleading internal memo.

Morton also revealed that Hess was living in a large estate near Glasgow reserved for higher German officers, but was apart from them in one of the servants' cottages. He had a radio and listened to both English and German broadcasts, and 'Every time someone says the word "Hitler", Hess jumps to his feet and says "Heil Hitler".'[41]

Morton evidently did not divulge that Hess was confined to bed with his leg in a splint after a suicide attempt.

Morton expected his remarks to reach Washington as he said that Hess was 'especially interested in getting Roosevelt's speeches on the short wave'.[42] It is significant that he also credited Hess with the words, 'we are obliterating the Jews'.[43] Churchill, of course, knew that; Hess may have revealed it, but Morton's lunchtime confidences are no evidence that he did.

Moscow received a report of the same farrago of Morton's inventions even before Washington, although it is not clear who the 'agent source' was.[44] No doubt this was also intended: the impression that the British government had turned down an invitation from Hess to join Hitler's anti-Bolshevik crusade might have been designed to defuse Stalin's suspicions about Hess's presence in Britain. Possibly it merely intensified them, for it was shortly afterwards that MI5 attempted to prosecute de Courcy,[45] seen by Moscow's friends as an enemy of Britain's alliance with Russia.

DISINFORMATION

London had suffered its most destructive bombing raid of the war on the night Hess landed in Scotland.[46] It is unlikely that this was coincidence. Assuming that Hess flew on Hitler's commission, the raid was designed to herald the envoy of peace with an apocalyptic vision of the consequences of rejection. Yet a curious feature of the mission is that, despite the British government's failure to respond, raids on London virtually ceased after 10/11 May 1941, not to be resumed until Hitler himself was facing defeat in 1943.

One reason may have been that British agents maintained the lines of communication used in the negotiations that brought Hess to Scotland in the first place. At all events there is evidence of a continuing British deception in a file of correspondence between the German Security Service and Foreign Ministry in summer 1942. It opens with a letter from Heydrich dated 4 May, addressed to Ribbentrop personally.[47] In mid-April, Heydrich wrote, one of his *Gewährsleute* (confidential agents) had discussed a number of questions with an Englishman who had been educated in Germany. They concerned an Englishman with first-rate connections in influential English circles who knew Rudolf Hess personally. He asked Ribbentrop to acquaint the Führer with the contents of the report, which he enclosed:

The Englishman stated that in December last year he had spent four days in London with Hess at his [Hess's] express wish with the approval of Churchill. Hess was housed in a villa in Scotland, had his personal servants and wanted for nothing. Churchill had expressly decreed that Hess, on account of his rank as *SS-Gruppenführer*, should be accommodated as a general. On the agent asking whether the Englishman had had the impression that Hess was, perhaps, somewhat mentally confused, he received the answer that the Englishman had not gained this impression. Hess enjoyed the best of health, was very lively and very concerned, on the one hand about the destructive fratricidal war between the best white races, on the other about the great losses in valuable human material allegedly caused the Germans by the enemy in the east. Hess's four days in London served the purpose, in accordance with his wishes, of showing him London and above all the havoc of the bomb damage. The Englishman and Hess, equipped with dark glasses, had moved about London freely and Hess had been shown everything he had wanted to see. He had then parted from him, by the Englishman's account, with the words, 'Work with me to bring about peace in the soonest possible time.'[48]

The report went on to mention other topics Heydrich's agent had discussed with the Englishman, first the Japanese campaign in the Far East. The previous December Japan had entered the war as an ally of the Axis by attacking US and British Eastern possessions, so bringing the United States into the war on the Anglo–Russian side. The Englishman stressed his countrymen's grave concern about Japanese successes, as a Japanese–Chinese–Indian bloc, rich in raw materials and cheap labour, would be a danger for the white races; Great Britain and Germany needed to unite quickly to save the predominance of the white races in Asia, although he saw no possibility of that at present.

The Englishman had gone on to specify three things that he considered most damaging for Germany:

a) The Jewish question, which in his opinion had to be solved internally instead of allowing them out of the country, where they would have the possibilities of using their connections and money to work systematically against Germany.

b) The bombardment of London had been mistaken since it had awakened feelings of hate against Germany in even the most simple Englishmen, which had not been present before ...

c) The unbelievable corruption spreading through Germany which is known everywhere abroad ...[49]

Ribbentrop requested more details on the source before he laid the report before Hitler. In the meantime Heydrich had been assassinated by Czech agents, and Schellenberg, who was expected to succeed him as chief of the Security Service, took up the case. Schellenberg had been in charge of the investigation into Hess's flight. The files have never been found, but in his post-war memoirs Schellenberg stated that Hess had been influenced for some years by agents of the British Secret Service and their German collaborators, who had played a large part in his decision to fly to Scotland; he named especially Professor Gerl, the Bavarian gland specialist with top-level British contacts from his pre-war practice, who was a particular friend of Hess.[50]

To the Foreign Ministry's request for information on the source of the recent report on Hess Schellenberg replied that it came from a trustworthy German businessman, who often travelled to Switzerland and had dealings with Swiss business leaders with good connections to England. His evidence came on the one hand from the circle of Hess's relations in Switzerland, on the other from their English associates. Among these the agent had met an Englishman 'who had himself talked exhaustively on political questions with Rudolf Hess, Winston Churchill, Eden, Greenwood, Dr. Thompson and leading representatives of the Labour Party'.[51]

It is not certain from the correspondence, but it seems probable that Ribbentrop then sent the report to Führer headquarters,[52] for that summer a high-ranking *Abwehr* agent visited Hess's elderly aunt, Emma Rothacker, in Zürich saying he was on a commission from the Führer to photocopy all the letters she had received from Rudolf Hess.[53]

The impression from these Security Service files is that Hess was kept at the centre of a deception campaign undertaken largely by Claude Dansey's agents in Switzerland with corroborating 'whispers' from London – no doubt co-ordinated by the Double-Cross

Committee, since both Desmond Morton and Heydrich's agent had Hess living in high style in a villa in Scotland. The Nazi mindset on race, Jews and the Japanese threat to white supremacy in the East was indulged in order to promote the idea that Hess was in contact with leading Englishmen and in position to open peace negotiations when the time was right – precisely what Stalin feared – and further, that bombing London would not help this cause. It may partly explain why Göring's massed raids on the capital were not continued after the night of 10/11 May 1941. If so, this must surely rank as an outstanding, hitherto unknown success for British intelligence.

THE NUCLEAR THREAT

Germany had entered the war with an office for the military application of nuclear fission; German scientists had already split the uranium nucleus. Churchill and Roosevelt faced the nightmare possibility that Hitler would develop a nuclear weapon before their own scientists. Frank Foley had been personally involved in the question: he had flown 26 canisters of heavy water – the moderating agent essential to the German line of research – out of Norway during the German invasion of that country, and had done the same from France before the fall of Paris.[54] The nuclear question must surely have been one of his priorities when interviewing Hess. Asked about Germany's 'secret weapons' on one occasion in November 1941, Hess had replied he knew there was one but had no idea what it was; and Hitler would only use it as a last resort.[55]

In reality German nuclear scientists had hardly progressed. On 4 June 1942 Albert Speer, Hitler's Minister of Armaments, chaired a conference on the question in Berlin and offered considerable resources for nuclear weapon development. Werner Heisenberg, speaking for the scientists, had to confess they would not know how to use the money. Five days later Foley's scientific contact in Berlin from before the war, Paul Rosbaud, flew to Oslo and told his MI6 contact there that German nuclear research remained at a preliminary stage; minimal resources had been allotted.[56]

Later the same month Hess had been moved from Mytchett Place into a ground-floor suite in the wing of Maindiff Court mental hospital, Abergavenny, south Wales. It was entirely coincidental. Foley had given him up as a useful source some months before Rosbaud's revelation. Hess was continuing to deflect all sensitive questions by saying he knew nothing of military matters, and his mental state had deteriorated alarmingly, or so it appeared. After his splint had been removed in September 1941 he had complained of headaches, eye, stomach, liver and gall bladder pains and the medical orderlies saw him hallucinating, waving his hands and whispering in the direction of blank walls.[57] In December he had told the surgeon treating his leg that he was losing his memory.[58] Like much of his behaviour, this was assumed as a defence against the constant probing to which he was subject. He freely admitted this later.[59]

By the end of 1941 at the latest Foley had been forced to admit defeat. He left Mytchett Place in March 1942 to return to normal duties. In May Maindiff Court was approved as a new and quieter home for Hess, and he was moved there on 26 June.

STALIN'S SUSPICIONS

By summer 1942, in Poland, death camps designed for industrial murder were replacing the first, *wild* phases of Heydrich's final solution to the Jewish problem. Meanwhile, early that year representatives of the European countries occupied by Germany had met in London and issued what was termed the St James' Declaration, calling for retributive justice after the war for those responsible for acts of violence against civilian populations. Great Britain was an observer, not a signatory. It will be recalled, however, that the previous year Churchill, when considering how Hess should be detained, had anticipated post-war trials of 'war criminals'.[60]

He took the idea to Washington in June 1942, apparently under pressure from the Polish, Czech and other exiled governments in London, and suggested the establishment of a 'United Nations Commission on Atrocities'. Subsequently Lord Simon was appointed to chair a British Cabinet Committee on the Treatment of War Criminals. This proposed a United Nations Commission to investigate war crimes. Washington supported the principle, and on 7 October Roosevelt joined Simon in a public announcement to that effect.

It touched Stalin on a raw nerve. The Soviet government had not responded to Simon's soundings on war crimes; and for his two major allies to come to an agreement without his concurrence seems to have stirred all his suspicions about Churchill's treatment of Hess – probably aggravated by the recent British disinformation campaign which must have been picked up by his agents in Switzerland – and his doubts about British and American willingness to create a 'second front' in Europe to ease pressure on the Red Army.

His mistrust was expressed by *Pravda* in an explosive article on 19 October, repeated by Moscow Radio the same night. This asked whether Hess was being harboured in Britain as Hitler's plenipotentiary, and accused Churchill's government of transforming Britain into 'an asylum and refuge for gangsters'.[61]

Two days later the Soviet Security Service, NKVD, received a wire from one of its most trusted sources in London, Colonel Frantisek Moravetc, head of military intelligence in the exiled Czech government, to the effect that the current view that Hess had arrived in Britain unexpectedly was not correct:

> Long before his flight HESS had discussed his mission with the DUKE OF HAMILTON. The correspondence covered in detail all the questions involved with organisation of this flight. But HAMILTON himself did not participate personally in the correspondence. All HESS's letters to HAMILTON ... were intercepted by the intelligence service where the answers to HESS were also elaborated in the name of HAMILTON ...[62]

In this way, Moravetc stated, Hess was lured to England; he had personally seen the correspondence. The letters from Hess had, he said, concerned the necessity of stopping the war between Britain and Germany and had linked this to the planned German attack on Russia. Therefore, he concluded, the British possessed written proofs of the guilt of Hess and other Nazi leaders in preparing the attack on the Soviet Union.[63]

The timing of this wire suggests Moravetc must have been prompted by the *Pravda* outburst, which had been reported in British newspapers. Possibly he sought to reassure the Russians that the British, having proofs of Hess's complicity in the assault on the Soviet Union, would send him for trial after the war. Possibly he was shown the Hess–Hamilton letters for this purpose by MI6 – assuming they had indeed conducted such a correspondence. His source has never been discovered. But it is strange, if Hess wrote about Hitler's plans to attack Russia before flying to Scotland, that he said nothing about them after his arrival, even denying they existed – that, at least is the clear impression given by all the open papers on the subject, including memos by Desmond Morton and Henry Hopkinson, both of whom were close to Menzies.

His information on Hess falling into a British intelligence trap is more plausible. The diaries of Eduard Taborsky, personal secretary to Eduard Benesch, President of the Czech government in exile, show that Hess's arrival in Britain had prompted Benesch to question whether the British government was preparing another 'Munich' settlement with Hitler; and on 31 May Taborsky had noted it was clear that 'the Nazi No. 3 was enticed into an English trap'.[64] His source was a top-secret report from a British military department. Which department and how he obtained it is not known, but Robert Bruce Lockhart, SOE's liaison with the provisional Czech government, has been suggested as the informant; his name often appeared in Taborsky's diary. Taborsky's evidence is almost contemporary with Hess's arrival in Britain, and more persuasive therefore than Moravetc's account of over a year later; it also conforms with the September 1941 report the NKVD had received from an agent in Vichy France.[65] At all events, Moravetc's despatch convinced NKVD analysts, who used it as the basis for a top-secret report for Stalin and his Foreign Minister dated 24 October.

The British Ambassador in Moscow, Sir Archibald Clark Kerr, registered a strong protest over the language used in the *Pravda* article, and on 25 October sent a series of wires to the Foreign Office expressing his puzzlement at the Russian government attitude and reporting two theories behind their mistrust:

Before he went to Scotland Hess had been in touch with certain influential people in England belonging to a group who still believed it was possible and wise to compound with Hitler, who gave him to understand that, if he came on a special embassy with certain proposals H.M.G. would not only make peace but would join the Germans in a crusade against Bolshevism. The people concerned are so powerful that H.M.G., while rejecting their proposals at the time they were made did not dare to expose their sponsors, preferring to be distrusted by their Ally, Russia, and to leave her in the lurch, for it is these people who are ... standing in the way of a second front ...

2) That is one theory. Another suggests that H.M.G. are foreseeing the day when it might suit them to compound with Hitler, biding their time against it and keeping Hess up their sleeve for the purpose ...[66]

To the obvious answers against these ideas, he reported, the Russians counter by asking why there was any mystery about Hess and why they had not been told what had happened; 'Finally they claim that since Hess went to the U.K there have been no serious bombings, and they hold this to be significant.' To calm them, Clark Kerr suggested the publication of a white paper with a full description of Hess's arrival and the proposals he had brought, which reiterated the government's intention to put him on trial when the time came. He went on:

If these [Hess's] alleged proposals were indeed (as was suggested to me at the time) that in exchange for the evacuation of certain of the occupied countries we should withdraw from the war and leave Germany a free hand in the East, our declared rejection of them should be enough to satisfy the most difficult and suspicious of the Russians outside the Kremlin ...[67]

How had Clark Kerr heard of the proposal that Germany would evacuate certain occupied countries if Britain withdrew from the war and left her a free hand in the east? It does not appear in Kirkpatrick's or Hamilton's or Foley's or any Guards' officers records of their conversations with Hess, nor in the transcripts of Simon's or Beaverbrook's interviews, nor indeed in any papers in the open files.

In the event, this crucial disclosure did not appear in the report on Hess's mission and proposals that the former Ambassador to Moscow, Sir Stafford Cripps, was asked to prepare from documents made available to him by the British government in response to this suggestion of Clark Kerr's for appeasing Moscow.[68] This report was wired to Clark Kerr in summary on 4 November for communication to Stalin. It stated:

> Hess proposed a peace settlement on the following basis:
> (1) Germany to have a free hand in Europe and to receive her colonies back;
> (2) England to have a free hand in the British Empire;
> (3) Russia to be included in Asia, but Germany intended to satisfy certain demands upon Russia either by negotiation or war. Hess denied that Hitler contemplated an early attack on Russia.'[69]

The first public allusion to Hess proposing German withdrawal from occupied western Europe was to appear in an American journal the following spring, as will appear. More recently, both the anonymous informant who claimed to have been conscripted by Kirkpatrick to translate Hess's formal proposals[70] and Kenneth de Courcy, who received information from Lieutenant Loftus, cited German evacuation of occupied western Europe as fundamental to Hess's peace plan.[71]

However, it is evident that with the presence in London of the exiled governments of the German-occupied countries, many possibly suspecting another 'Munich', Churchill, if he wished to maintain their support and continue the war, had to conceal Hess's offer to liberate their homelands. He did so, if the anonymous informant and Kenneth de Courcy are to be believed, by placing the formal, typed proposals Hess brought with him under the strictest secrecy, and speaking only of what he referred to as the 'conversational aspects'[72] of the offer. This must of necessity have involved Hamilton and Kirkpatrick amending their reports; it is known that Hamilton did so, and his original report is missing from the files.[73] It is, nonetheless, curious that Hess does not appear to have mentioned his formal peace proposals to any of the people he spoke to subsequently.

The one phrase from Clark Kerr's despatch from Moscow which appears to lift a corner of the veil of secrecy Churchill placed over the formal proposals is so vital to the elucidation of the mystery still surrounding Hess's mission it bears repetition:

> If these alleged proposals were indeed (as was suggested to me at the time) that in exchange for the evacuation of certain of the occupied countries we should withdraw from the war and leave Germany a free hand in the East ...[74]

This appears to be the only phrase in the official files open to scrutiny which indicates the full scope of Hess's peace plan.

CHAPTER SIXTEEN

The real story?

IN MAY 1943 a sensational article in the popular US journal *American Mercury* purported to tell 'The Inside Story of the Hess Flight'. The editor vouched for its anonymous author as 'a highly reputable observer', and expressed 'full faith' in the sources used.[1]

The article itself claimed to reveal 'one of the most fascinating tales of superintrigue in the annals of international relations', resulting in 'a supreme British coup', and for the Nazis the equivalent of a shattering military defeat. A few details were still obscure, others had to be suppressed for policy reasons, but on the basis of 'reliable information from German sources and from indications given by Hess himself' it could be stated that Hess came to Britain on Hitler's explicit orders; the outlines of his mission were known in advance by a limited number of Britishers and his arrival was expected – even to the extent of an RAF escort for the final stage of his flight.

In January 1941, the article stated, Hitler, determined on pursuing his 'holy war' against Russia, had used 'an internationally known diplomat' to extend a feeler towards an influential group in Britain, formerly members of the Anglo-German Fellowship, including the Duke of Hamilton. This initial sounding by the 'eminent diplomat' in person was intercepted by the Secret Service. They responded using the names and handwriting of the Duke of Hamilton and others of the group. 'Replies designed to whet the German appetite, replies encouraging

the supposition that Britain was seeking a way out of its military difficulties, were sent to Berlin. The hook was carefully baited.'² A German
proposal of negotiations on neutral soil was rejected. Berlin then
offered to send a delegate to England, selecting Ernst Wilhelm Bohle
for the purpose and planting stories in Turkish and South American
newspapers that he was being groomed for an important and mysterious job abroad. Lack of reaction from the British Press showed the
Germans that the British were indifferent to Bohle, upon which Hitler
decided to send 'a really big Nazi' whose presence could not fail to
command attention: his own deputy, Rudolf Hess.

It is worth noting that this account loosely fits Bohle's own post-
war testimony that when translating Hess's letters to Hamilton he had
believed Hess was acting on Hitler's authority and that he (Bohle)
would be flying to a meeting in a neutral country, possibly Switzerland.³
More significantly, perhaps, Bohle's name was completely unknown in
England, and only someone fully briefed in the detail of these top-
secret negotiations either from the British or German side could
possibly have known he was involved. It is also worth recalling the
remarkable preparations for receiving Hitler's Condor aircraft at
Lympne aerodrome in Kent, which were called off after Hess's arrival.⁴

Professor Karl Haushofer's post-war testimony also bears a resemblance to this *American Mercury* account:

> At that time Hess initiated peace feelers to be put forward, and the
> responsible man in dealing with these peace feelers was my murdered
> son [Albrecht]. He was in Switzerland and talked with Burckhardt
> and Burckhardt told him to come back again to Switzerland and
> there he would be flown to Madrid, and would there have a confer-
> ence with Lord Templewood [as Sir Samuel Hoare became]. When
> my son returned from Switzerland Hess spoke to him again and it
> was after that that he flew to England. I don't know what he spoke to
> him about at this discussion.⁵

Carl Burckhardt certainly fits the *American Mercury* description of an
'eminent' and 'internationally known diplomat'. As to the reason and
objective of Hess's flight, Karl Haushofer's 'firm conviction' was that

he had been impelled by 'his [Hess's] own sense of honour and his desperation about the murders going on in Germany. It was his firm belief that if he sacrificed himself and went to England he might be able to do something to stop it.'[6]

A 28-page statement written by Hess's adjutant, Karl-Heinz Pintsch, while in Soviet captivity after the war has recently been discovered in the Russian State Archives. Hitler knew about Hess's proposed flight, Pintsch wrote, because Berlin had been negotiating with London for some time: 'The flight occurred by prior arrangement with the English.'[7] The mission Hess undertook, he went on, was to achieve a military alliance with England against Russia, or at least the neutralisation of England. Scholars have doubted the statement on the grounds that Pintsch was telling his Soviet captors what he knew they wanted to hear at the beginning of the Cold War in order to procure his release – namely that the British had been in secret negotiations with Nazi Germany to attack Russia.

Yet this claim had been asserted as early as October 1942 by the Swedish Nazi newspaper *Dagsposten*, controlled and financed from Berlin. An article obviously inspired by Berlin had claimed that it was time to lift the secrecy about Hess's flight to Britain. This had not been Hess's independent venture but part of Hitler's considered plan to form an alliance with Britain against Russia. To protect himself against a possible failure Hitler had agreed in advance to deny all knowledge, and to give this plausibility had subsequently punished those who helped Hess. The article stated that Churchill had turned down the offer without consulting Parliament or informing the British people of the proposal. He did consult Roosevelt, however, who emphatically opposed the Hess plan.[8]

Following this article the British German-language magazine *Die Zeitung*, published for Germans living in Britain, had stated that 'well-informed observers in London' believed the *Dagsposten* version of events was 'on the whole correct'.[9] Cadogan had commented, 'I do not know who the "well-informed political observers" were, but I am quite sure that they were not "well-informed".'[10]

Yet this is what the *American Mercury* article also claimed implicitly: that all details of Hess's mission were arranged with the British side before he took off on 10 May and 'a kind of official reception committee composed of Military Intelligence officers and Secret Service agents was waiting at the private aerodrome on the Hamilton estate [Dungavel].'[11] It will be recalled that long after the war two members of the women's services who had been stationed at Dungavel told the authors of *Double Standards* that a number of people, including the Duke of Kent, had been waiting in a small house adjacent to the Dungavel airstrip that night; further, that they had seen the landing lights switched on briefly and off again, and heard a low-flying aircraft shortly afterwards.[12]

Because of Hess's forced parachute landing ten miles from Dungavel, the article continued, by the time the official 'reception committee' found him he was in Home Guard custody; otherwise his arrival might have been kept dark for some time, if not for the duration. As we have seen, he was driven to Maryhill Barracks near Glasgow, thence to a military hospital, where his injured ankle was treated, and the next day Churchill sent Ivone Kirkpatrick up to Scotland to receive his proposals. The article presented these in general outline, withholding details:

> Hitler offered a total cessation of the war in the West. Germany would evacuate all of France except Alsace and Lorraine, which would remain German. It would evacuate Holland and Belgium, retaining Luxembourg. It would evacuate Norway and Denmark. In short, Hitler offered to withdraw from Western Europe, except for the two French provinces and Luxembourg, in return for which Great Britain would agree to assume an attitude of benevolent neutrality towards Germany as it unfolded its plans in Eastern Europe. In addition, the Führer was ready to withdraw from Yugoslavia and Greece ...[13]

Hess had refused to be drawn on military plans, the article stated, but had explained the importance of 'Hitler's Eastern mission "to save humanity" [from Bolshevism]', and promised that Germany would take the full production of British and French war industries until they could be converted to a peacetime basis, in effect using 'the arsenals of free capitalism against Asiatic Bolshevism'.

Churchill had communicated Hess's proposals to Roosevelt, who had agreed with his decision to reject them and avoid open discussion, instead accepting 'the insanity explanation fed to the German people'. The article concluded that this episode was not the first time England had reduced a German stronghold by audacious Secret Service work.

Although the author claimed information from German sources and indications from Hess himself, it is evident that many details could only have come from British insiders, Ivone Kirkpatrick's role as a particular example. It is unlikely that MI6 officers would have talked: the service still refuses to open its files on the affair. The two most likely candidates are Churchill's intelligence adviser, Desmond Morton, or his Minister of Information and confidant, Brendan Bracken. Both were capable of the more extravagant flourishes in the story – that Hess had an RAF escort on the final leg of his journey surely overstates Fighter Command's contribution.

Whoever the source, Churchill must have been behind it. The war had turned in his favour: in February 1943 what remained of the German 6th Army besieging Stalingrad had been forced to surrender; in the Pacific US forces had broken the domination of the Japanese carriers and taken Guadalcanal; Atlantic U-boats had suffered record losses; in North Africa Axis forces were trapped between Anglo–American armies advancing from east and west. The arguments for a compromise peace with Hitler had been demolished on battlefield and ocean and it was safe at last to reveal the terms Hess had offered. There must also have been a purpose. Perhaps it was to reassure Stalin, still fretting about the Western Allies' failure to open a 'second front' in Europe. The article stated initially that 'most of those in possession of the true story' of Hess's mission felt it should now be told:

> For one thing, it would place before critics of the Anglo-American policy towards Soviet Russia the vital and silencing fact that at a difficult moment, when he might have withdrawn his country from the war at Russia's expense, Churchill pledged Britain to continue fighting as a full ally of the newest victim of Nazi duplicity. There would have been some semblance of poetic justice to such a withdrawal – was it not Stalin who set the war in motion by signing a friendship

pact with Hitler in 1939? But the British Prime Minister never even considered such action.[14]

Later that summer Brendan Bracken spoke about the affair in America, admitting that Hess had flown over 'expecting to find quislings who would help him to throw Churchill out and make peace', also that the Duke of Hamilton had met Hess before the war, thereby contradicting earlier statements in the Commons designed to protect Hamilton's reputation.[15]

On 1 September the *Daily Mail* published a more sensational disclosure, 'The Daily Life of Hess in Prison Camp', describing his confinement in the wing of a former lunatic asylum, and presenting him as a 'paranoiac, suffering from persecution mania, convinced that people are in league against him, hearing voices which do not exist'.[16] It is evident the author had inside information from an orderly or officer at Maindiff Court: this was indeed how Hess was reacting to the ever-worsening news for the Axis.[17]

These revelations revived interest in the case; questions were put down for the Commons, and the War Cabinet decided an official statement could no longer be resisted.[18] Eden was asked to produce one on the lines of the report Stafford Cripps had compiled for Stalin; he delivered it to the House on 22 September. It was the official version based primarily on the reports from Hamilton and Kirkpatrick available in the open files today. He made no mention of prior negotiations, bogus or otherwise, but expected the House to believe that Hess had flown to see the Duke of Hamilton simply because his friend Haushofer had told him that 'the wing commander was an Englishman who would understand his point of view'.[19] Nor did Eden mention a formal offer from Germany to evacuate occupied western Europe. According to his statement, the 'solution' Hess had proposed amounted to nothing more than Germany being given a free hand in Europe, England a free hand in the British Empire, which 'so-called "terms"' had been restated by Hess in a signed document dated 10 June.

The account may have been true so far as it went: it asserted that Hess had arrived with photographs of a small boy and the visiting cards of the Haushofers; 'No other documents or identifications were found on the prisoner'.[20] No mention was made of the documents now known to have been found afterwards on the site of his crashed Messerschmitt.[21] And it was these, if the anonymous informant is to be believed, not Hess's own statements, which carried Germany's official terms offering evacuation of the occupied countries of western Europe.[22]

Whether the House or the country were satisfied, Stalin did not believe it. Churchill visited Moscow the following year, and during a dinner in the Kremlin expatiated on Hess's motives and simple belief that if he could see the Duke of Hamilton, who was Lord Steward, he would immediately be taken to the King and everything would be settled. Instead, he was put in prison. 'He is now completely mad,' he concluded.

At this, according to the recollections of the British Ambassador, who was at the dinner, 'Marshal Stalin rather unexpectedly proposed the health of the British Intelligence Service which had inveigled Hess into coming to England.' Churchill protested that the British government had known nothing of his flight beforehand. 'The Russian Intelligence Service,' Stalin replied, 'often did not inform the government of its intentions, and only did so after their work was accomplished.'[23]

THE END OF THE REICH

In April 1945, as the Red Army closed in on Berlin, the Duke of Hamilton called on Brendan Bracken at the Ministry of Information to tell him that the RAF had released him for a month so that he could visit the United States to attend a conference of airline operators in a civilian capacity. He asked him for a note from the Prime Minister. Bracken wrote to Churchill's private secretary to pass on the request, adding that Hamilton was bound to be pursued by a host of reporters 'who will wish to extract the "low down" on Hess'.[24] He enclosed a draft testimonial of the kind Hamilton sought, stating that the Duke's actions 'were in all respects becoming to a loyal serving officer'.[25] He also provided Hamilton with character references of his own addressed to influential Americans, including Roosevelt's aide, Harry

Hopkins: 'The bearer of this letter is the Duke of Hamilton, a great friend of mine. He is not a teetotaller and he would enjoy being shown the beauties of New York.'[26]

Meanwhile Hamilton had prepared 'Additional Notes on the Hess Incident' to use as a basis for his replies to questions he knew he would be asked, and he sent these to the Foreign Office. An official there pencilled brackets around two passages it was thought should be omitted. These passages do not appear on the present file copy, although one phrase has been underlined: '*He* [Hess] *made no remark at all on Russia*, which then had a non-aggression pact with Germany ...'[27]

Churchill lost no time in vetoing Hamilton's trip:

> Surely it is not necessary for the Duke to undertake this particular task. I quite agree that he will most certainly be badgered by American and Canadian reporters about Hess, and excitement would all the more be increased if I took the most unusual course of giving him a special testimonial of this kind. I have never been asked to do such a thing before ...[28]

The Russians, he went on, were most suspicious about the Hess episode, and he had had a lengthy argument about it with Marshal Stalin in October. It was not in the public interest that the affair should be stirred up at the present time. He concluded: 'I desire therefore that the Duke should not, repeat not, undertake this task.'

* * *

A month later, after Berlin had been overrun and Hitler had taken his own life, Germany surrendered to the Allies. In September Japan surrendered; the most destructive world war in history was over. The following month Rudolf Hess, dressed in his Luftwaffe uniform with flying boots, was taken from Maindiff Court and flown to Nuremberg to stand trial with other captured Nazi leaders as a war criminal, as Churchill had foreseen almost from the day of his arrival in Scotland.

In July 1942, after his move from Mytchett Place to south Wales, Hess's health and disposition had improved remarkably. He had liked the doctors there, describing them in recollection to Ilse as 'especially nice types', cultivated and many-sided in their interests.[29] He had enjoyed walking with them in the countryside, and had become especially friendly with an older lieutenant, Walter Fenton, who had a car allotted especially to drive him to local sites of interest. Years later Fenton looked back on this period as his best time in the war. 'I got to like the old boy very much,' he recalled, 'he thought a lot of England and thought it was a great shame we ever came to war.'[30]

Hess read much during this time, including the complete works of Goethe and books on British naval history; he made architectural drawings, painted and received and wrote letters to Ilse and Buz and friends and relations, remembering their birthdays, recalling old times and looking forward to refreshing them in the future. The letters showed no trace of the persecution complex he still exhibited to his captors when it suited him.

In autumn 1943 his earlier black moods had returned. Whether triggered by a letter from Ilse about the treatment of his personal staff, who, she told him, had been expelled from the party, arrested and if male sent to punishment battalions on the eastern front, or by increasingly grim war news for Germany, or by a Parliamentary debate on the trial of war criminals which he probably read in *The Times* on 21 October,[31] he reverted to the kind of psychotic behaviour he had displayed at Mytchett Place; and in November he again began faking amnesia. His performances were so convincing that the psychiatrists who examined him were completely taken in. He also faked pains, groaning and calling out for water. 'It was grand theatre,' he was later to recall for Ilse, 'and a complete success!'[32]

As Germany's situation grew worse, his behaviour grew more bizarre, almost as if he were willing himself to suffer with his country and his Führer. The abdominal pains he complained of grew worse, his hallucinations more graphic. He raged and shouted at himself and his attendants, wrapped up portions of supposedly poisoned food and forgot where he put them, forgot what he had been told or people he had seen only five minutes before. As he was to explain to Ilse, it was a desperate act to gain repatriation to Germany.[33]

In February 1945, as the ring of Allied forces closed on the Reich, he borrowed a bread knife, changed into his Luftwaffe uniform, sat in his armchair and stabbed himself twice in the left chest, without, however, penetrating his heart, then screamed out for the attendant. He said afterwards the Jews had placed the bread knife near him to tempt him to take his life. While convalescing from the apparent suicide attempt he refused to wash or shave and announced he had decided to fast to the death; at the same time he sealed his drinking glass with paper and string to prevent poison being administered in his water.

In early April, after giving up his fast, he began writing a long memoir of his flight to Scotland and subsequent captivity and the secret chemical poisons administered to him. He continued over the following days as if consumed by the need to unburden himself before the end, as one attendant put it, seemingly 'working against time'. He ascribed everything to the Jews:

> the Jews were behind all this ... The British government had been hypnotised into endeavouring to change me into a lunatic ... to revenge on me the fact that National Socialist Germany had defended itself from the Jews ... revenge on me because I had tried to end the war too early which the Jews had started with so much trouble, whereby they would have been prevented from reaching their war aims ...[34]

Manifestly the ramblings of a deranged mind. Perhaps not: the letters he wrote at this time give no hint of madness. Taken together with his increasingly extreme behaviour as the Reich went down to disaster and Hitler finally committed suicide beneath the rubble of his Chancellery, the manic tone of the document suggests a lover's cry of despair and affirmation, for he believed what he wrote about the Jews. Hitler made a similar statement in his last testament on 30 April, enjoining the nation to 'merciless resistance to the world-poisoner of all peoples, international Jewry.'[35]

In June Hess, continuing to behave like a lunatic, although several of his captors were now convinced he was putting it on, wrote to Ilse about the Führer he had known and adored:

> It has been granted to few to take part as we have from the outset in the development of a unique personality, in joy and sorrow, cares

and hopes, hates and loves and all the marks of greatness – and also in all the little signs of human weakness which alone make a man wholly lovable.[36]

NUREMBERG

Hess arrived in Nuremberg for the war crimes trial with a large number of the statements, depositions and letters he had written in captivity, together with samples of food, medicines and chocolate carefully wrapped in tissue, sealed, numbered and signed, for use as proof that the British had tried to poison him.[37]

Colonel Burton C. Andrus, the US commandant of the prison block attached to the courthouse, told him he would have to hand it all in. Hess tried to impress Andrus with his status as an officer, but made no impression; he had to surrender it all. His prison cell provided further proof of his dramatically reduced circumstances: instead of the comfortable furnishings of the rooms he had inhabited in Britain, there was a steel cot with straw mattress, a straight wooden chair, flimsy table, wash basin and lavatory bowl without seat or cover; instead of windows looking out on trees and a flower garden, a high, barred window admitted thin daylight. In the oak door opposite, a small aperture permitted the guards to observe him at any time they chose.

Not unnaturally, perhaps, given the shock, when an American psychiatrist, Major Douglas Kelly, came to assess him he said he had forgotten every detail of his former life.[38] The following day he was taken before the chief American interrogator, Colonel John H. Amen, and played the same game, able to remember nothing; yesterday the doctor had even had to tell him where he was born, he said. It was terrible for him because he would have to defend himself in the trial that was coming up.

'How do you know that any kind of trial is coming up, as you say?'

'This trial has been talked about all the time. I have seen it in the newspapers ...'[39]

He had been putting on the act so long in Britain it must have become second nature. After stonewalling for one and a half hours he was taken back to his cell. Later he was led out again to the Colonel's office; this time Göring was present. Hess affected not to notice him, and when Amen pointed him out pretended not to know who he was.

'Don't you know me?' Göring asked.

'Who are you?'[40]

Göring reminded him of events in which they had both taken part, but Hess claimed he could remember nothing, not even going to England to bring about peace. Eventually Göring gave up. Colonel Amen motioned him aside and called in Karl Haushofer. Hess repeated his act. Haushofer told him they had been friends for 22 years, assured him his wife and son were well on the farm at Hartschimmelhof, and like Göring, reminded him of times they had shared before the war, then of the letters Hess had written during his captivity in Britain, to all of which Hess insisted he had no knowledge.

'Don't you remember Albrecht, who served you very faithfully? He is dead now.'

In the final days of the war Albrecht had been taken from prison and shot by a special commando, no doubt to Himmler's orders. Haushofer did not tell him this.

'I am terribly sorry,' Hess said, 'but at the moment all this doesn't mean a thing to me.'[41]

After Haushofer, von Papen was brought in and Hess repeated his act, then Ernst Bohle. Göring told Bohle to remind Hess that he had translated his letter.

'Don't you remember,' Bohle said, 'that I translated your letter to the Duke of Hamilton?'

'No.'

'Don't you remember that you took this letter to the Duke of Hamilton, and that it was I who translated it?'

'I don't remember that. I just don't have the least recollection of that.'

Bohle broke into English, 'This is flabbergasting.'[42]

Despite the emotional turmoil Hess must have experienced at meeting his old colleagues and intimates, he managed to preserve an expressionless, detached manner, and certainly convinced Haushofer, who was devastated. It was the last time Haushofer spoke to his disciple, friend and protector. He was a spiritually broken man. Five months later he would leave instructions to his surviving son, Heinz, that no identification should ever be placed on or near his grave, then set out with his 'non-Aryan' wife, Martha, to a favourite stream near their house to take poison together.[43]

Hess continued his charade of amnesia through October and November. An extension of the strategy he had employed to resist questioning in Britain, it was no doubt also a way of striking back at fate and his jailors in the ruins of his world. Since it carried profound implications for his ability to defend himself, an international panel of psychiatrists was convened to examine him. They failed to agree a unanimous report, but all accepted that Hess was not insane. One report from a French, a British-Canadian and two American psychiatrists postulated:

> Rudolf Hess is suffering from hysteria characterised in part by loss of memory ... In addition there is a conscious exaggeration of his loss of memory and a tendency to exploit it to protect himself against examination. We consider that the hysterical behaviour ... was initiated as a defence against the circumstances in which he found himself in England; that it has now become in part habitual and that it will continue for as long as he remains under the threat of imminent punishment.[44]

* * *

The trial opened on 20 November 1945. Twenty-two of Hitler's former ministers and leaders of the armed forces were led into the courtroom to seats on two straight-backed benches, one behind the other near the wall opposite the judges' dais, separated from it by ranks of counsel and officials in the body of the chamber. Göring, senior surviving member of the Nazi regime, occupied the premier position at the right-hand end of the front bench; Hess sat next to him with Ribbentrop on his left, two grand admirals of Hitler's navy behind.

For those who had seen them strutting beside the Führer in their days of glory, the transformation was astonishing. 'How little and mean and mediocre they look,' William Shirer, formerly a US correspondent in Berlin, thought. Göring, in a faded Luftwaffe uniform, without his galaxy of medals, reminded him of a genial ship's radio operator; and he wondered how Hess could have been at the pinnacle of a great nation – seemingly a broken man with a gaunt face like a skeleton, his mouth twitched and his eyes stared 'vacantly and stupidly around the courtroom'.[45] Hess had adopted a pose of complete indifference as an expression of his conviction that the court was invalid – and, of course, he could not remember what he was being tried for.

The entry of the judges of the victorious Allied powers and the opening speeches for the prosecution outlining the scale of horror visited on the world and Germany itself by Nazism, and appealing to visions of a new world order in which such things could not occur, left the principal defendants unmoved, Göring cockily defiant, Hess exaggerating his air of detachment.

His affectation slipped briefly on the third day. One of the American prosecution team outlining the structure of the German government referred to Hess as Hitler's successor-designate, and Göring as next after Hess. This reversed the actual order, and Göring started waving his arms and pointing to himself, saying repeatedly, '*Ich war der Zweiter*!' ('I was the second' – or successor-designate). Hess turned to look at him and burst out laughing. Telford Taylor, assistant to the chief US Counsel, studying the two men from his seat barely twenty feet away, 'inferred from this occurrence that Hess's amnesia was not as complete as he had given out'.[46]

On the afternoon of the tenth day the defendants were shocked abruptly out of their attitudes. The main courtroom lights were extinguished for the projection of a film taken as US troops entered German concentration camps in the closing stages of the war; only fluorescent lights built into the ledges of the dock cast an eerie glow on the faces of the defendants. Two US psychiatrists stationed themselves with notebooks and pencils at either end of the dock to observe the defendants' reactions.

The film began with scenes of victims burned alive in a barn. Hess's attention was caught at once. The observers noted him glaring at the screen 'looking like a ghoul with sunken eyes over the footlamp'. Others bowed their heads, covered their eyes or looked away as the film ran. Göring leant on the ledge before him, eyes cast down, 'looking droopy'. Hess kept looking bewildered, the observers noted, as piles of dead were shown in a slave labour camp.[47] Walther Funk, formerly head of the Reichsbank, cried openly. Crematorium ovens appeared on the screen, then a lampshade made from human skin, which drew audible gasps from the body of the court.

The end of the film was followed by a stunned silence as the lights went on again. Hess, who had shown sustained interest throughout, said, 'I don't believe it.'[48] Göring, whose former insouciance had vanished, whispered to him to keep quiet. The judges rose, forgetting even to adjourn the session, and strode out without a word.

The two American psychiatrists visited Hess afterwards in his cell. He seemed confused and kept mumbling, 'I don't understand –'[49]

The next day, 30 November, General Erwin Lahousen, who had been one of Canaris's confidants in the *Abwehr*, testified for the prosecution. He gave an account of his former chief's reaction to the massacres of the intelligentsia, nobility, clergy and Jews in the Polish campaign, and quoted his words: 'One day the world will also hold the *Wehrmacht*, under whose eyes these events occurred, responsible for such methods.'[50] During the afternoon session he described the mass murders committed by Heydrich's *Einsatzkommandos* in the Russian campaign.

When he stood down a recess was announced, during which the judges were to consider a submission from Hess's counsel, Dr Günther von Rohrscheidt, that his client was unfit to stand trial. The dock was cleared, apart from Hess himself. Von Rohrscheidt had had an impossible task preparing a defence since Hess had continued to maintain to him that he had lost all memory. As he was about to rise Hess told him he had decided to say his memory had returned. Von Rohrscheidt got up anyway and began his prepared statement to the effect that his client's amnesia made it impossible for him to defend himself adequately.[51]

It is not clear why Hess decided to drop his pretence. The prison commandant, Colonel Andrus, had told him to his face that he was feigning, and it was not a very manly thing to do.[52] The US psychiatrist, Dr Gustave Gilbert, had suggested that he might be excluded from the proceedings on the grounds of incompetence.[53] Perhaps the fear that he would be disqualified and have to suffer the reproach of evading his responsibilities, thus denying his Führer, caused him to change tactics. At all events, after von Rohrscheidt and the prosecution had exchanged arguments for about an hour Hess was given an opportunity to speak.

'Mr President!' He clicked heels and bowed his head towards the presiding judge, 'In order to forestall the possibility of my being pronounced incapable of pleading in spite of my willingness to take part in the proceedings and to hear the verdict alongside my comrades, I would like to make the following declaration before the Tribunal, although originally I intended to make it during a later stage of the trial. Henceforth my memory will again respond to the outside world. The reasons for simulating loss of memory were of a tactical nature ...'[54]

He went on to say that he bore full responsibility for everything he had done, signed or co-signed, but his statement did not affect his fundamental attitude that the tribunal was not competent.

As he finished speaking a buzz of talk and laughter rose from the Press benches, and reporters dashed for the door.

The following morning the presiding judge announced that, having heard Hess's statement, the tribunal was of opinion that he was capable of standing his trial; the motion of the counsel for the defence was therefore denied.

* * *

Recovering his memory did not affect Hess's attitude to the trial. He continued to feign indifference, not bothering to wear the headphones provided for translation, reading books during sessions, holding whispered conversations with Göring and others around him, grinning toothily, even laughing out loud. Beneath the act, to judge by letters he smuggled out to Ilse under the guise of notes for his counsel, he was quite aware of the proceedings. Thus the following January he described the trial as in part frightful, in part boring, but at times interesting.[55]

By this time he had replaced von Rohrscheidt with Dr Alfred Seidl, who was representing one of his co-defendants and had impressed him with his sharpness and aggression. Seidl advised him to continue his attitude of indifference to the proceedings.

The prosecution opened the case against him on 7 February. He was indicted under the four counts of conspiracy against peace and humanity; planning and initiating wars of aggression; war crimes including murder and ill treatment of civilian populations; crimes against humanity including deliberate and systematic genocide. Since few documents had been found connecting him with specific decisions, the prosecution insisted that he must have been involved because of his position and offices. However, in view of the race policies pursued in Poland and later in the whole of the occupied east, one document was particularly damaging: an order he had signed demanding support from the party for recruiting members of the *Waffen-SS* – the SS military units: 'The units of the *Waffen-SS* are more suitable than other armed units for the specific tasks to be solved in the occupied eastern territories due to their intensive National-Socialist training in regard to questions of race and nationality.'[56] He was not called to account for this order since Seidl did not put him on the witness stand, no doubt for the same reason he had advised him to continue his guise of indifference to the proceedings. In any case, by this time Hess's memory had begun to slip again. To the psychiatrists it appeared genuine; one believed it was a result of Hess's exposure to the mounting evidence of the crimes and cruelties perpetrated by Nazism: 'he took flight into amnesia to escape the dreadful reality presented [in Court].'[57]

The descriptions of hideous tortures, mass sadism, slave labour in unimaginably degrading conditions, the reduction of human beings to so-called *Muselmänner* with vacant eyes, lacking the will to live, horrific medical experiments on concentration camp inmates, mass shootings, gassing in mobile vans and purpose-built gas chamber-incinerator plants run as production lines of death day after day, week after week built up a totality of horror numbing the strongest nerves. For a man as sensitive as Hess who was regarded by his colleagues as 'soft' and who knew at one level of his mind that his Führer had been ultimately responsible and that this was the necessary end of the creed to which he himself adhered, it can be imagined that he did indeed take flight into unreality. One defence he raised, as he had in Britain, was that it was all the work of the Jews; another, again as in Britain, was to pretend he had lost his memory – although this hardly squares with the rationality of his letters home. In August his memory duly returned: he wrote to Ilse that the 'miracle has occurred again ... vvvvv [Hess family laugh sign].'[58]

Meanwhile, conducting his defence, Seidl had ambushed the tribunal, particularly the Soviet component, by presenting the hitherto secret protocol attached to the Nazi–Soviet pact of August 1939; this had divided Poland and other east European countries between Germany and Russia.[59] Despite this proof of their own complicity in 'conspiracy against peace and humanity', the Soviet contingent – which had argued vigorously against its admission to the proceedings – felt no compulsion to withdraw, and the trial continued.

On 31 August, after counsel had made their final speeches, the defendants were each permitted a brief statement, Göring first, and after him Hess, who was allowed to remain seated because of his state of health.

At the start of the trials, he began, he had predicted certain things, as some of his comrades here could confirm: witnesses would appear and make untrue statements while creating an absolutely reliable impression; some defendants would act rather strangely, make shameless utterances about the Führer and would incriminate their own people and each other. These predictions had come true, he said, then referred the court to the Moscow show trials of 1936–38 when some 'mysterious means' had been used to make defendants accuse themselves in an extraordinary way.[60]

After some twenty minutes' rambling discourse he was cut short and reminded that the tribunal could not allow speeches of great length. In that case, he replied, he would forego the statement he had wanted to make; instead, he said, he would not defend himself against accusers whom he denied the right to charge him and his fellow countrymen, and would not discuss accusations on purely German matters. 'I was permitted to work for many years of my life under the greatest son my *Volk* has brought forth in its thousand year history,' he continued, reprising the sentiments in his earlier letter to Ilse. 'Even if I could, I would not want to erase this period of time from my existence.

I am happy to know that I have done my duty to my *Volk*, my duty as a German, as a National-Socialist, as a loyal follower of the Führer. I regret nothing.'

He went on, invoking the omnipotent Creator in whom he believed, 'If I were to begin again, I would act as I have acted, even if I knew that in the end I should meet a fiery death on the pyre. No matter what humans do, some day I shall stand before the judgement of the Eternal. I shall answer to Him, and I know He will judge me innocent.'

Verdicts were announced on 1 October. Hess, who had prepared himself for a death sentence, continued to play his role of indifference and did not put his headphones on. He was adjudged to have participated fully and willingly in all the German aggressions which had led to the war. There was evidence showing the participation of his office in the distribution of orders connected with war crimes, but this was not sufficiently connected with the crimes themselves to sustain a finding of guilt. He was, therefore, judged guilty on the first two counts, conspiracy and crimes against peace, but not guilty of war crimes or crimes against humanity.[61]

Sentences were handed down that afternoon. Again Hess did not bother to put on the headphones.

'Defendant Hermann Wilhelm Göring, on the counts of the indictment on which you have been convicted, the International Military Tribunal sentences you to death by hanging.'[62]

'Defendant Rudolf Hess, on the counts of the indictment on which you have been convicted, the Tribunal sentences you to imprisonment for life.'[63]

The US psychiatrist, Gilbert, was waiting by the cells as the prisoners were led down one by one after hearing their sentences. Göring's face was pale, his eyes moist and he was evidently fighting back an emotional breakdown as he asked Gilbert in an unsteady voice to leave him alone for a while. He was later to cheat the hangman by taking poison smuggled in to him. By contrast Hess 'strutted in, laughing nervously', and told Gilbert he had not been listening; he didn't know what his sentence was.[64]

The Russian team had wanted the death penalty. In addition to his flight to Britain in the hope of 'facilitating the realization of aggression

315

against the Soviet Union by temporarily restraining England from fighting', it was argued that Hess, as the third most significant Nazi, had played a decisive role in the crimes of the regime. That his counsel had exposed the hypocrisy of the Soviet presence on the tribunal was, perhaps, a further consideration.[65]

CHAPTER SEVENTEEN

Spandau

SEVEN OF THE DEFENDANTS at Nuremberg were sentenced to varying terms of imprisonment: the one-time Foreign Minister, Konstantin von Neurath; Hitler's architect and Minister of Armaments, Albert Speer; the former Minister of Economics and President of the Reichsbank, Walter Funk; the Reich Youth Leader and Gauleiter of Vienna, Baldur von Schirach; the two Grand Admirals, Erich Raeder and Karl Dönitz; and the former Deputy Führer, Rudolf Hess.

Spandau jail in West Berlin was adapted to accommodate them. It was a fitting choice. Built in the late 19th century like a red-brick fortress with castellated towers and walls, it had been used during the Nazi period as a collecting point for political prisoners before despatch to concentration camps. It had also served for executions, one of several prisons in Berlin equipped with a newly designed guillotine and sloping, tiled floor to drain blood, and a beam with hooks for the simultaneous strangulation of eight persons by hanging. This apparatus was removed during the refit to accommodate the Nuremberg prisoners.

The small single cells in which they were to live were modified to prevent suicide, and outside a high, barbed-wire fence was erected beyond the red-brick boundary wall, together with an electric fence carrying a 4,000-volt charge. This was designed to prevent rescue attempts. Timber watchtowers were built at intervals atop the wall from which floodlights could be played over the entire perimeter.

At the end of the war Germany had been occupied by the victorious Allies – the United States, the Soviet Union, Great Britain and France – and divided into sectors, each controlled by one of the occupying powers; Berlin, although inside the Soviet sector, was similarly divided. Spandau jail stood in the British sector, but was run jointly by the four powers, each providing a director, a deputy director and 32 soldiers for external guard duty for one month in four in a continuous cycle. Besides the external guards there were some eighteen internal guards or warders in control of the prisoners, and a number of ancillary staff.

Not until July 1947 were the modifications to the building complete; then the seven prisoners were flown from Nuremberg to Berlin and bussed at speed through the still-ruined city to the jail, each handcuffed individually to guards. The handcuffs were removed once the main gates had closed behind them, and they were shepherded over a cobbled yard to the main cell block. There, in the chief warder's room, they were made to strip and don rough blue-grey convict uniform that had come from a concentration camp. Each set was stencilled with a different number; the prisoners would be known by these numbers for their whole time inside. Hess, gaunt and pale, his once-luxuriant dark hair now touched with grey, became 'Number Seven'.

The cell to which he was led was almost nine feet by seven-and-a-half and just twelve feet high to the curved ceiling. Judging from Albert Speer's description, the bare walls were painted a muddy yellow with white above. Opposite the door was a small, high window, its glass replaced by brownish celluloid, barred outside; below it against the left wall stood a narrow iron bed with grey blankets. Otherwise there was only a small, chipped, brown-varnished table, an upright wooden chair, an open cupboard with a single shelf on the wall above, and in the corner by the door a flush lavatory bowl with a black seat.[1]

* * *

While still in Nuremberg after the sentences had been handed down Hess had escaped into a fantasy world in which the Western powers had released him to lead a new Germany to counteract the 'Bolshevisation' of Europe that he had predicted in Britain. Now the danger was obvious: Churchill had spoken of the 'iron curtain' that had fallen across the continent. The vision had been so real to him he had spent the months before his transfer to Spandau typing press releases about his new government on a typewriter allowed him by the authorities. He had also composed his first speech to the Reichstag, beginning with a eulogy for the dead, and 'above all of the *one* among the dead, the originator and leader of the National-Socialist Reich, Adolf Hitler'.[2]

The state Hess imagined himself leading had been scarcely distinguishable from Hitler's Führer state, but without the excesses: the Jews, for instance, might ask to go to protective camps 'to save themselves from the rage of the German people', and in these camps conditions were to be 'as humane as possible'.[3] He was not insane: Dönitz was occupying himself with much the same fantasy of being called to head a new German regime.

Spandau brought Hess, Dönitz and their fellow prisoners down to cold reality. Reduced to the anonymity of numbers, they were not allowed to speak to one another during their supervised times together or during their 30-minute exercise period circling an old linden tree in the prison yard, hands clasped behind their backs, wood-soled prison shoes clomping the hard ground. The guards held aloof in the early months, visiting on them the hatred accumulated by the Nazi regime. The meals they ate from tin trays alone in their cells were so meagre they lost weight steadily, and soon the prison clothes hung shapelessly on their bony figures.

At night their sleep was interrupted constantly by warders turning up the cell lights to 'inspect' them. The Russian warders made a point of doing this up to four times an hour, according to a report on the 'mental torture' of the prisoners made by the French prison chaplain in 1950.[4] The one letter they were allowed to write home each month was censored to eliminate references to the Third Reich or its personalities, Nuremberg, or contemporary politics, as was the one incoming letter permitted each month.

Books were the chief escape from utter tedium and loneliness. Another escape was the garden. On arrival this consisted mainly of nut trees and lilac bushes amid a wilderness of waist-high weeds and grasses. The first summer they dug in the weeds and planted vegetables under the direction of von Neurath, the only one among them who knew anything of gardening. Albert Speer used his architectural talents to draw up plans for landscaping the area. 'How we sweated!' Hess wrote home describing their labour creating the new garden.[5] He was not writing about himself. He refused all work on the twin principles that he had not been sentenced to hard labour, and in any case the trial had been invalid. When summoned by the warders for some task, he pretended stomach cramps, and moaned and groaned, establishing a pattern of non-cooperation from the start. Sometimes he refused to get up in the morning and lay groaning until the warders tipped him out. On one occasion when it was raining, Speer recorded, he refused to go outside for the exercise period.

'Seven!' a warder called out, 'You'll be put in the punishment cell.'

Hess rose and walked into the punishment cell himself.[6] He spent much time there in solitary confinement.

The attention he attracted to himself from the prison staff by his eccentricity and prickliness distanced him from the other prisoners. Yet, difficult, pathetic and at times peremptory, as if assuming his former role as Deputy Führer, he remained consistent in his attitude to the Nuremberg trial, refusing to recognise its legality, refusing to repent, refusing to allow his counsel, Dr Seidl, to enter a plea for mercy[7] – desperately though he wanted to be free with Ilse and his growing son – refusing to allow his family to visit him in prison since it would be dishonourable for him to meet them under such conditions with witnesses listening to every word in case the forbidden topics were mentioned. He rejoiced when Ilse wrote to say she understood his reasons: it showed that she, too, considered their 'own and German honour higher than personal wishes and feelings'.[8]

* * *

After some two-and-a-half years in Spandau Hess's amnesia returned. The rule of silence had been relaxed by this time. He pointed to the British prison director making his rounds in the garden, which he did every day, and asked Speer who that stranger was.[9] He had played the trick so often he could hardly have expected to be taken wholly seriously. Nor could he have expected to gain release. No doubt it was a ploy to gain attention and defeat monotony. As Speer recorded later, the days were so numbing in their evenness and emptiness, he could not find words to convey 'the forever unchanging sameness'.[10]

Hess regained his memory within four months, proving it with an outburst of esoteric information on history and literature. He then began experiencing crippling stomach cramps, and wailed and moaned at night. The eerie lament proved so distressing to his fellow prisoners that the current director ordered his mattress and blankets removed to prevent him lying in bed wailing all morning as well; he wailed from his chair instead.[11] The two admirals, contemptuous of his lack of self-control and bearing, virtually broke off relations with him.[12]

All the other cranky or paranoiac patterns he had displayed in captivity in Britain returned in cycles: the obsession with poison in his food, black depressions when he refused to eat, stomach pains for which the doctors could find no organic cause. Like the recurrent periods of amnesia he experienced, these were surely symptoms of despair.

In November 1954 von Neurath was released on grounds of age and ill health after serving only nine of the fifteen years to which he had been sentenced. Hess, who had perhaps hoped that he, too, might be allowed home on compassionate grounds, suffered badly afterwards, scarcely eating, complaining of unbearable pains and wailing again at night. The following year Raeder was freed and after him Dönitz; and in May 1957 Funk, who was serving life, was released on grounds of ill health, leaving only Hess and the two younger men, Speer and von Schirach, inside.

Hess fell into a cycle of deep depressions, refusing food, suffering stomach cramps and wailing, which culminated in the morning of 26 November 1959 with an apparent suicide attempt. While the other two prisoners were in the garden with the duty warder he broke a lens of his glasses and used the jagged edge to open a large vein in his wrist. The warder found him shortly after noon, curled up in bed with blood seeping through the blanket and sheet. After his wrist had been stitched Hess appeared much calmer, as often happened after his outbursts, and he began eating heartily. The warder did not consider the incident a genuine suicide attempt, merely one of Hess's ways of draw-ing attention to himself;[13] Speer had the impression of a child who had just carried off a prank.[14]

On the 25th anniversary of his flight to Scotland, 10 May 1966, Hess remained in his cell all day, according to Speer sitting bolt upright at his table, staring at the wall.[15] He had by now far surpassed the normal span for a life sentence in Western penal systems; moreover, he knew that his two remaining compatriots were due to be released in less than six months' time. Any hope that he might be allowed out with them was extinguished two weeks later with the arrival of a motor lawnmower for the warders to use to keep the garden going for him when the working prisoners left.

That day arrived on 1 October. Hess was left sole inmate of the prison designed originally for 600. The establishment of directors, guards and warders was left unchanged, rotating by nationality on a monthly basis as before. Hess appeared to accept it philosophically. He had recently allowed his lawyer, Dr Seidl, to appeal on his behalf, and when Seidl visited him to tell him of a letter he had addressed to the heads of state of the four occupying powers requesting a review of his case, he said he did not want a plea for mercy based on his mental condition; there was nothing wrong with him mentally.[16]

His son, Wolf Rüdiger, whom he had not seen since he was three-and-a-half years old, had formed a 'Freedom for Rudolf Hess' association with Ilse, other family members and Dr Seidl, and had already addressed innumerable appeals to the governments of the four powers, human rights organisations and religious leaders. These had received wide international support, and Western governments had accepted the case for mercy. The Russians had remained unmoved. They had lost twenty million dead in the 'great patriotic war'; they believed Hess had flown to Scotland specifically to gain British acquies-cence in Hitler's assault on their country; besides, it was unimaginable that the last living symbol of the highest echelons of the Nazi regime should be released.[17] And without Russian agreement the Western powers had declared themselves unable to act.

Wolf Rüdiger believed that the Western powers, especially Britain, were using the Russian veto as an excuse to ensure that Hess never left Spandau alive. The files remain closed, so the question cannot be resolved.[18] It seems likely, however, that Hess was a pawn in the Cold War. The Western powers needed to maintain the four-power status of Berlin to preserve their rights of access to West Berlin, and since Spandau was one of only two remaining four-power institutions, they feared a quarrel over its continuing use. Spandau also served the Russians as a useful listening post in the western sector of the city.

In addition, Hess refused to express repentance or accept the validity of the Nuremberg trial; Seidl reinforced his conviction that the trial lacked legal validity and made the political mistake of using this argument in his submissions to the four powers.[19] Hess, caught in a three-way bind between the visceral enmity of the Russians, the tensions of the Cold War and the blind refusal of his own supporters to accept the legitimacy of his trial, seemed destined to spend the rest of his life in Spandau.

THE DIRECTOR AND THE PASTOR

It is often said of Hess that he was kept in captivity because of what he might divulge if released. Yet if he had explosive secrets to reveal there were plenty of opportunities to make them known while still inside. He could have told Dr Seidl – when at length he agreed to see him. He could have told Albert Speer, probably closer to him than the others in the cell block, or any of his fellow prisoners, who could have released them to the outside world when they were freed. Their silence is evidence that he did not do so. Speer, who wrote of life in Spandau and of his experiences in the Third Reich,[20] would certainly have used any revelations from Hess to boost sales.

Could Hess have been dissuaded from talking by threats of dire consequences for his family? The system widely used in Nazi Germany would surely not have been contemplated by the British government or secret services. More likely, perhaps, in view of the notions of honour that prevented Hess from seeing his family in prison, he might have considered anything he had to say from a prison cell worthless or demeaning. This was his attitude towards making a public condemnation of the Nazi slaughter of the Jews – as will appear. Certainly, Ilse Hess thought that if he were allowed home he might open up.[21]

More profound questions concern the extent of his amnesia: how much he wanted to forget, how much he pretended to forget, how much he really had forgotten. This is illustrated by his replies to two men who had opportunity to probe him closely and who wrote books afterwards attempting to explain his mission and his character: the US director of Spandau, Colonel Eugene Bird, and after Bird retired, the French pastor, Charles Gabel. Several of Hess's answers to Bird are plainly untrue: for instance, it is known from his own letters home and reports of his conversations in England that Karl Haushofer told him of a dream in which he had seen him striding through the halls of tapestried English castles; it is also known from his own letters and the German investigation into his flight that he consulted astrologers. Yet, tackled by Bird on both matters, he denied being especially interested in astrology, he had never asked an astrologer to read his horoscope, and he knew nothing about Haushofer's dream.[22]

Relatively unimportant as they were, his denials suggest he had either lost all memory of the circumstances of his flight or was, as so often, playing games. On the important question of whether he had known about Operation 'Barbarossa', Hitler's planned assault on Russia, when he flew to Scotland, he initially misled Bird. His first response was that he was sorry, he didn't know; he couldn't remember: 'But in any case I did not fly to England for this reason. I only flew to make peace.'[23] He continued to maintain this attitude whenever Bird pressed him on the subject, yet in the end, when he had to make a decision on the story that would appear in Bird's book, he admitted, yes, he had known of Barbarossa.[24]

* * *

Lieutenant Colonel Eugene Bird had been appointed US Director and Commandant of Spandau in 1964 when only Hess, Speer and von Schirach remained in the cells. He had soon decided to write a book to record the story of the secret institution for posterity, but almost inevitably the focus shifted to the prison's most enigmatic inmate and his wartime peace mission to Britain. This was facilitated by Bird's discovery of a cardboard carton that had arrived with Hess on his transfer to Spandau in 1947 and was filled with papers he had written in Nuremberg. They included diary notes, plans for his new German government and a full account of his peace mission to Scotland. Allowing Hess to read them, Bird enlisted his co-operation in his own book, which became virtually a joint venture. Hess would read every page of Bird's typescript and if he approved initial it.[25]

Bird did not find Hess an easy man to know, but persisted in his quest for the hidden truth week after week, attempting to draw out memories from what he soon recognised were depths to which they had been purposely consigned.[26] He found him complex and intelligent, humorous and on occasion warm, far from the mad fantasist customarily portrayed, and formed a close relationship with him. But how far he succeeded in penetrating the shell of evasion and half-truth which Hess had grown to protect his Führer and, no doubt, his own self-respect from his wild miscalculation – the realisation, perhaps, that he had been gulled or had gulled himself into a fool's flight – must be questionable.

In November 1969 Hess fell into a decline, refusing to eat, wash or shave and groaning so loudly it could be heard by guards on the perimeter wall. After a while it was discovered this was not one of his tactical ploys; he was seriously ill and needed to be examined in hospital. He refused to go. He had been confined for so long he feared to leave the prison, and pleaded for treatment in his cell. Told he must go, he called for Colonel Bird, and when he arrived implored him, weeping, to go with him and visit him every day in the hospital. Bird agreed, after which he was rushed to the British Military Hospital nearby.[27]

There it was found he had a perforated duodenal ulcer and peritonitis had set in. After treatment he remained dangerously ill, and eight days later, on 29 November, became convinced he was about to die[28] – a fact which, as we have seen, was to acquire significance for the provenance of what was later presented as a suicide note. He demanded the attendance of a British and a German heart specialist, Dr Seidl and a German notary to witness a statement he wished to sign; he also asked that his son be informed.

He survived the night. Over the following days, seduced by the comfort and splendour of his hospital room after the stone walls of his cell, he weakened in his resolve not to see his family in the dishonourable condition of a prisoner, and allowed Bird to talk him into a Christmas visit from Ilse and his son. They arrived on 24 December, Ilse now grey-haired, Wolf Rüdiger a grown man of 32. As they entered the room where he waited tensely, he shot up like a spring from his chair and brought his hand up to his forehead in salute.

'I kiss your hand, Ilse!'

The two stared almost unbelievingly at one another before Ilse replied, 'I kiss your hand, father!'[29]

Her impulse to rush to him with outstretched arms was restrained by Wolf Rüdiger; physical contact was not permitted. They sat at opposite sides of a table set between partitions dividing the room. Hess put on a cheerful, confident performance, asking about their flight, talking about his illness, assuring them he was receiving 'absolutely overwhelming treatment', listening to their news of relations. After the allotted 30 minutes, stretched to 34, he returned to bed smiling contentedly.

'I'm so happy I've seen them,' he told Bird, 'I'm just sorry I waited so long ...'

One thing that occupied him during that first visit was the distress he had caused his former secretary, Hildegard Fath, known in his close circle as 'Freiburg' – her home town – when at Nuremberg he had pretended not to know her. He had been unable to explain or make his apologies as Nuremberg was one of the topics the prisoners were not permitted to write about; and almost the first thing he said to Ilse was to ask her to convey his greetings to Freiburg and say he was very sorry he had treated her very badly for over twenty years. Like his premonition of death the previous month, these words would acquire significance for the provenance of his later 'suicide note'. That he said them is not in doubt as they were published in a book Wolf Rüdiger wrote about his father in 1984, three years before his alleged suicide.[30]

That first visit broke Hess's resistance to seeing his family in prison. After he had recovered and been returned to Spandau Ilse, Wolf Rüdiger or other members of his family visited him every month.

Bird continued probing him about his mission to Britain. On 10 May 1971, the 30th anniversary of his flight, he brought a tape recording of a BBC documentary on the subject which he hoped might prick Hess's memory. They sat on a bench in the garden under the shade of a tall poplar Dönitz had planted years ago. As Bird fitted the cassette into his recorder Hess seemed nervous and told him his mission had been a great one; he was not ashamed of it. It was a mission for humanity. He had wanted to end the war and bring about an understanding with England to stop the bloodshed and end the suffering. He had taken it on himself to go, but it was too late. His mission had been a failure –

'Did you have high hopes of bringing about a settlement with the British?' Bird asked.

'Of course!' Hess laughed. 'Otherwise why would I have gone?'[31]

Bird switched on the recorder. He did not, according to the book he published later, ask him what reason he had for his high hopes, nor why he had chosen Hamilton.

On another occasion Bird showed him microfilm of captured correspondence between Hess and the Haushofers in the late summer and autumn of 1940. Hess agreed that the Haushofers had been working to find a basis for an understanding, but said that they had not known and could not have guessed that he himself would fly to conduct the negotiations.

> We had not heard from the Duke of Hamilton and it was becoming urgent that something had to be done soon or it would be too late. There was the danger that England would make her pact with America before we could get someone over to talk to her on the highest authority. That is why I decided to take it on myself to fly.[32]

Bird asked whether he had talked to Hitler about it first. Hess replied that Hitler had not known he planned to fly to England himself; but he himself had known that what he had to say would have the Führer's approval. Again, Bird apparently failed to ask him why, if he had not heard from Hamilton, he flew to see him. This was especially odd since Hess insisted during this same conversation that he had never met

Hamilton; he may have seen him across a room at a Berlin reception, but he had never met him and had not corresponded with him.[33]

In spring 1972 their talks came to an abrupt end. Bird was summoned to his commanding officer at US mission headquarters in Berlin and asked if he was responsible for a manuscript on Spandau written with Hess's co-operation. Bird agreed that he was. It was no secret among his colleagues; several of his fellow officers had read his chapters and made suggestions. Now it appeared that it had suddenly become a matter of grave official concern.

He was interrogated for several hours and when finally allowed home was placed under house arrest, and a team of officers searched every room and took away documents, letters and photographs. His phone was tapped, and although allowed to travel in Berlin in his car he was followed by three cars, each containing two secret service men. Finally, he was asked to resign his post as US Commandant of Spandau, made to sign a secrets act and told he would have to await official permission before he could publish his book.[34]

Undoubtedly Colonel Bird had broken the regulations governing Spandau and talked to Hess on all the forbidden topics. Whether his transgressions merited the extreme measures described seems doubtful. He was, however, given permission to publish, and his book, *The Loneliest Man in the World*, appeared in 1974, extending knowledge of Hess's plight internationally and increasing pressure for his release.

Bird did not reveal whether he had been made to cut out certain passages before he was allowed to publish, but Desmond Zwar, who helped him or even 'ghosted' his book, is positive that 'Bird and I were never "censored".'[35]

* * *

Five years after Bird was forced to resign, a French priest, Charles Gabel, took over as pastor for the lone prisoner in Spandau. By this time Hess was 83, but it is clear from the book Gabel published later that despite age and physical frailty and the psychic strain of endless years in captivity, he had retained mental acuity and balance.[36] When not indulging his extravagant theatre of distress during the early years or descending into spirals of ultimate despair, he had maintained internal discipline and succeeded in keeping mentally active, reading widely in history and philosophy, always making copious notes. The new science of space exploration particularly excited him, and he had studied and thought creatively about its problems. In addition, until prevented by age and stiffness, he had done daily physical exercises.

He had told Bird that his main source of strength was his strong belief in God – 'not in the Church, only in God.' His own philosophy, he had said, was based on Schopenhauer's concept that ultimately man was guided by fate, 'but really, isn't our fate in God's hands?'[37] Gabel had no doubt that he was completely sound in mind. He also discovered in him, little by little, a wry sense of humour he had not expected.

The visits he made once a week always followed the same pattern: first about twenty minutes listening on an old record player to the classical composers Hess loved, Mozart, Beethoven, Schubert in particular; next about quarter of an hour of reading, and afterwards they would walk in the garden whatever the conditions. Here, Gabel recorded, they could broach subjects of the moment, but also talk of personal and family affairs. Sometimes Hess sent messages to his family via Gabel, sometimes the family passed news to him through the pastor.

Hess was highly amused in May 1979 when Gabel told him of Hugh Thomas's book, *The Murder of Rudolph Hess*. Based on his observation that prisoner 'Number 7' in Spandau had no scar on his chest from a wound Hess had sustained in the first war, Thomas, a doctor, claimed that he was a double, substituted for the real Hess, who had been murdered. The argument was soon disposed of by two doctors from the British Military Hospital who examined Hess and found the scarcely visible scar.[38] It did not prevent the book from being an international sensation.

Some two years later Gabel told Hess that a former chief of British counter-espionage – Sir Maurice Oldfield – had revealed that Hess's intelligence chief had been a Soviet agent, and helped Hess to make his flight to Scotland. 'What interest would the Russians have had in sending me to England?' Hess very reasonably asked.[39]

One of the intriguing features of Gabel's book is the number of times he refers to Hess expressing profound regret for the Nazi programme of exterminating the Jews:[40] 'Hess likes to repeat that he himself bears no responsibility for what the Nazi leaders ... savagely baptised the *Endlosung*. He deeply regrets that which will never be erased from history.'[41] Gabel suggested to him that if he could publicly disassociate himself from these Nazi excesses he would render a great service to his country, even to himself. Hess declined on the grounds that prison was not the ideal place from which to make a statement that was 'truly and totally free'. Gabel understood the argument, but kept returning to the question, and put it to him later that a public declaration of his regret for the war and the sufferings it had brought, particularly to the Jews, would meet Russian objections that he had never expressed repentance, and might facilitate his release. Hess said he saw no need to put it in writing. He had always regretted the violence and excesses of the war. His commitment to peace had been sufficiently demonstrated on 10 May 1941.[42]

In Bird's book there is only one passing reference to Hess's regret for Nazi Jewish policy. It was after Bird told him that Ilse had referred to him as 'the conscience of the party'. Hess had chuckled, 'Yes, in many ways I was very much against treating the Jews the way they were treated.'[43] This is hardly the profound regret for the mass slaughter programme he regularly expressed during talks with Gabel. The want of any serious reference to the subject is so remarkable as to suggest that despite the denial of Bird's co-author Zwar, Bird himself might have been warned off any references to Hess's attitude to the extermination of the Jews. Yet there is nothing to substantiate that possibility.

Of his flight to Scotland, Hess maintained an obdurate silence. In June 1986 as Gabel's time in Spandau was coming to an end, the pastor reported, 'He has told me nothing [of his flight] and will never tell anything. One must not expect revelations.'[44]

Yet Gabel had, unwittingly, recorded one important revelation: two years earlier, on 16 May 1984, Hess had neatly side-stepped the question of whether Hitler had sent him to Britain by referring to documents in London which remained closed to the public. 'These,' he told Gabel, 'are without doubt the peace proposals I took. The English do not want it perceived that one could have stopped the war.'[45] Thus, from Hess's own lips, confirmation that he took peace proposals with him to Britain, proposals which have not surfaced to this day, and on which Kirkpatrick's, Hamilton's, Foleys, Simon's and Beaverbrook's reports are silent.

Hess made another reference to these documents in early 1987. His medical attendant, Abdallah Melaouhi, told him he had heard from one of the Soviet guards that the Russian leader, Mikhail Gorbachev, was prepared to release him on the next Soviet tour of duty at Spandau. Hess showed no reaction. Surprised, Melaouhi asked if he was not pleased by the news. Hess replied that if the Russians released him it would mean his death. 'He would only be pleased if the British published his documents internationally.'[46] If they did so it would mean he could be freed; but Hess cautioned Melaouhi to say nothing about this. Melaouhi claimed that it was not until after Hess's death that he understood what he had meant: that the British would never allow his release.

When Gabel heard the rumours that Gorbachev intended to propose Hess's release he wondered if it was, perhaps, disinformation designed to put pressure on the Allies.[47] He had kept in touch with his successor at Spandau, who informed him of a serious decline in Hess's health that summer; he did not expect him to survive the winter.

In August came the shocking news of Hess's suicide.

CHAPTER EIGHTEEN

Final audit

FIRSTLY, WHY HAMILTON? According to Eden's statement to the House of Commons Hess flew over to see the Duke because his friend, Haushofer, had told him that 'the wing commander was an Englishman who would understand his point of view'.[1] The explanation Hess gave Eugene Bird was scarcely more credible: he had not heard from the Duke, but took it upon himself to fly over to Scotland to see him because of the danger that England would make a pact with America before they (the Nazi government) could get someone over to talk to her on the highest authority.[2]

Bird, it will be recalled, asked Hess if he had had high hopes of success.

'Of course. Otherwise, why would I have gone!'

The statements appear contradictory. How could Hess have expected success if he had not heard from his would-be negotiating partner? Others must have told him then. He never revealed who – of which more later.

According to Hamilton's report of his first meeting with Hess alone in Maryhill Barracks Hospital soon after he landed, Hess requested two things: that Hamilton get together the leading members of his party to talk over peace proposals, and that he ask the King to give him parole as he had come unarmed and of his own free will.[3] At Mytchett Place Hess told Dr Gibson Graham that he could only gain access to the King through Hamilton;[4] later he asked Lieutenant Malone to request Hamilton to arrange an audience for him with the King;[5] and he told Lord Simon, 'I appealed to the gallantry of the King of England ... I thought the King and the Duke of Hamilton would take me under their protection.'[6] He said the same to Major Foley and to Lieutenant Loftus.[7]

This probably answers the question 'why Hamilton?' As Lord Steward in the Royal Household Hamilton had direct access to the King. Hess seems to have believed that an appeal to the King would allow him to circumvent the British diplomatic channels answerable to Churchill. It will be recalled that on the morning of 10 May, prior to taking off for Scotland, he had called a legal officer on Martin Bormann's staff to ask the position of the King of England.[8] He appears to have believed the King had the power to install a new administration in place of Churchill's.

Yet there was a serious flaw in Hess's plan: he regarded himself as a *Parlementär*[9] under a flag of truce, yet he could not say he came on behalf of the Führer, for that would indicate a weakening in Hitler's position of continental mastery; consequently he lacked the authority of a legitimate *Parlementär*, and Churchill could and did confine him as a prisoner of war, or as he termed it a prisoner of State.

* * *

What of Hamilton's own role? In the four months following the interception of Albrecht Haushofer's letter to him in November 1940 he took three unexplained periods of ten days' leave. The first, from 12 to 21 November may have been connected with the MI5 investigation into his 'bona fides'. The second, from 26 January to 4 February 1941, followed two meetings he had with the Duke of Kent on 20 and 23 January,[10] and coincided with an escalation of peace feelers from both sides – Dr Weissauer's Finnish emissary, Dr Henrik Ramsay, in London from 18 to 26 January, Claude Dansey's Finnish emissary, Tancred Borenius, in Geneva with Carl Burckhardt. In addition Albrecht Haushofer was in Sweden during this period from 2 to 5 February, probably for Hess in connection with King Gustav's peace mediation offer, which was the subject of Sir Stewart Menzies' note to Hopkinson of 19 February with the bottom half torn off.[11] That is speculation. Hamilton's third period of leave from 8 to 17 March was connected with the Air Intelligence scheme to send him to Lisbon to meet Albrecht Haushofer.

These three mostly unexplained periods of leave might seem to implicate Hamilton in the peace approaches of this period, yet 'Tar' Robertson's report after interviewing him on 25 April states that while still a member of the community willing to make peace with Germany, Hamilton 'now considers that the only thing that this country can do is to fight the war to the finish'.[12] Hamilton was an uncomplicated aviator. Robertson was a shrewd judge of men. It is, therefore, difficult to ascribe these three periods of leave to Hamilton's membership of a group plotting a negotiated peace.

Hamilton's activities, or lack of activity, on 10 May as Hess flew in to his command sector and bailed out do need explanation. His own account is quite inadequate. It must be assumed that whatever he was doing during the hours he failed to account for he was acting on the instructions of his superior officer at Fighter Command. Otherwise Churchill would not subsequently have made it known – as he did – that Hamilton had acted in all respects honourably. If a record was made of Hamilton's communications with Group or Fighter Command during this period it has not been released. Finally he was told to report in person to Sir Alexander Cadogan at the Foreign Office, but Churchill intervened.

* * *

Lord Simon concluded from his interview with Hess that he had come under the impression his chances of success were much greater than he now realised they were. 'He imagined there was a strong peace party and that he would have the opportunity of getting into touch with leading politicians who wanted the war to end now.'[13] Hess later told Lieutenant Loftus he was quite certain that if only he had been able to contact influential persons in Britain they could have stopped the war between them.[14]

It is apparent that there were numbers of hugely influential persons wanting a compromise peace, many in the House of Lords, several with grand houses and vast estates; yet there is no evidence of any coherent 'peace party' such as Hess apparently expected. It is clear from Guy Liddell's diary and the investigations launched by MI5 after the event that the internal Security Service had not anticipated Hess's arrival and had no intelligence of a 'peace party' gathering to greet him. They were either remarkably lax – for the Duke of Hamilton himself had been investigated in connection with the letter from Albrecht Haushofer – or there was no organised peace party waiting for Hess. Alternatively, it is possible that there was such a group led by someone so elevated he was not under surveillance, perhaps the King's younger brother, the Duke of Kent.

The authors of *Double Standards* allege that the Duke of Kent was indeed waiting with others, including Poles, in the cottage known as the Kennels adjacent to the airstrip at Dungavel.[15] Their informant wished to remain anonymous. It is significant, however, that the Duke's whereabouts on that weekend cannot be traced.

Equally significant is the testimony of retired squadron leader Frank Day, who as a young pilot stood guard duty on 13 May at what from his description and from post-war legend attached to the house seems likely to have been Craigiehall, outside a room where Hess was brought for a meeting with a high-ranking RAF officer with a gold-braided cap.[16] Day was told the officer was 'the Duke'; he assumed the Duke of Hamilton, yet Hamilton as a wing commander had no gold braid on his cap. On that evidence alone it was more likely to have been the Duke of Kent, an RAF group captain with the honorary rank of air commodore.

The official account has Hess at the Drymen Military Hospital on 13 May, yet Ivone Kirkpatrick, who had visited him in the early hours of that morning after flying up from London with Hamilton, and who had been ordered to stay in Scotland specifically to probe Hess on his proposals, did not visit him again until the next day, the 14th. Of course, it would have been difficult for him to have done so any sooner if Hess was brought to Craigiehall House on the 13th.

The only other trace of 'peace party' members in Scotland comes from the recollections of a former Royal Navy and British Airways pilot named Ronald Williams, who has not thus far appeared in the story. As a youngster in May 1941, he vividly recalls an unexpected and unusual journey with his parents by train to Glasgow. His father went off somewhere after arrival, while his mother took him for a cruise on the Loch Lomond steamer, and the following day down the Clyde to Rothesay, where electric motor boats were for hire. There the question arose as to whether, at seven, he was old enough to navigate a boat on his own. He caused laughter by asserting he was actually seven and a half, and was allowed to take one out. Judging by what happened next, it must have been Saturday 10 May:

> The next thing was that Dad returned in a stew. Although it was late at night we had to pack up to go to the station to try to get a sleeper back to Liverpool. I was warned not to open my smart alecky mouth about us using a false name for the cabin.[17]

His father, G.E. Williams, had been interned in a camp on the Isle of Man the previous year under the emergency Defence Regulation 18b on account of an association with the British Fascist leader, Oswald Mosley.[18] Williams was an economist with an enthusiasm for 'social credit' as a remedy for the ills of society, and Mosley had shown an interest in applying the idea.[19] Williams had been released after six months, but banned from all war-related work. He also had an association with the Duke of Bedford – formerly Marquis of Tavistock – the most outspoken aristocratic member of the peace movement, and it was this link which had probably drawn him up to Glasgow and subsequently been the cause of his hurried departure by the night train under an assumed name; for when, much later in life, Ronald Williams asked his mother about that night she told him that his father had been among the group waiting for Hess. He assumed they were waiting at Dungavel and the panic was the result of Hess landing some distance away and being taken into custody by the Home Guard. Ron Williams' sister remembers their mother telling her later that their 'dad went to the peace meeting to hear what Hess had to say' – an extraordinarily suggestive phrasing.

It is interesting that Bedford wrote to the Labour MP and peace campaigner Dick Stokes on that 10 May proposing that Lloyd George, 'so *obviously* the one man who could save the country!', should make a public statement setting out possible peace terms to which Germany could respond.[20]

* * *

Had Hess flown into enemy territory in wartime without prior negotiation or arrangement simply on the off chance of finding the Duke of Hamilton at home he would have been certifiable. Yet he could not have made such a difficult and dangerous flight with such precision if he had been mad; no one he spoke to after landing in Scotland gained that impression, and doctors who examined him specifically reported him as being of sound mind.[21]

Besides this obvious reason for doubting the official line that his flight was a lone endeavour and his arrival in Scotland a complete surprise, there were those who knew he was coming: Ernest Bevin, a member of Churchill's War Cabinet, received a coded message to that effect from a contact inside Germany; he apprised Churchill,[22] who the following morning, Sunday 11 May, asked his hostess at Ditchley Park for a room to be prepared for the Duke of Hamilton that night.[23] James Douglas, on duty on the evening of 10 May at the BBC's Mayfair Information Bureau, received intercepted reports that Hess had taken off on a flight from which he had not returned, and alerted the Air Ministry and Fighter Command.[24] Squadron Leader W. Geoffrey Moore, Deputy Commandant of the Royal Observer Corps, Scottish Command, told his daughter, Nancy Mary Goodall, in the strictest confidence after she came off duty from the Operations Room at Turnhouse that night that the German airman who had asked to speak to Hamilton was Rudolf Hess.[25] Sergeant Daniel McBride, one of the first servicemen to speak to Hess after he landed – to whom Hess for some unexplained reason confided his Iron Cross – stated 'with confidence' after the war that high-ranking government officials were aware that Hess was coming.[26]

Apart from this positive evidence, there is Hamilton's refusal to allow anti-aircraft batteries to open fire on an enemy aircraft approaching Glasgow or air-raid warnings to be sounded,[27] his baffling inaction later when told the German pilot had an urgent message for him,[28] and the equally puzzling inaction of the intelligence officer at RAF Ayr close to the site of Hess's landing.[29] And in London the next day Churchill's private secretary, Jock Colville, omitted any mention of the arrival of the Deputy Führer from his first diary entry for the 11th, only adding a demonstrably bogus account of this sensational event in an entry for the same day written at a much later date with borrowings from the leader column of *The Times*.[30]

The possibility that Hess may have been enticed to Britain by false promises was mooted in a German broadcast as early as 13 May – 'It is also conceivable that Hess was deliberately lured into a trap by a British party' – and this was echoed that evening in a broadcast by Goebbels' deputy, Hans Fritsche: 'unless he [Hess] has been consciously trapped by England ...'[31]

On 31 May Eduard Taborsky, personal secretary to the President of the Czech government in exile in London, wrote in his diary on the basis of a top-secret report he had been shown that 'it is clear the Nazi No. 3 was enticed into an English trap'.[32] In September a Soviet agent in Vichy France reported that Hess had been lured to England by MI6 in retaliation for their humiliation at Venlo.[33] And in October 1942 Colonel Moravetz, head of Czech military intelligence, reported to Moscow in the same vein: Hess had been lured to Britain through correspondence purportedly with Hamilton, but actually written by the Intelligence Service. He had personally seen the letters.[34]

In May 1943 the *American Mercury* magazine published a fuller account of the alleged sting: the Secret Service (MI6) had intercepted a peace feeler from Germany and responded, using the names of Hamilton and others to suggest Britain was seeking a way out of its military difficulties. The anonymous author's knowledge of figures like Ernst Bohle and Ivone Kirkpatrick who were unknown to the general public is proof of insider briefing, although whether genuine or disinformation is unknowable. The latter is more likely: for it will be recalled that an MI6 officer serving at the time of the Hess mission confirmed that his service was in the affair 'up to their necks', but that contrary to the story put out later for public consumption, 'there was never any conspiracy to lure Hess to Great Britain.'[35]

All that seems clear is that Stalin believed it, and when Churchill visited Moscow, proposed a toast 'to the British Intelligence Service which had inveigled Hess to Britain'.[36]

* * *

The indications are that Hess was entrapped. He seems never to have admitted this, perhaps not even to himself, and the details of the entrapment – directed by whom, when and where – are for the most part hidden. Only the background is clear: British ambassadors, particularly in Berne and Madrid, but also in Stockholm, Sir William Wiseman in San Francisco and double agents such as 'Dusko' Popov controlled by Menzies, 'Tar' Robertson and the Double-Cross Committee, consistently fed the Germans an exaggerated picture of British demoralisation under bombing, opposition to Churchill and the strength of the 'peace party', even names of potential quislings.

Beyond that there are flashes of suggestive detail. In January 1941 the art historian Tancred Borenius travelled to Geneva on the commission, by his son's account, of Claude Dansey, Assistant Chief of the Secret Service (MI6).[37] There he met Carl Burckhardt of the International Red Cross and, as is known from Ulrich von Hassell's diary, delivered a message supposedly from influential English circles that a reasonable peace could still be concluded, and there was a mood for compromise in Churchill's cabinet. Questioned by Burckhardt, Borenius stated the terms that might be acceptable to Britain. He had carried out with him a book, believed to have been a code book for Dansey's Swiss network of agents, and an oversize poison pill. Afterwards he travelled to Italy.

This establishes a link between MI6 and Burckhardt, who subsequently got word to Albrecht Haushofer that he had a message for him from his 'old English circle of friends'; so Albrecht stated in his subsequent report for Hitler. Albrecht visited Burckhardt in Geneva towards the end of April 'with a double face' – for Hess and for von Hassell's opposition circle. From this meeting, at which Burckhardt passed on Borenius's message that England was still prepared to conclude a reasonable peace, Albrecht travelled to Arosa and met Ilse von Hassell. He told her, according to von Hassell's diary entry, that Burckhardt had agreed to make further contact with the British and would meet him again in a few weeks' time.[38]

Compare this with Karl Haushofer's post-war testimony:

Hess initiated peace feelers ... and the responsible man in dealing with these peace feelers was my murdered son [Albrecht]. He was in Switzerland and talked with Burckhardt and Burckhardt told him to come back again to Switzerland and then he would be flown to Madrid and would there have a conference with Lord Templewood [as Sam Hoare had become]. When my son returned from Switzerland Hess spoke to him again, and it was after that that he flew to England.[39]

In another interrogation a few days earlier Karl Haushofer had said:

In 1941 Germany put out peace feelers to Great Britain through Switzerland. Albrecht was sent to Switzerland. There he met a British confidential agent – a Lord Templewood, I believe. In this peace proposal we offered to relinquish Norway, Denmark and France. A larger meeting was to be held in Madrid. When my son returned, he was immediately called to Augsburg by Hess. A few days later Hess flew to England.[40]

It is unlikely that Hoare flew to Switzerland for a meeting with Albrecht, or that Albrecht himself met Hoare in Madrid,[41] although there were credible reports, denied in Berlin, that Hess had flown to Madrid in April. Either Karl Haushofer had never been privy to the details of the negotiation, or his memory had slipped. Nonetheless, the sequence of documented events shows a clear link between Claude Dansey and his Swiss network, Carl Burckhardt in Geneva, Albrecht Haushofer on behalf of Hess, and Sam Hoare in Madrid.

In the meantime, in early February 1941, Albrecht had visited Sweden.[42] On 19 February Menzies wrote to Henry Hopkinson, his liaison with Cadogan, to say that the King of Sweden did not think the time opportune for mediating a peace move. Menzies probably wrote something by hand below the typed text as the bottom half of the letter from just above the green 'C' with which he signed all documents was torn off neatly before the file was opened to the public.[43]

Also in February preparations were made at Lympne aerodrome in Kent for Hitler's pilot, Hans Baur, to fly in with the Führer on board,[44] while in Madrid Herbert Stahmer contacted Sam Hoare on behalf of Albrecht Haushofer and the von Hassell circle of opposition-ists to arrange a meeting to discuss terms which might satisfy Britain if both Hitler and Churchill were removed.[45] According to Stahmer's post-war testimony such a meeting was arranged. There is no evidence that it took place.

However, in early March Hoare, contrary to his instructions to meet all approaches from the enemy with 'absolute silence', granted an interview to Ribbentrop's envoy, Prince Hohenlohe. The Prince's report of their conversation is missing from the Foreign Ministry files, but both the German and Italian ambassadors in Madrid reported Hoare saying that Churchill would soon have to resign and he, Hoare, would be called back to form a government with the specific task of concluding peace.[46]

Either Hoare was indulging treasonable speculation or he was party to the specific deception initiated by Claude Dansey that influ-ential British circles were prepared to remove Churchill and conclude peace. There are compelling grounds for believing the latter. On 4 May, a week before Hess's flight, Jock Colville recorded in his diary that Alan Hillgarth, one of Churchill's guests that weekend, was 'a fervent dis-ciple of Sam Hoare'.[47] Hillgarth was attached to the Madrid Embassy with special responsibility for counter-intelligence and had a direct line to Menzies at MI6; he of all people must have known what Hoare was up to. He was a friend of Churchill and surely loyal to him. Less than a fortnight before that Churchill himself had expressed full con-fidence in Hoare with a fulsome tribute in the House of Commons.[48] And after Hess's flight Hoare wrote to Eden about a personal note he had sent Churchill 'in view of the fact that he [Churchill] took so much interest last year in agreeing our secret plans'. That note to Churchill is missing from the files.[49]

From what Hess said after his arrival in Scotland there is no doubt he was convinced there was a powerful British peace party waiting to topple Churchill.

Besides these channels of disinformation through Switzerland, Spain and Sweden in particular, there are numerous other possible intermediaries: Kurt Jahnke, who worked more or less independently in Hess's intelligence department and often travelled to Switzerland, had many British contacts; the MI5 index shows that he was in touch with MI6 from February 1940 and again in early May 1941, although the papers recording these contacts have been removed from the file.[50]

A later head of MI6, Sir Maurice Oldfield, proffered the suggestion that Hess's flight might have been assisted by the head of his (Hess's) intelligence service, who was a KGB agent.[51] It is known that Jahnke, who was violently opposed to Hitler and National Socialism, had worked for Soviet Military Intelligence between the wars.

Walter Schellenberg, who headed Himmler's Security Service investigation into the flight, concluded that Hess had been influenced by British Secret Service agents and their German collaborators, in particular Hess's friend, the gland specialist, Dr Gerl, whose clients before the war had included many influential Englishmen.[52] Schellenberg's final report has not been found, but in his memoirs he recorded receiving 'a shattering secret report' in 1942 proving with detailed evidence that Jahnke was a top-level British agent. He failed to obtain confirmation from Jahnke.[53]

Others who might be considered as go-betweens include Air Vice Marshal Trafford Leigh Mallory who passed on warnings, apparently from Willi Messerschmitt, about parachutists landing to assassinate Hess at the Air Intelligence Interrogation Centre.[54] And since it was Leigh Mallory who oversaw the preparations for receiving Baur's aircraft with Hitler aboard at Lympne aerodrome it is possible he might also have been the channel through which Baur, or whoever was assuming Baur's identity, notified the Air Ministry of an alteration to the agreed arrival and landing signals.[55] That is speculation. Leigh Mallory died in an air crash before the end of the war.

Other possible go-betweens are the Duke of Kent and his cousin, Prince Philip of Hesse, with whom Kent took part in 1939 in fruitless

attempts to prevent the outbreak of war between their two countries. Philip of Hesse was one of Lonsdale Bryans' contacts when he
sought peace negotiations with the von Hassell group on behalf of
Lord Halifax.[56] He was, moreover, an art historian and married to the
daughter of King Emmanuel III of Italy, thus a possible contact for
Tancred Borenius when, after seeing Burckhardt in Geneva, he travelled on to Italy. Again, that is speculation.

Carl Eduard, Duke of Saxe-Coburg and Gotha, cannot be omitted
from a long list of possible go-betweens. He was a grandson of the
British Queen Victoria. Born in England, he attended Eton College
before being sent at the age of sixteen to preside over the German
Duchies from which his grandfather, Victoria's consort, Prince Albert,
had come. After the First World War he had been stripped of all his
English titles, and of his German titles after the 1918–19 revolution,
and he had become an early convert to Nazism. Appointed president
of the Anglo-German Fellowship in 1936, he had attempted to foster
permanent ties between the two countries. He was also president of
the German Red Cross, and although this became a Nazi association
disaffiliated from the International Red Cross, there were necessary
contacts during the war with that organisation in Geneva.

Another Swiss forum whose international members, including
British and German, met regularly during the war was the Bank for
International Settlements in Basel. Speculation is endless but, without
evidence, pointless.

* * *

There need be no speculation about whether Hess carried a letter or
other documents to Hamilton. MI5 files released recently show that
on 14 May Censorship intercepted photostat copies of a letter Hess
had brought with him, and sent a copy to Air Intelligence. MI5 investigated and documents were 'recovered from a ditch in the field where
Hess had landed',[57] or as the farmer's wife, Margaret Baird, put it in a
letter to a friend, 'the police was ordered to search for a valuable document which was missing, he found it over near the wee burn in the
park.'[58]

In Spandau prison Hess himself told Pastor Gabel that closed files held in London were 'without doubt the peace proposals' he took with him to Britain.[59] He also gave Abdallah Melaouhi to believe that if the British only published the closed documents he would be a free man; and conversely that the British would never allow his release until they were published.[60] Neither these documents, nor any mention of them have appeared in the files on his mission, and two inventories of his belongings when he landed are missing from the reports to which they were originally attached – clear proof of continuing official concealment.

The question of what is being concealed has been answered by the anonymous informant: an official proposal of peace in numbered clauses, typed on Chancellery paper, and a separate translation into English. Since the translation was somewhat stilted the informant was co-opted by Kirkpatrick into a small group to render the text into clear and comprehensible English.[61]

There are several reasons for accepting this account: Ernst Bohle translated Hess's letter or letters to Hamilton, but Bohle called on his half-brother, a translator in the language service of the Foreign Ministry, to help him.[62] Since Ernst Bohle was a fluent English-speaker, born in Bradford and educated in South Africa, it is difficult to see why he should have needed assistance from the Foreign Ministry unless it concerned the technical language and style of a proposed treaty.

From the English side there is Churchill's request to Cadogan after Kirkpatrick had returned from interviewing Hess in Scotland to 'make now a fairly full digest of the conversational parts of Hess's three interviews'.[63] The clear implication of the words 'conversational parts' is that Kirkpatrick had received documents as well. Churchill used English precisely.

The anonymous informant recalled that the first two pages of the proposed treaty detailed Hitler's plans for the conquest of Russia and destruction of Bolshevism. Britain would show her benevolent neutrality during this process and keep out of Continental affairs; in return she would retain her Empire and armed forces intact. German forces would leave France.

Kenneth de Courcy, briefed on Hess's peace proposals by Lieutenant Loftus, wrote after the war that in return for peace with

England, Germany would evacuate France, Belgium, Holland, Norway and Denmark – and Jews would be deported to Palestine.[64]

Hess's brief memorandum written before his interview with Lord Simon – given the pseudonym 'Dr Guthrie' – refers to British scepticism, 'but position alters if E[ngland] learns *authentic conditions*'.[65] And during that interview he said, 'I don't know if Dr. Guthrie has been informed of these conditions.'[66]

The *American Mercury* article of 1943 stated that Hess brought Hitler's offer of a total cessation of the war in the west, and the evacuation of all western occupied countries – with the exception of Alsace, Lorraine and Luxembourg – in return for which Britain would agree to adopt a position of 'benevolent neutrality' towards Germany while she unfolded her plans in eastern Europe to 'save humanity from Bolshevism'.[67] This is lent credence by the fact that these were the terms Dr Weissauer had spelled out to Dr Ekeberg in Stockholm in September 1940.

None of these terms is to be found in any of the open files on Hess, nor in the report on his mission sent to the British Embassy in Moscow for transmission to Stalin,[68] nor in Eden's 1943 statement on Hess to the House of Commons.[69] The clinching proof that Hess did bring such proposals – which have since been comprehensively excised from the official record – appears in the despatch wired to the Foreign Office by the British Ambassador in Moscow, Sir Archibald Clark Kerr, in October 1942:

> If these [Hess's] alleged proposals were indeed (as was suggested to me at the time) that in exchange for the evacuation of certain of the occupied countries we should withdraw from the war and leave Germany a free hand in the East, our declared rejection of them should be enough to satisfy the most difficult and suspicious of the Russians ...[70]

* * *

It is not difficult to see why these proposals had to be buried. If they had leaked to the governments of the occupied western countries in exile in London, and to the dedicated advocates of compromise

346

peace in Parliament and the City of London and among the country's great landowners, or to isolationists in the United States, then arming Britain to continue the struggle, Churchill would have been in dire trouble. The plan Hess brought with him showed diabolical ingenuity: the proposals could hardly be refused, yet they came from a man, Hitler, who had broken every treaty and solemn undertaking he had made, and could not be trusted.

Accepting that Churchill, Menzies and Cadogan had to conceal Hess's peace plan, even from Foreign Office ministers such as R.A. Butler, the question is why the veil is yet to be lifted decades after the affair passed into history. There are several possibilities: official inertia, reluctance on the part of MI6 to reveal operational secrets, or the involvement in negotiations of members of the Royal family such as the Duke of Windsor and the Duke of Kent and their German relatives – in which connection it is believed that when Anthony Blunt, one of the Cambridge ring of five Russian agents and Guy Liddell's personal assistant in MI5, finally admitted his traitorous activities, he gained immunity from prosecution because of a mission he had undertaken for King George VI in the immediate aftermath of the war to recover sensitive royal correspondence with Hitler and other leading Nazis from Schloss Friedrichshof, seat of the Princes of Hesse near Frankfurt am Main.[71]

There is another possible reason for the continuing secrecy over Hess's mission: that is, if he brought a warning about the impending fate of European Jewry.

Hess knew of Hitler's plans for Operation 'Barbarossa' and it appears he revealed them when he came to Britain; the informant claimed this, as did Kenneth de Courcy with his inside information from Loftus; so did the 1943 *American Mercury* article; and Alan Clark, once a minister at the War Office with access to the files, stated in his book *Barbarossa* that Hess revealed the German order of battle for Russia.[72] Hess also knew of the preparations for the *Endlösung*, the 'final solution' to the Jewish problem in Europe. If he revealed that too, Churchill's failure either to denounce or act to stop the coming slaughter could so damage perceptions of his and Britain's wartime record as to justify hiding the fact for ever.

There was, of course, nothing Churchill could have done. Had he accepted the peace plan it would only have made the assault on Russia more certain, and Hitler could not have been relied on to keep any promise to deport rather than physically annihilate the Jews. As for making an announcement, when towards the end of August 1941 Churchill had proof from intercepts that Jews were being massacred, he denounced the historic scale of the atrocity but did not specify its anti-Jewish character, referring to the victims as Russian peasants, as many were.[73]

There are indications that Hess may indeed have revealed Hitler's plans for the Jews: on one typed copy of the statement to Parliament Churchill never delivered regarding Hess's arrival in Britain, he wrote a comment in the margin: 'He [Hess] has also made other statements which it would not be in the public interest to disclose.'[74] Churchill's intended statement includes everything contained in the open records of Kirkpatrick's talks with Hess. Of course Hitler's coming attack on Russia is not disclosed, so if Hess did reveal it – as the informant and Kenneth de Courcy asserted – Churchill might have been referring to 'Barbarossa'. But the Jewish question is not mentioned either, and another curiously ambiguous statement Churchill made at about this time could refer to the fate of the Jews: 'This man, like other Nazi leaders, is potentially a war criminal, and he and his confederates may well be declared outlaws at the end of the war. In this case his repentance would stand him in good stead.'[75] Neither Kirkpatrick's nor Hamilton's reports on their interviews with Hess in the open files mention him expressing repentance of any kind; on the contrary, they recorded him blaming Britain for the war and threatening her with destruction and starvation by U-boat blockade. So, when and for what did Hess express remorse?

There is also Hess's comment to Lieutenant Robert Shaw, one of the officers guarding him at the Drymen Military Hospital – admittedly recalled long after the war – that the atrocities they were beginning to hear about were not typical of the German people.[76] Later at Mytchett Place Foley reported to Menzies on a conversation with Hess, 'We have been asking ourselves whether his [Hess's] expose [*sic*] was a pose which he had assumed for our benefit. We are inclined to think it was not and that he had been shocked by what he had seen in Poland and the West.'[77] There is no indication of what Hess had 'exposed', suggesting the file was 'weeded' before it was opened to the public, but evidently his comments concerned the brutalities of German occupation.

While whatever has been concealed cannot be known, there is no doubt about its extreme sensitivity. When, immediately after the war, Hamilton was due to travel to America for an airline operators' conference he asked Churchill for a reference. Fearful of what avid US reporters might extract from him, Churchill would not hear of him attending the conference: 'I desire therefore that the Duke should not, repeat not, undertake this task.'[78] That 'repeat not' is surely an indication of the gravity of the secrets Hamilton might inadvertently disclose.

Later, the treatment of Colonel Eugene Bird by the US authorities when they learned of his collaboration with Hess on a book seeking to set out the truth of his mission appears so disproportionate to the offence[79] – besides being so long after the end of the war – that it leaves the same impression of a secret so monstrous it could never be released to the world. Pastor Gabel's subsequent account of conversations with Prisoner Number 7 allows no doubt that the systematic massacre of European Jewry weighed heavily on Hess's mind; he repeatedly expressed remorse for that which could never be expunged from history,[80] yet Bird's book made no mention of the *Endlösung* or Hess's contrition, leading to the suspicion that, despite co-author Desmond Zwar's denial, Bird was warned off referring to the fate of the Jews.

In any event, the anxiety shown by the US authorities over Bird's book suggests that the feared potential revelations were unlikely to have concerned the British Royal family: the reputation of the House of Windsor hardly touched American interests. On the other hand, if Hess gave advance warning of German preparations for genocide in the east Churchill would certainly have communicated this explosive information to Roosevelt, and both would have borne equal responsibility for the subsequent silence and inaction.

* * *

The question arises as to whether the need to conceal pre-knowledge of the coming 'holocaust' – if Hess did indeed reveal it – could have been a sufficient motive for murder. Indications were that the Soviets intended to sanction Hess's release. He might then have been expected to tell the world all he knew. He had, of course, had opportunity to do so from his prison cell, yet outside he would have more credibility. He would certainly have faced persistent questioning.

However, the recent release of the British Military Police Reports into his death, and more importantly the witness statements taken during the investigation, show that no unauthorised persons were in the grounds that day; there were no SAS assassins acting on the commission of the British Home Office, as alleged by the late Wolf Rüdiger Hess,[81] supported by Abdallah Melaouhi.

Doubts were certainly raised by the German forensic pathologists, Professors Eisenmenger and Spann, who carried out a second post-mortem and concluded that strangulation should not have been ruled out as a possible cause of death.[82] They were supported by an eminent British pathologist, Professor Bowen, who suggested in particular that the bruising to Hess's deeper neck tissues was unlikely to have occurred in a suicidal hanging, but was a feature of strangulation.[83] Yet Jordan, the only person in the right place at the right time to have strangled Hess, was shown by the testimony of the US guards to have been sitting calmly immediately after his brief opportunity, and subsequently running in circles in complete panic. Such a dramatic reversal would have been hard for the most accomplished actor to have staged.

The obviously bogus 'suicide note'[84] remains the chief obstacle to believing the official verdict of suicide; this is removed if the note was written by Hess himself in a deliberately outdated form to suggest a forgery and so get back at the authorities who had kept him incarcerated for so long. Bizarre as this might appear, it would be in character – very much in the hysterical character he had displayed since his early days in captivity. Making out his weekly requisition, including three rolls of toilet paper, and sending Melaouhi to the shops to buy a new ceramic pot were, in that case, integral to the scheme to show he had no intention of taking his life that day – so must have been murdered.

* * *

Until the relevant documents are released the major questions surrounding Hess's mission can never be definitively resolved. Both Churchill and Hitler had, for very different reasons, to conceal the fundamental aim of the undertaking, and both constructed very similar official narratives of a crazed fanatic flying on a lone, unauthorised bid to regain the position he felt he had lost at the Führer's court. This explains a good deal of the mystification. It is difficult, nevertheless, to understand why Hess appears to have said nothing in any of his interviews in Britain with Kirkpatrick, Lords Simon and Beaverbrook or with his 'companions' or the young Guards officers at Mytchett Place of the official peace proposals he had brought with him. In part this may be explained by his refusal to negotiate with representatives of Churchill's 'clique of warmongers' or the Secret Service agents he believed were preventing him from seeing the King and members of the opposition to Churchill. In part it may be due to deliberate omissions from Kirkpatrick's and others' written reports, or to subsequent 'weeding' of the files to ensure no trace remained of any reference to his documents.

He may have told Hamilton, who was certainly made to rewrite his original, now missing report on his first interview with Hess,[85] and who was refused permission by Churchill to visit the United States at the end of the war.[86] What had Churchill feared he might give away? Only many years later in Spandau jail did Hess reveal to Pastor Gabel and Abdallah Melaouhi that he had taken documentary peace proposals to Britain, and that, if published, these could secure his freedom.[87] This suggests they must have been serious proposals.

* * *

Apart from the official cover-up of events so long ago, the most lamentable aspect of the Hess affair is the failure of the academic historical establishment to probe the unbelievable story they have been fed. Thus Ian Kershaw, Hitler's biographer, writes that news of Hess's flight struck the Berghof 'like a thunderbolt'.[88] In common with Rainer Schmidt, author of the most perceptive German account of the mission, he ascribes Hess's motive to a desire to restore his lost position at the Führer's court.[89] Both Kershaw and Schmidt accept the story that

Hess told until the end of his life, that he acted without Hitler's know-ledge, 'but in the belief he was carrying out Hitler's wishes'.[90] Kershaw states there is no evidence that Hess was enticed by the British Secret Service, basing this on an academic study of the records of MI5,[91] not the Secret Intelligence Service, MI6, whose records have not been released, and whose recent authorised historian has revealed nothing of the Service's involvement. On the other hand Schmidt does believe that British intelligence entrapped Hess by corresponding with him in Hamilton's name: 'It appears that the British hoaxed the Nazis and that they finally brought Hess to England on the presumption that the ground for peace negotiations was prepared and that he could really meet the Duke of Hamilton.'[92]

A British author, the late Alfred Smith, not a member of the academic establishment, viewed MI6's role in Hess's mission differ-ently. Smith saw the head of MI6, Sir Stewart Menzies, as 'perhaps the most prominent member of the British peace party', whose alle-giance was to the sovereign rather than to the government of the day, and who believed in rapprochement with Germany to defeat Britain's real enemy, Soviet Russia.[93] In short, Smith suggested that Menzies and at least parts of MI6 encouraged Hess's peace mission because they believed in it and wanted it to succeed.[94] Their plans went awry because Hess missed Dungavel and was taken prisoner by the Home Guard.

Smith provided a theoretical rationale for his thesis, but no evi-dence at all. While it does fit what are known of the facts it is difficult to accept since it implies the overthrow of Churchill and the installation in his place of a figure like Lloyd George – who was undoubtedly wait-ing for the call – or Sam Hoare, or even Halifax. Only the King could have brought this about, but it would have been a high-risk, virtually unprecedented use of the royal prerogative in the era of constitutional monarchy. Who could say if the Commons would have accepted it? Of course, if true, this theory could provide grounds for the continuing cover-up since it implies the participation of King George VI and his formidable wife, Elizabeth. Yet it is unsupported by evidence.

While there is no conclusive evidence for the part MI6 played in Hess's flight to Britain, there is no doubting the documents in the

German Foreign Ministry from 1942 that reveal British intelligence using Hess's presence in Britain to keep open German hopes of a compromise peace, and implying in this context that bombing London was counter-productive since it provoked hatred of Germany that did not otherwise exist.[95] It is a fact that London was spared further serious raids until 1943, leading Stalin to believe that Churchill was holding Hess in reserve if it became necessary to make peace with Germany. Apart from the work at Bletchley Park, this must be the most important, yet unknown achievement of British intelligence during the war.

* * *

The one constant against which all questions and all that is now known of the peace mission must be measured is Hess's personality. This does not appear to have changed much. After the war Karl Haushofer, who knew him better than most, said he had to admit that 'Hess had more heart and strength of character than intelligence'.[96] Undoubtedly his strength of character was borne out by his lone flight into enemy territory.

When Haushofer was asked why he thought Hess had made the flight, he replied, 'It was the escape of a heroic and idealistic man from an unbearable situation.'[97]

On another occasion Haushofer expressed his firm conviction that the reasons for Hess's flight were 'his own sense of honour and his desperation at the murders going on in Germany'.[98] The industrial phase of genocide had not begun at the time of his flight, but Hess was aware of routine atrocities committed in Poland by the SS and police against Jews and the educated classes. As arbiter between party and state he received complaints from the army about the damage to morale caused by these crimes. Karl Haushofer was equally aware: Albrecht wrote anguished letters to his parents about his own conflict of loyalties: 'An example: I sit at a table with a man whose task it will be to cause a great part of the Jews transported to the Jews' ghetto in Lublin to freeze and starve to death according to programme.'[99] Karl Haushofer may have used 'the murders going on in Germany' as a euphemism for the actions against Jews in Poland since he made the comment at a time when his former student, friend and protector was about to stand trial for war crimes.

All those who knew Hess testified to his sensitive moral character. Ernst Bohle described him as 'the biggest idealist we have had in Germany, a man of a very soft nature'.[100] And, as we have seen, his adjutant, Leitgen, stated that the example of Hitler's personal brutality during the purge of the leadership of the Nazi paramilitary *Sturmabteilung* (SA) on 30 June 1934, had 'deeply wounded his [Hess's] marked, almost feminine sensitivities'.[101]

The finance minister, Schwerin von Krosigk, made a more profound point:

> He [Hess] had recognized that the conflict between good and evil which ran through the whole development of the Nazi Party played itself out in the person of the Führer and had to be decided there. But his loyalty to the Führer prevented him interfering in the process. He suffered from this, but found no way out.[102]

In England Major Dicks, the army psychiatrist appointed to Mytchett Place, made a similar deduction: 'In Hitler Herr Hess has seen the perfect father authority who would make the bad world right. The moment he felt that Hitler was ruthless and destructive, he must have experienced great anxiety ...'[103] He could not, of course, admit this, Dicks went on, or even allow himself to know that he felt it. The Führer was still perfect, and he had to be loyal. But the internal conflict became so great he could only save his mental balance by a dramatic act of redemption.

Or, as Karl Haushofer put it, his flight was, 'the escape of a heroic and idealistic man from an unbearable situation.'[104]

It also seems true that he was assisted by the British Secret Service and was commissioned by Hitler; for it is inconceivable that in an informer society such as Nazi Germany neither Göring, head of the air force, nor Hitler was aware of Hess's flying preparations – although academic historians seem prepared to accept it. The more powerful point is that for Hess to have flown off without Hitler's knowledge or commission would have been a negation of his whole life purpose and indeed his personality. It would have been a betrayal. But Hess would never have betrayed his Führer. To believe that he did so on the word and play-acting of Hitler and Goebbels is risible.

The terms he carried – from Hitler – would have given Britain peace with some honour. Churchill, committed to the defeat of 'that man', Hitler, and Nazism, had to bury the message and write off the messenger; in doing so he almost single-handedly deflected the course of history – for realists would have accepted Hess's terms. This is the real significance of his story: as a pivotal moment when history did not turn as might have been expected.

CHAPTER NINETEEN

The answer?

Colonel Stewart Menzies belonged in the inner circle of the British ruling class. Moulded by Eton and the Guards, White's in St James' was his home from home, the Beaufort Hunt his enthusiasm when on occasion he could escape from London. Approaching 50 when appointed 'C', he was of medium height, slim, with a pale face, pale blue eyes and darkish blond hair. His voice was authoritative; he dressed elegantly and had an artless, even boyish manner. Underneath he was, in the words of one who worked with him, 'sphinx-like and cunning'.[1]

This was the spymaster who in December 1940 invited the young Yugoslav banker and *Abwehr* agent, Dusko Popov, only recently arrived in England and inducted by Major 'Tar' Robertson as a double agent against his German masters, to join him for a family New Year house party; who then drew Popov aside into a book-lined study with deep armchairs and, after giving him such an accurate assessment of his character Popov felt as if he were looking at himself for the first time in his life, proceeded to talk about the *Abwehr* and its enigmatic chief, Admiral Canaris.[2] He told Popov that he wanted information on anyone intimately connected with Canaris, mentioning particularly Colonel Hans Oster and Hans von Dohnanyi.

'We know that Canaris, Oster and Dohnanyi are not dyed in the wool Nazis,' Menzies went on, and said that Churchill had had an unofficial conversation with Canaris before the war and came to the conclusion that the admiral was a kind of catalyst for anti-Hitler elements in Germany. This was why he, Menzies, wanted to know more about the people around him. 'Eventually I may want to resume the conversation that Churchill started.'[3]

Popov gained the impression that Menzies contemplated a dialogue with Canaris aimed at removing Hitler. The immediate task Popov was given, however, was to convince his *Abwehr* handlers that British defences against invasion were far stronger than they actually were, and to pass on gossip he was supposed to have gathered in society that British morale was low as a result of bombing raids and many politicians thought it was time to overthrow Churchill and his warmongering 'clique' and negotiate peace. This was, of course, the central deception on which 'Tar' Robertson and the Double-Cross Committee were working.

Three days later Popov was flown to Lisbon, where he reported to his controller on these lines, thence travelled to Madrid to meet his *Abwehr* colleague and old university friend, Johann Jebsen, who had briefed him for his English mission in the first place. Jebsen, whose *Abwehr* mentor was the convinced anti-Nazi Colonel Oster,[4] was also pro-British and was soon to be recruited by Robertson as a double agent under the code name ARTIST. In his initial briefing for Popov he had told him that Rudolf Hess was talking of high personalities in Britain seeking contact with Germany.[5] It was a curious comment: Hess was about the only top Nazi whose name had not thus far appeared in connection with German peace feelers. In his memoirs Popov did not reveal whether he told Menzies of Hess's interest in British circles promoting peace, but it would be strange in view of the deception he was to promote if he had not done so.

Meeting Jebsen in Madrid Popov talked of the anti-Nazi officers in the *Abwehr,* and suggested there must be many others of influence in Germany who recognised Hitler's madness and wanted to stop the war. It seemed to him that the *Abwehr,* with its freedom of movement, would be the ideal instrument through which these people might negotiate with Britain.

Jebsen rejected the idea. There was no opposition in Germany, he said; it had either been smashed or reduced to complete impotence, while German youth had been raised from the cradle to believe in Hitler. He asked if there was one example in history of generals revolting when victorious. Yet some minutes later, after reflection, he said that madly idealistic as the idea was, it was so attractive he would not be able to put it from his mind: 'It is worth living or dying for.'[6] And he promised to sound people out and let Popov know how things stood when next they met. Popov had pledged absolute secrecy to Menzies, so felt he could not tell Jebsen that the chief of MI6 was ready to join hands with him.

Later in his memoirs after a conversation about Hess's peace mission, Popov speculated whether the planted reports of low British morale might have influenced Hess, whether indeed British intelligence had unwittingly inspired the Hess incident.[7] Did he insert the word 'unwittingly' to hide the fact that Menzies' idea of using the *Abwehr* as a bridge to negotiations had indeed been tried and had brought Hess to Britain?

* * *

Stewart Menzies' biographer refers to strong circumstantial evidence for Menzies' involvement in the Hess affair and holds it 'undeniable' that the Double-Cross Committee was implicated.[8] The late Alfred Smith asserted that an MI6 officer of that time had assured him 'in the most categorical terms' that MI6 was 'in the Hess thing up to their necks', although there was never any plan to lure Hess over to Britain.[9]

Claude Dansey, Menzies' chief of staff, sent the art historian, Borenius, to Geneva to open a peace channel to Carl Burckhardt at about the time Menzies briefed Popov on his wish for dialogue with Canaris, whom he saw as the key to contact with anti-Hitler elements in Germany. This seems like a reversion to the Chamberlain–Halifax policy of supporting a generals' revolt against Hitler, and is hard to understand in view of the Führer's apparently unassailable position after his victorious campaigns in the west.

Nonetheless, accepting on the one hand that Menzies was attempting to build a bridge to Canaris, on the other that Hess had been trying to build a bridge to anti-Churchill elements in Britain for some months beforehand; accepting, too, the assertion of Alfred Smith's MI6 officer that there was never any plan to lure Hess to Britain, the simple hypothesis presents itself that Hess learned of MI6's channel to Canaris and linked in to it for his own purposes.

In such case Kurt Jahnke enters the picture. Until recently he had been the real force in Hess's intelligence organisation; he had previously worked for Canaris and loathed the Nazis; and it is known from the MI5 registry that he was in contact with MI6 through 1940 and in early May 1941. Menzies' biographer speculates that he 'may have been one of Dansey's most important informants'.[10] Walter Schellenberg, chief of Himmler's Security Service, stated in his memoirs that in 1942 he received a 30-page compilation of evidence proving that Jahnke was a top-level British agent.[11] Then there is the suggestion of Sir Maurice Oldfield after retiring as chief of MI6 that the head of Hess's intelligence service had been a Soviet agent, and might have been behind Hess's flight to Britain.[12] Between the wars Jahnke had worked for Soviet Military Intelligence.

There is no doubt that Menzies, like his great friend Buccleuch, believed Soviet Russia a far greater threat to the British Empire than Nazi Germany and wanted peace with Germany so that Hitler could attack Russia. He believed the German Army would take Moscow in a matter of weeks, then become sucked into a guerrilla war which would bleed both nations.[13] To argue from this, as two recent books have, that Hess's arrival was the result of a genuine peace move by Menzies in opposition to Churchill's policy[14] seems far-fetched, and fails on the simple fact that Churchill not only retained Menzies in post, making him responsible for isolating and interrogating Hess, but he and Menzies remained on intimate terms for the rest of the war and for a time afterwards[15] – something inconceivable if Churchill had suspected him of treachery.

The hypothesis advanced here that Hess used contacts between Menzies and Canaris to advance his own mission is supported in the post-war testimony of Kenneth de Courcy. It will be recalled that de Courcy learned of Hess's peace proposals from a Guards officer at Mytchett Place, Lieutenant Loftus. He never admitted this publicly, and in an *Intelligence Digest* he produced in 1984 claimed he had learnt details of Hess's mission from Colonel W.S. Pilcher, commanding the Grenadier Guards at Windsor. He quoted from a note he had made on 28 May 1941 allegedly based on what Pilcher had told him:

> the one man in all Europe who certainly knows the innermost details of the whole [Hess] business is Admiral Canaris ... I suggest that there was little if anything known to Canaris which was not also known to Menzies and that secret agents of both men (Canaris and Menzies) frequently met in Spain and that Canaris was determined that Hitler should NOT, repeat NOT, defeat England.
>
> If Hess came with the knowledge of Canaris and his real object was to topple Hitler before total war further developed, then it was of crucial importance to the Russian party to stop Hess ...[16]

De Courcy then developed his theory that the Russian party headed by Lord Rothschild forced Churchill to banish Pilcher to Scotland.

It is difficult, if not impossible, to accept de Courcy's main premise that Hess was prepared for Hitler's removal, but this does not invalidate his claim, as repeated in a subsequent *Intelligence Digest*, that 'Hess flew to Britain with the knowledge of Admiral Canaris, who worked closely with Sir Stewart Menzies.'[17]

If so, the answer may be that Hess tapped into a peace channel between Menzies and Canaris without realising that Hitler was to be sacrificed; the facilitator who deceived him was no doubt the Nazi-hating Jahnke, who had many contacts in Switzerland, and had been the real brains in Hess's own intelligence service. There is only de Courcy's testimony to support the hypothesis, but he was privy to high secrets, the confidant of many besides Lieutenant Loftus, and was undoubtedly targeted by MI5 and the Russians. He was certain that Canaris and Menzies were involved in Hess's mission; further, it is known that Canaris supplied information to MI6, and MI5 records show that Jahnke was in touch with MI6 at the relevant dates. Until the vital documents are released, the presumption that Hess came at the invitation of Stewart Menzies with the agreement of Canaris for the purpose of toppling Hitler – although it is unlikely Hess was aware of that – is probably as close as it is possible to approach to the truth.

* * *

Two stories Kenneth de Courcy used to tell: Menzies was asked by King George VI what he would do if he (the King) required him to reveal his top man in Germany (Canaris, according to de Courcy). Menzies replied that his head would roll with his lips still sealed.[18]

Towards the end of the war in Europe de Courcy was dining at White's with the Duke of Buccleuch when Menzies came up to them and said, 'I have just lost my greatest friend.'[19] He meant Canaris, hanged at Flossenburg concentration camp the day before with, according to de Courcy, eight strangulations – brought down and revived seven times before the end.

Notes

Books are referenced by author; if more than one book by that author is listed in the Bibliography, by author and key words in the title. The following abbreviations are used:

F & CO   Foreign and Colonial Office, London
FO   Foreign Office, London
IMT   The International Military Tribunal, *Trial of the Major War Criminals*, Nuremberg, 1947 (English language edition)
IWM   Imperial War Museum, London (or Duxford)
TNA   The National Archives, Kew, London

Chapter 1: Death in the summer house

1. See E. Bird, p. 237; C. Gabel, p. 172; T. Le Tissier, p. 56 states that there were 27 appeals to the Soviet authorities, and that the UK was alone in appealing at ministerial level, doing so routinely from 1970 on thirteen occasions.
2. See *Der Spiegel*, 16, 41 *Jahrg.*, 13 Apr. 1987, p. 151; also Richard von Weizsäcker to Adrian Liddell Hart, June 1987; A. Liddell Hart to author, 27 June 1990; and Abdallah Melaouhi, p. 101
3. 21 June 1987; cited W.R. Hess, *Mord*, p. 153
4. Civilian staff in/out book, Spandau prison; Special Investigation Branch RMP BAOR 53052/7 (MOD reference pending transfer to TNA), Final Report, p. 41
5. Abdallah Melaouhi, solemn declaration before notary, Reinhard Gizinsky, Berlin, 17 Feb. 1994

6. Entries in Chief Warder's log, Spandau prison; photocopy in *Figaro Magazin*, Paris, 1 Apr. 1989, copy in W.R. Hess, *Mord*, p. 244

7. R. Hess, '*Gesuch an den amerikanischer director, Herr Keane*', 4 Apr. 1987; copy in *ibid.*, p. 243 (from photocopy in *Figaro Magazin*)

8. Entry in Chief Warder's log, *op. cit.* ref. 6 above

9. Special Investigation Branch RMP BAOR 53052/7, Interim Report, pp. 1, 8, 28, Final Report, p. 5

10. This and all subsequent citations from witness statements attached to Special Investigation Branch RMP BAOR 53052/7 Interim Report, unless otherwise referenced.

11. Chief Warder's log, *op. cit.*, ref. 6 above

12. A. Melaouhi, p. 111

13. A. Melaouhi, solemn declaration, *op. cit.*, ref. 5 above

14. W.R. Hess, *Mord*, p. 47

15. *Ibid.*, p. 50; *The Daily Telegraph*, 19 Aug. 1987

16. W.R. Hess, *Mord*, pp. 50 f

17. Prof. J.H. Cameron, 'Autopsy Report on Allied Prisoner No. 7', undated; Special Investigation Branch RMP BAOR 53052/7, Addendum Report

18. The give-away phrase was, 'Tell Freiburg that, to my immense sorrow, since the Nuremberg trial I had to act as if I didn't know her ...' Yet he had told Ilse, his wife, and his son on his first meeting with them on 24 Dec. 1969 to pass this on to 'Freiburg', his former secretary – see p. 326 below. For full text of note see plate section 8

19. Profs W. Eisenmenger and W. Spann, '*Zusammenfassung der Befunde*'; cited W.R. Hess, *Mord*, p. 215

20. Prof. J.H. Cameron, *op. cit.*, ref. 17 above

21. Cited W. Schwarzwäller, p. 1

22. Document examiner's statement, 26 Aug. 1987; Special Investigation Branch RMP BAOR 53052/7, Final Report, pp. 15–17

23. Profs W. Eisenmenger and W. Spann, *Zusammenfassung, op. cit.*, ref. 19 above

24. Profs W. Eisenmenger and W. Spann to author, 17 Sept. 1990

25. Obituary Prof. David Bowen, *The Daily Telegraph*, 13 Apr. 2011

26. W.R. Hess, *Mord*, pp. 97, 101–3; W.R. Hess obtained 'the information personally by mouth from an official of the Israeli [Secret] Service on Tuesday 18 August 1987 at 08.00 South African Time. I had known this officer professionally and personally for four years.' He was told that the two SAS men were already in Spandau prison on the night of Saturday/

Sunday, 15/16 August 1987, and the US CIA gave approval for their murder mission on Monday 17th. However, the witness statements from the British Military Police investigation show there were no SAS or indeed any unauthorised persons within Spandau prison grounds at these dates.

Chapter 2: The big question

1. R.J. Aldrich, p. 6
2. See p. 224–5, 344–5 below

Chapter 3: Hess

1. Rudolf Hess Service Record, Berlin Document Center
2. I. Hess, *Gefangener*, p. 29. The poem 'Before Verdun' is given in full in author's translation in P. Padfield, *Hess: Disciple*, p. 8
3. R. Hess to F. & K. Hess (father and mother), 10 Aug. 1917; W.R. Hess, *Briefe*, p. 204
4. R. Hess to F. & K. Hess, 6, 11 Oct. 1918, *ibid.*, pp. 222–3
5. See N. Goodrick-Clarke, pp. 144 ff
6. Testimony of Alfred Leitgen, 3 Dec. 1965; *Inst. für Zeitgeschichte*, Akz 4501/70, ZS 262, f. 99
7. I. Hess, *Gefangener*, p. 19
8. R. Hess to K. & F. Hess, 17 June 1920; W.R. Hess, *Briefe*, p. 261
9. 'Interview with Professor Karl Haushofer', 28 Sept. 1945, p. 2; Office of Strategic Services, Washington; US National Archives RG 226, E 19, Box 315, XL.22853
10. I. Hess, *Gefangener*, pp. 24–5
11. R. Hess to K. Hess (mother), 12 May 1924; W.R. Hess, *Briefe*, p. 322
12. R. Hess to Ilse Pröhl, 18 May 1924; *ibid.*, p. 326
13. R. Hess to K. Hess, 16 May 1924; *ibid.*, pp. 323–4
14. E. Hanfstaengl, p. 165
15. Interrogation of Karl Haushofer, 5 Oct. 1945, p. 6; IWM FO 645, Box 157
16. *Ibid.*, p. 5
17. R. Hess to K. Haushofer, 11 June 1924; W.R. Hess, *Briefe*, pp. 334–5
18. A. Hitler, p. 772
19. R. Hess to Ilse Pröhl, 29 June 1924; W.R. Hess, *Briefe*, p. 342
20. See A. Bahar, W. Kugel
21. See von Pfeffer to Dr Bennecke, 21 Apr. 1963; *Inst. für Zeitgeschichte*, Akz. 4653/71, ZS 177, f. 069

22. *N-S Jahrbuch*, 1939, p. 189

23. Testimony of Alfred Leitgen, 19 Dec. 1952; *Inst. für Zeitgeschichte*, 743/52 ZS 262, p. 2, f. 13

24. *Ibid.*, 1 Apr. 1952, p. 6, f. 10

25. *Ibid.*, 19 Dec. 1952, *op. cit.* ref. 23 above

Chapter 4: The Jewish question

1. See R.G.L. Waite, pp. 152 ff, 442–5

2. A. Speer, p. 353

3. See R.G.L. Waite, pp. 152 ff

4. Cited *ibid.* p. 440

5. A. Hitler, p. 447

6. See R.J. Lifton, p. 31

7. *Ibid.*, pp. 35, 40–1, 129–30

8. See *ibid.*, pp. 25, 36

9. Geoffrey Shakespeare memo. to Sec. of State, 14 May 1941, p. 1; Geoffrey Shakespeare papers, GHS2, IWM

10. Erika Mann, 'Hess meeting in Spain was fixed', *Glasgow Evening Citizen*, 1945 (month and date missing); Ian Sayer archive

11. G. Shakespeare memo.; *op. cit.*, ref. 9 above

12. See Scott Newton, p. 26

13. See F.W. Winterbotham, pp. 83 ff

14. See B. Fromm, pp. 194 ff

15. That they met is confirmed by one of the first German broadcasts after Hess's flight: Bremen 16.30, 13 May 1941; BBC Written Archives Centre, Reading; also TNA INF 1/912, f. 6; see also Karl Haushofer interrogation confirming this, 9 Oct. 1945; IWM FO 695 Box 157; and R.C. Langdon to author, 13, 17 May 1991, states that Lord Malcolm Douglas-Hamilton left him in no doubt that Clydesdale and Hess met in Berlin in 1936

16. See J. Douglas-Hamilton, *The Truth*, pp. 68 ff

17. A. Haushofer to R. Hess, 7 Sept. 1933; U. Laack-Michel, p. 316

18. A. Haushofer to M. & K. Haushofer, 27 July 1934; *ibid.*, p. 321

19. A. Haushofer to M. Haushofer, 18 Aug. 1934; *ibid.*, p. 322

20. W. Stubbe, p. 245

21. A. Haushofer to M. & K. Haushofer, 27 July 1934; U. Laack-Michel, p. 321

22. Sir Nevile Henderson, British Ambassador to Berlin, 1937–39; cited A. Roberts, p. 49

23. Cited J. Douglas-Hamilton, *The Truth*, p. 70

24. *Ibid.*, pp. 73–4
25. Part of A. Haushofer's speech; cited *ibid.*, p. 75
26. A. Haushofer to Clydesdale, 27 Nov. 1937; cited *ibid.*, p. 77
27. Nesta Webster (Mrs Arthur Webster), 'Germany and England', *The Patriot*, Wikipedia
28. See J. Douglas-Hamilton, *The Truth*, pp. 77–8
29. See 'Hossbach Memorandum', 5 Nov. 1937; IMT 386-PS
30. 19 Nov. 1937; cited A. Roberts, p. 72
31. See *ibid.*, p. 73
32. See *ibid.*, p. 129
33. 29 Dec. 1938; U. v. Hassell, *Andern Deutschland*, p. 43
34. See A. Roberts, p. 136
35. See M.J. Cohen, p. xvii
36. A. Eichmann, 'Palästinareise Bericht', undated, pp. 31–2, *Sicherheitsdienst der RFSS*; David Irving archive

Chapter 5: Struggle for peace

1. See A. Roberts, p. 151
2. Kenneth de Courcy to author, 8, 14 Jan. 1990, 25 Nov. 1995
3. A. Haushofer to Clydesdale, 16 July 1939, J. Douglas-Hamilton, *The Truth*, pp. 94 ff
4. There is no record of these meetings in the Foreign Office files open to the public, nor in Halifax's private papers: see Andrew Roberts, 'The plot to betray Poland', *The Sunday Telegraph*, 8 Aug. 1999, 'Review', p. 1
5. Andrew Roberts, 'The plot to betray Poland', *ibid.*
6. See *ibid.*; and D. Cameron Watt to *The Sunday Telegraph*, 15 Aug. 1999; Andrew Roberts to *The Times*, 11 Aug. 1999; obituary Lord Aberconway, *The Times*, 5 Feb. 2003
7. See 'Summary of principle peace feelers September 1939–March 1941', TNA FO 371/26542, C4216/324/18, ff. 96–7; and R. Lamb, pp. 112 ff
8. E. St. J. Bamford (Ministry of Information) to A. Cadogan, 19 Oct. 1945; TNA KV 2/2839, f. 69
9. Special Branch, Straits Settlement Police to Sir Vernon Kell (Director MI5), 21 Aug. 1939; *ibid.*, f. 256
10. E. St. J. Bamford to A. Cadogan, *op. cit.*, ref. 8 above
11. TNA KV 2/2839, f. 4
12. *Ibid.* passim
13. 'Extract from Passport Papers'. *ibid.*, ff. 254, 249–50

14. 'L'AFFAIRE CHARLES', in *ibid.*, f. 91
15. E.B. Stamp ('B' div. MI5) to SIS (MI6), 14 Mar. 1941; *ibid.*, f. 166
16. 'L'AFFAIRE CHARLES', *op. cit.*, ref. 14 above
17. IMT, vol. 38, pp. 172–3
18. Cited D. Irving, *War Path*, pp. 255–6
19. N. Henderson, p. 287
20. W. Shirer, *Berlin Diary*, pp. 161
21. See P. Padfield, *Himmler*, pp. 270 ff
22. J. v. Lang and C. Sibyll, p. 92
23. J. Colville, p. 28
24. See A. Roberts, p. 179
25. Adrian Liddell Hart to *The Sunday Telegraph*, 26 Nov. 1989
26. 12 Aug. 1939, Nigel West, p. 11
27. Cited J. Costello, p. 55
28. 6 Oct. 1939; cited J. Douglas-Hamilton, *Motive*, pp. 105–6
29. 24 Oct. 1939; E. Fröhlich, *Teil 1, Band 3*, p. 619
30. 7 Nov. 1939; *ibid.*, p. 633
31. Report of US Minister in Berne to Sec. of State, 11 Nov. 1939; 862.002 Hitler, Adolf, f. 228, Confidential File RG 59, Nat. Archives, Washington; cited J. Costello, p. 59
32. See Bob de Graaff, 'The Venlo Incident'; www.georg-elser-arbeitskreis. de/texts/graaff.htm
33. See K. Jeffery, p. 383
34. 9 Nov. 1939; E. Fröhlich, *Teil 1, Band 3*, p. 636
35. *Ibid.*, pp. 636–7
36. *Ibid.*, p. 637
37. See S. Payne Best, pp. 157 ff; O. Strasser, p. 146
38. See Peter Steinbach, Johannes Tuchel, '*"Ich habe den Krieg verhindern wollen": Georg Elser und das Attentat vom 8 November 1939*'; www.georg-elser.de/dok/index.html; and Christopher Glazek, 'Remembering Georg Elser', *Spiegel* (online), 23 Oct. 2008
39. See E. Calic, pp. 319 ff; and A. Cave Brown, p. 326
40. See K. Jeffery, p. 385. Payne Best had a list of agents' names and addresses with him
41. 'Extract from Passport Papers, James Lonsdale Bryans'; TNA KV 2/2839, f. 254
42. J. Lonsdale Bryans to Halifax, 28 Feb. 1940; *ibid.*, f. 140
43. Facsimile of the conditions in U. v. Hassell, *Tagebücher*, pp. 171–2

44. *Ibid.*, p. 169
45. *Ibid.*, p. 170
46. J. Lonsdale Bryans to Halifax, 28 Feb. 1940; *op. cit.* ref. 42 above
47. J. Lonsdale Bryans' own account, 'L'AFFAIRE CHARLES'; TNA KV 2/2839, f. 91; and see confirmation in U. v. Hassell, *Tagebücher* p. 189. 'Another group in Germany' referred to Admiral Wilhelm Canaris and co-conspirators in the *Abwehr*, whose representative, Josef Müller, was attempting to obtain British governmental support for a coup against Hitler through the Vatican; see M. Mueller, p. 180
48. See Beaverbrook–Liddell Hart correspondence; Beaverbrook Papers, House of Lords Record Office, C/159; and see P. Padfield, *Hess*, p. 115
49. 19 Mar. 1940; E. Fröhlich, *Teil 1, Band 4*, p. 80
50. 30 Mar. 1940; *ibid.*, p. 91
51. U. v. Hassell, *Andern Deutschland*, pp. 148–9; and see R. Lamb, pp. 133 ff

Chapter 6: Churchill – and the Jews

1. 21 Apr. 1940; E. Fröhlich, *Teil 1, Band 4*, p. 121
2. 25 Apr. 1940; *ibid.*, p. 126
3. Cited M. Cohen, p. 5
4. Cited *ibid.*, p. 277
5. M. Gilbert, pp. 919 f
6. See M. Cohen, p. 3
7. *Der Halt Befehl*, 24 May 1940; cited A. Seidl, p. 85
8. See B. Bond, pp. 104–5
9. Cited A. Seidl, pp. 82–3
10. B. Liddell Hart, pp. 114–5
11. 4 June 1940; cited M. Gilbert, p. 468
12. By July a peak of 753 members of the BUF had been interned; C. Andrew, p. 227
13. See TNA PREM 5/209. Buccleuch relinquished his appointment in audience with the King on 26 June 1940; *The Times*, 27 June 1940
14. 24 May 1940; TNA PREM 5/209
15. Guy Liddell's diary, 12, 17, 19 May 1940; 13 May: 'I have got Sneath and Dickson to prepare a case on the B.U.F. in order to show the whole organisation is a hostile association'; 16 May: 'the case against the B.U.F. is being worked up ...'; TNA KV 4/186, pp. 451 ff
16. See www.oswaldmosley.com/regulation18b.htm
17. TNA KV 2/841; cited C. Andrew, p. 225

18. TNA KV 4/227; cited *ibid.*; and see B. Clough, pp. 127, 129 ff, 142 ff, 187, 254

19. Maxwell Knight's report to Brig. O.A. Harker, 31 Jan. 1945 in TNA KV 2/545, reproduced in B. Clough, p. 266; and see B. Clough, pp. 47, 241

20. Guy Liddell's diary. 21 May 1940; TNA KV 4/186, pp. 466 f

21. See C. Andrew, p. 226; and Guy Liddell's diary, 23 May 1940; TNA KV 4/186, pp. 469–70

22. Nat. Archives Washington, RG 59, US Emb. London Confidential File 1939–40; cited J. Costello, p. 136

23. Guy Liddell's diary, 12 Feb. 1940; TNA KV 4/185, p. 134

24. *Ibid.*, 14 Feb. 1940; *ibid.*, p. 140

25. *Ibid.*

26. *Idem.*, 18, 22, 23 Feb., 20 Apr. 1940, pp. 146, 157–8, 432

27. Cited in *Bild-Zeitung*, 16 Mar. 1981; and see Richard Deacon, *'C': A Biography of Sir Maurice Oldfield, Head of MI6*, Macdonald, 1985, pp. 86–7

28. Report P.F.37755 on Jahnke; TNA KV 2/755

29. Walter Schellenberg's report on Jahnke; *ibid.*

30. W. Schellenberg, p. 304

31. See TNA KV 2/755

32. H. Kravsnick, *'Denkschrift Himmlers über die Behandlung der Fremdvölkischen im Osten'*; *Viertelsjahrsheft für Zeitgeschichte*, 5, 1957, p. 195

33. *Ibid.*, p. 197

34. F. Kersten, p. 88

35. *Ibid.*, pp. 334–6

36. 17 Aug 1940; E. Fröhlich, *Teil 1, Band 4*, p. 284

37. J. v. Lang, C. Sibyll, pp. 92–3

38. See http://frank.mtsu.edu/~baustin/madagascar.html

39. P. Longerich, *Holocaust*, p. 164

40. Bundesarchiv Koblenz, R 49/157; cited R. Giordano, pp. 154 ff

41. See P. Longerich, *Himmler*, pp. 527–9; P. Longerich, *Holocaust*, p. 217

42. Cited Peter Longerich, *Unwritten Order*, p. 71; German text in R. Calic, p. 400

43. See P. Padfield, *Himmler*, pp. 260 ff, 303 ff

44. R.J. Lifton, p. 14

45. 9 Nov. 1939; E. Fröhlich, *Teil 1, Band 3*, p. 636

46. 10 Sept. 1940; *ibid.*, *Teil 1, Band 4*, p. 317

47. Hohenlohe to W. Hewel, 23 June 1940; F & CO 1504 371077
48. K. de Courcy to A. Liddell Hart, 2 Feb. 1988; to author 30 Nov. 1990, 13 Jan. 1993 (and see R.A. Butler to K. de Courcy, 6 June 1940; Trinity College Lib.)
49. K. de Courcy to author, *ibid.*
50. Prytz told K. de Courcy that the meeting was arranged; K. de Courcy to author, 30 Nov. 1990
51. R. Lamb, pp. 143–6; A. Roberts, pp. 231–2; *'Prytz-Telegramm' Der Spiegel*, No. 40, 19 *Jahrg.*, 29 Sep. 1965, p. 103; von Weizsäcker to Ribbentrop, 19, 22 June 1940; F & CO B15 B002529, B002530; Tel. No. 723, 17 June 1940; Swedish Staatsarchiv/HP 39 A XXXIII/UDA; cited Gellermann, p. 26
52. Gellermann, p. 26
53. M. Gilbert, pp. 598–9; A. Roberts, pp. 234–6
54. 28 June 1940; E. Fröhlich, *Teil 1, Band 4*, p. 221
55. Hohenlohe to W. Hewel, 18 July 1940; *Documents on German Foreign Policy, Series D*, p. 202
56. See Lord Vansittart, *Lessons*, pp. 185–6
57. See *ibid.*, pp. 186 f, 205; and Lord Vansittart, *Black Record*, pp. 33, 79
58. See Lord Vansittart, *Mist Procession*, pp. 497, 512–3, 550 ff; and A. Roberts, p. 81
59. A. Liddell Hart to author, 6 Dec 1989. Vansittart remained at the highest level of intelligence/Foreign Office co-ordination (see K. Jeffery, pp. 548, 738) and was particularly involved in the evaluation of German peace feelers; see TNA FO 371/24251, FO 371/24405, FO 371/24407. As a recipient of political reports on Hess's mission, his name appears second, after 'C's liaison, Henry Hopkinson, and before Churchill's intelligence adviser, Major Desmond Morton; see MI6 Political Report No. 25, 19 May 1941; TNA WO 208/4471
60. R. Vansittart (later Lord), 'Desolation'; *The Times*, 31 July 1940
61. Hohenlohe to W. Hewel, 18 July 1940, *op. cit.*, ref. 55 above, p. 203
62. Sir David Kelly, *The Ruling Few*, Hollis & Carter, 1952, pp. 372–3; cited A. Roberts, p. 245
63. H. Nicolson to V. Sackville-West, 19 June 1940; H. Nicolson, p. 96
64. Cited J. Colville, p. 186
65. 31 July 1940; F. Halder, p. 48
66. Carl Aschan, 'Reminiscences of the Second World War 1926–1945' (translated from Swedish text), unpublished, 12 Dec. 1995, pp. 13–14; author's collection

67. C. Aschan to author, 17 Apr. 1996
68. See I. Kershaw, *Nemesis*, pp. 303–4
69. 24 July 1940; E. Fröhlich, *Band 1, Teil 4*, p. 250
70. Köcher to *Auswärtiges Amt*, 18 July 1940; F & CO B15 B002566
71. 22 July 1940; E. Fröhlich, *Band 1, Teil 4*, p. 250
72. *Ibid.*, p. 242
73. Ilse to K. Hess, 20 Oct., 3 Nov. 1937; TNA FO 371/26566
74. E. Bohle evidence, 26 Sept. 1945, pp. 10–11; IWM FO 645 box 155
75. See P. Ziegler, p. 421
76. A.W. Weddell to Sec. of State: *Foreign Relations of the United States 1940, vol. III*, 1939/4357, p. 41; cited *ibid.*
77. Stohrer to Ribbentrop, 2 July 1940, No. 2088; F & CO, B15 B002538
78. S. Hoare wire No. 437, 27 Jan. 1940; cited M. Gilbert, p. 613
79. W.S.C. minute of 28 June 1940; Churchill Papers, 20/9; cited *ibid.*
80. See *ibid.*, pp. 699–701; and P. Ziegler, pp. 426–8
81. See Stohrer to Ribbentrop, 9 July 1940; F & CO B15 B002545
82. Ribbentrop to Stohrer, 11 July 1940, wire No. 1023; *ibid.*, B002549
83. Stohrer to Ribbentrop, 23, 25 July 1940, wires Nos 2474, 2495; *ibid.*, B002582, B002588
84. Huene (German Ambassador in Lisbon) to Ribbentrop, 2 Aug. 1940, wire No. 800; *ibid.*, B002632-3
85. 1 Aug. 1940; E. Fröhlich, *Band 1, Teil 4*, p. 260

Chapter 7: Clandestine approaches

1. Cited M. Gilbert, *Finest Hour*, pp. 694–5; and see TNA FO 371 26542, C4216/324/18, ff. 106 f
2. '*Aufnahme inoffizieller Friedensverhandlungen mit England*' (almost certainly written by Dr Weissauer), p. 1, in *SS-Brigadeführer* Jung to *Gesandten* Luther, *Auswärtigen Amt*, 23 Oct. 1940; *Politischen Archiv des Auswärtigen Amtes*, Berlin, Inl. Hg Bd. 476
3. See G. Gellermann, pp. 19 ff
4. V. Mallet to Foreign Office, No. 1011, 5 Sept. 1940; TNA FO 371 24408, C/1973
5. '*Aufnahme inoffizieller Friedensverhandlungen ...*', *op. cit.* ref. 2 above, pp. 2–3
6. Foreign Office to Mr Mallet, No. 726, 6 Sept. 1940; TNA FO 371 24408, C/1973
7. R. Vansittart to Foreign Secretary, 6 Sept. 1940; *ibid.*

8. V. Mallet to A. Cadogan, 7 Sept. 1940; *ibid.*

9. See R. Giordano, pp. 226 ff. This quotation from *Denkschrift, Gesellschaft für europäische Wirtschaftsplanung und Grossraumwirtschafts*, 31 May 1940, p. 227

10. V. Mallet to A. Cadogan, 7 Sept. 1940; *op. cit.* ref. 8 above

11. Foreign Office (draft signed 'A.C.') to V. Mallet, 11 Sept. 1940; *ibid.*

12. Simon interview transcript, 9 June 1941, Copy No. 2; Simon Papers, Bodleian Library, Oxford, Box 88, f. 76

13. *Ibid.*, f. 78

14. See R.C. Nesbit and G. v. Acker, pp. 35–8

15. Ingeborg Sperr sworn statement, Nuremberg, 5 Mar. 1946; IWM FO 645/31

16. Hildegard Fath sworn statement, Nuremberg, 5 Mar. 1946; *ibid.*

17. Dr F.S. to Georges van Acker, 10 July 1993; cited R.C. Nesbit and G. v. Acker, p. 44

18. *Ibid.*

19. Albrecht to Karl Haushofer, 2 Aug. 1940; H.-A. Jacobsen, p. 402

20. Karl to Albrecht Haushofer, 3 Sept. 1940; F & CO, C109 C002185

21. *Ibid.*

22. Martha Haushofer's diary, 14 Aug. 1925, '*Die Bekanntschaft mit der Familie R. datierte aus der Vorkriegszeit*'; H.-A. Jacobsen, p. 453 note

23. '*Gibt es möglichkeiten eines deutsch–englischen Friedens*', Albrecht to Karl Haushofer, Berlin, 15 Sept. 1940; F & CO C109 C002193

24. R. Hess to K. Haushofer, 10 Sept. 1940; *ibid.* C002188

25. Albrecht Haushofer to R. Hess, 19 Sept. 1940; *ibid.* C002198

26. Albrecht Haushofer to R. Hess, 23 Sept. 1940; *ibid.* C002203

27. 10 Sept. 1940; E. Fröhlich, *Teil 1, Band 4*, p. 316

28. H. Nicolson, p. 114

29. Lord Simon interview transcript; *op. cit.*, ref. 12 above, f. 79; Hess said the same to the psychologist, J.R. Rees on 12 May 1941; see http://propaganda3.tripod.com/nur01.html

30. 15 Oct. 1940; E. Fröhlich, *Teil 1, Band 4*, p. 365

31. 26 Nov. 1940; *ibid.*, p. 411

32. Robert Kempner testimony; see http://propaganda3.tripod.com/nur01.html; and E. Bohle's interrogation, 26 Sept. 1945; IWM FO 645, Box 155

33. 4 Nov. 1940; cited I. Hess, *Schicksal*, p. 81

34. TNA INF 1/192 150028

35. *Ibid.*

36. *Ibid.*
37. 13 May 1941; N. West, p. 147
38. Operations Record Book (ORB) RAF Turnhouse, Appendix; TNA AIR 28/864
39. Room 055 (MI5) to H. Hopkinson, 22 Nov. 1940; cited J. Douglas-Hamilton, *The Truth*, p. 128
40. Cited *ibid.*, p. 129
41. Cited U. Laack-Michel, p. 229
42. Lord Simon interview transcript, 9 June 1941; IWM FO 645/31, p. 150. In another copy of the transcript Hess gives the date as 7 Jan. 1941, and three pages later as 10 May 1941; Simon interview transcript, Copy No. 2; *op. cit.*, ref. 12 above, pp. 60, 63. Are the differences due to transcription errors or deliberate amendments?
43. J. Leasor, pp. 69 ff
44. E. Bohle to Robert Kempner at Nuremberg Trials of the Major War Criminals; http://propaganda3.tripod.com/nur01.html
45. R. Nesbit and G. v. Acker, pp. 38–9
46. *The Times*, London, 10 Jan. 1941, p. 4
47. R. Nesbit and G. v. Acker, p. 42
48. See ref. 42 above
49. 'The Secret Dossier Prepared for Stalin', see H. Eberle and M. Uhl; and K.-H. Pintsch's statement; see J. Friedmann and K. Wiegrefe
50. J. Friedmann and K. Wiegrefe
51. 11 Jan. 1941; TNA KV 2/1684, ff. 3–5
52. 11 Jan. 1941; N. West, p. 123
53. Maj. Robertson internal note, 20 Jan. 1941; TNA KV 2/1684, f. 5
54. See J. Douglas-Hamilton, *Motive*, pp. 159 ff
55. Internal note re. Mrs Roberts' address, 29 Nov. 1940; TNA KV 2/1684, f. 7A; letter to Regional Security Officer, Cambridge, 23 Mar. 1941; *ibid.* f. 19A; J.H. Marriott to Major Robertson, 24 Mar. 1941; *ibid.*, f. 37A; Capt. C.M. Hughes to J.H. Marriott, 14 May 1941; *ibid.* f. 54A
56. C. Andrew, p. 222
57. 'Communication with Blenheim Palace is frightful. At the moment there are only two lines and one of them is not working. Whenever you ring up you are told that your name will be put on the waiting list ...'; Guy Liddell's diary, 7 Oct. 1940; N. West, p. 101
58. *ibid.*, pp. 146–7
59. Anonymous MI6 officer to Alfred Smith; A. Smith, p. 309

60. C. Andrew, p. 203; and see K. Jeffery, p. 306

61. H. Höhne, p. 361

62. G. Kiesel states that one channel led through the Vatican, another through Sir Samuel Hoare in Madrid. He also conveyed information via the wife of the former Polish Military Attaché in Berlin, for whom he had secured safe passage to Switzerland in summer or autumn 1940; G. Kiesel, pp. 5 ff; about which, see K. Jeffery, pp. 380–1; and see M. Mueller, p. 171

63. Interrogation of TRICYCLE, 30 Apr. 1941; TNA KV 2/847, p. 5

64. D. Popov, pp. 44–5

65. *Ibid.*, p. 53

66. C. Andrew, pp. 211–2, 248; J.C. Masterman, p. 40

67. D. Popov, p. 62

68. *Ibid.*, pp. 69–70

69. Michael Smith, 'Mrs Foley's diary solves the mystery of Hess'; *The Daily Telegraph*, 27 Dec. 2004, p. 14

70. J. Maude to T.A. Robertson, 11 Jan. 1941; TNA KV 2/1684 ff. 3–5; see p. 106 above

71. See Michael Smith; *op. cit.*, ref. 69 above

72. See P. Padfield, *Hess*, p. 156

73. 'C' to H. Hopkinson, 19 Feb. 1941; TNA FO 371/26542, C1687 (released Nov. 2007)

74. Bickham Sweet-Escott to Elizabeth Sparrow, 4 Aug. 1981; cited E. Sparrow, p. xiv

75. See J. Harris and M.J. Trow, pp. 6, 101, 123, 137–9

76. *Ibid.*, p. 139

77. Internal note, 29 Nov. 1940; TNA KV 2/1684 Doc. 19A

78. Minute sheet, 23 Mar. 1941; *ibid.*, f. 6; and Capt. C.M. Hughes to J.H. Marriott, 14 May 1941; TNA KV 2/1685, Doc. 54A

79. Capt. C.M. Hughes to J.H. Marriott; *ibid.*

80. *Ibid.*

81. *Ibid.*

82. Ernst Haiger (Albrecht Haushofer biographer) to author, 11 Feb. 2011

83. *Ibid.*

84. John Maude to Maj. T.A. Robertson, 11 Jan. 1941; KV 2/1684, Doc. 29, ff. 3–4; and Guy Liddell's diary, 11 Jan. 1941; N. West, p. 123

85. Col. T.A. Robertson to J. Douglas Hamilton; cited J. Douglas-Hamilton, *The Truth*, p. 132; and Col. T.A. Robertson to author, 3 July 1992

86. J. Douglas-Hamilton, *The Truth*, p. 129

87. L. Picknett, C. Prince and S. Prior, p. 156

88. For Hamilton's periods of leave see ORB RAF Turnhouse; TNA AIR 28/863

89. Statement of Wing Cdr, the Duke of Hamilton, Provost Marshal's Dept., Air Ministry, 11 Mar. 1941; TNA KV 2/1684, Doc. 35a

90. 13 May 1941; N. West, p. 147

91. J. Douglas-Hamilton, *The Truth*, p. 129; J. Leasor, p. 59

92. J. Leasor, p. 59

93. J.H. Marriott to Maj. Robertson, 24 Mar. 1941; TNA KV 2/1684, Doc. 37A

94. T.A. Robertson to Group Capt. G.S. Stammers, 25 Mar. 1941; *ibid.*, Doc. 38A

95. T.A. Robertson to Air Commodore Boyle, 7 Apr. 1941; *ibid.*, Doc. 41A

96. Air Commodore Boyle to Maj. T.A. Robertson, 9 Apr. 1941; *ibid.*, Doc. 42A

97. Internal note signed T.A.R., 29 Apr. 1941; *ibid.*, Doc. 45A

98. Duke of Hamilton's Flying Log, 24–26 Apr. 1941; photocopy sent to author by Lord James Douglas-Hamilton, 28 Dec. 1991

99. J. Douglas-Hamilton, *The Truth*, p. 130

100. Wing Cdr the Duke of Hamilton to Group Capt. D.L. Blackford, 28 Apr. 1941; cited *ibid.*, pp. 130–1

101. Group Capt. D.L. Blackford to Wing Cdr the Duke of Hamilton, 3 May 1941; TNA KV 2/1685, Doc. 65A

102. T.A. Robertson to Group Capt. W. (*sic*) Blackford, 6 May 1941; *ibid.*, Doc. 49A

103. Internal note to Major Robertson, 11 May 1941; *ibid.*, Doc. 50; confirmed in note by the Security Service, 'Albrecht Haushofer', unsigned, undated; *ibid.*, Doc. 57A

104. J. Douglas-Hamilton, *The Truth*, p. 132

105. See C. Andrew, p. 255

106. Wing Cdr the Duke of Hamilton to Group Capt. D.L. Blackford, 10 May 1941; cited J. Douglas-Hamilton, *The Truth*, p. 133

Chapter 8: Deception operations

1. Air Vice Marshal Sir Arthur Harris to Air Marshal Sir W.S. Douglas, 21 Feb. 1941; TNA AIR 16/619; A. Crawley, pp. 160 ff

2. ORB RAF Lympne; TNA AIR 28/509

3. TNA AIR 16/619

4. Air Vice Marshall Sir Arthur Harris to Air Marshal Sir W.S. Douglas, 17 Mar. 1941; *ibid.*

5. Group Capt. Sanders to Air Vice Marshal Evill, 17 May 1941; *ibid.*

6. R. Schmitt, p. 162

7. See obituary Hans Baur; *The Times*, 17 Mar. 1993; and R. Schmidt, p. 161; Dr Wilhelm Höttl to author, 20 Feb. 1940

8. See D. Irving, *Hess*, p. 61

9. 22 Dec. 1940; E. Fröhlich, *Teil 1, Band 3*, p. 442

10. See I. Kershaw, *Nemesis*, pp. 335–6

11. Haberlein to *Auswärtiges Amt*, 19 Aug. 1940, No. 2825; F & CO B15 B002661

12. Huene, Lisbon to *Auswärtiges Amt*, 29 Aug. 1940, No. 971; F & CO, 3084 613477

13. K. de Courcy saw Buccleuch at White's Club intermittently throughout the war; K. de Courcy to author Jan. 8 1990; and see, for instance, Buccleuch to Lord Brocket, 16 Feb. 1941, 'I am at 2 Gros Pl [Grosvenor Place] Slo 6612 till fr morning'; TNA KV 2/2839, f. 178; and see visitors' book, Drumlanrig Castle (Buccleuchs' main residence) for 1941

14. Stohrer, Madrid, to *Auswärtiges Amt*, 2 Sept. 1940, No. 2979; F & CO B15 002687

15. Huene, Lisbon, to *Auswärtiges Amt*, 10 Sept. 1940, No. 1049; *ibid.* D 613498-500

16. Huene to *Auswärtiges Amt*, 17 Sept. 1940, No. 1907; *ibid.* D613511

17. 2 Sept. 1940; cited J. Colville, p. 239

18. 17 Sept. 1940; H. Nicolson, p. 114

19. Thomsen, Washington, to *Auswärtiges Amt*, 30 Sept. 1940, No. 2093; F & CO B15 002794-5

20. Huene, Lisbon, to *Auswärtiges Amt*, 19 Sept. 1940, No. 1181; *ibid.* D613522

21. K. Jeffery, p. 113

22. 'Both my predecessors made it clear that in their view Wiseman should never be employed again by this organisation. They had their reasons', Menzies to Gladwyn Jebb, 21 June 1940, cited K. Jeffery, p. 440

23. See J. Costello, pp. 400 ff

24. H. Hoover to Berle, 30 Nov. 1940, 'Meeting in Mark Hopkins Hotel 7.30–1.0 pm, 27.11.1940'; Nat. Archives, Washington RG 59 741.6211/11-2940; cited R.E. Schmidt, p. 143; and see J. Costello, p. 402

25. *Ibid.*

26. Hohenlohe to W. Hewel, '*Betr: Britische Gesandschaft*, Mr Kelly', 6 Dec. 1940; F & CO 371047

27. TNA FO 371 26542, C610/324/18, C1705/324/18

28. 13 Feb. 1941; *ibid.*, C1426/324/18

29. 17 Jan. 1941; *ibid.*

30. 11 Jan. 1941; *ibid.*, C324/324/18, C610/324/18

31. 28 Jan. 1941; *ibid.*, C610/324/18

32. See D. Day, pp. 35–6

33. 20 Jan. 1941; TNA FO 371 26542, C610/324/18

34. *Ibid.*

35. Huene (Lisbon) to *Auswärtiges Amt*, 23 Jan. 1941, No. 934/41; F & CO D613659-67

36. *Ibid.*, D613667

37. See Ian Kershaw, *Making Friends with Hitler: Lord Londonderry and Britain's Road to War*, Allen Lane, 2004

38. See p. 204 f above

39. Cited by Bryans in 'L'AFFAIRE CHARLES', p. 2; TNA KV 2/2839, f. 92

40. Cited by Bryans in *ibid.*, f. 91

41. *Ibid.*

42. Bryans to *Direktor*, Schwarzhaupter Verlag, 8 Oct. 1940; TNA FO 371/26542, C1072/324/18

43. See interrogation of O.E. Anderson, 17 Dec. 1940, p. 36; TNA KV 2/2839, f. 231; and report on Bryans by E.B. Stamp, MI5, 28 Aug. 1941, reverse of p. 1 in *ibid.*, f. 103

44. Further interrogation of James Lonsdale Bryans, 4 June 1941, p. 8; *ibid.*, f. 132; also Bryans, 'L'AFFAIRE CHARLES', *ibid.* p. 2, f. 92

45. U. v. Hassell, *Tagebücher*, p. 227

46. *Ibid.*, p. 228

47. *Ibid.*, pp. 228–9

48. Bryans to Buccleuch, 22 Feb. 1941 (cable); TNA FO 371/26542, C1954/324/18

49. Brig. O.A. Harker (Acting D.G. MI5) to Cadogan, 22 Feb. 1941; *ibid.*; and Buccleuch to Brocket, 16 Feb. 1941; TNA KV 2/2839, f. 177

50. Cadogan minute, 3 Feb. 1941; TNA FO 371/26542, C1072/324/18

51. Report on Bryans by E.B. Stamp (MI5), 28 Aug. 1941, reverse p. 1; TNA KV 2/2839, f. 103

52. Interrogation O.A. Anderson, 17 Dec. 1940, pp. 10, 13, 41 ff; *ibid.*, ff. 205, 209, 226 ff

53. *Ibid.*, f. 214
54. See p. 127 above
55. Interrogation of O.A. Anderson, 17 Dec. 1940; TNA KV 2/2839, f. 228; and see resumé of above interrogation, 24 Jan. 1941, p. 2; *ibid.*, f. 189
56. See E.B. Stamp (MI5) to MI6, 14 Mar. 1941, p. 2; *ibid.*, f. 167; and Cadogan to Brig. O.A. Harker (acting D.G. MI5), 7 Apr. 1941; *ibid.*, f. 150
57. See MI6 to D.G. White (MI5), 3 May 1941; *ibid.*, f. 149
58. See *ibid.*
59. See p. 111 above
60. See p. 124–5 above
61. See p. 125 above
62. See p. 125–6 above
63. See J. Harris, *Illusion*, p. 185
64. U. v. Hassell, *Tagebuücher*, p. 228
65. *Ibid.*
66. *Ibid.*, p. 229
67. J. Harris and D. Wilbourn, *Illusion*, pp. 181–3
68. See K. Jeffery, pp. 314–5, 343
69. See *ibid.*, pp. 361–3
70. For his charm, see *ibid.*, p. 314; for his hatred of Vivian, *ibid.*, pp. 365, 380, 403
71. See *ibid.*, pp. 378–81. The official was Hans-Bernd Gisevius of the Prussian Interior Ministry
72. See pp. 123–4; and see TNA FO 371 26542, C4216/324/18
73. See G. Gellermann, p. 43
74. See K. Jeffery, p. 403
75. D. Eccles, p. 158
76. J. Colville, p. 770
77. Lord Templewood, p. 275
78. H.W. Stahmer, pp. 4–5; cited R. Schmidt, p. 163
79. H.W. Stahmer Affidavit, Hamburg, 20 May 1948, *Politisches Archiv des Auswärtigen Amts; Akten betr. Weizsäcker Prozess*, Bd, 10/2; cited R. Schmidt, pp. 164, 323
80. H.W. Stahmer; cited R. Schmidt, p. 164
81. '*halb kaltgestellten, halb auf Lauer liegenden*'; A. Haushofer, '*Gibt es nach Möglichkeiten eines deutsch–englischen Friedens?*', 15 Sept. 1940; cited H.-A. Jacobsen, Bd. 2, p. 459; also W. Stubbe, p. 247

82. A. Haushofer, '*Englische Beziehungen und die Möglichkeit ihres Einsatzes*', Obersalzberg, 12 May 1941; *Akten zur Deutschen Auswärtigen Politik 1918–1945*, Serie D, Frankfurt, 1963, Bd. 12, No. 500, pp. 654–5

83. Sir H. Knatchbull-Hugessen to Sir A. Eden, 8 Jan. 1941; TNA FO 371/26542 C1118/324/18

84. See, for instance, M. Gascoigne (British Consul in Tangiers) to R.M. Makins, 21 Apr. 1941; TNA FO 371/26945, C4456/306/41; 'he [Hoare] has built up so much personal prestige vis-à-vis the Spaniards in Spain ...'

85. D. Eccles, p. 158; and see *ibid.*, pp. 101–2

86. R.M. Makins minute on two wires from Hoare to Churchill, 2 Mar. 1941, 3 Mar. 1941; TNA FO 371/26945 C2065/306/41

87. R.M. Makins minute, 25 Apr. 1941; TNA FO 371/26905 C4161/46/41

88. P. Padfield, *Hess*, p. 156

89. See p. 112 above; 'C' to H. Hopkinson, 19 Feb. 1941; TNA FO 371/26542 C1687

90. U. v. Hassell's diary 16 Mar. 1941; U. v. Hassell, *Tagebücher,* pp. 232–3

91. See W.R. Hess, *My Father*, p. 70

92. Martha Haushofer's diary 15 Apr. 1941; cited R. Schmidt, p. 166

93. *Ibid.* 26 Apr. 1941; cited *ibid.*

94. See E. Haiger, pp. 112–3

95. No. 31 Secret; TNA FO 371/26542 C610/324/18

96. FO to Sir R. Craigie (Tokyo), 24 Feb. 1941; *ibid.* C2189/324/18

97. A. Cadogan to S. Hoare, 28 Feb. 1941; *ibid.*

98. S. Hoare to A. Cadogan 'Personal & Secret', 6 Mar. 1941; *ibid.* C2505/324/18 f. 75

99. R. Makins' minute, 15 Mar. 1941; *ibid.*

100. A. Cadogan to S. Hoare 'Personal & Secret', 21 Mar. 1941; *ibid.* f. 78

101. S. Hoare to A. Cadogan, 6 Mar. 1941; *ibid.*

102. *Ibid.*

103. V. Lequio to Ministry of Foreign Relations, 14 Mar. 1941; *Documenti Diplomatici Italiani 1939–1943*, 9th Series; cited Scott Newton, p. 20

104. Stohrer to *Auswärtiges Amt*, 13 Mar. 1941, No. 987; *Politische Archiv des Auswärtigen Amtes, Büro Staatsekretär, England*, Bd. 4, f. 108677; cited R. Schmidt, p. 164

105. Huene to *Auswärtiges Amt*, 29 Mar. 1941, No. 635; *ibid.* f. 108683

106. R. Nicolson, p. 149

107. See p. 139 above

108. See p. 140 above

109. See FO to Madrid, 22 Apr. 1941, No. 592 *Important*; TNA FO 371/26945 C4140/306/41, and C4147/306/41

110. S. Hoare to FO, 25 Apr. 1941, No. 641; *ibid.* C4245/306/41

111. S. Hoare to FO, 25 Apr. 1941, No. 148 (by bag); *ibid.* C4613/306/41

Chapter 9: Two-front war

1. E. Fröhlich, *Teil 1, Band 4*, p. 557

2. Albrecht Haushofer, '*Gibt es noch Möglichkeiten eines deutsch–englischen Friedens?*', 8 Sept. 1940; cited W. Stubbe, p. 246

3. See C. Thorne, pp. 77–8

4. See p. 80 above

5. See, for instance, Viktor Brack's evidence at the Nuremberg Trials of the Major War Criminals: 'it was no secret in Party circles by March 1941 that the Jews were to be exterminated'; W. Laqueur, p. 196

6. IMT PS 447; and see F. Halder, 13 Mar. 1941, p. 419, note 1

7. Testimony of *Sonderkommando* commander; cited H. Krausnick and others, pp. 62–3

8. Cited M. Gilbert, *Holocaust*, p. 152; and see J. v. Lang and C. Sibyll, p. 73

9. See P. Padfield, *Hess*, pp. 132–3

10. *Centre de Documentation Juive Contemporaire, CXLVI-23*; cited R. Cecil, pp. 195, 227; and see R. Bollmus. p. 120

11. Karl Haushofer interrogation, 5 Oct. 1945; IWM FO 645 box 155

12. 'Studies in Broadcast Propaganda: Rudolf Hess'; TNA INF 1/192, f. 27

13. *Ibid.*

14. See pp. 143–4 above

15. Martha Haushofer's diary, 26 Apr. 1941; Bundesarchiv Koblenz, *Nachlass Haushofer* 128

16. Diary 18 May 1941; U. v. Hassell, *Andern Deutschland*, p. 207

17. Albrecht Haushofer, '*Englische Beziehungen ...*', *op. cit.* Chapter 8 ref. 82; and see W. Stubbe, pp. 254–5

18. Carl Burckhardt to Walter Stubbe; cited W. Stubbe, pp. 251–2

19. U. v. Hassell's diary, 18 May 1941; U. v. Hassell, *Tagebücher*, p. 252

20. Interrogation of Karl Haushofer, 5 Oct. 1945; IWM FO 645 box 155

21. See Erica Mann, 'Hess Meeting in Spain was Fixed', *Glasgow Evening Citizen*, 20 Sept. 1945

22. Martha Haushofer's diary, 3–5 May 1941; Bundesarchiv Koblenz, *Nachlass Haushofer 128*

23. R. Hess to Ilse Hess, 12 Feb. 1950, Spandau; I. Hess, *Schicksal*, pp. 211–2

24. See R. Schmidt, p. 170
25. *Ibid.*
26. See A. Masters, pp. 127–8; according to which Ian Fleming, later the 'James Bond' author, then in naval intelligence, conceived the idea of resurrecting the extreme right-wing British organisation, The Link, to create a picture of a group powerful enough to overthrow Churchill and negotiate peace; then briefed an astrologer via a Swiss contact to infiltrate Hess's astrological circle and let it be known via MI6 that the Duke of Hamilton would be sympathetic to meeting Hess as a peace negotiator
27. See H.-A. Jacobsen, *Band I*, pp. 403 f; *Band II*, pp. 523 ff; and see D. Irving, *Hess*, pp. 60–1
28. Col. Gibson Graham, 'Memorandum on Herr Rudolf Hess', undated, p. 3; TNA 1093/11, f. 75
29. R. Hess to Ilse Hess, 2 Feb. 1942, England; TNA FO 1093/3, f. 19
30. W.R. Hess, *My Father*, pp. 60–2; citing Hess's flying mentor Helmut Kaden's report under oath, 4 May 1981
31. See I. Kershaw, *Nemesis*, p. 368; citing Gen. Halder's KTB (war diary)
32. *Völkischer Beobachter*, 2 May 1941; and see Hess personal file; IWM FO 643/31
33. *Ibid.*
34. *Aktenvermerk*, W. Messerschmitt to Caroli, No. 92/41, 2 May 1941; IWM FO 4355/45, vol. 4, box 5206, *Handakten Messerschmitt*; cited D. Irving, *Hess*, p. 63
35. See D. Irving, *Hess*, p. 63
36. Hitler's speech 4 May 1941; http://der-fuehrer.org/reden/english/41.05.04.htm
37. Hans Frank diary, *Anlage*: IWM AL 2525; cited D. Irving, *Hess*, p. 64
38. IMT doc. M-117
39. Cited *Sunday Dispatch*, 30 Sept. 1945; copy in TNA FO 371/46780, C4725
40. *Ibid.*
41. Anthony Eden, 'Why Hess came to England', *The Times*, 23 Sept. 1943
42. W.R. Hess, *Mord*, p. 148; and W.R. Hess, *My Father*, pp. 68, 341–2
43. See p. 32 above
44. J. Colville, p. 383
45. See W.R. Hess, *My Father*, p. 83
46. Log of *Flugkapitän* Helmut Kaden; cited R.C. Nesbit and G. v. Acker, pp. 154–5

Chapter 10: Take off!

1. I. Hess, *Schicksal*, pp. 67–8
2. 7 May 1941; H. Nicolson, p. 164
3. *Hansard*, 7 May 1941; cited M. Gilbert, *Finest Hour*, p. 1084
4. Diary 7 May 1941; J. Colville, p. 384
5. 7 May 1941; E. Fröhlich, *Teil 1, Band 4*, p. 627
6. 8 May 1941; H. Nicolson, p. 165
7. 9 May 1941; E. Fröhlich, *Teil 1, Band 4*, pp. 631–2
8. See D. Irving, *Hess*, p. 64
9. W.R. Hess, *Mord*, p. 149; and Dr Koeppen (Rosenberg's adjutant in 1941) to L. Charlton; L. Charlton to author, 22 June 1990
10. W. Bechtold (on staff of legal officer, Dr Gerhard Klopfer), 30 Apr. 1946; Nat. Archives, Washington, RG 238 box 180; cited D. Irving, *Hess*, p. 64
11. K.-H. Pintsch statement to J. Leasor; J. Leasor, p. 80; confirmed by Dr Gibson Graham, 'Memorandum on Herr Rudolf Hess', May 1941, p. 3; TNA FO 1093/11 f. 75
12. R. Hess to W. Darré, 9 May 1941; Bundesarchiv Koblenz, Schumacher collection; cited W.R. Hess, *My Father*, p. 83
13. K.-H. Pintsch to J. Leasor; J. Leasor, p. 82
14. Rosenberg interrogation, 16 Nov. 1945, p. 12; IWM FO 645 box 160
15. Dr Koeppen, *op. cit.* ref. 9 above
16. I. Hess, *Schicksal*, pp. 69–70
17. See J. Leasor, p. 85
18. *Ibid.*
19. I. Hess, *Schicksal*, p. 70
20. K.-H. Pintsch to J. Leasor; J. Leasor, pp. 88–90
21. *Ibid.*
22. See R.C. Nesbit and G. v. Acker, pp. 51–3
23. H. Colyton, pp. 177–8
24. R. Hess to '*Meinem Sohn*', 15 June 1941, England; TNA FO 1093/1 ff. 38–42
25. Len Deighton, 'Hess the Aviator', unsourced, in D. Stafford (ed.), p. 131
26. R. Hess to Ilse Hess, letters May–July 1947, Nuremberg; I. Hess, *Schicksal*, p. 82
27. R. Hess to Ilse Hess, 9 May 1948, Spandau; *ibid.*, pp. 180–1
28. R. Hess to Ilse Hess; *op. cit.* ref. 26 above, p. 84
29. R. Hess to '*Meinem Sohn*'; *op. cit.* ref. 24 above
30. *Ibid.*

31. *Ibid.*; and R. Hess to Ilse Hess; *op. cit.* ref. 26 above, p. 86

32. R. Hess to Ilse Hess, 1947, Spandau; I. Hess, *Schicksal*, p. 163. Explanation of how Hess arrived at his stall by Ron Williams, ex-Fleet Air Arm and British Airways pilot

33. R. Hess to Ilse Hess; *op. cit.* ref. 26 above, p. 87

34. *Ibid.*, p. 82; see Air Vice Marshal Sandy Johnstone's similar view of Hess's chances of landing at Dungavel, ref. 35 below

35. R. Hess to Ilse Hess, 9 May 1948; I. Hess, *Schicksal*, p. 180; Air Vice Marshal Sandy Johnstone, a friend of Hamilton, wrote in his memoirs that Hess told Hamilton he had intended to land at Dungavel, have a talk with him, then return to Germany. Yet, Johnstone continued, 'the small landing strip Douglo [Hamilton] had laid down there ... would have been totally inadequate for a fast military aircraft and, in all probability Hess plus Messerschmidt [*sic*], would have ended up in a ball of fire'; Sandy Johnstone, *Diary of an Aviator*, Airlife Publishing, 1993, p. 43

36. Hess's pilot's notes; from late Prof. A.W. Brian Simpson, Ann Arbor, Michigan, who received them from a former commanding officer of RAF Navigators' School, to author, 5 May, 18 Aug. 2008

37. L. Heydrich, *Leben mit einen Kriegsverbrecher*, 1976, p. 72; cited E. Calic, p. 380

38. E. Calic, p. 426; E. Calic to author, 14 Dec. 1989

39. A. Galland, p. 108

40. See J. Leasor, pp. 94–5

41. *The Yorkshire Post*, 4 Nov. 1969

42. See *The Times*, 12 May 1941

43. J. Douglas to author, 13 May 1991; the former head of the London Information Bureau, John Keyser, wrote, 'Knowing Jim [Douglas] I would think his memory was likely to be correct'; J. Keyser to author, 20 Sept. 1991

44. BBC Monitoring Service 'flash', 12 May 1941; IWM Box A 216

45. J. Douglas to author, 13 May, 2 Aug., Oct. 1991: 'There is no possible doubt about my recollection of the Hess affair. I would not have awakened my wife in bed at Richmond after midnight on 10 [11] May to tell her that Hess had gone missing if there had been any doubt. As regards the 'flashes' they were probably removed by Intelligence.'

46. See F. Ashbee (Filter Room 'teller' at Bentley Priory, 10 May 1941), 'the thunderstorm that was Hess', *Aeroplane Monthly*, Oct. 1987, p. 530;

and 'Report No. 195 Operational Research Section', 18 May 1941; cited
R.C. Nesbit and G. v. Acker, pp. 156–7

47. 'Report No. 195'; *op. cit.* ref. 46 above
48. RAF Ouston ORB, 10 May 1941; TNA AIR 28/624
49. RAF 72 Squadron ORB, 10 May 1941; TNA AIR 27/624.
50. Maurice Pocock to author, 16 Apr. 1990
51. 'An Observer's Diary', *Airfix Magazine*, Dec. 1985, p. 157
52. *Ibid.*; and T.W. Dobson (Duty Controller ROC Ops Room, Durham,
10 May 1941) to author, 16 May 1991
53. See 'Report No. 195'; *op. cit.* ref. 46 above; and No. 30 Observer Centre
recording of Raid 42; 23 Group ROC Historical Archive Committee
54. 'Report No. 195'; *op. cit.* ref. 46 above
55. RAF Ouston ORB, 10 May 1941; *op. cit.* ref. 48 above
56. RAF 72 Squadron ORB, 10 May 1941; *op. cit.* ref. 49 above
57. No. 30 Observer Centre recording; *op. cit.* ref. 53 above
58. 'An Observer's Diary'; *op. cit.* ref. 51 above, pp. 157–8
59. RAF Ayr ORB, 10 May 1941, 22.34; TNA AIR 28/40: 'This raid, numbered
42J ... was thought to be an Me110'
60. Sqdn Ldr R.G. 'Tim' Woodman to author, 24 June 1941, citing personal
information from Wing Cdr Wolfe, C.O. of 141 Squadron and on duty
with Cuddie on standby.
61. Maurice Pocock to author, 16 Apr. 1990
62. Jiri Rajlich, *Stíhací Pilot*, Prague, 1991
63. Vaclar Baumann's flying log, 10 May 1941; photocopy sent to author by
Andrew Rosthorn, 4 Oct. 2000, together with translation of relevant
section of Rajlich's book.
64. The translation (ref. 63 above) has this significant passage: 'after dark
[there] landed a liaison Anson [aeroplane] with several strange RAF
officers who immediately summoned both Czech sergeants. They were
separately subjected to intensive interrogation, they asked them about
impossible details ...'
65. So Hamilton told author James Leasor after the war; J. Leasor, p. 105;
Hamilton's flying log confirms that he did fly a Hurricane for one hour on
10 May 1941
66. Joseph W. Debney (junior NCO at 42 AA Brigade office, King's Park,
Glasgow, 10 May 1941) to author, 14 May 1991
67. *Ibid.*

68. Dennis Rose (Duty Officer Ops Room 42 AA Brigade, King's Park, Glasgow, 10 May 1941) to author, 12 May 1941

69. 'An Observer's Diary'; ref. 51 above, p. 158; R.G. Woodman (ref. 60 above) to author, 11 June 1991

70. D. Wood, p. 3; 'An Observer's Diary'; ref. 51 above, p. 158

71. 'Rudolf Hess in Scotland'; *The Bulletin & Scots Pictorial*, 13 May 1941; reproduced in J. Douglas-Hamilton, *Motive*, endpapers; I. Hess, *Schicksal*, p. 88; J. Leasor, p. 26; *The Times*, 14 May 1941 report omits any mention of Dungavel or the Duke of Hamilton

72. Alan Starling, 'In the Home Guard', *Everyone's War*, 25, Summer 2012, p. 23

73. L. Picknett, C. Prince, S. Prior, p. 203, citing account adapted from *Hong Kong Telegraph*, 6 Mar. 1947 in McBride's papers in S. Prior's possession

74. Alan Starling, *op. cit.*, ref. 72 above

75. L. Picknett, C. Prince, S. Prior, pp. 206–7

76. *Ibid.*, p. 199

77. See pp. 168–9 above

78. See pp. 169–71 above

79. 'Extract from Duty Officer's [Clyde Sub-Area] Report for night of 10/11 May '41'; TNA WO 199/3288A

80. 'German P.O.W. Captured Night 10/11 May '41 – Report by Night Duty Officer'; *ibid.*

81. Col. R.C. Firebrace, Scottish Area Command (Intelligence) memo., 18 May 1941; *ibid.*

82. *Ibid.*

83. Col. J.P. Duke, Scottish Command, memo., 31 May 1941; *ibid.*

84. I. Hess, *Schicksal*, pp. 88–9

85. Report by O.C. 3rd Battalion Renfrewshire Home Guard of the incidents of the night 10th, 11th May 1941; TNA WO 199/3288A

86. I. Hess, *Schicksal*, p. 89

87. Report by O.C. 3rd Battalion ..., *op. cit.* ref. 85 above

88. 'German P.O.W. captured ...', *op. cit.* ref. 80 above

89. 'Extract from Duty Officer's Report ...'; *op. cit.* ref. 79 above

90. Report by O.C. 3rd Battalion ...; *op. cit.* ref. 85 above

91. J. Leasor, pp. 37–8

92. See Spence (?) to Maj. P.C. Perfect, 19 May 1941; TNA KV 2/34 f. 3; and 'Report on the Collection of Drugs etc. belonging to the German Airman Prisoner, Capt. Horn', H.H. Duke, 27 May 1941; TNA FO 1093/10 f. 178

93. Report by O.C. 3rd Battalion ..., *op. cit.* ref. 85 above, p. 2: 'Copy of the inventory is attached to this report.'; Major James Barrie to O.C. 3rd Battalion Renfrewshire Home Guard, p. 4: 'handed over to him all the articles removed from the prisoner and obtained the accompanying receipt.'; Lt Whitby to O.C. 11th Battalion Cameronians: 'The Duty Officer took an inventory of the prisoner's effects ... a receipt for these was given to Maj. Barrie.'

94. Spence (?) to Maj. P.C. Perfect, 19 May 1941; TNA KV 2/34 f. 1

95. See 'An Observer's Diary'; ref. 51 above, pp. 157 ff; and letter Group Capt. C. Murray to author, 12 May 1991: 'a fellow officer was Flying Officer Malcolm. Malcolm was on leave at his house in Scotland after Hess landed very close by. As an RAF officer he was summoned to interview Hess ...'

96. City of Glasgow Police to Maj. P. Perfect, 17 May 1941: 'Mr Fairweather of Farside, Newton Mearns, Renfrewshire, a fluent German speaker ... was sent a request to act as interpreter but was ill in bed and forced to refuse. BATTAGLIA, who is a lodger with the Fairweather family ... offered his services ...'; TNA KV 2/34; alternatively Spence (?) to Major P. Perfect, 19 May 1941, p. 2: 'Col. Hardie thought it advisable to have an interpreter present. He telephoned to Roman Battaglia, a Pole employed in the Polish Consulate in Glasgow'; *ibid.*

97. Lt John Mair, 'The Interrogation of Rudolf Hess by Roman Battaglia'; TNA KV 2/35

98. *Ibid.*

99. Maj. Graham Donald to Scottish Area Commandant ROC, 11 May 1941, p. 2; TNA AIR 16/266; and see Commandant ROC to C.-in-C. Fighter Command, 18 May 1941; *ibid.*

100. I. Hess, *Schicksal*, pp. 89–90

101. Report by O.C. 3rd Battalion ...; *op. cit.* ref. 85 above, p. 2

102. Maj. Graham Donald to Sir Harry Greer, 19 May 1941, enclosing a piece of metal from Hess's Me 110; IWM Exhibit ref. 268/67

103. See ref. 99 above

104. Major Barrie to O.C. 3rd Battalian Home Guard Renfrewshire, 11 May 1941: 'I left Battalion Headquarters ... at 02.15'; TNA WO 199/3288A

105. *Ibid.*

106. *Ibid.*, p. 4

107. *Ibid.*

108. See p. 119

109. See p. 174

110. 'Report on Interview with Herr Hess by Wing Commander the Duke of Hamilton, Sunday, 11 May 1941'; TNA FO 1093/1
111. Mrs N.M. Goodall to author, 26 May, 12, 14 June 1991
112. See 'An Observer's Diary'; ref. 51 above, p. 157; D. Wood, p. 2; Sqdn LDr R.G. Woodman to author, 11 June 1991; R.C. Nesbit and G. v. Acker, p. 66
113. Mrs N.M. Goodall to author, 26 May 1991
114. Elizabeth Hamilton to author, 12 July 1992
115. Mrs N.M. Goodall to author, 26 May, 12, 14 June 1991
116. Elizabeth Hamilton to author, 12 July 1992
117. See p. 182 above; Major Barrie to O.C. 3rd Battalion; *op. cit.* ref. 104 above
118. J. Harris and D. Wilbourn, p. 228
119. 'Report on Interview ...'; *op. cit.* ref. 110 above
120. I. Hess; *Schicksal*, May–July 1947, p. 90
121. *Ibid.*, 9 May 1948, p. 179
122. See Duke of Hamilton to P.M.'s private office, 18 May 1941: 'As you know the Prime Minister saw some rough notes about my first meeting with Herr Hess. I now enclose a more detailed report compiled from these notes which I think the Prime Minister might like to see; TNA PREM 3 219/7, f. 137; and Mrs I. Pyne to author, 12 July 1992
123. 'Additional Notes on the Hess Incident by Group Captain the Duke of Hamilton'; TNA INF 1/912
124. Draft statement by W. Churchill, 13 (?) May 1941; TNA PREM 3 219/4
125. FO to Moscow, 4 Nov. 1942; TNA FO 371/30920, C10635/61/18
126. 'Additional Notes ...'; *op. cit.* ref. 123 above
127. Mrs I. Pyne to author, 12 July 1992
128. Elizabeth Hamilton to author, 12 July 1992
129. 'Additional Notes ...'; *op. cit.* ref. 123 above
130. Lord Sherfield (formerly R. Makins) to author, 7 Mar. 1991; and see J. Colville, p. 734
131. A. Cadogan's diary, Sun. 11 May 1941; Churchill College Archives Centre, Cambridge, ACAD 1/10

Chapter 11: Reactions

1. 11 May 1941; Colville diary (unpublished), vol. 4, p. 157, Churchill College Archive Centre, Cambridge, CLVL 1
2. *Ibid.*

3. 17–18 May 1941; *ibid.*, pp. 199–200. The 'red pocket diary' is not in the archive

4. 11 May 1941; *ibid.*, p. 196

5. J. Colville, p. 385

6. 11 May 1941; Colville diary, *op. cit.* ref. 1 above, p. 197

7. *Ibid.*, pp. 158, 197; J. Colville, p. 386

8. Colville diary; *op. cit.* ref. 1 above, p. 197

9. J. Colville, p. 387

10. 11 May 1941; Cadogan diary, *op. cit.* Chapter 10 ref. 131

11. J. Costello, pp. 416–7, citing Lawford's unpublished diary and Lawford interview

12. *The Times*, 14 May 1941, p. 5

13. J. Douglas-Hamilton, *Motive*, p. 178, citing account given in writing by Jock Colville, summer 1969

14. See M. Gilbert, *Finest Hour*, pp. 841, 900

15. See Martin Wood, 'The Queen of Chintz', *Telegraph Magazine*, 17 Sept. 2005, pp. 62–3

16. Ronald Tree, *When the Moon was High: Memoirs of Peace and War 1897–1942*, London, 1962, p. 130; cited J. Costello, p. 417

17. See pp. 168–9 above

18. See p. 189 above; Cadogan diary, 11 May 1941; *op. cit.* Chapter 10, ref. 131

19. 'Additional Notes ...'; *op. cit.* Chapter 10 ref. 123, p. 2

20. *Ibid.*

21. *Ibid.*

22. Cadogan diary, Mon, 12 May 1941; *op. cit.* Chapter 10 ref. 131

23. 'Additional Notes ...'; *op. cit.* Chapter 10 ref. 123, p. 3

24. *Ibid.*

25. See pp. 159–60 above

26. F. Halder, 15 May 1941, *Band 2*, pp. 413–4

27. See p. 147 above

28. Lippert's statement to W.R. Hess, 29 Feb. 1984; W.R. Hess, *My Father*, pp. 343–4, ref. 1

29. K.-H. Pintsch to James Leasor; J. Leasor, pp. 94–6

30. *Ibid.*, pp. 97–192

31. *Ibid.*, p. 102. This account corresponds with a statement Pintsch wrote in Soviet captivity in 1948: 'The Führer had known about Hess's flight for a while because Berlin had been negotiating with London for some time';

Jan Friedmann and Klaus Wiegrefe, 'Historian Uncovers New Account', *Spiegel* (online), 30 May 2011

32. Engel's diary, 11 May 1941; H. v. Ketz (ed.), *Heeresadjutant bei Hitler 1938–1943*, Stuttgart, 1974, pp. 103–41; cited R. Schmidt, p. 190

33. Bormann's *Notizkalendar*, 11 May 1941; Nat. Archives, Washington, T-84, EAP 105/18; cited R. Schmidt, p. 189

34. Engel's diary, 11 May 1941; *op. cit.* ref. 32 above

35. CSDIC (UK) G.G. Report, S.R.G.G 1236© 20.5.1945; TNA WO 208/4170; cited R. Schmidt, p. 189

36. See W. Schwarzwäller, p. 175

37. A. Speer, *Errinerungen*, p. 189

38. H. Linge (ed. W. Masur), *Bis zum Untergang: Als Chef des persönlichen Dienstes bei Hitler*, Munich/Berlin, 1980, pp. 141 f; cited R. Schmidt, pp. 186–7

39. H. Eberle and M. Uhl, p. xxvi

40. *Ibid.*, pp. 69–70

41. I. Hess, *Schicksal*, p. 78

42. See, for instance, I. Kershaw, *Nemesis*, pp. 371–7; and R. Schmidt, esp. pp. 187–90

43. Joachim Fest, *The Face of the Third Reich*, Harmondsworth, 1972, p. 292; cited I. Kershaw, *Nemesis*, p. 375

44. '*Rede Hans Franks über Wirkung des Englandflugs von Rudolf Hess*', IfZ (Munich) MA 120/5, Fol. 480: '*Der Führer war so vollkommen erschüttert, wie ich das eigentlich noch nicht erlebt habe.*'

45. G. Halder's Journal, p. 388; cited J. Costello, p. 422

46. N. v. Below, *Als Hitlers Adjutant 1937–1945*, Mainz, 1980, pp. 273–4; IfZ ED 100 *Hewel Tagebuch*, Irving *Sammlung, 12 Mai 1941*: '*Der Führer entschliest sich zur Veröffentlichen. Passus, dass es sich um eine Wahnsinntat handelt, wurd von F*[ührer] *durchgesetzt*'; cited I. Kershaw, *Nemesis*, p. 938, ref. 190

47. *Deutschlandsender*, 12 May 1941, 20.00; BBC Written Archives Centre, Reading; and TNA INF 1/192

48. Martha Haushofer diary, 11 May 1941; H.-A. Jacobsen, p. 509

49. IMT doc. Ps-1671; Bundesarchiv Koblenz HC 833

50. W. Stubbe, p. 251

51. See U. Laack-Michel, p. 233

52. See pp. 168–9 above

53. 13 May 1941; E. Fröhlich, *Teil I, Band 4*, pp. 638–9

54. BBC Written Archives Centre, Reading
55. I. Kirkpatrick, 'Record of an Interview with Herr Hess on May 13 1941'; IMT vol. 38, p. 177, doc. 117-M
56. 'Additional Notes ...'; *op. cit.* Chapter 10 ref. 123
57. I. Kirkpatrick, *op. cit.* ref. 55 above
58. *Ibid.*, pp. 179–80
59. *Ibid.*, p. 180
60. A. Cadogan (untitled) Report to P.M., 13 May 1941, p. 2; TNA PREM 3 219/7, f. 172
61. Mrs I. Pyne to author, 12 July 1992
62. See *The Times*, 12 June 1992
63. Sqdn Ldr F. Day to author, 16 June 1992, 15 May 2001: 'The Air Force officer had lots of medals and gold braid on his cap; the gold braid particularly struck me.'
64. See C.F. Innes, *Craigiehall: The Story of a fine Scots Country House*, 1966, p. 76
65. Scott Newton, *Profits of Peace*, p. 83
66. Peter Millar, 'The Other Prince', *The Sunday Times* (News Review), 26 Jan. 2003, p. 2
67. See p. 128 above
68. L. Picknett, C. Prince, S. Prior, p. 269
69. *Ibid.*, pp. 268–9
70. Roy Nesbit to author, 17 Sept. 2012; and J. Harris and R. Wilbourn, pp. 27–8; R. Williams to author, 3 Oct. 2012, states, 'An airfield lighting system for night landings was developed at RAF Drem in 1940, and was so successful ... it became the basis for all subsequent RAF airfield lighting.' Williams points out that RAF Drem was Hamilton's 602 Squadron base before he moved to Turnhouse, thus it seems very possible that he had the system installed on his landing strip at Dungavel.
71. L. Picknett, C. Prince, S. Prior, p. 285
72. See J. Harris and D. Wilbourn, *Illusion of Peace*, p. 69
73. Peter Millar; *op. cit.* ref. 66 above, p. 2
74. I. Kirkpatrick; *op. cit.* ref. 55 above, p. 181
75. 'Additional Notes'; *op. cit* Chapter 10 ref. 123, p. 4
76. I. Kirkpatrick; *op. cit.* ref. 55 above, p. 182
77. Col. Duke to Undersecretary of State War Office, 15 May 1941; TNA WO 199/3288A
78. R. Grenfell, p. 252

Chapter 12: Conflicting statements

1. 13 May 1941, 10.30, Bremen, in English; IWM BBC flash form
2. 14 May 1941 ('Yesterday'); E. Fröhlich, *Teil 1, Band 4*, pp. 639–40
3. *Deutschlandsender*, 13 May 1941, 14.00; IWM (Duxford) Box A 216
4. Bremen, 13 May 1941, 16.30, in English; IWM BBC flash form
5. *Deutschlandsender*, 13 May 1941, 19.45; IWM (Duxford) Box A 216
6. *Ibid.*
7. See R. Schmidt, p. 199
8. Unknown signature to *Hauptbefehlshaber* Saupert, 2 Dec. 1941, '*Anschluss aus der NSDAP Pg Franz von Pfeffer am 24 Nov. 1941*'; Berlin Document Center
9. See R. Schmidt, pp. 199–200
10. See R. Heydrich to *Reichsführer*, 15 May 1941, telegram 2020; Bundesarchiv Koblenz NS 19/3872
11. See R. Schmidt, p. 202
12. *Reichsführer-SS* to Ilse Hess, 29 Apr. 1943; cited H. Heiber, p. 211: '*Die Entscheidung in der Sache Ihres Hauses von Seiten des Führers ist eine ganz klare. Sie sollen das Haus in Harlaching behalten ...*'
13. 14 May 1941; E. Fröhlich, *Teil 1, Band 4*, p. 640
14. Cadogan's diary, Monday 12 May 1941; Churchill College Archives Centre, Cambridge ACAD 1/10
15. See p. 185 above
16. Cadogan's diary, Monday 12 May 1941; *op. cit.* ref. 14 above
17. 14 May 1941, 13.55, Berlin; TNA PREM 3 219/4, f. 12
18. Cadogan's diary, Wednesday 14 May 1941; *op. cit.* ref. 14 above
19. 10 Downing Street, typed: TNA PREM 3 219/4, ff. 16–17
20. *Ibid.*, f. 15
21. Cadogan's diary, Wednesday 14 May 1941; *op. cit.* ref. 14 above
22. *Op. cit.* ref. 19 above, f. 7
23. See pp. 207–9 above
24. President to Former Naval Person, 15 May 1941; TNA PREM 3 219/7, f. 197
25. I. Kirkpatrick, 'Record of an Interview with Herr Hess', 15 May 1941; IMT vol. 38, doc. 119-M, pp. 183–4
26. *Ibid.*
27. International Committee of the Red Cross, Geneva, to the authors of *Double Standards*, 28 July 2000, Picknett, Prince, Prior, p. 306
28. ORB RAF Turnhouse, appendices, 15 May 1941; TNA AIR 28/864

29. Cadogan's diary, 15 May 1941; *op. cit.* ref. 14 above
30. W. Monckton to Duff Cooper, 27 May 1941; Ian Sayer archive
31. W. Armstrong, p. 129
32. Duff Cooper to P.M., 16 May 1941; TNA INF 1/912; and see TNA FO 371/26565, C5562/5188/18
33. A. Cadogan 'Most Secret' circular to Berne, Madrid etc., 17 May 1941; TNA FO 371/26565, C5421/5188/18
34. *Ibid.*
35. P.M.'s personal minute to Foreign Sec., M 540/1, 13 May 1941; TNA PREM 3 219/7, f. 167
36. Robert Shaw to Stephen McGinty; cited in 'Flight to Nowhere', *The Sunday Times*, 11 Apr. 1999
37. Hamilton to J.M. Martin, Air Ministry, 18 May 1941; TNA PREM 3 219/7, f. 137; and J.M. Martin to W.I. Mallet, 10 Downing Street, 18 May 1941; TNA FO 1093/11, f. 107
38. Letter dated 15 May 1941; TNA INF 1/192
39. Maj. Sheppard, 'My Impressions of X', 21 May 1941; TNA PREM 3 219/7, f. 144
40. Maj. Sheppard, 'Report on the Conduct of X', 17 May 1941; *ibid.*, f. 147
41. Col. R.A. Lennie, C.O. Military Hospital, 'Special Report – Prisoner of War – No. 3', 17 May 1941; TNA WO 199/3288A
42. 'Helping Hess', *The Daily Telegraph*, 15 Oct. 2009
43. See, for instance, *The Herald*, Glasgow, 2 Feb. 2009
44. Guy Liddell's diary, 13 May 1941; N. West, pp. 146–7
45. Report signed T.A. Robertson, 13 May 1941; TNA KV 2/34; T.A. Robertson to author, 2 Oct. 1992
46. See Maj. P. Perfect to A.S. MacIver, 17 May 1941; TNA KV 2/34
47. Buyers to Spence (?), 19 May 1941; *ibid.*
48. Spence (?) to Major P. Perfect, 19 May 1941; *ibid.*
49. Cited John Harris, 'Witness'; *BBC History Magazine*, May 2001, p. 53
50. See pp. 187–9 above
51. See pp. 179–80, 182
52. John Howell in conversation and letters to the author, 19 Feb.–10 July 1992
53. R. Kempner, *Das Dritte Reich im Kreuzverhör: Aus den Vernehmungsprotokollen des Anklägers*, Athenäum/Droste, 1980, pp. 104 ff; cited A. Seidl, p. 70
54. A. Seidl, pp. 70–1

55. H. Bohle's testimony, 10 July 1945; TNA KV 2/38
56. E.W. Bohle interrogation by Col. H.A. Brundage, 11 Sept. 1945, p. 2; IWM FO 645, Box 155
57. H. Bohle's testimony; *op. cit.* ref. 55 above
58. See pp. 153–5 above
59. Beaverbrook to J. Leasor, 20 Feb. 1961; Beaverbrook Papers, House of Lords Record Office, C/216
60. Beaverbrook to J. Leasor, 13 Feb. 1961; *ibid.*
61. Lawrence Burgis (Assistant to Deputy Secretary to the War Cabinet) docket, 15 May 1941, p. 2; Lawrence Burgis Papers, Churchill College Archives Centre, Cambridge, BRGS 2/4
62. *Ibid.*, p. 4
63. MI6 Political Report No. 225, 19 May 1941; TNA WO 208/4471
64. Lord Vansittart, *Black Record*, p. 43
65. *Ibid.*, p. 45

Chapter 13: Negotiations?

1. Received 5 June 1941; TNA FO 371/26542, C6049/324/18
2. Enclosed in *ibid.*
3. See Dill Papers, King's College London, 3/2/7
4. See pp. 138–9 above
5. See Hoare, Madrid, Nos. 320, 321, 20 Feb. 1941; TNA FO 371/26939, C1713/222/41; Hoare, Madrid, No. 631, 23 Apr. 1941; TNA FO 371/26905, C4161/46/41
6. See p. 138 above
7. See pp. 133–5 above
8. See pp. 141–3 above
9. See p. 142 above
10. See p. 139 above
11. Hoare, Madrid, No. 641, 25 Apr. 1941; TNA FO 371/26945, C4245/306/41; Hoare, Madrid, No. 148, 25 Apr. 1941; *ibid.*, C4613/306/41
12. 'Questions in Parliament'; *The Times*, 23 Apr. 1941
13. 16 May 1941; TNA PREM 3 219/7, f. 146
14. See pp. 226–8 above
15. Cadogan's diary, 19 May 1941; Churchill Archives Centre, Cambridge, ACAD 1/10
16. *Ibid.*

17. See A. Kramish, pp. 97, 200–1
18. See pp. 111, 132 above
19. See K. Jeffery, p. 301
20. See S. McGinty, p. 8
21. See Col. Scott's diary, 'Camp Z'. 7 July 1941; IWM 69/66/1; G. Liddell's diary, 9 June, 3 July 1941; N. West, pp. 153, 158; Gen. A. Hunter to H. Hopkinson, 5 July 1941; TNA F0 1093/12, f. 190; Michael Evans, 'Poles plotted to kidnap and beat up Hess', *Daily Telegraph*, 3 July 1992
22. Col. N. Coates to Col. A.M. Scott, 18 May 1941; Col. Scott's diary; *op. cit.* ref. 21 above
23. 'he was convinced he was surrounded by the sinister forces of the secret service, who desired his death ...', Col. G. Graham, 'Memorandum on Rudolf Hess'; TNA FO 1093/11, f. 74
24. R. Hess to Hamilton, '*Persönlich, Dem Herzog von Hamilton*', London, 19 May 1941; TNA FO 1093/11, ff. 64–8
25. Cadogan memo., 25 May 1941, initialled 'A.E.'; *ibid.*, f. 69
26. Col. Scott's diary, 20 May 1941; *op. cit.* ref. 21 above
27. *Ibid.*, 21 May 1941; and see D. Irving, *Hess*, p. 105
28. See S. McGinty, pp. 14–16
29. Col. Scott's diary, 24 May 1941; *op. cit.* ref. 21 above
30. Lt W.B. Malone diary, 28 May 1941; *The Observer*, London, Sept. 1987, cited D. Irving, *Hess*, p. 110
31. Col. Scott's diary, 24 May 1941; *op. cit.* ref. 21 above
32. Lt W.B. Malone's diary, 28 May 1941; *op. cit.* ref. 30 above
33. Translation of Deposition handed to Lt Loftus; Col. Scott's diary, 1 Aug. 1941; *op. cit.* ref. 21 above
34. See D. Popov, p. 240; and G. Thomas, pp. 74 f
35. Lord Beaverbrook believed this, according to Robert Bruce Lockhart, head of Foreign Office political intelligence dept., who after talking about Hess with him, wrote in his diary, 'Max thinks he [Hess] was probably given some kind of drugs by our people to make him talk'; *The Diaries of Sir Robert Bruce Lockhart, vol. II; 1939–1945*, London, 1984, cited D. Irving, *Hess*, p. 197 note
36. R. Hess to Ilse Hess, 8 Jan. 1948; I. Hess, *Schicksal*, p. 166
37. Lt W.B. Malone, 'Report on last night's incidents'; Col. Scott's diary, 29 May 1941; *op. cit.* ref. 21 above
38. *Ibid.*
39. Col. Scott's diary, 29 May 1941; *op. cit.* ref. 21 above

40. Col. G. Graham, 'Memorandum on Herr Rudolf Hess'; TNA FO 1093/11, f. 73
41. *Ibid.*, f. 76
42. J. Leasor to *The Times*, 20 Aug. 1987
43. Col. Scott's diary, 29 May 1941; *op. cit.* ref. 21 above
44. *Luton Herald*, 8 Feb. 1979
45. G. Liddell's diary, 28 May 1941, vol. 3, p. 919; TNA KV 4/187
46. *Ibid.*, 27 May 1941
47. *Ibid.*, 28 May 1941
48. *Luton Herald*, 8 Feb. 1979
49. See G. Liddell's diary; N. West, p. 315
50. *Luton Herald*, 8 Feb 1979
51. Lt Col. J. McCowen to author, 10 June 1990
52. N. West, p. 151 skips from 27 to 29 May 1941
53. See p. 162 above
54. J.R. Rees, 'Tentative Conclusions from my Interview', 31 May 1941; TNA FO 1093/10, f. 159
55. 'Report No. 16' unsigned (by F. Foley), 30 May 1941; TNA FO 1093/11, f. 85
56. *Ibid.*
57. R.A. Butler to A. Cadogan, 22 May 1941; Cadogan minute, 22 May 1941; *ibid.*, f. 90
58. A. Eden to Lord Simon, 28 May 1941; Simon Papers, Bodleian Library, Oxford, Box 88, f. 39
59. I. Kirkpatrick to Lord Simon, untitled, 29 May 1941; *ibid.*, ff. 47 ff
60. See, for instance, pp. 96, 142 above
61. R.H. Dicks, 'Preliminary Medical Notes on Herr Rudolf Hess', 9 June 1941; TNA FO 1093/10, ff. 98 ff
62. Col. Scott's diary, 9 June 1941; *op. cit.* ref. 21 above
63. 'Dr. Guthrie, Dr. Mackenzie and Jonathan ...', 9 June 1941, 14.30–17.30 hrs, transcript, copy No. 2; Simon Papers, Bodleian Library, Oxford, Box 88. All subsequent quotations from this source
64. H. Boberach, p. 2272
65. See pp. 244–5, 248–50, 253, 255, 259 above
66. IMT, Defence Document Book 'Rudolf Hess'; IWM FO 645/31, p. 150
67. See p. 104 above
68. These notes in TNA FO 1093/1, ff. 135–6

69. Lord Simon, 'Rudolf Hess – Preliminary Report' (m.s.), 10 June 1941; TNA FO 1093/1, ff. 2 ff; typed copy in PREM 3 219/7, f. 104

70. 'Dr. Guthrie, Dr. Mackenzie ...'; *op. cit.* ref. 63 above

71. See D. Irving, *Hess*, p. 135

72. Col. Scott's diary 'Camp Z', 9 June 1941, *op. cit.* ref. 21 above

73. 7 July 1941; TNA KV 2/37, f. 55c

74. M. Evans to G.M. Liddell, 25 July 1941; *ibid.*, f. 62a

75. 'Dr. Guthrie, Dr. Mackenzie ...'; *op. cit.* ref. 63 above, p. 70, f. 144

76. MI6 (illegible green ink signature) to Capt. Guy Liddell, 29 Aug. 1941; TNA KV 2/37, f. 66c

Chapter 14: The story leaks

1. 'Rudolf Hess – Preliminary Report', 10 June 1941; TNA FO 1093/1, ff. 2 ff; also PREM 3 219/7, ff. 103 ff

2. *Ibid.* (PREM 3 219/7), f. 104

3. 'To Sec. of State re. "Jonathan"', undated, unsigned minute in Cadogan's hand; TNA FO 1093/10, ff. 86–7

4. Prime Minister's 'Personal Minute' to Foreign Secretary, 14 June 1941; TNA PREM 3 219/5, f. 3

5. Col. Scott's diary, 14 June 1941; *op. cit.* Chapter 13, ref. 21

6. *Ibid.*, 15 June 1941

7. Lt W.B. Malone's report; in *ibid.*

8. R. Hess to A. Hitler, 14 June 1941; TNA FO 1093/1, ff. 47–50

9. *Ibid.*, f. 50

10. R. Hess to Ilse Hess, 14 June 1941; *ibid.*, f. 51

11. Erika Mann, 'Hess meeting in Spain was fixed'; *Glasgow Evening Citizen*, (date missing) 1945, Ian Sayer archive

12. R. Hess to '*Meinem Sohn*', 10–15 June 1941; TNA FO 1093/1, ff. 38–42

13. R. Hess, '*Aussergewöhnlich Zusammenkunft ...*', 9 June 1941; TNA FO 1093/1, f. 55

14. R. Hess, untitled note, 15 June 1941; TNA FO 1093/10, f. 78

15. Col. Scott's diary, 16 June 1941, p. 24; *op. cit.* Chapter 13, ref. 21; Lt J. McI. Young's account in *ibid.*; Maj. Dicks' account in J.R. Rees, pp. 47–8

16. Maj. Dicks' account in *ibid.*, p. 48

17. Lt W.B. Malone's report, 16 June 1941, in Col. Scott's diary, pp. 26–8; *op. cit.* Chapter 13, ref. 21

18. Col. J.R. Rees to Col. Coates, 19 June 1941; TNA PREM 3 219/3, f. 15

19. See p. 256 above

20. Mallett to FO (wire), 9 June 1941; cited D. Irving, *Hess*, pp. 136, 352; and see I. Kershaw, *Nemesis*, p. 379

21. Maj. Dicks; cited D. Irving, *Hess*, p. 150

22. 22 June 1941; E. Fröhlich, *Teil 1, Band 4*, p. 710

23. *Hansard*, 19 June 1941, pp. 886 ff.

24. Cited D. Day, p. 184

25. *Hansard*, 19 June 1941, pp. 900–1

26. See J. Harris and M.J. Trow, p. 124

27. K. Young, p. 98

28. See S. McGinty, p. 187

29. Lt M. Loftus, 'Report on Conversation with Z', 17 July 1941; Col. Scott's diary, *op. cit.*, Chapter 13, ref. 21

30. *Ibid.*

31. Col. Scott's diary, 20 July 1941; *op. cit.* Chapter 13, ref. 21

32. *Ibid.*, 27 July 1941

33. 'Copy of Translation of Deposition by Z handed to 2nd Lt Loftus'; 1 Aug. 1941; *ibid.*

34. R. Hess, '*Deutschland–England unter dem Gesichtswinkel des Krieges gegen die Sowjet-Union*', '*Beaverbrook übergeben* [handed to Beaverbrook] *9 Sept 1941*'; Beaverbrook Papers, House of Lords Record Office, D/443; English translation in Col. Scott's diary, 7 Aug. 1941; also in TNA FO 1093/12, ff. 115–26

35. 'C' to Maj. F. Foley, 11 Aug. 1941; TNA FO 1093/12, f. 127

36. F. Foley to 'C', 12 Aug. 1941; *ibid.*, f. 131

37. *Ibid.*

38. Lt M.P.M. Loftus memo., undated; *ibid.*, ff. 128–9

39. K. de Courcy, *Special Office Brief*, 6 June 1984; and *Special Office Brief Extra*, 1 Mar. 1989; K. de Courcy to Anthony Pilcher (son of Col. W.S. Pilcher), 10 Nov. 1986; Jeremy Pilcher (son of Col. W.S. Pilcher) to Duc de Grantmesnil (K. de Courcy), 20 May 1986; K. de Courcy to author, 16 Apr. 1989, 26 Apr. 1990

40. See TNA DPP 2/1056

41. 25 Nov. 1942; TNA DPP 2/1056

42. *Ibid.*

43. G.M. Liddell to Brig. S.C. Menzies, 4 Dec. 1942; TNA KV 2/37, f. 128A

44. Richard Ford, 'Nazi fraudster wins a reprieve from the grave', *The Times*, 15 Mar. 2001. The present author comments, de Courcy was no Nazi.

45. Duc de Grantmesnil-Lorraine (K. de Courcy), 'Confidential memo. on Col. W.S. Pilcher'; author's collection; Grantmesnil, 'The Hess Story', *Special Office Brief*, 6 June 1984

46. See R. Perry, pp. 36–7, 44–5

47. K. de Courcy to author, 26 Apr. 1990

48. M. Riley and S. Dorrill, p. 3

49. R. Perry, *passim*

50. See obituary Lord Rothschild, Alan Hodgkin, *The Independent*, 22 Mar. 1990; and R. Perry, pp. 78, 88

51. See R. Perry, pp. 91–3

52. Guy Liddell's diary, 21 Apr. 1940; N. West, p. 77

53. 2 Mar. 1940; *ibid.* p. 70

54. Grantmesnil (K. de Courcy) note, 2 Aug. 1984, attached to note from Lord Newall, July 1984; author's collection

55. Grantmesnil (K. de Courcy), 'Confidential memo. on Col. W.S. Pilcher' 19 June 1981; author's collection; and Grantmesnil to Anthony Pilcher, 10 Nov. 1986

56. Grantmesnil (K. de Courcy) to author, 26 Apr. 1990

57. M. Riley and S. Dorrill, p. 3

58. Grantmesnil (K. de Courcy), 'The Hess story: the background'; *Special Office Brief*, No. 249 (new series), 8 June 1984

59. *Ibid.*

60. Grantmesnil (K. de Courcy), 'Confidential memo ...'; *op. cit.* ref. 45 above

61. See pp. 109, 135 above

62. See pp. 227–8 above

63. Grantmesnil (K. de Courcy), m.s. draft for *Special Office Brief*, 1 Mar. 1989; author's collection

Chapter 15: The 'final solution'

1. See pp. 57, 146 above

2. Cited M. Gilbert, *Holocaust*, p. 152

3. Schellenberg circular, 10a Js 39/60, p. 239; *Landgericht München II*; cited G. Fleming, pp. 44–5

4. Note by the Prime Minister, 'Syrian Policy', 19 May 1941; cited M. Gilbert, *Finest Hour*, p. 1090

5. See R. Breitman, esp. pp. 35–42

6. 20 June 1941; E. Fröhlich, *Teil 1, Band 4*, p. 705

7. Lt W. Malone's report, 13/14 July 1941; Col. Scott's diary, *op. cit.* Chapter 13, ref. 21, p. 44

8. See S. McGinty, pp. 183–4

9. Col. Scott's diary, 11 Aug. 1941, p. 92; *op. cit.* Chapter 13, ref. 21, p. 92

10. Typed memo. signed F.F., 16 Aug. 1941: TNA FO 1093/12, f. 130

11. Report from Stephen Laird, 16 Aug. 1941; *ibid.* ff. 111–3

12. F.H. Hinsley, p. 671

13. Cited R. Breitman, p. 93

14. *Ibid.*, p. 94

15. F.H. Hinsley, p. 671

16. Summary of Police Decodes 324–343 (3 July–14 Aug. 1941); TNA HW 16/6, part 1; cited R. Breitman, p. 96

17. David Cesarini, 'Secret Churchill Papers Released', *The Journal of Holocaust Education 4*, No. 2 (1995), p. 226; cited *ibid.*

18. Col. Scott's diary, 21 Aug 1941, p. 95; *op. cit.* Chapter 13, ref. 21

19. Lord Beaverbrook to Hess, 1 Sept 1941; Beaverbrook Papers, House of Lords Record Office, D443

20. R. Hess to Beaverbrook, 4 Sept. 1941; *ibid.*

21. Col. Scott's diary, 2 Sept. 1941, p. 101; *op. cit.* Chapter 13, ref. 21; and see 5 Sept. 1941, *ibid.*, p. 102

22. *Ibid.*, 8 Sept. 1941, p. 103

23. Transcript 'Dr. Livingstone and Jonathan' 9 Sept. 1941, 19.30 hrs, p. 1; Beaverbrook Papers, House of Lords Record Office, D443

24. *Ibid.*, pp. 4–5

25. R. Hess, '*Deutschland–England ...*'; *op. cit.* Chapter 14, ref. 34

26. 'Dr. Livingstone and Jonathan'; *op. cit.*, ref. 23 above, p. 8

27. Col. Scott's diary, 9 Sept. 1941; *op. cit.* Chapter 13, ref. 21, p. 103

28. Bruce Lockhart's diary, 4 Sept. 1943; K. Young, p. 256; see also Beaverbrook to J. Leasor, 20 Feb. 1961; Beaverbrook Papers, *op. cit.* ref. 19 above

29. J. Leasor to author, 22 June 1990

30. See Sir S. Cripps (Moscow) to FO, No. 502, 13 May 1941; TNA FO 1093/11, ff. 146–7

31. Vadim to Moscow, No. 376, 14 May 1941; NKVD file No. 20566 'Black Bertha', released to Press June 1990

32. *Ibid.*, No. 338, 18 May 1941

33. Reports from agents 'GIT', 'JUN', 'FRANKFURTER', 'EXTERN' from *ibid.*; cited J. Costello, pp. 437, 577

34. 'ANGLETERRE Affaire Hess', No. 398/B, 5 Sept. 1941; cited J. Costello, pp. 452–3, 581

35. *Evening Standard*, 15 Sept. 1959; cited J. Leasor to Lord Beaverbrook; Beaverbrook Papers, ref. 19 above

36. Lord Beaverbrook to J. Leasor, 20 May 1961; *ibid.*

37. Raymond Lee to Brig. Gen. Sherman Miles, 5 Nov. 1941; Nat. Archives, Washington, B8 026020; and see J. Leutze, pp. 437, 441–2

38. *Ibid.*, p. 2

39. See p. 244 above

40. H. Hopkinson memo., 10 June 1941; TNA FO 1093/10, f. 94

41. Raymond Lee to Sherman Miles; *op. cit.* ref. 37 above, p. 7

42. *Ibid.*

43. *Ibid.*, p. 4

44. See J. Costello, pp. 447–8, 550

45. See pp. 269, 273 above

46. See Jock Colville's account pp. 191 ff above; and see Raymond E. Lee's account in J. Leutze, pp. 270–4

47. R. Heydrich to *Reichsaussenminister*, 4 May 1942; F & CO 434005

48. Annex, pp. 1–2; *ibid.*, 434006-7

49. pp. 4–5; *ibid.*, 434009-10

50. W. Schellenberg, pp. 200–2

51. W. Schellenberg to *Unterstaatssekretär* [*Auswärtigen*], 10 Aug. 1942; F & CO 434016-7

52. See Luther to von Rintelen, 27 June 1942; *ibid.*, 434013

53. See Ilse Hess to *RFSS* (*Reichsführer-SS* – Himmler), 16 May 1943; Nat. Archives, Washington, T-175, Roll 65, ff. 2581214-5; and see letter (signature indecipherable) from *Reichssicherheitshauptamt* to *SS-Obersturmbannführer* Brandt, 3 Aug. 1943; IWM H/28/431

54. See A. Kramish, pp. 81–7

55. Col. Scott's diary, 19 Nov. 1941; *op. cit.* Chapter 13, ref. 21, p. 125

56. A. Kramish, pp. 126–9

57. See, for instance, medical orderly's report, 2 Sept. 1941; cited D. Irving, *Hess*, p. 17

58. Col. Scott's diary, 4 Dec. 1941; *op. cit.* Chapter 13, ref. 21, p. 132

59. R. Hess statement at Nuremberg IMT; cited J.R. Rees, pp. 96 ff

60. See p. 222 above

61. See Dominions' Office to Dominion Governments, 5 Nov. 1942; TNA FO 371/30920, f. 219; and A. Eden to Sir A. Clark Kerr, 22 Oct. 1942; TNA PREM 3 319/6, f. 39

62. NKVD rezident London to Moscow, N.450, 21 Oct. 1942; file No. 20566 'Black Bertha', NKVD Archives, Moscow

63. *Ibid.*

64. Cited R. Schmidt, pp. 148, 319

65. See p. 284 above

66. Sir A. Clark Kerr to FO, No. 281, 25 Oct 1942; TNA PREM 3 219/6, f. 34

67. *Ibid.*, No. 280, f. 33

68. Memorandum by the Lord Privy Seal, 'The facts about Rudolf Hess', printed for the War Cabinet, W.P.(42)502, 2 Nov. 1942; TNA FO 371/30920, ff. 263 ff

69. FO to Moscow, No. 332, 4 Nov. 1942; *ibid.*, ff. 217–8

70. See pp. 226 ff above

71. See p. 274 above

72. See p. 234 above

73. See pp. 207, 223 above

74. Sir A. Clark Kerr to FO; *op. cit.* ref. 66 above

Chapter 16: The real story?

1. Anonymous, *American Mercury,* May 1943; reprinted in *The Journal of Historical Review*, Autumn 1982, pp. 291–99

2. *Ibid.*, p. 295

3. Ernst W. Bohle interrogation, 26 Sept. 1945; IWM FO 645 Box 185, pp. 6–7, 10–11; and see p. 298 above

4. See pp. 121 ff above

5. Karl Haushofer interrogation, 5 Oct. 1945; IWM FO 645 Box 155, p. 15

6. *Ibid.*

7. J. Friedmann and Klaus Wiegrefe, 'Historian Uncovers New Account', *Spiegel* (online), 30 May 2011; and see Matthew Day, 'Hitler knew of Hess's 1941 peace flight to Britain ...', *The Daily Telegraph*, 1 June 2011

8. See *The Times*, 5 Oct. 1942; and Mallet (Stockholm) to FO, 23 Oct. 1942, No. 779; TNA FO 371/30941

9. Translation in *ibid.*

10. *Ibid.*

11. *Journal of Historical Review, op. cit.* ref. 1 above, pp. 294, 296

12. See p. 209 above

13. *Journal of Historical Review*, *op. cit.*, ref. 1 above, p. 297

14. *Ibid.*, p. 292

15. See *The Scotsman*, 23 Sept. 1943; and W.R. Hess, *My Father*, p. 186; and TNA INF 1/912, ff. 76–9

16. Guy Ramsay, 'The Daily Life of Hess in Prison Camp', *Daily Mail*, 1 Sept 1943

17. See D. Irving, *Hess*, pp. 238 ff

18. See draft wire to Washington, 3 Sept. 1943; TNA INF 1/912, f. 75

19. Eden's statement in the Commons; *The Times*, 23 Sept 1943

20. *Ibid.*

21. See pp. 302–3 above

22. See pp. 227 ff above

23. 'Record of talks at the Kremlin at supper, 18 Oct. 1944' compiled (from memory) by Sir A. Clark Kerr and Mr Birse; TNA PREM 3 434/7

24. BCS (?) to J.M. Martin, 6 Apr. 1945; TNA INF 1/912, f. 80

25. *Ibid.*, f. 81

26. *Ibid.*, ff. 83–6

27. 'Additional Notes ...' *op. cit.* Chapter 10, ref. 123

28. Prime Minister's personal minute to Sec. of State for Air, 7 Apr. 1945; TNA INF 1/912, f. 97

29. R. Hess to Ilse Hess, 8 Jan 1948; I. Hess, *Schicksal*, p. 166

30. P. Bloom re. Walter Fenton, *Deben Journal*, Suffolk, 5 Dec. 1985

31. See D. Irving, *Hess*, p. 244

32. R. Hess to Ilse Hess, 10 Mar. 1947; I. Hess, *Schicksal*, p. 123

33. *Ibid.*

34. Cited J.R. Rees, p. 114

35. Cited A. Bullock, p. 226

36. R. Hess to Ilse Hess, 18 June 1945; I. Hess, *Schicksal*, p. 102

37. D. Kelley, pp. 22–3

38. *Ibid.*, p. 23

39. Testimony of Rudolf Hess, 9 Oct. 1945; IWM FO 645 Box 155

40. *Ibid.*

41. *Ibid.*

42. *Ibid.*

43. K. Haushofer to Max Hofweber, 14 Nov. 1945; H.-A. Jacobsen, *Band* 2, p. 442

44. Dr J. Delay and others, 20 Nov. 1945; Prosecution Document File, IWM FO 645 Box 151

45. W. Shirer, *End of*, p. 293
46. T. Taylor, pp. 177–8
47. G. Gilbert, pp. 29–30
48. *Ibid.*
49. *Ibid.*
50. IMT vol. 2, p. 447
51. 30 Nov. 1945; *ibid.*, pp. 479 ff
52. B.C. Andrus, *The Infamous of Nuremberg*, 1969; cited J. Douglas-Hamilton, *Motive*, p. 276
53. G. Gilbert, p. 36; and see E. Bird, p. 57
54. IMT vol. 22, pp. 368–73
55. R. Hess to Ilse Hess, 25 Jan. 1946; I. Hess, *Schicksal*, p. 104
56. IMT 3245-PS; quotation from IMT vol. 7, p. 136
57. Lt Col. William H. Dunn, 'Report on present mental state of Rudolf Hess'; Medical Reports File, Quinlan Papers, IWM FO 645, Box 455; and see D. Kelley, p. 30
58. R. Hess to Ilse Hess, 31 Aug. 1946; I. Hess, *Schicksal*, p. 110
59. See A. Seidl, pp. 11 ff; see D. Irving, *Hess*, p. 329
60. IMT vol. 22, pp. 368–73
61. Judgement, 30 Sept. 1946; IMT vol. 22, pp. 487–9
62. Sentence, 1 Oct. 1946; *ibid.*, p. 529
63. *Ibid.*
64. G. Gilbert, p. 272
65. I.T. Nikitchenko, 'Concerning the sentence on the defendant, Rudolf Hess', in 'Dissenting Opinion of the Soviet Member of the International Military Tribunal', IMT vol. 22, pp. 540–1

Chapter 17: Spandau

1. A. Speer, *Spandau*, pp. 71–2
2. Cited E. Bird, p. 70
3. Cited *ibid.*, p. 69
4. Pastor Casalis to Prison Directorate, Apr. 1950; cited W.R. Hess, *My Father*, pp. 264 ff
5. R. Hess to Ilse Hess, 5 Oct. 1947; I. Hess, *Schicksal*, p. 158
6. A. Speer, *Spandau*, p. 124
7. R. Hess to Ilse Hess, 13 Oct. 1946; I. Hess, *Schicksal*, p. 118
8. R. Hess to Ilse Hess, 26 Sept. 1946; *ibid.*, p. 113

9. A. Speer, *Spandau*, p. 147: 'I wonder what is prompting Hess to come out with all these old crazy tricks again.'

10. *Ibid.*, p. 400; and see p. 429

11. *Ibid.*, p. 196

12. *Ibid.*, p. 270

13. E. Bird, p. 137

14. A. Speer, *Spandau,* p. 343

15. *Ibid.* p. 442

16. See E. Bird, p. 164

17. See *ibid.*, p. 237; and C.A. Gabel, p. 172

18. But see T. Le Tissier, p. 56: 'A summary made from F & CO records shows that there were a total of 27 Allied appeals to the Soviet authorities, and that the British government participated in all but three of them. The UK was alone among the Western Allies in appealing at Ministerial level, and did so routinely from 1970 on 13 separate occasions.'

19. See E. Bird, pp. 152–3

20. A. Speer, *Spandau*; *Erinnerungen*

21. C.A. Gabel, p. 239, 7 Sept. 1983

22. E. Bird, pp. 225–6

23. *Ibid.*, p. 226

24. *Ibid.*, p. 275

25. *Ibid.*, pp. 10–11, 222

26. *Ibid.*, p. 12

27. *Ibid.*, pp. 171–2

28. *Ibid.*, pp. 173–4

29. *Ibid.*, pp. 194 ff

30. W.R. Hess, *My Father*, p. 286

31. E. Bird, p. 252

32. *Ibid.*, pp. 264–5

33. *Ibid.*, p. 265

34. *Ibid.*, pp. 280–1

35. Desmond Zwar to author, 12 Mar. 2012

36. See C.A. Gabel, p. 22

37. E. Bird, p. 223

38. C.A. Gabel, p. 73

39. *Ibid.*, p. 151

40. See, for instance, *ibid.*, pp. 59, 90, 197, 254–5, 290

41. *Ibid.*, p. 59, 14 Feb. 1979

42. *Ibid.*, pp. 290–1, 3 Oct. 1984
43. E. Bird, p. 276
44. C.A. Gabel, p. 351
45. *Ibid.*, p. 174
46. A. Melaouhi, *Rudolf Hess*, pp. 101–2
47. C.A. Gabel, p. 394

Chapter 18: Final audit

1. Eden's statement, *The Times*, 23 Sept. 1943
2. E. Bird, p. 252
3. TNA FO 1093/1
4. S. McGinty, pp. 14–16
5. Col. Scott's diary, 'Camp Z', 29 May 1941; *op. cit.* Chapter 13, ref. 21
6. 'Dr. Guthrie and Jonathan', transcript 9 June 1941; Bodleian Lib., Oxford, Box 88, ff. 53 f
7. Col. Scott's diary, 'Camp Z', 1 Aug. 1941; *op. cit.* Chapter 13, ref. 21
8. Von Bechtold statement, 30 Apr. 1946; Nat. Archives, Washington, RG 238 Box 180; cited D. Irving, *Hess*, p. 64
9. R. Hess, '*Aussergewöhnlich Zusammenkunft ...*', 9 June 1941; TNA FO 1093/1, f. 55
10. Hamilton's diary 1941; 20 Jan. 'Duke of Kent. Lunch'; 23 Jan. 'Duke of Kent. Prestwick'; cited Picknett, Prince, Prior, p. 282
11. See p. 112 above; TNA FO 371 26542, C1687 (released Nov. 2007)
12. TNA KV 2/1684, Doc. 45A
13. 'Rudolf Hess – Preliminary Report', 10 June 1941; TNA FO 1093/1, ff. 2 ff
14. Lt Loftus report, 'Conversation with Z'; Col. Scott's diary, 'Camp Z', 17 July 1941; *op. cit.* Chapter 13, ref. 21
15. L. Picknett, C. Prince, S. Prior, p. 269
16. Sqdn LDr F. Day to author, 11 June 1992, 15 May 2001
17. R. Williams to author, 7 Oct. 2009, 1 Oct. 2011
18. See TNA KV 3/277
19. Hitler and Mussolini had used 'social credit' principles to turn round their devastated economies; R. Williams to author, 1 Oct. 2011
20. Duke of Bedford to R.R. Stokes, 10 May 1941; copy sent to Lloyd George by Stokes 5 June 1941; Lloyd George Papers, G/19/3/26, House of Lords Record Office; cited D. Day, p. 184
21. Letter dated 15 May; TNA INF 1/912
22. *The Yorkshire Post*, 4 Nov. 1969

23. Ronald Tree, *When the Moon was High: Memoirs of Peace and War 1897–1942*, London, 1962, p. 130; cited J. Costello, p. 417

24. J. Douglas to author, 13 May 1991

25. Mrs N.-H. Goodall to author, 26 May, 12, 14 June 1991

26. *Hong Kong Telegraph*, 6 Mar. 1947; cited Picknett, Prince, Prior, p. 199

27. See pp. 174–5 above

28. See pp. 177–8, 183–4 above; Duty Officer Clyde Sub-Area Report night 10th May 1941; TNA WO 199/3288A

29. See pp. 177–8 above

30. See pp. 191–4 above

31. *Deutschlandsender* 14.00, 13 May 1941; IWM (Duxford) Box A 216

32. Cited R. Schmidt, pp. 148, 319

33. Cited J. Costello, pp. 452–3, 581

34. NKVD resident London to Moscow, Nr. 450, 21 Oct. 1942; file No. 20566 'Black Bertha', NKVD archives, Moscow

35. See p. 108 above

36. Record of talks at the Kremlin at supper, Oct. 18 1944; TNA PREM 3 434/7

37. See pp. 133–5 above

38. See p. 149 above

39. Interrogation of Karl Haushofer by Col. Howard A. Brundage, 5 Oct. 1945, p. 15; IWM (Duxford) FO 645, Box 155

40. 'Interview with Professor Karl Haushofer' 28 Sept. 1945, Office of Strategic Services, Washington, p. 4; US Nat. Archives, RG 226, E19, Box 315, XL22853

41. See Ernst Haiger, p. 113; and Ernst Haiger to author, 17 Mar. 2008

42. See pp. 111–2 above

43. TNA FO 371 26542, C1687

44. See pp. 121–3 above

45. See pp. 131, 137–8 above

46. See pp. 142–3 above

47. J. Colville, p. 383

48. See p. 233 above

49. TNA FO 371 26542, C6049/324/18

50. See pp. 231–2 above

51. See Richard Deacon, *'C': A Biography of Sir Maurice Oldfield Head of MI6*, Macdonald, 1985, pp. 86–7; and cited in *Bild-Zeitung*, 16 Mar. 1981

52. See p. 288 above

53. See p. 76 above
54. See p. 242 above
55. See pp. 121–2 above
56. See p. 128 above
57. Spence (?) to Maj. P. Perfect, 19 May 1941; TNA KV 2/34
58. Cited John Harris, 'Witness'; *BBC History Magazine*, May 2001, p. 53
59. C. Gabel, p. 174
60. A. Melaouhi, *Rudolf Hess*, pp. 201–2
61. See p. 207 above
62. See p. 228 above
63. TNA PREM 3 219/7, f. 146
64. See p. 273 above
65. See p. 259 above; R. Hess, '*Aussergewöhnlich Zusammenkunft ...*', TNA FO 1093/1, f. 55
66. See p. 248 above
67. See p. 300 above
68. See p. 294 above
69. See p. 302 above
70. Sir A. Clark Kerr to FO, 25 Oct. 1942, No. 281; TNA PREM 3 219/6, f. 34
71. See J. Costello, 'Royal insurance for a traitor', *The Times*, 13 Oct. 1988; also Richard Brooks, 'Traitor Blunt apologises from beyond grave', *Sunday Times*, 21 Oct. 2001
72. A. Clark, *Barbarossa*, p. 40
73. See p. 280 above
74. TNA PREM 3 219/4, ff. 16–17
75. TNA PREM 3 219/7, f. 167
76. See p. 223 above
77. TNA FO 1093/12, f. 130
78. Prime Minister's personal minute to Sec. of State for Air, 7 April 1945; TNA INF 1/192, f. 97
79. See p. 328 above
80. See p. 330 above
81. See W.R. Hess, *Mord*, pp. 101–2
82. Prof. W. Eisenmenger and W. Spann, '*Zusammenfassung der Befunde*'; cited W.R. Hess, *Mord*, p. 215
83. Obituary, Professor David Bowen, *The Daily Telegraph*, 13 Apr. 2011
84. See p. 14 above

85. See Hamilton to J. Martin, 18 May 1941; TNA PREM 3 219/7, f. 137; J.M. Martin to W.I. Mallet, 10 Downing Street, 18 May 1941; TNA FO 1093/11, f. 107

86. B.C.S. to J.M. Martin, 6 Apr. 1945; TNA INF 1/912, f. 80

87. C. Gabel, p. 174; A. Melaouhi, *Rudolf Hess*, pp. 101–2

88. I. Kershaw, *Nemesis*, p. 369

89. *Ibid.*, p. 378; R. Schmidt, pp. 271–2

90. I. Kershaw, *Nemesis*, p. 379

91. *Ibid.*, pp. 377, 939; his authority is Ted Harrison, '*wir wurden schon viel zu oft hereingelegt*', (unpublished); cited I. Kershaw, *Nemesis*, p. 939, n. 216

92. R. Schmidt, p. 149

93. A. Smith, pp. 273, 310, 319

94. *Ibid.*, p. 309

95. See p. 288 above; R. Heydrich to Reichsaussenminister, 4 May 1942; F & CO 434005

96. 'Interview with Professor Haushofer', *op, cit.* ref. 40 above

97. *Ibid.*, p. 3

98. Interrogation of Karl Haushofer, *op. cit.* ref. 39 above

99. A. Haushofer to M. Haushofer, 13 Dec. 1939; cited U. Laack-Michel, p. 346

100. E. Bohle interrogation, 16 Oct. 1945; IWM (Duxford) FO 645, Box 155

101. Leitgen 'Statement', 1 Apr. 1952; IfZ ZS/262, f. 10

102. S. v. Krosigk, p. 159

103. TNA FO 1093/10, ff. 100 f

104. 'Interview with Professor Karl Haushofer', *op. cit.* ref. 40 above

Chapter 19: The answer?

1. Sir James Easton, ACSS; cited A. Cave Brown, p. 11

2. D. Popov, pp. 59 ff

3. *Ibid.*, p. 62

4. See G. Ritter, pp. 146–7

5. D. Popov, p. 44

6. *Ibid.*, p. 87

7. *Ibid.*, p. 115

8. A. Cave Brown, pp. 349–50

9. A. Smith, p. 309

10. A. Cave Brown, p. 211

11. W. Schellenberg, p. 304

12. See Richard Deacon, *'C': A Biography of Sir Maurice Oldfield, Head of MI6*, Macdonald, 1985, pp. 86–7; and cited in *Bild-Zeitung*, 16 Mar. 1981
13. K. de Courcy to author, 8 Jan. 1990
14. A. Smith, pp. 309, 322; L. Picknett, C. Prince, S. Prior, pp. 91, 260, 287
15. A. Cave Brown, p. 317
16. K. de Courcy, *Special Office Brief*, 6 June 1984
17. *Ibid.*, 1 Mar. 1989
18. K. de Courcy to author, 30 Nov. 1990
19. K. de Courcy to author, 8 Jan. 1990

Bibliography

Confined to works referenced in the text. Works published in London unless otherwise stated.

Akten zur Deutschen Auswärtigen Politik, 1918–1945, Serie D, Frankfurt, 1963

Aldrich, Richard J., *The Hidden Hand: Britain, America and Cold War Secret Intelligence*, John Murray, 2001

Andrew, Christopher, *The Defence of the Realm: The Authorized History of MI5*, Allen Lane, 2005

Armstrong, W. (ed.), *With Malice Toward None: A War Diary by Cecil H. King*, Sidgwick & Jackson, 1970

Bahar, Alexander and Kugel, Wilfred, *Der Reichstagsbrand: Wie Geschichte gemacht wird*, edition q, Berlin, 2001

Best, S. Payne, *The Venlo Incident*, Hutchinson, 1950

Bird, Eugene, *The Loneliest Man in the World: The Inside Story of the 30-Year Imprisonment of Rudolf Hess*, Secker & Warburg, 1974

Boberach, Heinz, *Meldungen aus dem Reich*, Pawlak, Herrsching, 1984

Bollmus, Reinhard, *Das Amt Rosenberg und seine Gegner*, Deutsche Verlags Anstalt, 1970

Bond, Brian, *Britain, France and Belgium 1939–1940*, Brasseys, 1990

Breitman, Richard, *Official Secrets: What the Nazis Planned, What the British and Americans Knew*, Allen Lane, 1998

Brown, Anthony Cave, *The Secret Servant: The Life of Sir Stewart Menzies*, Michael Joseph, 1988

Bullock, Alan, *Hitler: A Study in Tyranny*, Odhams, 1952

Burns, Jimmy, *Papa, Spy: A True Story of Love, Wartime Espionage in Madrid, and the Treachery of the Cambridge Spies*, Bloomsbury, 2010

Calic, Eduard, *Reinhard Heydrich: Schlüsselfigur des Dritten Reichs*, Droste, Düsseldorf, 1982

Cecil, Robert, *The Myth of the Master Race: Alfred Rosenberg and Nazi Ideology*, Batsford, 1972

Clark, Alan, *Barbarossa: The Russian German Conflict 1941–1945*, Weidenfeld & Nicolson, 1965

Clough, Brian, *State Secrets: The Kent–Wolkoff Affair*, Hideaway Publications, 2005

Cohen, Michael J., *Churchill and the Jews*, Cass, 1985

Colville, Jock, *The Fringes of Power: Downing Street Diaries 1939–1955*, Hodder & Stoughton, 1985

Colyton, Henry, *Occasion, Chance and Changes: A Memoir 1902–1946*, Michael Russell, Norwich, 1993

Costello, John, *Ten Days that Saved the West*, Bantam Press, 1991

Crawley, Aidan, *Leap Before You Look*, Collins, 1988

Douglas-Hamilton, James, *Motive for a Mission*, Macmillan, London, 1971

——, *The Truth about Rudolf Hess*, Mainstream, Edinburgh, 1993

Day, David, *Menzies & Churchill at War*, Angus & Robertson, 1986

Eberle, Henrik, and Uhl, Matthias (eds), *The Hitler Book: The Soviet Dossier Prepared for Stalin* (transl. G. MacDonagh) John Murray, 2005

Eccles, David, *By Safe Hand: Letters of Sybil & David Eccles, 1939–42*, The Bodley Head, 1983

Fleming, G., *Hitler and the Final Solution*, Hamish Hamilton, 1985

Fröhlich, Elke, *Die Tagebücher von Joseph Goebbels*, K.G. Saur, Munich, 1987

Fromm, Bella, *Blood and Banquets: A Berlin Social Diary*, Geoffrey Bles, 1941

Gabel, Charles, *Conversations Interdite avec Rudolf Hess 1977–1986*, Plon, Paris, 1988

Galland, Adolf, *The First and the Last: The German Fighter Force in World War Two* (transl. M. Savill), Methuen, 1953

Gellermann, Günther W., *Geheime Wege zum Frieden mit England ...: Ausgewählte Initiativen zur Beendigung des Krieges 1940/42*, Bernard & Graefe, Bonn, 1995

Gilbert, G., *Nuremberg Diary*, Eyre & Spottiswoode, 1948

Gilbert, Martin, *Finest Hour: Winston S. Churchill 1939–41*, Heinemann, 1983

——, *The Holocaust: The Jewish Tragedy*, Collins, 1986

Giordano, Ralph, *Wenn Hitler den Krieg gewonnen hätte: Die Pläne der Nazis nach dem Endsieg*, Kiepenheuer & Witsch, Köln, 2000

Goodrick-Clarke, Nicholas, *The Occult Roots of Nazism: Secret Aryan Cults and their Influence on Nazi Ideology*, Tauris, 1992

Grenfell, Russell (as T-124), *Sea Power*, Jonathan Cape, 1940

Halder, Franz, (ed. Jacobsen, H.-A.), *Kriegstagbuch, vol. II*, Kohlhammer, Stuttgart, 1963

Hanfstaengl, Ernst, *15 Jahre mit Hitler*, Piper, Munich, 1980

Harris, John, and Trow, M.J., *Hess: The British Conspiracy*, André Deutsch, 1999

——, and Wilbourn, D., *The British Illusion of Peace*, Jema Publications, Northampton, 2010

Hassell, Ulrich von, *Vom Andern Deutschland*, Atlantis Verlag, Zürich, 1946

——, *Die Hassell-Tagebücher 1938–1944*, Siedler Verlag, Berlin, 1988

Heiber, Helmut, *Reichsführer: Briefe an und von Himmler*, Deutsche Verlags Anstalt, Stuttgart, 1968

Henderson, Sir Nevile, *Failure of a Mission: Berlin 1937–1939*, Hodder & Stoughton, 1940

Hess, Ilse, *Ein Schicksal in Briefen*, Druffel, Leoni, 1971

——, *Gefangener des Friedens*, Druffel, Leoni, 1955

Hess, Wolf Rüdiger, *Mord an Rudolf Hess? Der geheimnisvolle Tod meines Vaters in Spandau*, Druffel, Leoni, 1989

——, *My Father Rudolf Hess* (transl. Crowley, Frederick & Christina), W.H. Allen, 1986

—— (ed.), *Rudolf Hess: Briefe 1908–1937*, Müller, Munich, 1987

Hinsley, F.H. Thomas, E.E., and others, *British Intelligence in the Second World War, vol. 2*, H.M.S.O., 1981

Hitler, Adolf, *Mein Kampf*, Zentralverlag der NSDAP, Munich, 1924

Höhne, Heinz, *Canaris: Patriot im Zweilicht*, Bertelsmann, Munich, 1976

Howe, Ellic, *The Black Game: British Subversive Operations Against the Germans during the Second World War*, Michael Joseph, 1982

IMT, *Trial of the Major War Criminals before the International Military Tribunal*, Nuremberg, 1947

Irving, David, *Churchill's War*, Veritas Publishing, W. Australia, 1987

——, *Hess: The Missing Years 1941–1945*, Macmillan, London, 1987

——, *The War Path: Hitler's Germany 1933–1939*, Michael Joseph, 1978 (refs. from Papermac ed. 1983)

Jacobsen, Hans-Adolf, *Karl Haushofer: Leben und Werk, Band II*, Boldt, Boppard am Rhein, 1979

Jeffery, Keith, *MI6: The History of the Secret Intelligence Service, 1909–1949*, Bloomsbury, 2010

Kelley, Douglas, *22 Cells in Nuremberg*, W.H. Allen, 1947

Kershaw, Ian, *Hitler: 1889–1936: Hubris*, Allen Lane, 1998

——, *Hitler: 1936–1945: Nemesis*, Allen Lane, 2000

Kersten, Felix, *The Kersten Memoirs 1940–1945*, Hutchinson, 1956

Kilzer, Louis, *Churchill's Deception: The Dark Secret that Destroyed Nazi Germany*, Simon and Schuster, 1994

Kramish, Arnold, *The Griffin*, Macmillan, London, 1986

Krausnick, H., and others, *Anatomy of the SS State*, Collins, 1968

Krosigk, Schwerin von, *Es geschah in Deutschland*, Wunderlich, Tübingen, 1951

Laack-Michel, Ursula, *Albrecht Haushofer und der National-Sozialismus*, Klett, Stuttgart, 1974

Lamb, Richard, *The Ghosts of Peace*, Michael Russel, Wiltshire, 1987

Lang, J. von, and Sibyll, C. (eds.), *Eichmann Interrogated*, The Bodley Head, 1982

Laqueur, Walter, *The Terrible Secret*, Weidenfeld & Nicolson, 1980

Leasor, James, *Hess: The Uninvited Envoy*, Allen & Unwin, 1962

Leutze, James (ed.), *The London Observer: The Journal of General Raymond E. Lee 1940–1941*, Hutchinson, 1972

Liddell, Guy, diaries – see West, Nigel

Liddell Hart, Basil H., *The German Generals Talk*, Berkley, New York, 1988

Lifton, Robert J., *The Nazi Doctors: Medical Killing and the Psychology of Genocide*, Macmillan, 1986

Longerich, Peter, *Heinrich Himmler* (transl. Jeremy Noakes, Lesley Sharpe), Oxford University Press, 2012

——, *Holocaust: The Nazi Persecution and Murder of the Jews*, Oxford University Press, 2010

——, *The Unwritten Order: Hitler's Role in the Final Solution*, Tempus, Stroud, 2001

Masterman, J.C., *The Double-Cross System*, Yale University Press, 1972

Masters, Anthony, *The Man who was M: The Life of Maxwell Knight*, Blackwood, Oxford, 1984

McGinty, Stephen, *Camp Z: The Secret Life of Rudolf Hess*, Quercus, 2011

Melaouhi, Abdallah, *Rudolf Hess – His Final Years and his Sudden Death* (English translation, 2011, of *Ich sah den Mördern in die Augen*, Märkische Raute, 2008)

Mueller, Michael, *Canaris: The Life and Death of Hitler's Spymaster* (transl. Geoffrey Brooks), Chatham Publishing, 2007

Nesbit, Roy C., and van Acker, Georges, *The Flight of Rudolf Hess: Myths and Reality*, Sutton Publishing, Stroud, 1999

Newton, Scott, *Profits of Peace: The Political Economy of Anglo-German Appeasement*, Oxford University Press, 1996

Nicolson, Harold, *Diaries and Letters 1939–45*, Collins, 1967

Padfield, Peter, *Hess: The Führer's Disciple*, Cassell, 2001

——, *Himmler, Reichsführer-SS*, Macmillan, 1990

Payne Best, S., *The Venlo Incident*, Hutchinson, 1950

Perry, Roland S., *The Fifth Man*, Sidgwick & Jackson, 1994

Popov, Dusko, *Spy Counterspy*, Weidenfeld & Nicolson, 1974

Picknett, Lynn, Prince, Clive, and others, *Double Standards: The Rudolf Hess Cover-up*, Little, Brown, 2001

Rees, J.R. (ed.), *The Case of Rudolf Hess*, Heinemann, 1947

Ritter, Gerhard, *The German Resistance*, Allen & Unwin, 1958

Roberts, Andrew, *The Holy Fox: A Biography of Lord Halifax*, Weidenfeld & Nicolson, 1991

Schellenberg, Walter, *The Schellenberg Memoirs* (transl. L. Hagen), André Deutsch, 1956

Schmidt, Rainer F., *Rudolf Hess: 'Botengang eines Toren?'*, Econ, Düsseldorf, 1997 (3rd edn 2000)

Schwarzwäller, Wulf, *Rudolf Hess: The Deputy*, Quartet, 1988

Seidl, Alfred, *Der verweigerte Friede: Deutschlands Parlementär Rudolf Hess muss schweigen*, Universitas Verlag, Munich, 2nd edn 1985

Shirer, William, *Berlin Diary*, Hamish Hamilton, 1941

——, *End of a Berlin Diary*, Hamish Hamilton, 1947

Smith, Alfred, *Rudolf Hess and Germany's Reluctant War*, The Book Guild, Lewes, Sussex, 2001

Sparrow, Elizabeth, *Secret Service: British Agents in France 1792–1815*, Boydell, Woodbridge, 1999

Speer, Albert, *Erinnerungen*, Ullstein, Frankfurt/Berlin, 1972

——, *Spandau: The Secret Diaries*, Macmillan, New York, 1976

Strasser, Otto, *Mein Kampf: eine politische Autobiographie*, H. Heine, Frankfurt, 1969

T-124 – see Grenfell, Russell

Taylor, Telford, *The Anatomy of the Nuremberg Trials*, Knopf, New York, 1992

Templewood, Lord, *Ambassador on a Special Mission*, Collins, 1946

Thomas, Gordon, *Journey into Madness: Medical Torture and the Mind Controllers*, Bantam, 1986

Thorne, Christopher, *Allies of a Kind, The United States, Britain and the War against Japan, 1941–1945*, Oxford University Press, 1978

Tissier, Tony Le, *Farewell to Spandau*, Buchan & Enright, Leatherhead, Surrey, 1994

Vansittart, Lord, *Lessons of My Life*, Hutchinson, 1943

——, *The Black Record of Germany: Past, Present and Future*, Hamish Hamilton, 1941

——, *The Mist Procession*, Hutchinson, 1958

Waite, Robert G.L., *The Psychopathic God: Adolf Hitler*, Basic Books, New York, 1977

West, Nigel (ed.), *The Guy Liddell Diaries, vol. 1, 1939–1942*, Routledge, 2005

Winterbotham, F.W., *The Nazi Connection*, Weidenfeld & Nicolson, 1978

Wood, Derek, *Attack, Warning, Red*, Macdonald & Jane's, 1976

Young, Kenneth (ed.), *The Diaries of Sir Robert Bruce Lockhart*, Macmillan, London, 1980

Ziegler, Philip, *King Edward VIII*, Collins, 1990

Zwar, Desmond, *Talking to Rudolf Hess*, The History Press, Stroud, 2010

ARTICLES

'An Observer's Diary, Jan. 6 1941–May 2 1942', *Airfix Magazine*, Dec. 1945

Anonymous, 'The Inside Story of the Hess Flight', *American Mercury*, May 1943; reprinted in *The Journal of Historical Review*, Autumn 1982, pp. 291–9

Ashbee, Felicity, 'The Thunderstorm that was Hess', *Aeroplane Monthly*, Oct. 1987

Friedmann, Jan, and Wiegrefe, Klaus, 'Historian Uncovers New Account', *Spiegel* online, 30 May 2011

Haiger, Ernst, 'Fiction, Facts and Forgeries: The "Revelations" of Peter and Martin Allen', *The Journal of Intelligence History*, vol. 6, No. 1 (2006)

Kiesel, Georg, '*SS Bericht über den 20 Juli; aus den Papiere Dr. Georg Kiesel*', *Nordwestdeutsche Hefte*, 2 Jahrg., No. 1, Jan. 1947

Mann, Erica, 'Hess Meeting in Spain was Fixed', *Glasgow Evening Citizen*, 20 Sept. 1945

Newton, Scott, 'The economic background to appeasement and the search for Anglo-German détente before and during World War 2', *Lobster*, 20 Nov. 1990

Riley, Morris, and Dorrill, Stephen, 'Rothschild, the right, the far right and the Fifth Man', *Lobster*, 16 June 1988

Stahmer, H.W., '*Wahrheit und Irrtum um Rudolf Hess*', unpublished
    m.s., 1959
Stubbe, Walter, '*In Memoriam Albrecht Haushofer*', *Vierteljahrshefte
    für Zeitgeschichte, 8 Jahrg.*, 1960

Index